Karoline von Günderrode
Philosophical Romantic

LEGENDA

LEGENDA is the Modern Humanities Research Association's book imprint for new research in the Humanities. Founded in 1995 by Malcolm Bowie and others within the University of Oxford, Legenda has always been a collaborative publishing enterprise, directly governed by scholars. The Modern Humanities Research Association (MHRA) joined this collaboration in 1998, became half-owner in 2004, in partnership with Maney Publishing and then Routledge, and has since 2016 been sole owner. Titles range from medieval texts to contemporary cinema and form a widely comparative view of the modern humanities, including works on Arabic, Catalan, English, French, German, Greek, Italian, Portuguese, Russian, Spanish, and Yiddish literature. Editorial boards and committees of more than 60 leading academic specialists work in collaboration with bodies such as the Society for French Studies, the British Comparative Literature Association and the Association of Hispanists of Great Britain & Ireland.

The MHRA encourages and promotes advanced study and research in the field of the modern humanities, especially modern European languages and literature, including English, and also cinema. It aims to break down the barriers between scholars working in different disciplines and to maintain the unity of humanistic scholarship. The Association fulfils this purpose through the publication of journals, bibliographies, monographs, critical editions, and the MHRA Style Guide, and by making grants in support of research. Membership is open to all who work in the Humanities, whether independent or in a University post, and the participation of younger colleagues entering the field is especially welcomed.

ALSO PUBLISHED BY THE ASSOCIATION

Critical Texts
Tudor and Stuart Translations • New Translations • European Translations
MHRA Library of Medieval Welsh Literature

MHRA Bibliographies
Publications of the Modern Humanities Research Association

The Annual Bibliography of English Language & Literature
Austrian Studies
Modern Language Review
Portuguese Studies
The Slavonic and East European Review
Working Papers in the Humanities
The Yearbook of English Studies

www.mhra.org.uk
www.legendabooks.com

GERMANIC LITERATURES

Editorial Committee
Chair: Professor Ritchie Robertson (University of Oxford)
Professor Jane Fenoulhet (University College London)
Professor Anne Fuchs (University College Dublin)
Professor Karen Leeder (University of Oxford)
Dr Jakob Stougaard-Nielsen (University College London)
Dr Ernest Schonfield (University of Glasgow)
Professor Annette Volfing (University of Oxford)
Professor Susanne Kord (University College London)
Professor John Zilcosky (University of Toronto)

Germanic Literatures includes monographs and essay collections on literature originally written not only in German, but also in Dutch and the Scandinavian languages. Within the German-speaking area, it seeks also to publish studies of other national literatures such as those of Austria and Switzerland. The chronological scope of the series extends from the early Middle Ages down to the present day.

APPEARING IN THIS SERIES

11. *E.T.A. Hoffmann's Orient*, by Joanna Neilly
12. *Structures of Subjugation in Dutch Literature*, by Judit Gera
13. *Isak Dinesen Reading Søren Kierkegaard:*
On Christianity, Seduction, Gender, and Repetition, by Mads Bunch
14. *Yvan Goll: The Thwarted Pursuit of the Whole*, by Robert Vilain
15. *Foreign Parts: German and Austrian Actors on the British Stage 1933–1960*, by Richard Dove
16. *Paul Celan's Unfinished Poetics*, by Thomas C. Connolly
17. *Encounters with Albion: Britain and the British in Texts by Jewish Refugees from Nazism*, by Anthony Grenville
18. *The Law of Poetry: Studies in Hölderlin's Poetics*, by Charles Lewis
19. *Georg Hermann: A Writer's Life*, by John Craig-Sharples
20. *Alfred Döblin: Monsters, Cyborgs and Berliners 1900–1933*, by Robert Craig
21. *Confrontational Readings: Literary Neo-Avant-Gardes in Dutch and German*, edited by Inge Arteel, Lars Bernaerts and Olivier Couder
22. *Poetry, Painting, Park: Goethe and Claude Lorrain*, by Franz R. Kempf
23. *Childhood, Memory, and the Nation: Young Lives under Nazism in Contemporary German Culture*, by Alexandra Lloyd

Managing Editor
Dr Graham Nelson, 41 Wellington Square, Oxford OX1 2JF, UK
www.legendabooks.com

Karoline von Günderrode

Philosophical Romantic

Joanna Raisbeck

Germanic Literatures 26
Modern Humanities Research Association
2022

Published by Legenda
an imprint of the Modern Humanities Research Association
Salisbury House, Station Road, Cambridge CB1 2LA

ISBN 978-1-83954-025-7 (HB)
ISBN 978-1-83954-026-4 (PB)

First published 2022

All rights reserved. No part of this publication may be reproduced or disseminated or transmitted in any form or by any means, electronic, mechanical, photocopying, recording or otherwise, or stored in any retrieval system, or otherwise used in any manner whatsoever without written permission of the copyright owner, except in accordance with the provisions of the Copyright, Designs and Patents Act 1988, or under the terms of a licence permitting restricted copying issued in the UK by the Copyright Licensing Agency Ltd, Saffron House, 6–10 Kirby Street, London EC1N 8TS, England, or in the USA by the Copyright Clearance Center, 222 Rosewood Drive, Danvers MA 01923. Application for the written permission of the copyright owner to reproduce any part of this publication must be made by email to legenda@mhra.org.uk.

Disclaimer: Statements of fact and opinion contained in this book are those of the author and not of the editors or the Modern Humanities Research Association. The publisher makes no representation, express or implied, in respect of the accuracy of the material in this book and cannot accept any legal responsibility or liability for any errors or omissions that may be made.

Trademark notice: Product or corporate names may be trademarks or registered trademarks, and are used only for identification and explanation without intent to infringe.

© Modern Humanities Research Association 2022

Copy-Editor: Dr Nigel Hope

CONTENTS

	Acknowledgements	ix
	Notes on Editions and Translations	xi
	Introduction	1
1	Biography and Myth	9
2	Pantheism and Panentheism: From the *Spinozastreit* to Günderrode	21
3	'Vieles werd' ich können, weil ich will': Fatalism, Agency, and Autonomy in Günderrode	36
4	From Political to Religious Revolution: The Rise of Muhammad and the Fall of Napoleon	80
5	Ascent and Descent: Platonism and Cognition in Günderrode	121
6	The Practice of Poetry in *Melete*	157
7	Perspectives on Pantheism: Mereau, Hölderlin, Novalis	191
	Conclusion	225
	Bibliography	231
	Index	256

ACKNOWLEDGEMENTS

Above all, I would like to thank my doctoral supervisor Kevin Hilliard, for his generosity, encouragement, and dedication over the course of work on the original thesis and on subsequent revisions, and for the years beforehand. I could not have asked for a better supervisor and academic mentor. I am also grateful to the examiners of the thesis, Ritchie Robertson and Claudia Nitschke, for a very productive discussion during the viva and for their incisive comments. Ritchie Robertson has supported the project with enthusiasm from its inception as a Master's dissertation through to its eventual publication, and I would also like to thank the reader for the Germanic Literatures series for the invaluable suggestions that have sharpened the project as it developed beyond the confines of a doctoral thesis. My thanks go to Graham Nelson, the Managing Editor of Legenda, for his invaluable advice in preparation of this book, and also to Nigel Hope for his copy-editing and keen attention to detail.

The Faculty of Medieval and Modern Languages and Somerville College, University of Oxford, provided a stimulating environment in which to pursue research. I am particularly thankful to Almut Suerbaum and Joanna Neilly for their advice and encouragement. I am grateful to the Georg-August-Universität Göttingen, the Goethe-Universität Frankfurt am Main, and the Graduiertenkolleg 'Modell Romantik' at the Friedrich-Schiller-Universität Jena, and particularly to Anne Bohnenkamp-Renken, Gerhard Kaiser, and Dirk von Petersdorff for their constructive comments. Joanna Neilly, Charlie Louth, Stephanie Galasso, Anna Ezekiel, Svenja Frank, Steffan Davies, and Alison Sage all read substantial parts of the original thesis, and I would like to thank them for the astute critical eye they cast over my work. Jordan Lavers was an excellent interlocutor for discussing all matters relating to Günderrode. Work on revising the thesis was undertaken during lectureships at Wadham College and St Hilda's College at the University of Oxford, and I am grateful to Carolin Duttlinger and Georgina Paul in particular for their advice, generosity, and good humour.

My doctoral research was generously funded by the Faculty of Medieval and Modern Languages and Somerville College on a Heath Harrison-Somerville College Studentship, by the Alfred Toepfer Stiftung F.V.S., and by the Alexander von Humboldt-Stiftung. I am grateful too to the librarians and archivists at the Universitätsbibliothek Johann Christian Senckenberg and the Freies Deutsches Hochstift in Frankfurt am Main, particularly Raschida Mansour and Bettina Zimmermann, for their support. I would also like to thank the Modern Humanities Research Association for awarding me a Research Scholarship in 2020–21, which facilitated the revisions to the original manuscript.

Parts of Chapter 5 (on Kantian epistemology and Platonism) have already been published as '"Diese Unwissenheit ist mir der unerträglichste Mangel, der gröste Widerspruch": The Pursuit of Pre-rational Knowledge in Günderrode', in *Anti\ Idealism: Re-interpreting a German Discourse*, ed. by Juliana de Albuquerque and Gert Hofmann (Berlin: De Gruyter, 2019), pp. 131–45. Parts of Chapter 7 (on Hölderlin) are scheduled to appear in 'Daimonic Energies in Hölderlin's *Tod des Empedokles*', in *Forces of Nature: Dynamism and Agency in German Romanticism*, ed. by Adrian Renner and Frederike Middelhoff (Berlin: De Gruyter, 2022), pp. 127–46. I am grateful to De Gruyter for permission to reproduce the material here.

★ ★ ★ ★ ★

Innumerable friends and colleagues have contributed to this project, directly or indirectly. I would like to give my especial thanks to Fergus Cooper, Ben Lambert, Jean-Michel Johnston, Katharine Lauderdale, and Martin Urschel, for being there from the start; finally, to my family — my parents, John and Sue, and my brother, Gary — for their unwavering support and love. My book is dedicated to my parents, who not only endlessly encouraged me, but also instilled in me the importance of pursuing whatever enthused me. This book would not have been possible without them.

J.R., Oxford, July 2022

NOTES ON EDITIONS AND TRANSLATIONS

❖

The edition used to refer to Günderrode's works here is Karoline von Günderrode, *Sämtliche Werke und ausgewählte Studien*, ed. by Walter Morgenthaler, 3 vols (Frankfurt a.M.; Basel: Stroemfeld/Roter Stern, 2006), referenced as *SW* in the body of the text, followed by volume number, page number, and also by line number if the text in question contains verse. If it is does not, the reference is to the volume and page number only.

The edition used of Günderrode's *Studienbuch* is Max Preitz and Doris Hopp, 'Karoline von Günderrode in ihrer Umwelt, III. Karoline von Günderrodes Studienbuch', *Jahrbuch des freien deutschen Hochstifts* (1975), 223–323, referenced as Preitz/Hopp III in the footnotes. Günderrode's letters are taken from a variety of sources. Alongside archival sources, Günderrode's correspondence is taken from Karoline von Günderrode, *Ich sende dir ein zärtliches Pfand: Die Briefe der Karoline von Günderrode*, ed. by Birgit Weißenborn (Frankfurt a.M.: Insel, 1992), referenced as Günderrode, *Briefe* in the footnotes. The correspondence between Friedrich Creuzer and Günderrode is taken from Karl Preisendanz, *Die Liebe der Günderode: Friedrich Creuzers Briefe an Caroline von Günderode* (Berlin: Lang, 1975), referenced as Preisendanz in the footnotes.

English translations from German and French are my own, unless otherwise indicated. English translations of quotations from 'Mahomed, der Prophet von Mekka' and 'Hildgund' are taken from Karoline von Günderrode, *Poetic Fragments*, trans. by Anna Ezekiel (Albany: SUNY Press, 2016), referenced as Günderrode, *Poetic Fragments* in the footnotes.

The cover image of this book is a small oil painting on canvas, and the only existing painting of Karoline von Günderrode, which is held in the collection of Historisches Museum, Frankfurt am Main (photo by Horst Ziegenfusz). It is attributed to Günderrode's sister, Charlotte von Günderrode (1783–1801). I am grateful to the Historisches Museum, Frankfurt am Main, for permission to reproduce the image as the cover of this book.

INTRODUCTION

Karoline von Günderrode offers a particularly acute example of how the biographical images of a poet consistently overshadow the reception of his or her literary work. Whilst her collections of poetry, prose, and plays had received some critical attention during her lifetime, and her suicide in July 1806 caused consternation among intellectual circles, as well as her acquaintances and family, Günderrode's literary fame had its origins not in her lifetime but rather in the middle of the nineteenth century, through Bettine von Arnim, and in the twentieth century, through the efforts of Christa Wolf.

Yet the publication of a critical edition of Günderrode in 1991, the *Sämtliche Werke und ausgewählte Studien* edited by Walter Morgenthaler, ushered in a period of critical appreciation of all aspects of Günderrode's work. Previously, the pull of Günderrode's attractive biography had delayed the scholarly reception of her literary *oeuvre*.[1] One of the merits of the critical edition has been to draw attention to her previously neglected dramas, which form two thirds of the literary *oeuvre*. Longer studies have emerged that encompass the entirety of Günderrode's work. These are often thematically driven: how nature is conceptualised,[2] how nature, sense perception and cognition are mythologised,[3] or whether Günderrode constructs a specific kind of aesthetics.[4] Shorter pieces are similarly constructed around themes, such as the presentation of the Orient,[5] or how death is represented in mythologised form.[6] These are valuable contributions which illustrate how Günderrode engages

---

[1] As late as 1986, Helene C. Kastinger-Riley stated that 'Die derzeitige Forschungslage ist immer noch [...] primitiv' [The current state of research ist still [...] basic], in 'Zwischen den Welten: Ambivalenz und Existentialproblematik im Werk Caroline von Günderrodes', in *Die weibliche Muse: Sechs Essays über künstlerisch schaffende Frauen der Goethezeit* (Columbia, SC: Camden House, 1986), pp. 91–119 (p. 119).
[2] Wolfgang Westphal, *Karoline von Günderrode und 'Naturdenken um 1800'* (Essen: Blaue Eule, 1993).
[3] Helga Dormann, *Die Kunst des inneren Sinns: Mythisierung der inneren und äußeren Natur im Werk Karoline von Günderrodes* (Würzburg: Königshausen & Neumann, 2004).
[4] Lucia Maria Licher, *Mein Leben in einer bleibenden Form aussprechen: Umrisse einer Ästhetik im Werk Karoline von Günderrodes (1780–1806)* (Heidelberg: Winter, 1996).
[5] For example: Ingeborg H. Solbrig, 'Die Orientalische Muse Meletes: Zu den Mohammed-Dichtungen Karoline von Günderrodes', *Jahrbuch der deutschen Schillergesellschaft*, 33 (1989), 299–322; Annette Simonis, '"Das verschleierte Bild": Mythopoetik und Geschlechterrollen bei Karoline von Günderrode', *Deutsche Vierteljahrsschrift für Literaturwissenschaft*, 74.2 (2000), 254–78.
[6] Barbara Becker-Cantarino, 'The "New Mythology": Myth and Death in Karoline von Günderrode's Literary Work', in *Women and Death 3: Women's Representations of Death in German Culture since 1500*, ed. by Claire Bielby and Anna Richards (Rochester, NY: Camden House, 2010), pp. 51–70.

with topics familiar to the intellectual and literary historiography of the late eighteenth century.

Yet few critical attempts have been made to integrate Günderrode into a coherent narrative of contemporary literary and philosophical developments, and one that would establish Günderrode's significance as a poet and philosopher in the formidable intellectual landscape around 1800. This lack is, in part, a reflection of the corpus itself: slight, but so formally and thematically diverse that it resists a comprehensive interpretation. This critical focus on particular themes in Günderrode is one productive method of navigating textual diversity. The disadvantage of these approaches is that they present a collection of related material, without accounting for the significance of Günderrode above and beyond the topic at hand. What is lacking is a main narrative thread, in the vein of the method of conceptual history, of the history of a particular problem, which has acquired the name *Problemgeschichte*. Such a conceptual history encompasses the majority of Günderrode's corpus and would serve as an anchoring point that would link these themes together.

This book reads Günderrode through the lens of the reinterpretation of Spinoza that was ushered in by the *Pantheismusstreit* [pantheism controversy] of the 1780s. Looking at Günderrode's work through this lens, as I will show, reveals the remarkable consistency of Günderrode's metaphysical commitments to panentheism and pantheism — the idea that God and nature are the same. Chapter 2 outlines what is at stake in this controversy, and how Günderrode intervenes in these debates. By contextualising Günderrode in the literary and intellectual landscape of the end of the eighteenth century, the aim of this book is to establish Günderrode as a figure of philosophical and literary significance in her own right. Whilst this study is not a comprehensive interpretation of all of Günderrode's literary and philosophical work, it does intend to demonstrate the development of Günderrode as a poet and philosopher over the course of her short period as an active writer, from around 1800 to 1806.

Before turning to the particulars of the pantheism controversy itself, it is worth attending to the interactions between philosophy and literature. Metaphysical ruminations are not just philosophical abstractions for Günderrode. They are concepts central to her literary work. This book, therefore, is concerned with how they achieve a variety of manifestations in poetic form. At the heart of such considerations is how poetry and philosophy interact in Günderrode's work. My contention is that Günderrode is both a philosopher and a poet. Her philosophical interests should not be considered as conceptual, nor is her literary work a mere vessel for representing concepts. The interactions between the two are more complex. We need to consider these interactions on two levels: on the metalevel of disciplinary practices, of how, in particular, German Romanticism has been conceptualised over the past thirty years, and secondly, on the historical-contextual level — that is, what can be inferred from Günderrode's own writings.

What differentiates Günderrode's poetics from those of the Jena Romantics is that Günderrode's literary work is not expressly developed in philosophical terms.

The creative reception of Fichte in the *Fichte-Studien* [Fichte Studies] (1795–96) laid the foundations for Novalis's poetics.[7] Equally, Friedrich Schlegel's own critique of Fichte gave rise to the idea that the Idealist system lacked the capacity to ground itself. Schlegel's resulting anti-foundationalism fed directly into his aesthetics and poetics.[8]

The lack of an explicit philosophical foundation for Günderrode's poetics is something of a virtue, particularly with regard to the reception of German Romanticism over the past thirty years. The ground-breaking work by Manfred Frank and Frederick C. Beiser has rehabilitated the Jena Romantics as, alongside their literary achievements, a legitimate philosophical movement.[9] This philosophical approach is both welcome and extremely fruitful, especially following Dieter Henrich's research, which reconstructs the social networks that allowed philosophical ideas to develop, known by the name of *Konstellationsforschung*. It can, however, have the effect of giving primacy to philosophical interests above all else. To give an extreme example of this tendency: Philippe Lacoue-Labarthe and Jean-Luc Nancy's rigorous postmodern reading of Jena Romanticism, *L'Absolu littéraire: théorie de la littérature du romantisme allemand* (1978; English translation 1988) distils its essence into philosophy, insofar as Romanticism's condition of possibility is to be found in Kant's allegedly problematic construction of the subject, to the point that philosophy, in a rhetorically hyperbolic gesture, *determines* Romanticism:

> Philosophy, then, controls romanticism. In this context, and crudely translated, this means that Kant opens up the possibility of romanticism. [...] however accurate historico-empirical geneses of the origins of romanticism may be [...] the romantics have no predecessors.[10]

As Christoph Bode has highlighted in an ironic (and Schlegelian) critique of Lacoue-Labarthe and Nancy's work, whilst these theorists object to both an historical reading of German Romanticism and its wholesale appropriation for contemporary purposes, the effect of *L'Absolu littéraire* is to empower criticism, and in doing so denies literature and art precisely the kind of autonomy that the Jena Romantics ascribed to them.[11] The end result is for philosophy to question the utility of literature itself.[12] In the end, the effect of Lacoue-Labarthe and Nancy is

---

7 Nicholas Saul, 'The Pursuit of the Subject: Literature as Critic and Perfecter of Philosophy 1790–1832', in *Philosophy and German Literature, 1700–1900*, ed. by Nicholas Saul (Cambridge: Cambridge University Press, 2002), pp. 57–101 (pp. 70–72).
8 See Elizabeth Millán-Zaibert, *Friedrich Schlegel and the Emergence of Romantic Philosophy* (Albany: SUNY Press, 2007), pp. 159–74.
9 This rehabilitation assumes its most polemical form in the introduction to Manfred Frank, '*Unendliche Annäherung*': *Die Anfänge der philosophischen Frühromantik* (Frankfurt a.M.: Suhrkamp, 1997), pp. 17–25.
10 Philippe Lacoue-Labarthe and Jean-Luc Nancy, *The Literary Absolute: The Theory of Literature in German Romanticism*, trans. by Philip Barnard and Cheryl Lester (Albany: SUNY Press, 1988), p. 29.
11 Christoph Bode, 'Absolut Jena: A Second Look at Lacoue-Labarthe's and Nancy's Representation of the Literary Theory of *Frühromantik*', in *Romanticism and Philosophy: Thinking with Literature*, ed. by Thomas Constanticso and Sophie Laniel-Musitelli (New York: Routledge, 2015), pp. 19–39 (p. 33).
12 Daniel J. Hoolsema, 'The End of an Impossible Future in "The Literary Absolute"', *Modern Language Notes*, 110.4 (2004), 845–68 (p. 868).

to utilise a small segment of Jena Romanticism — they refer to only twelve texts from the *Athenaeum* (1798–1800) — in order to make a point about the primacy of criticism over literature.

Günderrode's work offers scholarship on Romanticism a way of backing out of this over commitment to philosophy.[13] To move away from this metalevel and towards a historical and contextual focus: if philosophy was no doubt a significant influence on the Romantic generation (and indeed beyond), what specific role do poetry and art assume for Günderrode? The answer is twofold, and both answers rest on the valorisation of art, and by extension, poetry as a kind of aesthetic or poetic evangelism.

Firstly, Günderrode's *Nachlass* poem 'Tendenz des Künstlers' [The Artist's Tendency] (*c.* 1799–1802) bears an unmistakeable debt to the vocabulary of Schiller's philosophical poetry, specifically to 'Die Künstler' [The Artists] (1789) and in particular to 'Das Ideal und das Leben' [The Ideal and Life] (1800). Like Schiller, Günderrode programmatically exhorts the reader to flee material reality into the immortal realm of beauty, which allows for thought to be represented in eternal form: 'Bleibend will sein der Künstler im Reiche der Schönheit | Darum in dauernder Form stellt den Gedanken er dar' [The artist wants to be lasting in the realm of beauty | For that reason he portrays thoughts in permanent form] (*SW* I, 378, ll. 11–12). This is not merely a banal matter of the enduring fame of the artist; rather, as David Pugh has shown for Schiller, it proceeds from Platonic ontology and grants beautiful art a dignified status in opposition to material reality.[14]

The second role that poetry takes on for Günderrode is structurally linked to Schiller's valorisation of art and poetry, but one that brings Günderrode closer to the Jena Romantics: that is, that art and poetry function as equivalents to religion. Günderrode's poem 'Der Dom zu Cölln' [The Cathedral at Cologne] (1800–1802) articulates a form of *Kunstreligion* [art religion].[15] The experience of art and specifically of poetry functions by analogy with religious experience, and poetry gives rise to revelatory insights into higher truths that lie beyond the material realm: 'Dichtkunst! Du Seele der Künste, du die sie alle gebohren, | Du beseelest das Grab steigest zum Himel empor' [Poetry! You soul of the arts, you who gave birth to them all | You ensoul the grave, ascend to heaven] (*SW* I, 379, ll. 22–23). Günderrode's aphorisms feature ruminations on the role of the artist as the higher, if ascetic, form of life. The artist assumes the role of the priest, if not the new Messiah (*SW* I, 437) and this transforms poetic production metaphorically into evangelism.

---

13 Schlegel's anti-foundationalism corresponds to deconstruction: see Andrew Bowie, 'The Philology of Philosophy: The Early Romantic Critical Heritage and Contemporary Literary Theory', *Publications of the English Goethe Society*, 65 (1996), 116–35 (pp. 122–23). Part of the impetus for Manfred Frank's examination of philosophical Romanticism, to whom Bowie is indebted, is to protect it against contemporary French philosophy. See William Large's review: William Large, 'From German Romanticism to Critical Theory, by Andrew Bowie', *Journal of the British Society for Phenomenology*, 31.1 (2000), 108–09.

14 David Pugh, *Dialectic of Love: Platonism in Schiller's Aesthetics* (Montreal: McGill-Queen's University Press, 1997), pp. 55–56.

15 For the broader eighteenth-century context of *Kunstreligion*, see Bernd Auerochs, *Die Entstehung der Kunstreligion* (Göttingen: Vandenhoeck & Ruprecht, 2006).

The truths that are proclaimed by the prophetic speakers throughout Günderrode may be associated with Spinozist panentheism, but this philosophical element becomes enmeshed in a specific understanding of poetry that grants it an epiphanic function. Therefore, this book will attend to the literary qualities of Günderrode's exploration of Spinozist panentheism and pantheism, but also to how this interacts with other philosophical traditions, such as the legacy of Idealist philosophy, Platonism, and with Günderrode's political, at times republican, interests.

The Scope of this Study

The first chapter outlines the important stages in Günderrode's reception history, through examining the importance of Bettine von Arnim and Christa Wolf in shaping images of Günderrode in the nineteenth and twentieth centuries. This is complemented by a brief overview of Günderrode's biography. The second chapter outlines the conceptual framework of this study: it traces the contours of the *Pantheimusstreit* and demonstrates how and why Günderrode has to be read in this context.

The third chapter is concerned with human agency across Günderrode's plays and poetry, and how these coincide with Günderrode's political leanings towards Republicanism. The play 'Magie und Schicksal' [Magic and Fate] (1805) functions as a negative example of Spinozism, specifically of the kind of fatalism that Friedrich Heinrich Jacobi accused Spinoza of during the pantheism controversy; the focus on fatalism also befits the subgenre of the *Schicksalsdrama* [fate drama]. The protagonist Ligares has to acknowledge the inherent limitations of his own agency, and how his agency is neutralised by the interventions of fate. What is at stake in this chapter is not only the possibility of individual agency, but also what historical development may mean — and this is where the argument leads back to Republicanism, but also to the eighteenth-century notion of perfectibility and its ambivalences. Günderrode's poems dedicated to Brutus, Caesar's assassin, complement the failings of Ligares by presenting a similar character type of unbridled agency, albeit in idealised form. The poems uphold ideals of Republicanism and valorise Brutus's world-historical agency, whilst lamenting how Brutus becomes a victim to history, which functions as a parallel to the French Revolution's bloody descent into terror and failure.

The chapter further investigates how Günderrode explores the possibilities of human agency in two plays: 'Nikator' and 'Hildgund'. Both the protagonists of 'Nikator' and 'Hildgund' are revolutionary in function by committing tyrannicide. Like Brutus, their agency is unconstrained by conventional norms of authority. But what has been previously overlooked is how their agency is grounded. There are textual clues that link back to a metaphysical understanding of the world: both Hildgund and Nikator invoke the notion of an inner voice — an allusion to Rousseau — but one that also suggests that this inner voice corresponds to the voice of the divine operating within the individual. That is, there is a form of moral universalism at work which implies a metaphysical, teleological structure to the world. The end of the *telos*, or, in this sense, of revolutionary action, remains unexplored in both 'Hildgund' and 'Nikator': both are marked by non-closure, an inability to realise the promise of revolutionary hopes.

The fourth chapter builds on this interaction between politics and metaphysics to chart the transformation of political hopes into hopes for a new Spinozist religion, which also continues the argument about the question of agency. The German intelligentsia became disillusioned with Napoleon after a period of feverish excitement in 1799, and particularly after he had himself crowned Emperor in 1804. Günderrode participates in an oblique critique of Napoleon by staging his literary fall from grace in the poem 'Der Franke in Egypten' [The Frenchman in Egypt], written in the same year. The utopian hopes that had once been associated with Napoleon become displaced thereafter onto the figure of the Prophet Muhammad: there are clear textual and contextual commonalities to help clarify why Napoleon should be transfigured into Muhammad in Günderrode's *oeuvre*. What distinguishes Muhammad and indeed becomes problematic in some ways is how he is an agent of and conduit for divine will.

Günderrode's most substantial work, 'Mahomed, der Prophet von Mekka' [Mahomed, the Prophet of Mecca] (1805), is a systematic *apologia* for revealed religion, but in the form of Spinozism. Mahomed's own agency as the true prophet of Islam is displaced: his surrender to divine will maps onto the etymological meaning of Islam as submission. What is significant about the Spinozism of the play is not just the fact that it clarifies the function of panentheism in general as a heterodox form of religion, but also that Günderrode makes the claim that Spinozism is the universal religion that was given to mankind in antiquity in the form of a primordial revelation. All religious and philosophical traditions in 'Mahomed' confirm the notion of perennial philosophy. This is a point also confirmed in the companion piece to 'Mahomed', 'Geschichte eines Braminen' [Story of a Brahmin] (1805), whose protagonist embodies the *vita contemplativa* to Mahomed's *vita activa*. Both the play 'Mahomed' and 'Geschichte eines Braminen' share the notion that presenting a return of religion to its prelapsarian state, before it disintegrated historically into factionalism or into separate religions, has the effect of uncovering the highest truths of how the individual should relate the world, and of anchoring the individual in nature. In the case of 'Geschichte eines Braminen', this becomes explicitly a project of naturalisation: the individual exists in complete harmony with the cosmos; indeed, the protagonist rejects all social bonds in favour of a metaphysical variant of cosmopolitanism that allows for the unimpeded development of the self. As this chapter argues, 'Geschichte eines Braminen' contains textual and structural allusions to Johann Joachim Spalding's *Betrachtung über die Bestimmung des Menschen* [Consideration on the Destination of Man] (1748), which was a popular and influential text in the latter half of the eighteenth century. Where the 'Mahomed' problematises the agency of its protagonist, 'Geschichte eines Braminen' makes use of the same metaphysical underpinnings to explore the possibility for absolute self-development.

The fifth chapter examines how Günderrode responds to Kantian epistemology, and how forms of cognition and sense perception make possible insights into the first cause or unmoved mover. To do this, Günderrode moves away from Kantian epistemology and instead adopts a Platonic model, where the 'fall' of the individual into consciousness creates a cognitive barrier to apprehending the panentheistic whole. This barrier is almost impossible to overcome without undoing the process of individuation entirely. This chapter covers the prominent trope of the epistemological quest in Günderrode and demonstrates how it operates according to poetic models of ascent and descent. What is important about this chapter is how the tensions in this poetic movement of ascent and descent derive from the conception of the individual as a Leibnizian monad, as being invulnerable and yet reflecting the entirety of the cosmos. Even the most successful form of ascent and apprehension of the whole in 'Ein apokaliptisches Fragment' [An Apocalyptic Fragment] (1804) comes at a great cost: it is only through death that the individual can commune with the elements and come to understand its own origins. The tensions evident throughout the poems discussed in this chapter, many of which make use of Platonic vocabulary, prepare the ground for the dissolution of the barrier between subject and object in *Melete* (1806), where all becomes subsumed into nature, or, in Günderrode's terminology, into dynamic and ever-gestating 'Leben' [life].

The sixth chapter examines the function of poetry in Günderrode's final collection, *Melete*, and how poetry becomes a means of achieving epistemological insight: the aesthetic act of reading itself means that there is reciprocity between the reader and poet in creating the meaning of the texts, but this is also couched in terms of poetry conveying esoteric knowledge. This distinguishes *Melete* from Günderrode's preceding poetry. What also distinguishes *Melete* is also how nature is posited as a subject, rather than as an object. This is simply presented to the reader as a given in the three-poem cycle 'Der Nil', 'Aegypten', and 'Der Caucasus', rather than being discursively stated.

The sixth chapter also argues that Günderrode's interest in Spinozist panentheism becomes modified through her enthusiasm for Schelling's philosophy of nature. This enthusiasm, in part, derives from Günderrode's interest in late eighteenth-century philosophical and scientific theories of life. The idea of perfection was previously formulated in Platonic and Neoplatonist terms as the (vertical) return to the divine animating principle of the universe. In Günderrode's most expansive cosmology, 'Briefe zweier Freunde' [Letters between Two Friends], perfection becomes flattened out, or rather becomes immanent as cosmic perfectibility and as the historical process that, it is posited, would lead to the absolute harmony of the spiritualised and organic universe. Each individual's impulse towards self-development and self-perfection inherently contributes to the perfectibility of the whole: this absolute reciprocity between the individual and the whole draws on a Spinozist concept of human freedom. In this manner of naturalising the individual into the whole, panentheism also becomes pantheism, as transcendence collapses into the immanent world.

The seventh chapter moves away from looking at Günderrode to examine the reception of Spinozism and pantheism in the period more generally, by looking at the works of Sophie Mereau, Friedrich Hölderlin, and Novalis. The purpose of this chapter is to distinguish Günderrode from her contemporaries, since it has been a temptation in scholarship to compare Günderrode to both Hölderlin and Novalis, whom she read and admired. The aim of the chapter is to show how Günderrode is more consistent than these three writers in pursuing a positively connoted form of Spinozist panentheism and pantheism.

CHAPTER 1

Biography and Myth

Günderrode's reception history demonstrates the undeniably attractive pull of biography. In the pointed words of Hannelore Schlaffer in the afterword to her Reclam selection of Günderrode's works: 'Die Günderrode ist eine Dichterin ohne große Dichtung, jedoch mit großem Schicksal' [Günderrode is a poet without great poetry, but with a great destiny].[1] Or, in Gerhard Schulz's more charitable account, a sensational biography is 'Das Schlimmste, was einem literarischen Werk widerfahren kann [...] von solcher Belastung emanzipiert es sich nur schwer' [The worst thing that can happen to a literary work [...] it can be freed from this burden only with difficulty].[2] The appeal of Günderrode's biography stems from her suicide at the age of twenty-six. This was made particularly dramatic by its manner — a combination of drowning in the Rhine and stabbing — and by its purported stimulus: Friedrich Creuzer's rejection of Günderrode. He was also known as a professor of philology, known for his seminal publications on comparative mythology, at the University of Heidelberg. To be sure, it is a truism that any writer, poet, or philosophy is constituted by their reception and its attendant myths. The image of Novalis, as is well known, was posthumously crafted — and politically neutered — by Friedrich Schlegel and Ludwig Tieck, who edited the first edition of his works.[3] Novalis's works, however, enjoyed posthumous success on the book market.

Günderrode's collections received faintly well-meaning reviews upon publication as well as after her death. Goethe referred to her first collection somewhat uneasily as: 'wirklich eine seltsame Erscheinung und die Recension brauchbar' [truly a curious publication and should be reviewed].[4] Her works did not, however, have a lasting impact and enjoy the publishing success of Novalis's works. Ludwig Geiger, the literary historian and founder of the *Goethe-Jahrbuch* [Goethe Yearbook], had acquired Günderrode's *Nachlass* and noted that the two collections published during

---

1   Karoline von Günderrode, *Gedichte, Prosa, Briefe* (Stuttgart: Reclam, 1998), p. 131.
2   Gerhard Schulz, 'Träume eines Stiftfräuleins: Zum 200. Geburtstag der Karoline von Günderrode', *Frankfurter Allgemeine Zeitung*, 9 February 1980, p. 23. For an overview of the myths that have proliferated around Günderrode, see Adrian Hummel, 'Lebenszwänge, Schreibräume, unirdisch: Eine kulturanthropologische orientierte Deutung des "Mythos Günderrode"', *Athenäum*, 13 (2003), 61–91 (p. 67).
3   Erika Thomalla, *Anwälte des Autors: Zur Geschichte der Herausgeberschaft im 18. und 19. Jahrhundert* (Göttingen: Wallstein, 2020), pp. 372–83.
4   Johann Wolfgang Goethe, *Werke, herausgegeben im Auftrage der Großherzogin Sophie von Sachsen*, 143 vols (Weimar: Hermann Böhlau, 1887–1919), IV.XVII: *Goethes Briefe. Anfang 1804–9. Mai 1805* (1895), 131f.

Günderrode's lifetime had become so rare by the end of the nineteenth century as to be considered prized collectors' items.[5]

This means that Günderrode's reception history is based on and a symptom of nineteenth- and twentieth-century practices of literary memorialisation and canonisation. Günderrode becomes a useful point of reference and identification for women writers, most prominently for Bettine von Arnim and Christa Wolf, which will be the subject of discussion below. More generally speaking, the narrative of Günderrode's biography becomes an object of fascination not just because of her manner of death, but also because of what it represents. According to Birgit Wagenbäur, its symbolic power lies in Günderrode's uncompromising attitude and rejection of social norms — in the affair with Creuzer, and in the presumed logic of the suicide following Creuzer's rejection.[6] Günderrode's unwavering autodidacticism, literary and intellectual ambition, and attempts to overcome the restrictions of her patrician status make her into a victim of her social standing and of society more generally.[7] This reading of Günderrode as a victim of history can be intensified through an appreciation of the discomfort around female erudition in the latter half of the eighteenth century.[8] Christian Nees von Esenbeck, one of Günderrode's erstwhile literary mentors and a well-known botanist, lamented her masculine desire to write poetry — one that was necessarily doomed to failure — in an 1807 review of her second collection, *Poetische Fragmente* [Poetic Fragments] (1805), which he had advised Günderrode on during its composition.[9] Or: in a literary-historical reading, Günderrode's correspondence betrays the instability of Romantic notions of subjectivity, where the longing for the absolute becomes transfigured into a longing for death.[10]

Günderrode's biography is a narrative constituted by a series of tropes, which have turned Günderrode into a product of projections made by critics.[11] The problem lies not only the sensational aspects of the biography itself, but also in the substantial gaps in the extant archival materials and published editions of her works. The archival information still extant about Günderrode, her immediate social circle

---

5   Ludwig Geiger, *Karoline von Günderode und ihre Freunde: Mit dem Porträt der Dichterin* (Stuttgart: Deutsche Verlags-Anstalt, 1895), p. 1.
6   Birgit Wagenbäur, '"habe getaumelt in den Räumen des Aethers": Karoline von Günderrodes ästhetische Identität', in *Frauen: MitSprechen — MitSchreiben: Beiträge zur literatur- und sprachwissenschaftlichen Frauenforschung*, ed. by Marianne Henn and Britta Hufeisen, Stuttgarter Arbeiten zur Germanistik, 349 (Stuttgart: Heinz, 1997), pp. 201–21 (p. 201).
7   A typical example of this narrative is laid out by Andreas Hansert, in the context of the Günderrode family as a whole: Andreas Hansert, *Geburtsaristokratie in Frankfurt am Main* (Vienna: Böhlau, 2014), p. 443.
8   Silvia Bovenschen, *Die imaginierte Weiblichkeit: Exemplarische Untersuchungen zu kulturgeschichtlichen und literarischen Präsentationsformen des Weiblichen*, 3rd edn (Frankfurt a.M.: Suhrkamp, 2016), pp. 158–64.
9   'Frankfurt a. M., b. Wilmanns: Poetische Fragmente von Tian', *Jenaische Allgemeine Literatur-Zeitung*, 138, 13 June 1807, pp. 489–91.
10 Karl Heinz Bohrer, *Der romantische Brief: Die Entstehung ästhetischer Subjektivität* (Munich: Hanser, 1987), p. 179. See also: Walter Rehm, *Der Todesgedanke in der deutschen Dichtung vom Mittelalter bis zur Romantik*, 2nd edn (Darmstadt: Wissenschaftliche Buchgesellschaft, 1967).
11 Marina Rauchenbacher, *Karoline von Günderrode*: *Eine Rezeptionsstudie* (Würzburg: Königshausen & Neumann, 2014), p. 13.

as well as her family, is incomplete. A section of the family archive, which, the local historian Max Preitz noted in 1938, happened to contain a wealth of information on Günderrode's childhood, was destroyed in the series of bombing raids that razed the centres of Frankfurt am Main and Darmstadt in spring 1945 and autumn 1944.[12] Whilst a historical-critical edition was published by Stroemfeld in 1991, the three-volume edition does not include all of Günderrode's studies. To be sure, the publication of a critical edition makes Günderrode's works more accessible to scholarship and a broader readership when compared to other female writers of the period, such as Therese Huber, Sophie Mereau, or Caroline Schlegel-Schelling, or even to well-known male writers such as Ludwig Tieck. What is still lacking is a reliable and complete edition of Günderrode's correspondence.[13]

The overall purpose of the present volume is to move away from biographically determined readings of Günderrode's work and to account for her significance in the literary and intellectual climate of her time. By way of introduction to Günderrode, it is nonetheless worth briefly attending to a sketch of Günderrode's biography and the most important interpreters of her reception history. What follows is therefore a tentative reconstruction given the current material available, which still requires sustained scholarly attention. Following a brief overview of Günderrode's biography, I will turn to two of the most important figures in Günderrode's reception history in the nineteenth and twentieth centuries: Bettine von Arnim and Christa Wolf.[14]

Karoline von Günderrode: Frankfurt Patrician

Karoline von Günderrode was born in Karlsruhe in 1780 as the eldest child of a patrician family with strong ties to Frankfurt am Main. As an imperial free city or *freie Reichsstadt*, Frankfurt had a privileged status in the Holy Roman Empire and its city council was controlled by a group of Lutheran patrician families. The Günderrode line was a prominent family in the Alten-Limpurg *Ganerbschaft* [a joint family estate], an alliance of patrician families, and particularly in the political life of the city in the eighteenth century.[15] Günderrode's youngest sibling and only brother, Hektor, went on to play an important role in the city's cultural and political life in the nineteenth century. He became a senator and a mayor of Frankfurt. He also corresponded with Otto von Bismarck in 1851, who was at the time the Prussian ambassador to the city of Frankfurt.[16]

---

12   Frankfurt a.M., Universitätsbibliothek J. C. Senckenberg (SUF), Ms. Ff. K. v. Günderrode Abt. 3. A selection of the notes that Max Preitz took of the Günderrode family archive survive and are held by the Freies Deutsches Hochstift in Frankfurt am Main.
13   As Dieter Burdorf notes, the most recent edition of Günderrode's correspondence — Birgit Weißenborn's *Ich sende Dir ein zärtliches Pfand* — does not conform to editorial standards expected in academic scholarship: Dieter Burdorf, ' "Diese Sehnsucht ist ein Gedanke, der ins Unendliche starrt": Über Karoline von Günderrode — aus Anlaß neuer Ausgaben ihrer Werke und Briefe', *Wirkendes Wort*, 43 (1993), 49–67 (p. 60).
14   For a detailed account of Günderrode's biography, see Markus Hille, *Karoline von Günderrode* (Reinbek: Rowohlt, 1999).
15   Hansert, pp. 387–88.
16   The Universitätsbibliothek Senckenberg in Frankfurt am Main has evidence of this

Although Karoline von Günderrode is the most famous literary figure in her family, she was by no means an exception in her intellectual and literary pursuits. Her paternal grandfather, Johann Maximilian von Günderrode, published writings on German constitutional law. Her father, Hektor von Günderrode, a court counsellor in Karlsruhe in Baden, was also legally trained. He wrote on numismatics and produced historical writings, such as a biography of a thirteenth-century king of the Germans, Adolph of Nassau, as well as an earlier *Versuch in Idyllen* [Essays in the Idyllic Genre] (1771), a series of prose idylls modelled on the works of Salomon Gessner.[17] His collected writings were published a year after his death from a haemorrhage at the age of thirty, and were collated by Ernst Ludwig Posselt, the private secretary to Markgraf Karl Friedrich in Karlsruhe. Günderrode's mother, Louise, too, wrote occasional poetry, including love poetry, and manuscripts survive of rhyming exercises that were intended to be completed socially by several members of the family, not just in each other's presence but also in their correspondence.[18] In short: the Günderrode family were not just politically and socially important in Frankfurt, but were also integrated into the literary and intellectual culture of the time.

After the premature death of her husband, Louise von Günderrode moved to Hanau with her six children and was supported by a modest pension from the state of Baden but also by the trust inherited through her husband. Three of Günderrode's sisters died young: Louise in 1794 at the age of thirteen, Amalie in 1802, at seventeen, and most importantly, Charlotte in 1801, at the age of eighteen. Charlotte and Karoline were alike in temperament, according to Günderrode (*SW* I, 444), and she nursed her sister on her deathbed.[19] The causes of death are believed to be related to tuberculosis, which may have in turn be the source of the eye condition that gave Günderrode difficulty when reading, writing, and studying.[20]

In 1797, Günderrode entered the Lutheran Cronstetten-Hynspergische Damenstift, a home for unmarried women of the Alten-Limpurg line situated on the Roßmarkt in the centre of Frankfurt. It had been founded earlier in the eighteenth century by Justina Katharina Steffan von Cronstetten through her bequest. The benefactress was herself a devout Pietist. Indeed, Frankfurt itself was one of the centres of Pietism in the mid-eighteenth century. Goethe's early acquaintance with Pietist circles in Frankfurt made its literary mark in the chapter 'Bekenntnisse einer schönen Seele' [Confessions of a Beautiful Soul] in *Wilhelm Meisters Lehrjahre* [Wilhelm Meister's Apprenticeship] (1795–96). By Günderrode's time, the Damenstift's rules had become more liberal, which facilitated theatre visits and

correspondence in its autograph collection: Autogr. O.v.Bismarck.

17 Hector Wilhelm von Günderrode, *Geschichte des römischen Königs Adolphs nach denen Urkunden und gleichzeitigen Geschichtsschreibern* (Frankfurt a.M.: Johann Philipp Reifferstein, 1779).

18 Jordan Ross Lavers, '*Schwesterstimme*: Gender, Emotion and Kinship in the Correspondence of the von Günderrode Sisters' (unpublished doctoral thesis, University of Western Australia, 2020), pp. 118–19; private correspondence with Jordan Lavers, with permission.

19 Max Preitz, 'Karoline von Günderrode in ihrer Umwelt. II. Karoline von Günderrodes Briefwechsel mit Friedrich Karl und Gunda von Savigny', *Jahrbuch des freien deutschen Hochstifts* (1964), 158–235 (pp. 167ff.).

20 Hille, pp. 92–93.

stays with family and personal friends, such as the legal scholar Friedrich Karl von Savigny and his wife Gunda (née Brentano) in their estate at Trages, or to stay with her ailing grandfather in Butzbach after the death of her great aunt in early 1800.[21] Günderrode's entry into the Damenstift was not, however, determined by financial impoverishment, as has been often assumed.[22] The Günderrode family were wealthy and owned lands and estates in Frankfurt and the surrounding area. The Damenstift instead fulfilled a pragmatic function: as an intermediary site for young women of the Alten-Limpurg line prior to marriage. As Jordan Lavers has recently demonstrated, Günderrode was engaged in legal disputes about securing her inheritance with the manager of her mother's estate.[23]

Günderrode was well-integrated into the social and cultural life of Frankfurt patricians and the aristocratic circles in Hessen more generally. Her social circle, as can be gleaned from extant correspondence, included members of the Leonhardi banking family and the Fichard family, as well as lively exchanges with Lisette von Mettingh, who would become the wife of Christian Nees von Esenbeck, about the constraints of middle-class gender roles.[24] Lisette's half-sister, Susanne von Heyden, collaborated with Günderrode on her philosophical studies. It was she who destroyed Günderrode's letters to Friedrich Creuzer after her death and was responsible for clearing her possessions from the Damenstift.

The genealogy of Günderrode's literary reception was shaped by her connections to the Brentanos, who had established itself as a successful merchant family in Frankfurt in the eighteenth century. Günderrode knew and corresponded with Gunda, Clemens, and Bettine von Arnim (née Brentano). Clemens Brentano's correspondence with Günderrode began in early 1802 with a remarkably erotically charged letter. Günderrode responded to this coolly and the letter may well have been less of a sexual advance than a self-conscious literary game on Brentano's part.[25] Clemens Brentano commented on the publication of *Gedichte und Phantasien* [Poems and Fantasies] (1804) and considered the poems to be too scholarly and masculine (*SW* III, 62–63). Günderrode responded by claiming that writing was a form of self-assertion (*SW* III, 63). Brentano would also later come to ask Günderrode in 1806 for material for the second volume of the *Des Knaben Wunderhorn* [The Boy's Magic Horn] (1808), which he was preparing with Achim von Arnim.[26]

---

21   Ibid., p. 29; p. 45.
22   See, for example, Lazarowicz, p. 176; Judith Purver, 'Revolution, Romanticism, Restoration (1789–1830)', in *A History of Women's Writing in Germany, Austria and Switzerland*, ed. by Jo Catling (Cambridge: Cambridge University Press, 2000), pp. 68–87 (p. 73); see also the account of Günderrode's life aimed at a popular readership, where the assumption of Günderrode's poverty facilitates parallels with Kleist: Dagmar von Gersdorff, *Die Erde ist mir Heimat nicht geworden: Das Leben der Karoline von Günderrode* (Frankfurt a.M.: Insel, 2011), p. 147.
23   Lavers, pp. 158–61.
24   Preitz/Hopp III, pp. 243f.
25   Wolfgang Bunzel, 'Bis(s) zum Morgengrauen. Clemens Brentanos erster Brief an Karoline von Günderrode: Kontext, Funktion, Materialität', in *Romantik kontrovers: Ein Debattenparcours zum zwanzigjährigen Jubiläum der Stiftung für Romantikforschung*, ed. by Gerhart von Graevenitz, Stiftung für Romantikforschung, 58 (Würzburg: Königshausen & Neumann, 2015), pp. 229–44.
26   Clemens Brentano, letter to Karoline von Günderrode, 1806, Freies Deutsches Hochstift

It is tempting to write Günderrode's biography as a series of episodes in unhappy or unreciprocated love. She fell in love with Savigny, but he married Gunda Brentano rather than Günderrode. Creuzer was already married by the time he first met Günderrode in 1804, and their intense relationship was brought to a halt by illness, which caused him to renounce Günderrode in July 1806. More important than any speculation about matters of the heart is how Günderrode necessarily relied on male mediators to organise the publication of her works, which were also published under pseudonyms, as was common for both female and some male authors at the time. For Günderrode there were several men who acted in this role: in the first instance, Christian Nees von Esenbeck for both *Gedichte und Phantasien* and *Poetische Fragmente* (1805), followed by Friedrich Creuzer for *Melete*, the publication of which was suppressed following Günderrode's death.

The circumstances of Günderrode's death in July 1806 are troubling for several reasons. Unlike Kleist, Günderrode left no final letter. The official documents about the necessary legal proceedings following Günderrode's death are also missing.[27] In the 1870s, Karl Schwartz attempted to reconstruct the official reports and specifically the results of the autopsy, whereby it had been determined that Günderrode suffered from a splenetic disease that — to use present-day legal terminology — meant that she lacked mental and legal capacity.[28] A splenetic disease would, according to the Galenic medical theory of the humours, lead to an excess of black bile and to a state of melancholy. This interpretation neatly sidestepped the taboo of suicide and legitimised Günderrode's burial in the churchyard at Oestrich-Winkel.

Images of Günderrode: Bettine von Arnim, *Die Günderode* (1840)

Whilst Günderrode's publications garnered comparatively little attention during her lifetime, her literary fortunes changed with the novel *Die Günderode* (1840), compiled by Bettine von Arnim.[29] *Die Günderode* proved fundamental to the renewal of interest in Karoline von Günderrode. Its model of female friendship was warmly greeted by female and feminist readers alike. This established a pattern in the reception of Günderrode focussed on the virtues of female friendship, which can be traced from the American Transcendentalist author Margaret Fuller's project to translate the novel prior to her untimely death in 1850, to Margarethe

---

(FDH), Frankfurt a.M., MS 8298. Achim von Arnim also paid tribute to Günderrode by copying the epigraph on Günderrode's grave to bring the novella *Isabella von Ägypten* to an elegiac conclusion: Achim von Arnim, *Werke in sechs Bänden*, ed. by Roswitha Burwick and others, 6 vols (Frankfurt a.M.: Deutscher Klassiker Verlag, 1989–92), III: *Sämtliche Erzählungen 1802–1817*, ed. by Renate Moering (1990), pp. 776–77.

27 Florian Kühnel, *Kranke Ehre? Adlige Selbsttötung im Übergang zur Moderne* (Munich: Oldenbourg, 2013), p. 31.

28 Karl Schwartz, 'GÜNDERRODE (Karoline Friederike Louise Maximiliane von)', in *Allgemeine Encyklopädie der Wissenschaften und Künste*, ed. by Johann Samuel Ersch and Johann Gottfried Gruber, 167 vols (Leipzig: Brockhaus, 1818–89), XCVII: *Gulaþingslög — Gussonea* (1878), pp. 167–231 (pp. 219–20).

29 For the sake of consistency, I shall refer to Bettine von Arnim by her married name, including when discussing the period before her marriage to Achim von Arnim in 1811.

von Trotta's film *Heller Wahn* [Sheer Madness] (1983).[30] *Die Günderode* functions as literary memorial to Günderrode and omits discussion of the suicide entirely.

Arnim had known Günderrode but was by no means one of her most intimate acquaintances. They were closest in 1805, when Günderrode had acted as an intellectual mentor and instructor to Arnim, who chafed against Günderrode's insistence on discipline when learning and studying. Indeed, this distance between them is noted in Arnim's account of Günderrode's suicide in the opening section of *Goethe's Briefwechsel mit einem Kinde* [Goethe's Correspondence with a Child] (1835), in a long letter addressed to Goethe's mother. Here Arnim mentions that she did not know if Günderrode was closer to Creuzer or Carl Daub, a professor of theology and a colleague of Creuzer's at Heidelberg.[31] This suggestion of relative distance from Günderrode complicates Arnim's portrayal of herself as Günderrode's confidante, manifest, for example, in Günderrode's confession to Arnim that she had asked a surgeon for advice on how to commit suicide. Regardless of the truth-value of the details of this letter, it is marked by the difficulties of how to make sense of and articulate personal loss.[32] Should the incident with the surgeon be little more than a retrospective and imaginative addition — it certainly cannot be empirically quantified — it does intensify the pathos of the letter.

Following the success of *Goethe's Briefwechsel*, Bettine von Arnim compiled a further novel dedicated to Günderrode, which was equally well received upon publication.[33] Arnim's compositional technique for her epistolary novels was to compile, edit, and expand on actual letters, which has inspired critics to decry Arnim's seemingly careless fusion of historical fact and imaginative interpolation.[34] Some parts of the novel have been used by critics as evidence of Günderrode's writings when they are not available elsewhere.[35] Since the novel is composed primarily of Arnim's letters, which increasingly come to dominate the novel in the second half, it is therefore less concerned with representing Günderrode than it is with constituting Arnim's philosophical and poetic project, which recovers elements

---

30 Charles Capper, *Margaret Fuller: An American Romantic Life*, 2 vols (Oxford: Oxford University Press, 1992–2007), II: *The Public Years* (2007), p. 74. Barbara Becker-Cantarino, 'Zur Rezeption "Bettinas" in England und in Neuengland', in *Bettina von Arnim Handbuch*, ed. by Barbara Becker-Cantarino (Berlin: De Gruyter, 2019), pp. 609–21 (p. 616). I am grateful to Georgina Paul for bringing *Heller Wahn* to my attention.
31 Bettine von Arnim, *Goethe's Briefwechsel mit einem Kinde* (Frankfurt a.M.: Deutscher Klassiker Verlag, 1992), pp. 72–73.
32 Ibid., p. 63.
33 Lisabeth M. Hock, *Replicas of a Female Prometheus: The Textual Personae of Bettin von Arnim*, Northern American Studies in Nineteenth-Century German Literature, 27 (Peter Lang: New York, 2001), p. 55.
34 Edith Waldstein, *Bettine von Arnim and the Politics of Romantic Conversation*, Studies in German Literature, Linguistics, and Culture, 33 (Rochester, NY: Camden House, 1988), pp. 43–51; Karin R. Daubert, 'Reflexive Authorship in Bettina Brentano-von Arnim's *Die Günderode*: Narrative Disunity, Hölderlin, and Günderrode', in *Gender, Collaboration, and Authorship in German Culture: Literary Joint Ventures, 1750–1850*, ed. by Laura Deiulio and John B. Lyon, New Directions in German Studies, 27 (New York: Bloomsbury Academic, 2019), pp. 253–72 (pp. 254–55).
35 See most recently, for example, the poem 'Lethe', not present in Morgenthaler's critical edition, given in Rüdiger Görner, *Romantik: Ein europäisches Ereignis* (Stuttgart: Reclam, 2021), p. 164.

from Romantic philosophy.[36] It is nonetheless an act of imaginative archaeology in epistolary dialogue with Günderrode.[37] Indeed, this act of recovery assumes a political dimension: the exploration of female friendship presents an egalitarian and idealised countermodel to the strict hierarchies of German-speaking lands during the Restoration.[38]

Whilst *Die Günderode* predominantly focuses on Arnim's poetic self-presentation, there are productive points of overlap between the historical Günderrode and the literary Günderrode of the novel, much as the literary Günderrode is Arnim's invention.[39] Arnim writes *Die Günderode* explicitly in dialogue with Günderrode's work. Not only does she enclose Günderrode's poems and dialogues in the correspondence, but also she responds directly to parts of Günderrode's work, such as 'Ein apokaliptisches Fragment', which the literary Arnim, in a moment of self-deprecation, claims is too numinous for her to understand.[40] There is also discussion of Frans Hemsterhuis's philosophy, Hölderlin's poetry, and the literary Arnim expresses her bewilderment at the abstractions of Idealist philosophy of Kant, Fichte, and Schelling, so favoured by Günderrode.[41] In short: there are resonances between the literary presentation of Günderrode and her actual work, and it is worth briefly attending to how Arnim reflects the historical Günderrode's interests in the *Briefroman*.

There is a metaphysical strand to Arnim's concept of a *Schwebereligion* [floating religion] in the novel, which Günderrode never quite wholeheartedly endorses. Yet in an intense exchange about the divine character of music and poetry that opens the second part of the novel and uses the example of Goethe's poem 'Nachtgesang' [Night Song] (1804) as a primary example, Arnim depicts Günderrode's synthesising pantheism. Poetry, music, and philosophy give way to a sense of all-unity:

> Denn; wie auch das Alllebendige sich berühre, es entsteigt Wahrheit aus ihm, aus dem chaotischen Wogen und Schwanken entstieg die Welt als Melodie?
> [...]
> So wär der Menschengeist durch sein Fassen, Begreifen, befähigt Geistesallheit, Philosophie zu werden; also die Gottheit selbst? — denn, wär Gott

---

36   Lauren Shizuko Stone, 'Beilage zum Brief: On "Epistolarity" and Materiality in Bettine von Arnim's *Die Günderode*', *Colloquia Germanica*, 47.3 (2014), 287–305; Catherine Grimm, '"Wie ist Natur so hold und gut, die mich am Busen hält": Nature Philosophy and Feminine Subjectivity in the Epistolary Memoirs of Bettine von Arnim', in *Schwellenüberschreitungen: Politik in der Literatur von deutschsprachigen Frauen 1780–1918*, ed. by Caroline Bland and Elisa Müller-Adams (Berlin: Aisthesis, 2007), pp. 151–68.
37   Karin Zimmermann, *Die polyfunktionale Bedeutung dialogischer Sprechformen um 1800. Exemplarische Analysen: Rahel Varnhagen, Bettine von Arnim, Karoline von Günderrode*, Europäische Hochschulschriften Reihe I: Deutsche Sprache und Literatur, 1302 (Frankfurt a.M.: Peter Lang, 1992), p. 164.
38   Anna K. Kuhn, 'The "Failure" of Biography and the Triumph of Women's Writing: Bettina von Arnim's *Die Günderode* and Christa Wolf's *The Quest for Christa T.*', in *Revealing Lives: Autobiography, Biography, and Gender*, ed. by Susan Groag Bell and Marilyn Yalom (Albany: SUNY Press, 1990), pp. 19–28 (p. 23).
39   Kari Lokke, *Tracing Women's Romanticism: Gender, History, and Transcendence* (London: Routledge, 2004), p. 84.
40   Bettine von Arnim, *Clemens Brentano's Frühlingskranz: Die Günderode* (Frankfurt a.M.: Deutscher Klassiker Verlag, 2006), p. 316.
41   Ibid., p. 307.

unendlich, wenn er nicht in jeder Lebensknospe ganz und die Allheit wär? —
so wär jeder Geistesmoment die Allheit Gottes in sich tragend, aussprechend?

[For however the all-living God may move, truth emerges from Him, and
did the world not emerge as a melody from this chaotic surging and swaying?
[...]
In this way, the human spirit would be capable through its grasp and
comprehension to become the totality of spirit and philosophy; and so to
become the divinity itself? — for, if God is not infinite, is He not completely
present in every bud of life and is everything at the same time? — so would not
every moment of spirit bear and express the idea of God as everything?][42]

Günderrode's point relates to human creation as a second act of creation, deriving from the original act of divine creation, but also works through the pantheistic idea of God being in all things. Therefore, every act of human creativity, whether philosophical or poetic, is itself an expression of the divine. As part of the most intense exchange of letters between Arnim and Günderrode, this section also generates the textual impression of dialogic creativity. Günderrode's enthusiasm fades throughout the second half of the novel. In a later letter she touches on the problem of epistolary subjectivity:

aber es kommt mir sonderbar vor daß ich zuhöre wie ich spreche, und meine
eignen Worte kommen mir fast fremder vor als fremde. — Auch die wahrsten
Briefe sind meiner Ansicht nach nur Leichen, sie bezeichnen ein ihnen
einwohnend gewesenes Leben, und ob sie gleich dem Lebendigen ähnlich
sehen, so ist doch der Moment ihres Lebens schon dahin; deswegen kommt es
mir vor wenn ich lese was ich vor einiger Zeit geschrieben habe, als sähe ich
mich im Sarg liegen, und meine beiden Ichs starren sich ganz verwundert an.

[but it seems strange to me that I listen to how I speak, and my own words seem
even more foreign to me than those of others. — Even the most truthful letters
are, in my opinion, nothing but corpses, they designate an idea of life that had
once been and inhabits them, and even if they bear some similarities with the
living, their time of living has already passed. For that reason, whenever I read
what I had written down some time ago, it seems to me that I can see myself
lying in a coffin, and my two selves stare at one other in great bewilderment.][43]

This offers an intriguing qualification to the historical Günderrode's otherwise stated desire to write and publish literary works, which constitutes an indirect form of permanence or immortality. This letter can be read on a self-reflexive and metapoetic level about how to fix an individual through writing, in the way that Arnim herself is memorialising Günderrode in the novel.[44] The comically bizarre final image has shades of the humour of Jean Paul Richter and functions as a phenomenology of the self. The self is constructed of a series of impressions

---

42   Ibid., pp. 576–77.
43   Ibid., p. 682. Here Bettine von Arnim reproduces a genuine letter by Günderrode: Karoline von Günderrode, letter to Clemens Brentano, Klassik Stiftung Weimar, GSA 3/1053.
44   Marianne Schuller, '". . . da wars mir immer als wär hinter mir der mirs einflüstre . . .": Schreibszenen in Bettine von Arnims Günderode-Buch', in *'Mir ekelt vor diesem tintenklecksenden Säkulum': Schreibszenen im Zeitalter der Manuskripte*, ed. by Martin Stingelin (Fink: Munich, 2004), pp. 238–44 (p. 244).

and sensations that can be recorded but these lack coherence. Written memory and writing as a form of memory are, in this context, both alienating and moribund.

Images of Günderrode: Christa Wolf, *Die Schatten eines Traumes* (1979)

The question of memory and how to write historical narrative takes on importance for the most significant twentieth-century figure in Günderrode's reception, Christa Wolf. Wolf's selection of Günderrode's works, *Der Schatten eines Traumes. Gedichte. Prosa. Briefe* [The Shadow of a Dream. Poems. Prose. Letters] (1979) repeats the structure of Bettine von Arnim's reception, by omitting Günderrode's dramas entirely. For Wolf, this is a matter of aesthetic judgement.[45] Wolf was engaged in an explicitly feminist archaeology, recuperating Günderrode as a female poet and intellectual. Equally, Günderrode is useful for Christa Wolf as a parallel to her own disillusionment with the East German regime in the late 1970s, following Wolf Biermann's forced exile in 1976.[46] In this sense, as is the case with Bettine von Arnim, Wolf is engaged, if far more indirectly, in an act of double biography in her presentation of Günderrode's life.[47] Christa Wolf would also draw Günderrode and Kleist together as protagonists divided against themselves and against society in the novel *Kein Ort. Nirgends* [No Place on Earth] (1979), which extensively quotes and creatively condenses Günderrode's letters.[48]

Wolf's essay, 'Der Schatten eines Traumes: Karoline von Günderrode — ein Entwurf' [The Shadow of a Dream: Karoline von Günderrode — an Essay], which opens the volume of the same name, is polemical in character. It is revealing as an attempt write Günderrode into narratives of literary historiography, since Wolf presents Günderrode as a victim of her inner life and of society in general.[49] Whilst Wolf writes against the myth of Günderrode as an otherworldly figure, she is still cast as a historical failure, and thus her biography is read retrospectively through the circumstances of her death. In her opening sketch of Günderrode, Wolf outlines this double failure to evoke pathos:

> Die Dissonanz ihrer Seele [...] ist, aber, das weiß sie noch nicht, die Unstimmigkeit der Zeit. Gezeichnet von einem unheilbaren Zwiespalt, begabt, ihr Ungenügen an sich und die Welt auszudrücken, lebt sie ein kurzes, ereignisarmes, an inneren Erschütterungen reiches Leben, verweigert den Kompromiß, gibt sich selbst den Tod, von wenigen Freunden betrauert, kaum gekannt, hinterläßt, zu wichtigen Teilen ungedruckt, ein schmales Werk.

---

45   Karoline von Günderrode, *Der Schatten eines Traumes. Gedichte. Prosa. Briefe*, ed. by Christa Wolf (Berlin: Buchverlag der Morgen, 1979), p. 63.
46   John D. Pizer, *Imagining the Age of Goethe in German Literature, 1970–2010* (Rochester, NY: Camden House, 2011), p. 51.
47   See Helga G. Braunbeck, 'Das weibliche Schreibmuster der Doppelbiographie: Bettine von Arnims und Christa Wolfs Günderrode-Biographik', in *Frauen — Literatur — Revolution*, ed. by Helga Grubitzsch and others, THETIS — Literatur im Spiegel der Geschlechter, 3 (Pfaffenweiler: Centaurus-Verlagsgesellschaft, 1992), pp. 231–44 (p. 233).
48   See Ute Brandes, 'Quotation as Authentication: *No Place on Earth*', in *Responses to Christa Wolf*, ed. by Marilyn Sibley Fries (Detroit: Wayne State University Press, 1989), pp. 326–48.
49   Stephanie Bird, *Recasting Historical Women: Female Identity in German Biographical Fiction* (Oxford: Berg, 1998), pp. 82–84.

> [The dissonance of her soul [...] is, though — and she does not know this yet — to do with the dissonances of her time. Characterised by incurable inner discord, and possessing the talent to express her dissatisfaction with herself and the world, she lives a short life, one devoid of incident but rich in inner turmoil, shuns compromise, gives herself over to death, is mourned by few friends, is barely known, and leaves behind a small body of work, mostly unpublished.][50]

Günderrode is a source of fascination for Wolf precisely because of her refusal to compromise and conform to the gendered expectations of her time, in her desire both to write and also to pursue various love interests. Wolf clarifies that Günderrode is little more than a sexual object to Clemens Brentano, Savigny, and Creuzer, and Günderrode's desire for intellectual, erotic, and emotional fulfilment must be thwarted.[51] This framing of Günderrode as a victim of history may well be a feminist lament, but it has the effect of emptying Günderrode of historical agency so that she must succumb to patriarchal structures.

The essay closes with a restatement of the opening thesis of Günderrode cast in the role of a victim but expands this thought to include all poets and writers: 'Die Literatur der Deutschen als ein Schlachtfeld — auch das wäre eine Weise, sie zu betrachten. Dichter sind, das ist keine Klage, zu Opfern und Selbstopfern prädestiniert' [German literature as a battlefield — and that too would be a way of viewing it. Poets are — and this is no lament — predestined to be victims and victims of themselves].[52] This is more than Wolf drawing a distinction between creative writers and society and pointing to the inner tensions within poets and writers. The notion of writers as victims is also embedded in a historical narrative about the inheritance of the Enlightenment and the French Revolution. Wolf makes recourse to a narrative of historical pessimism:

> Die bürgerlichen Verhältnisse, die sich schließlich auch ohne Revolution diesseits des Rheins ausbreiten, etablieren zwar keine kräftig neuen ökonomischen und sozialen Zustände, dafür aber eine durchdringende, auf Niederhaltung alles Unbeugsamen, Originalen gegründete Kleinbürgermoral. [...] Fremdlinge werden die [Intellektuellen] im eignen Land, Vorgänger, denen keiner folgt, Begeisterte ohne Widerhall, Rufer ohne Echo.
> [...]
> Der vulgäre Materialismus unsrer Zeit kann dem dürren Rationalismus ihrer Zeit nicht auf die Sprünge kommen, der rechthaberischen, alles erklärenden und nichts verstehenden Plattheit, gegen den die, von denen wir reden, sich ja grade zur Wehr setzen: gegen die eiskalte Abstraktion [...] gegen das erbarmungslose Zweckmäßigkeitsdenken, die sich als Angst, Depression, als Hang zur Selbstzerstörung in ihnen niederschlagen.
>
> [The bourgeois conditions which, in the end, establish themselves on this side of the Rhine without a revolution, admittedly do not bring about any forcefully novel economic or social conditions, but instead do bring about a petit-bourgeois morality, which is founded on suppressing anything uncompromisingly original. [...] The intellectuals become foreign in their own land,

---

50   Günderrode, *Der Schatten eines Traumes*, p. 5.
51   Ibid., p. 23.
52   Ibid., p. 65.

an avant-garde without followers, filled with inspiration but achieving no resonance, calling out with no echo.
[...]
The vulgar materialism of our time cannot see through the tricks of the arid rationalism of their time, that attitude of dogmatic banality that seeks to explain everything and understands nothing, against which those of whom we speak did indeed take a stand: against cold abstraction [...] against that type of merciless thinking that reduces everything to purposes, and such resistance manifests in these individuals as fear, depression, as a tendency towards self-destruction.][53]

This is a psychologised reading of the legacy of Enlightenment — one that is itself a caricature of the Enlightenment as restrictive hyperrationalism — and goes hand in hand with Marxist critiques of the Enlightenment from the twentieth century, most famously Theodor Adorno and Max Horkheimer's equally polemical *Dialektik der Aufklärung* [Dialectic of Enlightenment] (1944). Here Günderrode emerges as a parallel to writers such as Hölderlin, who also has been read as a melancholic following the failure of the French Revolution and its promise of social and political progress.[54] Given the prevailing conditions, not only is Günderrode's failure a symptom of the tendencies of her time, but it is, to an extent, strongly pre-determined.

To be sure, Christa Wolf is vital in reviving interest in Günderrode as a poet in the latter half of the twentieth century, but the historically pessimistic narrative that she draws of Günderrode has the effect of reducing Günderrode's own agency, thus disempowering her, both personally and creatively. Both Wolf and Arnim are exemplars of how difficult it is to extricate Günderrode's work from biography; indeed, they can serve as examples of what Susanne Kord rightly terms the 'Biographismus in der Kritik' [biographical approach in criticism].[55] To put it bluntly: it is the very fact that Günderrode's suicide resists any final interpretation that proves critically attractive. Arnim's report on the suicide in *Goethe's Briefwechsel* also serves as evidence of this difficulty of making any retrospective sense of suicide. Günderrode's works, however, are far more accessible to sustained critical interpretation than her life or death, as I will demonstrate throughout the rest of this book.

---

53   Ibid., pp. 8–11.
54   Hartmut Böhme, *Natur und Subjekt* (Frankfurt a.M.: Suhrkamp, 1988), p. 263.
55   Susanne Kord, *Sich einen Namen machen: Anonymität und weibliche Autorschaft, 1700–1900* (Stuttgart: Metzler, 1996), p. 147.

CHAPTER 2

Pantheism and Panentheism: From the *Spinozastreit* to Günderrode

There is one main thread that runs through the entirety of Günderrode's corpus, from the *Studienbuch* [study book] from 1799–1800 to her third and final collection *Melete*: the metaphysical commitments inspired by the reinterpretation of Spinoza that followed the pantheism controversy of the 1780s. How this manifested in Günderrode's *oeuvre* is the subject of the remaining chapters of the present volume, but before looking at Günderrode, it is worth outlining why the pantheism controversy proved to be of such significance in the intellectual history of the period.

So important was this intellectual dispute that Frederick C. Beiser has gone so far as to claim that the earliest interpretations of Kant's critiques — such as Karl Leonhard Reinhold's *Briefe über die kantische Philosophie* [Letters on Kantian Philosophy] (1786–88) — must be read in the context of the pantheism controversy.[1] Pantheism, once a position associated with radical strands of thought such as atheism and materialism in the early Enlightenment, had become respectable, and was conjoined with the name of Spinoza from the late 1780s onward.[2] The engagement with pantheism among German and English Romantics was so sustained as to lead scholars such as Nicholas V. Riasanovsky to argue that pantheism is the central vision of early Romanticism.[3]

Why did this come to be? The central question that animates pantheism is how to understand the relation between humanity and nature. The direct opponent of pantheism in this debate is a form of mechanistic naturalism that originates in materialist science. To see why, we can turn to Panajotis Kondylis's discussion of mechanistic naturalism in his seminal study *Die Aufklärung im Rahmen des*

---

1 Frederick C. Beiser, *The Fate of Reason: German Philosophy from Kant to Fichte* (Cambridge, MA: Harvard University Press, 1987), pp. 44–45.
2 Margaret C. Jacob, *The Radical Enlightenment: Pantheists, Freemasons and Republicans* (London: Allen & Unwin, 1981), p. 224.
3 Nicholas V. Riasanovsky, *The Emergence of Romanticism* (New York, Oxford: Oxford University Press, 1992), p. 71; see also Jack Forstman, *A Romantic Triangle: Schleiermacher and the Early German Romantics* (Missoula, MT: Scholars Press, 1977), p. 116. For the English context, see Herbert W. Piper, *The Active Universe: Pantheism and the Concept of Imagination in the English Romantic Poets* (London: Athlone Press, 1962).

neuzeitlichen Rationalismus [The Enlightenment in the Context of Rationalism in the Modern Period] (1981). Kondylis outlines the consequences of mechanistic naturalism in the eighteenth century, which resulted from the elevation of nature as an object of scientific study. This form of naturalism incorporates individuals into nature, rather than separating the analytical intellect from it:

> für sie [die antiintellektualistisch-naturalistische eingestellte Skepsis] steht der Mensch nicht der Natur gegenüber, sondern verschmilzt mit ihr bis zur Unkenntlichkeit seiner spezifischen Züge, er wird zu einem bloßen Anwendungsfall der Naturgesetze, zu einer weiteren Manifestation der Naturnotwendigkeit. [...] Denn die blinde Naturnotwendigkeit scheint nicht nur die Freiheit des Willens, ohne die nicht ernsthaft von Moral die Rede sein kann, zugrundezurichten, sondern auch die Welt jedes objektiven Sinnes zu berauben.
>
> [for this [a form of scepticism given over to anti-intellectualism and naturalism], man does not stand in opposition to nature, but melds with it to the point of its characteristics becoming unrecognisable; the individual becomes a test case of the applicability of natural laws, another manifestation of the necessity of nature [...] For the blind necessity of nature appears not only to destroy free will, without which it is nigh on impossible to consider the existence of morality, but also appears to strip the world of having any objective meaning.][4]

This naturalisation of the individual had implications that were alarming for some: humankind is incorporated into nature and therefore subject to all its laws. All is predetermined by blind necessity. With this, once cherished concepts are lost: there is no space for human freedom, nor any space for morality.

Mechanical philosophy and Cartesian dualism had sought to avoid this problem by insisting upon the radical separation of mind and matter in the form of mind–body dualism. But dualism brought its own insoluble problems and by 1770 had ceased to be a convincing option. To counter the dangers posed by this mechanistic naturalism, pantheism was warmly embraced among writers and thinkers such as Herder, Goethe, and Lessing because of the possibilities it presented. Pantheism combined naturalism and monism in a manner that made space for spiritualising matter itself: the perils of mechanistic naturalism could be safely avoided through replacing mechanism with a metaphysical element of spirit.

The groundwork for pantheism was laid by the rise of vitalism in the natural philosophy of the mid-eighteenth century. In conscious opposition to the inert conception of matter inherited from Newtonian science, vitalism developed an alternative to mechanism that reanimated matter so that it was filled with vital energies, indwelling forces, and drives.[5] This paradigm shift emerged partly from

---

4   Panajotis Kondylis, *Die Aufklärung im Rahmen des neuzeitlichen Rationalismus* (Stuttgart: Klett-Cotta, 1981), pp. 125–26.
5   Peter Hanns Reill, 'Between Mechanism and Hermeticism: Nature and Science in the Late Enlightenment', in *Frühe Neuzeit — Frühe Moderne? Forschungen zur Vielschichtigkeit von Übergangsprozessen*, ed. by Rudolf Vierhaus (Göttingen: Vandenhoeck & Ruprecht, 1992), pp. 393–421 (p. 402). See also Peter Hanns Reill, *Vitalizing Nature in the Enlightenment* (Berkeley: University of California Press, 2005).

the inability of mechanistic philosophy to account for phenomena that fell outside the scope of Newtonian science, such as electricity and chemical reactions and processes.[6] While pantheism derived some of its appeal from this scientific vitalism, it had a further attraction. For Günderrode in particular, it had a metaphysical dimension as well: pantheism absorbs and lends a certain metaphysical dignity to philosophical and scientific conceptions that stem from vitalism.

In this shift from mechanistic naturalism to pantheism or spiritualised naturalism, what is striking is how both sides appropriated the very same philosopher: Spinoza. Where Spinoza had once been derided for his alleged materialism, he became a useful ally for those who subscribed to spiritualised naturalism. This turn in thought was achieved in the revival of interest in Spinoza among Herder, Goethe, and the Jena Romantics.[7] It is this philosophical inheritance that takes on a significant role in Günderrode's thought.

Pantheism has previously received critical attention in Günderrode, particularly in analyses of the play 'Mahomed, der Prophet von Mekka'.[8] Whether this pantheism is Spinozist or not, or whether it is even pantheism at all, remains open to question in previous critical literature.[9] Günderrode does indeed adopt a form of Spinozist pantheism, but it has not been discussed as a central metaphysical construction that can be traced throughout the entirety of her literary work.

Why should Spinozist pantheism assume such a central role for Günderrode? As I will show, the fears associated with the materialist form of Spinozism did remain potent. The usefulness of pantheism lies in how it provided a remedy for materialism. This is the project to which Günderrode's work can be assigned. Part of her appeal is how she explores not just the philosophical hopes of the period, but also its philosophical anxieties.

The most significant figure in Günderrode's adaptation of pantheist thinking was Herder. Herder's 'vitalised' reading — or creative misreading[10] — of Spinoza from *Gott. Einige Gespräche* [God. Some Conversations] (1787) added a dynamic element of force to transform Spinoza's God into a vitalist primal force that corresponds to the emergent organic understanding of nature. The purpose of this volume is to demonstrate how Günderrode took up these ideas and developed them in poetic form. For the moment, it is sufficient briefly to highlight both the problems and the

---

6   Stephen Gaukroger, *The Collapse of Mechanism and the Rise of Sensibility: Science and the Shaping of Modernity, 1680–1760* (Oxford: Clarendon Press, 2010), p. 355.
7   See Hermann Timm, *Gott und die Freiheit*, Studien zur Religionsphilosophie der Goethezeit, 1 (Frankfurt a.M.: Klostermann, 1974); Hermann Timm, *Die heilige Revolution: Das religiöse Totalitätskonzept der Frühromantik. Schleiermacher — Novalis — Friedrich Schlegel* (Frankfurt a.M.: Syndikat, 1978); Miklós Vassányi, *Anima Mundi: The Rise of the World Soul Theory in Modern German Philosophy* (Dordrecht: Springer, 2011), p. 395.
8   Solbrig, 'Die Orientalische Muse', pp. 305, 310; Simonis, p. 271; Margarete Lazarowicz, *Karoline von Günderrode: Portrait einer Fremden* (Frankfurt a.M.: Peter Lang, 1986), pp. 153–54.
9   Anna Ezekiel comments on the alleged pantheism in Günderrode's 'Mahomed', without fully subscribing to the reading of Günderrode's metaphysics as pantheistic: Günderrode, *Poetic Fragments*, p. 148.
10 David Bell, *Spinoza in Germany from 1670 to the Age of Goethe*, Bithell Series of Dissertations, 7 (London, 1984), p. 144.

possibilities that come with pantheist metaphysics, and to demarcate the territory in which Günderrode's work can be situated.

For a generation in which many had lost their faith in revealed religion, its organised structures and the authority of the Bible, pantheism — or, to be more precise, panentheism[11] — carried an obvious attraction. Panentheism is a term coined in the nineteenth century by Karl Christian Friedrich Krause, who was himself a student of Schelling's. The danger Krause identified in pantheism is that it could lead to the conflation and indeed collapse of nature and God into another, which can be tantamount to atheism. To avoid this danger, panentheism allows for God to be present in nature, but also to extend beyond it, being both transcendent and separate. Günderrode's writings feature a predominantly panentheistic metaphysics, although in *Melete* they become increasingly pantheistic.

There are several reasons why pantheism or (in the case of Günderrode) panentheism proved to be useful. The God of orthodox theology was transcendent and separate from the created world, communicating with it through the revealed truth of scripture and by occasional miracles. The God of panentheism is conceived of as inherent within all the phenomena of nature. But what is no less important for the reception of pantheist thought in the period is that it facilitates a changed understanding of the relation between nature and humanity. In this sense panentheism is a project of naturalisation. It re-writes the individual back into nature to overcome the artificial separation between human intellect and a moribund form of nature, one that would be ripe for subdivision into the taxonomies and classifications of scientific and empirical enquiry. Or to phrase it in strictly philosophical terms: to overcome the division between subject and object to appreciate the fundamental unity of — for Günderrode — all animate life. The perceived inertness of nature, when reduced to a passive object of study, connects with the mathematical models and the conceptualisation of matter as passive and subject to the mechanistic causality of nature. An understanding of matter as animate, as vivified, manifests itself most clearly in Günderrode's post-1804 works, where the influence of Schelling can be most clearly detected. Schelling's early *Naturphilosophie* [philosophy of nature] combines the results of empirical science with the attempt to provide it with a metaphysical foundation, so that empiricism and metaphysics could reciprocally justify each other.[12]

Beyond this fusion of science and metaphysics, the *livingness* of the universe becomes a central principle for Günderrode: 'Leben' [life] and its associated synonyms form the most common semantic item across Günderrode (*SW* III, 391–96), and it is a term that often carries metaphysical weight.[13] Animating nature does

---

11 There is a link between panentheism and Neoplatonist emanationism: see Benjamin Lazier, *God Interrupted: Heresy and the European Imagination between the World Wars* (Princeton: Princeton University Press, 2008), pp. 74–75.

12 John H. Zammito, *The Gestation of German Biology: Philosophy and Physiology from Stahl to Schelling* (Chicago: University of Chicago Press, 2018), p. 305.

13 Barbara Becker-Cantarino has also commented on the centrality of this concept for Günderrode: see Becker-Cantarino, 'The "New Mythology"', pp. 66–67. Concepts of life, power, and force were also important to the British Romantic poets: see Denise Gigante, *Life: Organic Form and Romanticism*

not come at the cost of losing its spiritual dimension. For this reason, the Romantic adaptation of vitalist thought assumed the form of panentheism. Since divine spirit is inherent in all matter, matter itself could be redeemed because it contains a spiritual component. Collapsing the spatial hierarchy that formerly distinguished the theist or deist God and the world has the advantage of inoculating against materialism by divinising and *spiritualising* matter.

Günderrode's studies of Schelling's *Bruno, oder über das göttliche und natürliche Princip der Dinge* [Bruno, or on the Divine and Natural Principle of Things] (1802) prepare the ground for her own cosmology of *Jdee der Erde* [Idea of the Earth] (1806). They include an extract that, following Schelling precisely, reclaims matter as the eternal, fundamental principle: 'Die wahre Jdee des Materialismus ist früher verlohren gegangen ihm zufolge ist die Materie selbst das einfache Unwandelbare Ewige das Eine was über allen Gegensatz erhaben ist' [The true idea of materialism was lost early on, according to which matter itself was the simple, immutable, eternal substance, the One that existed above all opposition] (*SW* II, 404). Günderrode develops these thoughts on returning to a primordial understanding of materialism in 'Briefe zweier Freunde' (1806), where the unnamed speaker expounds upon the form of divine perfection that is 'ein wahrhaft verklärter Leib' [a truly transfigured body] (*SW* I, 360), liberated from the defects of corporeal matter, here with both philosophical and religious associations.

One advantage of spiritualising matter in this fashion is that it wards off the danger of the mechanical materialism that was associated in its extreme form with such French thinkers as La Mettrie. Though few in Germany shared this materialist view, it was an object of fear for many.[14] For Günderrode, an entirely materialistic account of the individual is impossible, because it eradicates individual autonomy and agency. If the individual is subsumed entirely into causally deterministic nature, then the concept of human agency becomes conditioned to the extent of becoming entirely determined by external laws.

This problem of determinism is laid out by Günderrode in a series of fragmentary texts from the *Nachlass*. These are a set of dream-narratives, which are, to a degree, oddities for Günderrode, since they have biographical import. All deal with the prophetic function of dreams, understood in a Leibnizian sense of disclosing truths about the universe,[15] and all are about determinism. The second of the fragments questions determinism and concerns the oneiric foreknowledge of the deaths of two of the speaker's sisters — here, two sisters who, albeit in fictionalised form, allude to two of Günderrode's sisters, who died in quick succession.[16] Determinism opens up a potent moment of *horror vacui*, not just at the death of relatives, but at the absence of God:

(New Haven: Yale University Press, 2009).
14 Jonathan B. Knudsen, *Justus Möser and the German Enlightenment* (Cambridge: Cambridge University Press, 1986), p. 4.
15 Matthew Bell, *The German Tradition of Psychology in Literature and Thought, 1700–1840* (Cambridge: Cambridge University Press, 2005), p. 59.
16 The youngest sister, Amalie, died in April 1802, and Charlotte in October 1801.

> Jch hatte zwei Schwestern, die Älteste liebte ich vorzüglich weil sie mit mir eine grosse Ähnlichkeit der Gesinung hatte; ich war seit mehrern Wochen von ihr entfernt und dachte oft mit Sehnsucht und Liebe an sie, da träumte mir einst diese beide Schwestern seyn gestorben, ich war sehr traurig darüber. Da erschienen mir ihre Geister in dem Hofe eines alten Hauses indem wir einen grossen Theil unserer Jugend verlebt haben. Sie traten beide aus einer dunkeln Kammer vor der ich immer einen gewissen Schauer gehabt hatte. Es war Nacht, eine feuchte Herbst-Luft wehte und reichlicher Regen fiel herab. Meine ältere Schwester nahte sich mir, und sprach: Eine ewige kalte Nothwendigkeit regiret die Welt, kein freundlich liebend Wesen. Jch erwachte; Es träumte mir noch mehrmals sie sei gestorben obgleich sie sehr gesund war. Nach zwei Jahren erfülte sich der Traum, beyde starben kurz nacheinander —
>
> [I had two sisters. I loved the eldest dearly because she was very similar in temperament to me; I was away from her for several weeks and often thought of her with love and longing, and once I had a dream that these two sisters had died, and I was very sorrowful about it. Then their spirits appeared to me in the courtyard of an old house in which we had spent a good part of our youth. They both emerged from a dark chamber that had I always been afraid of. It was night, there was a damp autumnal breeze and it was raining heavily. My older sister approached me and said: an eternal cold necessity rules the world, not a kind and loving being. I awoke; I had the same dream several times over that she had died although she was still quite healthy. After two years the dream came true, both died shortly after one another –] (*SW* I, 444)[17]

Beyond the initial portents of pathetic fallacy, what animates this text is the authoritative and unmotivated declaration of the older sister that 'Eine ewige kalte Nothwendigkeit regiret die Welt, kein freundlich liebend Wesen'. This horrific revelation, if the textual logic is followed, is, by implication, true, since the vision of the sisters' deaths becomes reality ('Nach zwei Jahren erfülte sich der Traum'). What is equally intriguing is the literary pedigree of this revelation: the phrasing of 'eine ewige kalte Nothwendigkeit' recalls Jean Paul's *Siebenkäs* (1797),[18] and specifically 'Die Rede des toten Christus vom Weltgebäude herab' [The Speech of the Dead Christ from the Universe Above]. This features a dream-narrative of Christ descending upon the Day of Judgment to declare that there is no God: the end of the dream is a chaotic vision of the cosmos annihilating itself. The frame narrative of the text, however, contains and controls the nihilistic elements of the dream, since the speaker's faith is reaffirmed upon waking by experiencing the natural world.

Günderrode's debt to Jean Paul is revealing, because it involves a selective quotation from the penultimate speech of the risen Christ: 'Starres, stummes Nichts!

---

17 Günderrode's orthography is at times idiosyncratic. Where it affects the understanding of the text, alterations will be made.
18 Günderrode reports reading *Siebenkäs* in July 1799: 'Ich lese seit mehreren Tagen in Jean Pauls Siebenkäs, er gefällt mir ganz außerordentlich. [...] Ich bin äußerst begierig auf den dritten Teil' [I have been reading Jean Paul's *Siebenkäs* for several days and I like it very much indeed [...] I am very eager to read the third part] (Karoline von Günderrode, *Ich sende dir ein zärtliches Pfand: Die Briefe der Karoline von Günderrode*, ed. by Birgit Weißenborn (Frankfurt a.M.: Insel, 1992), p. 53; henceforth referred to as Günderrode, *Briefe*). Jean Paul is also a popular choice in Günderrode's *Studienbuch*, where the majority of the extracts derive from *Hesperus* (1795).

Kalte, ewige Notwendigkeit! Wahnsinniger Zufall! Kennt ihr das unter euch? Wann zerschlagt ihr das Gebäude und mich' [Inanimate, dumb nothingness! Cold, eternity necessity! Insane chance! Do you know that among yourselves? When will you crush the edifice and me?].[19] Günderrode replaces Christ with the spirit of the elder sister, but also condenses the extended lamentations of Christ into a moment of such brevity that it increases the intensity of shock, which also works on a phenomenological level for the reader. The conclusion of the fragment proves bleaker than Jean Paul's reassertion of belief. The truth-value of the statement is not expressly refuted; it is simply left as it is — unqualified and unexplained.

The explicit statement made by the sister is, however, relativised by the fact that she is making it, and making it *post mortem*. What this means is that the subtext, or what is not said by the speaker, becomes significant. In the dream, the sisters have already died, and their spirits appear. In the dream itself, there is, it appears, afterlife and transcendence. Through the revelation proclaimed by the spirit of the dead sister, one aspect of materialism is confirmed discursively: determinism. The dark chamber that the speaker so fears stands for the fear of living in a deterministic world. The other part of materialism, namely transience, is denied, albeit only performatively, and only in the dream. What is true in the waking state is left unsaid. There are further dreams; and the sisters do die within a couple of years. Nothing is said about any real-life apparitions thereafter. Between the dream and the reality, the reader is left in a position of sceptical suspension of judgement about the promise of an afterlife, as an alternative to the bleak vista of determinism.

While life after death can neither be affirmed nor denied, what is being questioned here are the truths long provided by faith: there may be no resurrection, no eternal life, and no transcendence. Like Jean Paul, Günderrode's compact statement focuses on the absence of love: hence the juxtaposition of 'Notwendigkeit' and 'kein freundlich liebend Wesen'. What is lost in this process is relational: a meaningful, emotional connection to a personal God, — here couched in unusually orthodox terms for Günderrode.[20] By extension, what is lost is also the connection to the material reality that is also dependent on a loving deity.

What Günderrode expresses, through the absence of love, is also a form of mechanistic naturalism: if the individual is entirely subject to the laws of nature — in the form of necessity — then the individual is reduced to being a witness to their own existence, rather than its primary agent. The lament in Günderrode's text, therefore, is not so much for the prophesied deaths, but for the metaphorical death of the individual as a meaningful, independent construct, one that possesses the capacity for self-development and improvement.

The short dream-narrative points to a philosophical balancing act: elevating the individual intellect above nature ossifies nature as an object of study, whereas integrating the individual into nature runs the risk of making every individual

---

19   Jean Paul, *Sämtliche Werke*, ed. by Norbert Miller, 10 vols (Munich: Hanser, 1959–; repr. Darmstadt: Wissenschaftliche Buchgesellschaft, 2000), I.II: *Siebenkäs. Flegeljahre*, ed. by Norbert Miller (1987), p. 274.
20   The only other orthodox Christian text is 'Verschiedene Offenbahrungen des Göttlichen' [Diverse Revelations of the Divine] (c. 1799–1802), also from the *Nachlass*, but that is a text that predates these dream-narratives.

entirely conditioned by deterministic laws of nature. Günderrode consistently elucidates the limitations of the human intellect and knowledge-seeking *vis-à-vis* nature and its metaphysical core in her published work, from 'Der Adept' [The Adept], 'Des Wandrers Niederfahrt' [The Wanderer's Descent] (both 1804), to 'Magie und Schicksal' and 'Eine persische Erzählung' [A Persian Tale] (1806).

The dream-narrative is one of the few instances where Günderrode outlines the existential horror of determinism, but this is where the legacy of the pantheism controversy can be detected in her work. One of its central concerns was the freedom of the individual will, a freedom that Spinoza had expressly denied in his *Ethics*.[21]

As is well known, the thinker who raised the alarm about Spinoza, and thus inaugurated the pantheism controversy, was Friedrich Heinrich Jacobi. One of Jacobi's main charges against Spinoza's philosophy is its alleged fatalism. For Jacobi, fatalism operates according to blind necessity, without purpose or intelligent cause. Jacobi's concern lies in the problem of freedom and how it connects to the vexed issue of final causes, which bring an element of goal-directed purposiveness into causation.[22] Should final causes not exist, then freedom is a chimera, and becomes replaced by fatalism. Jacobi makes precisely the same point as is implied in Günderrode, that the individual becomes a passive observer of their own existence, who may think about what they do, but whose actions are determined by external causes, not by thoughts, affects, or passions:

> Wenn es lauter würkende und keine Endursachen giebt, so hat das denkende Vermögen in der ganzen Natur blos das Zusehen; sein einziges Geschäffte ist, den Mechanismus der würkenden Kräfte zu begleiten. Die Unterredung, die wir gegenwärtig miteinander haben, ist nur ein Anliegen unserer Leiber [...] Denn auch die Affekten und Leidenschaften würken nicht, in so ferne sie Empfindungen und Gedanken sind; oder richtiger — in so ferne sie Empfindungen *mit sich führen*. Wir *glauben* nur, daß wir aus Zorn, Liebe, Großmuth, oder aus vernünftigem Entschlusse handelten. Bloßer Wahn! In allen diesen Fällen ist im Grunde das was uns bewegt ein *Etwas*, das von allem dem *nichts weiß*, und das, *in so ferne*, von Empfindung und Gedanke schlechterdings entblößt ist.

> [If there are nothing but external causes and no final causes, then the capacity for thought only observes the entirety of nature; its only role is to run alongside the mechanism of external causes. The conversation which we are currently having is only caused by our bodies [...] For affect and the passions do not have an effect on us, insofar as they are sensations and thoughts — or more precisely: that they *bring about* sensations. We only *believe* that we might act out of fury, love, magnanimity, or from a rational decision. Pure delusion! In all these cases, what fundamentally moves us is *something* that *knows nothing* of these things, and that, in this respect, is absolutely devoid of sensation and thought.][23]

---

21   Robert S. Leventhal, '"Eins und Alles": Herders Spinoza-Aneignung in *Gott, einige Gespräche*', *Publications of the English Goethe Society*, 86.2 (2017), 67–89 (p. 68).
22   Beiser, *The Fate of Reason*, p. 66.
23   Friedrich Heinrich Jacobi, *Über die Lehre des Spinoza in Briefen an den Herrn Moses Mendelssohn*, in *Werke: Gesamtausgabe*, ed. by Klaus Hammacher and Walter Jaeschke, 7 vols (Hamburg: Meiner, 1998–), I.I: *Schriften zum Spinozastreit*, ed. by Klaus Hammacher, Irmgard-Maria Piske (1998), pp. 20–21.

This fatalism is one of the scandalous consequences of Spinoza's philosophy: Spinoza denies the qualities accorded to humanity in Cartesian philosophy — that the human being operates according to laws distinct from those of physical nature.[24] The implication of this would be that, as Hasana Sharp has illustrated, 'no volitional power, divine or human, can operate independent of the natural order of cause and effect'.[25] What is anathema to Günderrode is precisely the kind of radical naturalism that Jacobi associates with Spinoza.

It may therefore seem paradoxical, if not misplaced, to turn to Spinozism to move against the ills of materialism and determinism. Yet this is precisely what Lessing, Goethe, and Herder did, in a significant reinterpretation of Spinoza's philosophy.[26] Those who enthusiastically embraced Spinoza produced a heterodox reading of Spinoza in the form of panentheism, which moved away from its previous associations with mechanism, atheism, fatalism and nihilism.[27] Whereas Spinoza had previously been spoken of 'wie von einem todten Hunde' [like a dead dog],[28] as Lessing supposedly said to Jacobi, he was now recast in reverential terms among the Early Romantic generation and, most prominently by Hölderlin, particularly in *Hyperion, oder der Eremit in Griechenland* [Hyperion, or, the Hermit in Greece] (1797–99),[29] Schleiermacher,[30] Novalis, and Friedrich Schlegel.

The philosophical advantage of Spinozism is that *deus sive natura* satisfies the desideratum within Idealism and Romanticism of an absolute ground or unity of being. Frederick C. Beiser summarises precisely how Spinoza's monism appealed to this generation. This is partly because it assumed a religious function. Spinozism provided an alternative to the orthodoxy of theism on the one hand and scientific and empiricist forms of enquiry on the other:

> The romantics were especially attracted to two aspects of Spinoza's system. First, his monism, his belief that there is a single universe, of which the mental and physical are only different attributes. Spinoza's monism was the antithesis to the dualistic legacy of the Cartesian tradition [...] Spinoza [...] saw everything as a mode of the divine. The identification of the divine with nature seemed

---

24   Michael Della Rocca, *Spinoza* (Abingdon: Routledge, 2008), p. 6.
25   Hasana Sharp, *Spinoza and the Politics of Naturalization* (Chicago: University of Chicago Press, 2011), p. 2.
26   Herbert Lindner, *Das Problem des Spinozismus im Schaffen Goethes und Herders* (Weimar: Arion, 1960), p. 176.
27   John H. Zammito, 'Herder, Kant, Spinoza und die Ursprünge des deutschen Idealismus', in *Herder und die Philosophie des deutschen Idealismus*, ed. by Marion Heinz (Amsterdam: Rodopi, 1997), pp. 106–44 (p. 113).
28   Jacobi, *Werke: Gesamtausgabe*, I.I, 27.
29   See Jochen Schmidt, 'Stoischer Pantheismus als Medium des Säkularisierungsprozesses und als Psychotherapeutikum um 1800: Hölderlins *Hyperion*', *Jahrbuch der deutschen Schillergesellschaft*, 51 (2007), 183–204.
30   Schleiermacher lauds Spinoza in his *Reden über die Religion* [Speeches on Religion] (1799): 'Opfert mit mir ehrerbietig eine Locke den Manen des heiligen verstoßenen Spinoza!' [Offer with me a lock of hair in reverence to the *manes* of the holy, expelled Spinoza!], in Friedrich Daniel Ernst Schleiermacher, *Reden über die Religion: Reden an die Gebildeten unter ihren Verächtern*, in *Kritische Gesamtausgabe*, ed. by Hans-Joachim Birkner and others, 58 vols (Berlin: De Gruyter, 1980–), I.XII: *Über die Religion; Monologen*, ed. by Günter Meckenstock (1995), p. 58.

to be the only way to keep religion alive in an age of science. The old theism had collapsed under the strain of modern biblical criticism; and deism had faltered in the face of Humean and Kantian criticism. [...] The slogan *deus sive natura* seemed to make a science out of religion by naturalizing the divine, and a religion out of science by divinizing the natural.[31]

To be sure, the Romantic definition of religion and religiosity is slippery at best, since these concepts are embedded within a response to Kantian philosophy where religion, art, and a longing for the absolute reciprocally relate to each other.[32] In the case of Friedrich Schlegel, religion is provocatively aestheticised.[33] Fusing Spinozism with religion is a fruitful line of enquiry for Günderrode as well, not least because it finds expression as a form of religion in both 'Mahomed, der Prophet von Mekka' and 'Geschichte eines Braminen'. One of the reasons for this Romantic attraction towards Spinozism can also be found within radical strains of Lutheranism. A relationship with God can be generated not through study of the Bible, but through an immediate awareness of God within the individual.[34] Traces of precisely this line of thought can be found in Günderrode's *Studienbuch*, which dates from 1799.[35] Of particular importance is an extract from a sermon by Johann Georg Diefenbach, pastor at Butzbach,[36] who encouraged Günderrode to study Kantian philosophy. In the extract, internal contemplation allows the individual to realise that the divine law and God resides within them, and that therefore the entire world of rational beings is God's work.[37]

Whilst Günderrode's Lutheran environment may have similarly prepared the ground for her appreciation of Spinozist panentheism, the question still remains of how this new, enlivened Spinozism could, if at all, avoid the problem of determinism and fatalism. How the realms of human freedom and morality connect to the deterministic causality of nature was a question that assumed a particularly extreme form in discussions of Spinoza's fatalism. It was a question that also troubled Kant, who, in the third antinomy of *Kritik der reinen Vernunft* [Critique of Pure Reason]

---

31   Frederick C. Beiser, *The Romantic Imperative: The Concept of Early German Romanticism* (Cambridge, MA: Harvard University Press, 2003), pp. 141–42.
32   Barbara Thums, 'Religion — Kunst — Lebenskunst: Romantische Tendenzen aufs Unendliche', in *Romantische Religiosität*, ed. by Alexander von Bormann (Würzburg: Königshausen & Neumann, 2005), pp. 19–44 (p. 20).
33   Alongside her study of Schleiermacher, Günderrode makes notes on Schlegel's 'Ideen' in an unpublished part of the *Nachlass*: MS Ff. K. v. Günderrode Abt. 2 A2, fols 67^r–70^v.
34   Beiser, *The Fate of Reason*, pp. 51–52.
35   Günderrode selects aphorisms under a variety of headings from a volume compiled by Johann Hugo Wyttenbach, the head of a *Gymnasium* in Trier, *Aussprüche der philosophirenden Vernunft und des reinen Herzens über die der Menschheit wichtigsten Gegenstände, mit besonderer Rücksicht auf die kritische Philosophie zusammen getragen aus den Schriften älterer und neuerer Denker*, 2 vols (Leipzig, Vienna: Rötzel, 1796–98), I. One of the two aphorisms under 'Gott' is a quotation from Johann Heinrich Vogt (1749–89), professor of practical philosophy at Mainz: 'Gott kann nicht demonstrirt werden er muß im Herzen sein' [God cannot be demonstrated, He must be in one's heart], in Preitz/Hopp III, p. 266.
36   This extract is written in Diefenbach's hand. Günderrode had others write down quotations and aphorisms in the *Studienbuch* as well.
37   Preitz/Hopp III, p. 274.

(1781), sought to separate the contradictory realms of free will, morality and nature absolutely, albeit with the admission that they must interact in some way.[38]

What is at stake in these tensions between free will and deterministic laws of nature bifurcates into the following questions: firstly, whether the realm of human freedom could be subsumed into nature; secondly, whether Spinoza's fatalism could be remoulded into the more familiar and palatable concepts of teleology and benevolent providence.

Attempts had been made to salvage Christian concepts whilst retaining elements of Spinozism. Moses Mendelssohn had attempted to recast Spinoza in the form of so-called 'geläuterter Pantheismus' [purified pantheism] which 'gar wohl mit den Wahrheiten der Religion und der Sittenlehre bestehen könne' [which can exist alongside the truths of religion and morality].[39] What this involved was inserting a scale of perfection into Spinoza and reforming it in the mould of Leibniz-Wolffian optimism: that God had chosen the best of all possible worlds.[40] This purified Spinozism was made possible because Mendelssohn conceded that Jacobi's original charges of atheism and fatalism were correct: to purify it was to rid it of such contagion. To Mendelssohn, a deist, Spinoza amounted to a materialistic form of pantheism that collapsed the distinction between God and the world.[41]

Recuperating positive aspects of Spinoza's monism and fatalism in a manner that would coincide with Christianity is a task that falls to Herder, the central figure in the Spinoza renaissance. Herder was an attentive reader of Spinoza from the 1760s onward and had, according to Michael N. Forster, aligned himself with Spinozism in the decade prior to the pantheism controversy.[42] In the 'Viertes Gespräch' [Fourth Conversation] of *Gott. Einige Gespräche*, Herder systematically works through Lessing's responses to Jacobi. Quoting Lessing's cheerily Spinozist denial of free will, Herder elaborates upon the serfdom of the individual human will, and how in fact this leads to a higher form of freedom:

> Mir ist kein Weltmeister bekannt, der die Knechtschaft des menschlichen Willens gründlicher aus einander gesetzt und die Freiheit desselben vortrefflicher bestimmt habe, als Spinoza. Dem Menschen ist kein geringeres Ziel der Freiheit vorgesetzt, als die Freiheit Gottes selbst, durch eine Art innerer Notwendigkeit, d. i. durch vollständige Begriffe, die uns Erkenntnis und Liebe Gottes allein gewähren können, über unsre Leidenschaften, ja über das Schicksal selbst Herren zu werden. Gründlich beweiset es Spinoza, daß, wenn man Freiheit für tolle, blinde Willkür nehme, der Mensch eben so wenig als Gott selbst den edeln Namen der Freiheit verdiene; vielmehr gehöre es zur Vollkommenheit

---

38 John H. Smith, 'Living Religion as Vanishing Mediator: Schleiermacher, Early Romanticism, and Idealism', *The German Quarterly*, 84.2 (2011), 137–58 (p. 140).
39 Moses Mendelssohn, *Morgenstunden oder Vorlesungen über das Dasein Gottes*, in *Gesammelte Schriften: Jubiläumsausgabe*, ed. by Fritz Bamberger and others, 32 vols (Stuttgart-Bad Canstatt: frommann-holzboog, 1971–), III.II: *Schriften zur Philosophie und Ästhetik*, ed. by Leo Strauss (1974), p. 133.
40 Philip Clayton, *The Problem of God in Modern Thought* (Grand Rapids: Eerdmans, 2000), p. 433.
41 Mendelssohn follows Wolff in this assessment of Spinoza: see David Bell, p. 113.
42 Michael N. Forster, 'Herder and Spinoza', in *Spinoza and German Idealism*, ed. by Eckart Förster and Yitzhak Y. Melamed (Cambridge: Cambridge University Press, 2012), pp. 59–84 (p. 72).

der Natur Gottes, daß er auf diese Art nicht frei sei, daß er eine blinde Willkür nicht kenne, wie es denn auch zur Vollkommenheit seiner Werke gehört, daß eine solche tolle Willkür aus der ganzen Schöpfung verbannt sei.

[I know no philosopher who has expounded the bondage of the human will more thoroughly, and defined its freedom more excellently, than Spinoza. Man has been appointed no less a goal for his freedom than the freedom of God Himself. By means of a kind of inner necessity, that is, by means of perfect conceptions which only the knowledge and love of God can reveal to us, we become lords over our passions, yes, even over fate itself. Spinoza thoroughly proves that if one takes freedom to be senseless, blind caprice, man, as little as God Himself, deserves the high and noble name of freedom. Rather does it befit the perfection of God's nature that He should not be free in this manner, that He should know no blind caprice, even as it also befits the perfection of His works that such senseless caprice be banned from all creation.][43]

To avoid the charge of fatalism that Jacobi had previously attached to Spinozism, Herder attributes absolute freedom to God, and by extension, to nature. Freedom, it is implied, is both purposiveness and a form of determinism, in contrast to associations of freedom with arbitrariness ('tolle Willkür'). The human will is indeed enslaved by a global form of determinism. It is through recognising this enslavement that another, higher form of freedom is possible. The individual shares in divine freedom because it is a part of the whole: if the individual acts according to the necessity of its own nature ('durch eine Art innerer Notwendigkeit'), this is how the divine operates through the individual. Being determined by God and nature is, by analogy, one and the same as self-determination. Herder is following Spinoza's *Ethics* here: it is through cognition and love that the individual comes to control their passions and can act in accordance with internal necessity. This corresponds to and testifies to a fascination with Spinoza's doctrine of *amor dei intellectualis*, the intellectual love of God.[44]

Günderrode was aware of this appropriation of Spinoza's *amor dei intellectualis* by Herder and others of the early Romantic generation. The germ of this line of thought is inherent, in latent form, in Herder's vitalist interpretation of Spinoza. This is, as Hermann Timm summarises in a discussion of Herder's Spinozism, an ontology of force:

---

43 Johann Gottfried Herder, *Gott: Einige Gespräche*, in *Werke in zehn Bänden*, ed. Jürgen Brammack and Martin Bollacher, 10 vols (Frankfurt a.M.: Deutscher Klassikerverlag, 1985–2000), IV: *Schriften zu Philosophie, Literatur, Kunst und Altertum, 1774–1787*, ed. by Jürgen Brummack and Martin Bollacher (1994), pp. 679–794 (pp. 741–42); Johann Gottfried Herder, *God, Some Conversations*, trans. by Frederick H. Burkhardt (Bobbs-Merrill: Indianapolis, 1940), pp. 138–39.

44 Wolfgang Janke has traced this philosophy of love in German Romanticism and Idealism: Wolfgang Janke, 'Amor Dei intellectualis (Spinoza — Jacobi — Fichte — F. Schlegel — Schelling): Vom Aufstieg des Geistes zur Gottesliebe', in *Geist, Eros und Agape: Untersuchungen zu Liebesdarstellungen in Philosophie, Religion und Kunst*, ed. by Edith Düsing and Hans-Dieter Klein (Würzburg: Königshausen & Neumann, 2009), pp. 291–310. As Frederick C. Beiser has demonstrated, the Romantic generation of Friedrich Schegel, Novalis, and Schelling equally struggled with the concept of freedom within a vitalised form of Spinozism, and came to the conclusion that *amor dei intellectualis* was a means to avoid fatalism: see Beiser, *The Romantic Imperative*, pp. 150–52.

Das höchste Wesen ist reine selbstverwirklichende Tätigkeit. Deus est operari. 'Urkraft'. Spinozas Gotteslehre wird zum Prinzip einer generellen Macht- und Kraftontologie entwickelt. [...] Seine uniforme Struktur spezifiziert sich nur, nämlich unter der Tendenz kontinuierlicher Steigerung. [...] In der intuitiven Erkenntnis des 'natura sive Deus' findet diese Offenbarungsgeschichte des Universums die alles begreifende Vollendung.

[The highest being is pure, self-realising activity. Deus est operari. 'Primal force'. Spinoza's teachings on God become a principle of a general ontology of power and force [...] Its uniform structure becomes more specific, namely within the tendency towards continuous intensification. [...] In the intuitive knowledge of 'natura sive Deus', this history of revelation for the universe finds its completion, which allows for the comprehension of everything.][45]

We cannot be certain that Günderrode was familiar with Herder's *Gott. Einige Gespräche*, and indeed she adopts vitalist language in her early studies of Fichte's *Die Bestimmung des Menschen* [The Vocation of Man], which anticipates her later studies of Schelling's philosophy of nature.[46] But there is an indirect link to Herder in Günderrode's *Studienbuch*. In this Günderrode copied and adapted Ludwig Gotthard Kosegarten's translation of an ode to God by the notorious heretic Giulio Cesare Vanini (1585–1616), the Latin original of which Herder had included at the end of the 'Erstes Gespräch' [First Conversation] in *Gott*. The ode is associated with Herder's Spinozism insofar as he portrays Vanini's thought as an antecedent to Spinoza's non-theistic theology.[47] There are other textual links: Herder's terminology of force, specifically 'Urkraft' [primal force],[48] features in Günderrode's 'Des Wandrers Niederfahrt' and 'Geschichte eines Braminen' to designate the singular creative, generative principle of the universe (*SW* I, 72, l. 91). Herder's *Ideen zu einer Philosophie der Geschichte der Menschheit* [Ideas for a Philosophy of History of Mankind] (1784–91), which Günderrode read with great interest in

---

45   Timm, *Gott und die Freiheit*, p. 325.
46   'Das Universum ist eine thätige Kraft [...] Alles in der Natur läst sich durch die Kräfte erklären, sie selber bleiben unerklärbar. Alles was geschieht in der Natur, geschieht durch ihre Kräfte' [The universe is a active force [...] Everything in nature can be explained through forces, they themselves remain inexplicable. Everything that happens in nature, happens because of its forces] (*SW* II, 289). This is in part a distillation of Fichte's original, which equally makes recourse to vitalist language. Günderrode's formulations are sharper. The genealogy of this vitalist language is partly scientific, since Fichte was drawing on Blumenbach's physiology and his notion of *Bildungstrieb* [formative drive]: see Dalia Nassar, 'The Human Vocation and the Question of the Earth: Karoline von Günderrode's Philosophy of Nature', *Archiv für Geschichte der Philosophie*, 104.1 (2022), 108-30. Günderrode's studies of Schelling equally make use of vitalist language that fuses the philosophical with the scientific: see in particular the diagrams: *SW* II, 358–62.
47   Jan Rohls, 'Herders "Gott"', in *Johann Gottfried Herder: Aspekte seines Lebenswerks*, ed. by Martin Kessler and Volker Leppin (Berlin: De Gruyter, 2005), pp. 271–91 (p. 284).
48   'In der Welt, die wir kennen, steht die Denkkraft oben an; es folgen ihr aber Millionen andre Empfindungs- und Wirkungskräfte und Er, der Selbstständige, er ist im höchsten, einzigen Verstande des Wortes, *Kraft*, d. i. die Urkraft aller Kräfte, die Seele aller Seelen' [In the world that we know, the power of thought stands highest, but it is followed by millions of other powers of feeling and activity, and He, the Self-dependent One, is *Power* in the highest and only sense of the word, that is, the primal Force of all forces, the Soul of all souls] in Herder, *Werke in zehn Bänden*, IV, 710; Herder, *God, Some Conversations*, p. 104.

1799,[49] is suffused with Spinozism, in the form of a spiritualised, enlivened concept of nature, which proved to be influential for the nineteenth-century reception of Spinoza.[50]

What makes Herder's Spinozism so attractive for Günderrode is that it transformed necessity from a purely external influence into one that is also internalised within the individual. Herder's reformulation of the mechanistic, inert concept of substance that was part of Spinoza's Cartesian inheritance into dynamic, living force — by way of Leibniz[51] — makes the individual an active agent. This is because the individual's actions necessarily contribute to the development of the self and, by extension, the development of the whole. The entirety of divinised nature and the individual exist therefore in a relationship of reciprocity, of interdependence. The precise form of this relationship varies across Günderrode, but its fundamental structure is stable. By reformulating substance as force, necessity becomes internalised within the individual, and is no longer the abhorrent concept that empties the individual of meaning. Instead, the individual takes on a teleological function by contributing, in Herder, to divine 'reine selbstverwirklichende Tätigkeit' [pure self-realising activity], one whose end in Günderrode is formulated as a state of perfection.

Perfecting the self, for Günderrode, prepares the ground for a universal form of perfection. Whilst this state may be positively connoted insofar as it is longed for, it is also treated with ambivalence. It endangers the dynamism of Herder's Spinozist model by introducing a final moment of stasis. What remains is a dynamic process or — to borrow a phrase from Manfred Frank and, in turn, from Hölderlin — 'unendliche Annäherung' [infinite approximation]. As early as 1799, Günderrode's understanding of God was indebted to a notion that God exists within the world and develops over the course of history. When Günderrode copied Ludwig Gotthard Kosegarten's translation of Vanini's ode to God, she inserted in an otherwise anthropomorphised reading of God variants of the phrase 'Ich bin alles was ist, was war, und was sein wird' [I am all that is, that was, and what will be].[52] Originally

---

49   'Bisher las ich auch sehr viel in Herders Ideen zur Philosophie der Geschichte der Menschheit, bei allen meinen Schmerzen ist mir dies Buch ein wahrer Trost, ich vergesse mich, meine Leiden und Freuden in dem Wohl und Wehe der ganzen Menschheit, und ich selbst scheine mir in solchen Augenblicken ein so kleiner, unbedeutender Punkt in der Schöpfung, daß mir meine eignen Angelegenheiten keiner Träne, keiner bangen Minute wert scheinen.' [Hitherto I read a good deal of Herder's *Ideas for a Philosophy of the History of Mankind*, and in all my pain this book is a true solace to me, I forget myself, my suffering, and joy in the weal and woe of the entirety of humanity, and in such moments I seem to be such a small, insignificant part in creation, that my own affairs appear not to be deserving of any tears or a troubled minute.] (Günderrode, *Briefe*, pp. 53–55)

50   Wilhelm Schmidt-Biggemann, *Baruch de Spinoza, 1677–1977: Werk und Wirkung* (Wolfenbüttel: Herzog August Bibliothek, 1977), pp. 18–19.

51   See John H. Smith, 'Leibniz Reception around 1800: Monadic Vitalism and Aesthetic Harmony', in *Religion, Reason, and Culture in the Age of Goethe*, ed. by Elisabeth Krimmer and Patricia Anne Simpson (Rochester, NY: Camden House, 2013), pp. 209–43.

52   Preitz/Hopp III, pp. 274–75. See Ludwig Gotthard Kosegarten, 'Vanini's Hymne', in *Poesieen: Erster Band* (Leipzig: Gräff, 1798), pp. 35–38. These insertions are unusual for Günderrode's early studies around 1800. Later studies tend to be adaptations or summaries of the original text. With regard to literary rewritings, Günderrode rewrites Novalis's 'Lied der Toten' [Song of the Dead]: see Sabine I. Gölz, 'Günderrode Mines Novalis', in *'The Spirit of Poesy': Essays on Jewish and German*

derived from Plutarch, it is a phrase that betrays Spinozist sympathies at the end of the eighteenth century.[53] It suggests that the divine realises itself — whether in perfective form or not — throughout history. It is this narrative of progress, of perfectibility, which becomes a constituent linear structure across Günderrode's *oeuvre*, in her plays, such as 'Mahomed, der Prophet von Mekka', and also in her later philosophically inflected texts, such as 'Briefe zweier Freunde'. Whilst it reveals the self-sustaining character of Herder's Spinozism, it also interacts with Günderrode's understanding of the possibility of historical progress in the aftermath of the French Revolution.

Literature and Thought in Honor of Géza von Molnár, ed. by Richard Block and Peter Fenves (Evanston, IL: Northwestern University Press, 2000), pp. 89–130.
53   See Simonis, p. 261; Plutarch, *Plutarch's De Iside et Osiride*, ed. and trans. by J. Gwyn Griffiths (Cambridge: University of Wales Press, 1970), p. 131: 'At Saïs the seated statue of Athena, whom they consider to be Isis also, bore the following inscription: "I am all that has been and is and will be; and no mortal has ever lifted my mantle."'

CHAPTER 3

❖

'Vieles werd' ich können, weil ich will':
Fatalism, Agency, and
Autonomy in Günderrode

Panentheism has political ramifications. It did so in the early Enlightenment, where panentheism was associated with radical thought and atheism.¹ Even if panentheism became respectable after the 1780s, this did not neutralise its radical implications. As Frederick C. Beiser has argued, the interest in panentheism among the Jena Romantic circle can be read as a politically radical move to criticise the *ancien régime*: panentheism functioned as 'the ideal metaphysics for their political creed'.² Panentheism is egalitarian, since all individuals are equal by nature, which challenges vertical social or political hierarchies; it is ecumenical and cosmopolitan, and if the divine is present within every single person, this removes the need for any form of ecclesiastical authority.

Whilst Günderrode belongs to a younger generation than that of the Jena Romantics, Beiser's synthesising argument offers a means of bringing together panentheism as a metaphysical construct in Günderrode's work, including her studies, and its political resonances. Whilst her corpus would suggest a thematic break between the more metaphysical texts, such as 'Geschichte eines Braminen' and 'Briefe zweier Freunde', and the more political texts, such as the plays 'Hildgund' and 'Nikator', there are sufficient correspondences between Günderrode's panentheism and the understanding of human agency in these plays to suggest that there is a connection between the two. In both, Günderrode advances the idea of the self-determining individual that, when pursued to its logical conclusion, necessitates revolutionary action. At the same time, Günderrode's consistent recourse to panentheism complements this principle of a self-determining individual with an article of faith: that the same individual inhabits and is sustained by a universe tending towards perfection, without revealing what the ends of this teleology might be. Indeed, the end of this teleology may never be reached. The need for metaphysical reassurance arises partly because Günderrode is aware of the pitfalls of agency in the political sphere, and partly because panentheism was itself open to

1   Jacob, p. 224.
2   Frederick C. Beiser, *Enlightenment, Revolution, and Romanticism: The Genesis of Modern German Political Thought, 1790–1800* (Cambridge, MA: Harvard University Press, 1992), p. 243.

the charge of fatalism. I shall proceed by examining some of her works on political themes and return to a fuller account of her metaphysics at the end of the chapter.

It is first important to elucidate what Günderrode's political affiliations may be, as far as they can be established, and how these link to Günderrode's construction of agency in her texts that concern liberation and emancipation. These comprise the two poems dedicated to Brutus, one of Caesar's murderers, and the aforementioned 'Hildgund' and 'Nikator'.

Günderrode was by no means as politically active as figures such as Therese Huber and Caroline Schlegel-Schelling, who were part of the intellectual circle of the Mainz Republic. Nor does Günderrode interrogate the question of the emancipation of women at the same time as expressing sympathy for the Revolution, as Huber and Sophie Mereau do.[3] Attempts to establish connections between her social circle and known Jacobin sympathisers like Isaac von Sinclair and Joseph von Görres have been inconclusive, but there are some incipient textual suggestions about her own republican leanings.[4] Writing to her sister Charlotte of a journey through the Bergstraße region of Hessen, Günderrode describes beholding Mainz from afar, some six years after the failure of the Mainz Republic. Mainz was also part of the territories on the left bank of the Rhine annexed by the French,[5] so both Mainz and the Rhineland carried republican associations: 'in der Ferne glänzt der Rhein wie ein breiter Silberfaden, einige Turmspitzen in ungewissem Nebel verraten Mainz und die Grenzen des Landes der Freiheit' [in the distance the Rhine shines like a wide silver thread, some tower tops in the diffuse fog reveal Mainz and the borders of the land of freedom].[6]

Like her contemporaries, Günderrode enthusiastically greeted the rise of Napoleon during the success of his Egyptian expedition of 1798 onward and hailed him as a world-historical figure who brought light and liberation to the oppressed and, by extension, was seen to revive values that drove the Revolution. In this Messianic portrayal, Günderrode is contributing to the contemporary image of Napoleon — an image he himself carefully crafted — of a divinised military leader, comparable to Charlemagne, and as a new Prometheus.[7]

---

3   Todd Kontje, *Women, the Novel, and the German Nation 1771–1871: Domestic Fiction in the Fatherland* (Cambridge: Cambridge University Press, 1998), p. 42.
4   Licher, *Mein Leben*, pp. 50–55.
5   Joachim Whaley, *Germany and the Holy Roman Empire*, 2 vols (Oxford: Oxford University Press, 2012), II: *The Peace of Westphalia to the Dissolution of the Reich, 1648–1806*, p. 579.
6   Günderrode, *Briefe*, p. 45.
7   Barbara Beßlich, *Der deutsche Napoleon-Mythos: Literatur und Erinnerung 1800 bis 1945* (Darmstadt: Wissenschaftliche Buchgesellschaft, 2007), p. 41. A copy of a paean to Napoleon by Karl Christian Wolfart, in Wolfart's hand, features in Günderrode's *Studienbuch*. The only explicit reference to Republicanism occurs in the letters when Friedrich Karl von Savigny jokingly scolded Günderrode for allowing republican tendencies to affect her conception of friendship: 'Sie haben ja ordentlich republikanische Gesinnungen, ist das vielleicht ein kleiner Rest von der französischen Revolution?' [Do you really have republican sympathies, is that perhaps a small remainder of the French Revolution?], Friedrich Karl von Savigny, letter to Karoline von Günderrode, 8 January 1804, Freies Deutsches Hochstift (FDH), Frankfurt a.M., MS 8305, fol. 1^r.

Whilst not programmatic, these scattered comments suggest that Günderrode, like many among the educated middle classes in German-speaking lands, was ideologically attracted to the values of the French Revolution, and to Republicanism in particular. These comments also point tentatively to two features that occur in the literary work and will be discussed further: an attraction to a slogan-like concept of freedom and narratives of liberation.

There are a cluster of texts by Günderrode that are shaped by liberation narratives and that draw on the idea of revolution brought about by tyrannicide: two poems dedicated to Brutus, the assassin of Caesar, and the dramas 'Nikator' and 'Hildgund'.[8] The Brutus poems are expressly republican, but also demonstrate an ambivalence about human agency and the possibility of realising republican ideals. In the two dramas, political liberation is brought about by the protagonists' ability to liberate themselves from all external and therefore oppressive social structures. In both, the focus lies on how they ground and justify their agency as individuals, and how this specific understanding of agency is a necessary precursor to overturning or flattening out political hierarchies.

Even if the implications of both 'Nikator' and 'Hildgund' are egalitarian, the focus on individual development as a precursor to revolutionary action raises the following question: how can this idea be squared with panentheist metaphysics? Whilst neither play contains a metaphysical framework, other dramas by Günderrode combine the question of how to ground individual agency in an underlying Spinozist panentheism. These comprise Günderrode's longest drama, 'Mahomed, der Prophet von Mekka' (1805), which will be discussed in the next chapter, and the only complete drama by Günderrode, 'Magie und Schicksal' (1805).

'Magie und Schicksal' explores the question of individual agency by negating its very possibility. Günderrode makes recourse to a metaphysical framework of Spinozist fatalism that spells out the dangers that were associated with Spinozism in the pantheism controversy of the 1780s. The main point of contention relevant to 'Magie und Schicksal' is when determinism tips into fatalism. Spinoza's philosophy, as outlined in the introduction, had fatalistic implications, which proved untenable for Jacobi. At best, Herder's solution to the problem depended on an idea of global determinism. Both these stances have the potential to undermine the understanding of an individual who has the capacity to determine their existence, free from any physical compulsion or external influence.

George di Giovanni identifies this disparity between the concept of a self-determining individual and determinism as a specific problem of the late Enlightenment, and considers it a problem that was taken up by Kant and his successors:

> The problem was that, on the view of humans as individuals, the human being emerges as the responsible master of his own destiny; on the deterministic view, as a piece of the greater organization of matter by which he is determined from beginning to end. Or again, on the one view, God — if a human individual

---

[8] Tyrannicide proved to be a popular theme after the French Revolution: see Annette Runte, *Über die Grenze: Zur Kulturpoetik der Geschlechter in Literatur und Kunst* (Bielefeld: transcript, 2006), p. 181.

still cares for him — has to be sought within the individual's own heart, as if an extension of his private conscience; on the other, the same individual finds himself externally caught up in this God's cosmic designs without having any effective say about them at all.[9]

One potential solution to this problem would be to argue that the fear of determinism becomes irrelevant if the individual nurtures the illusion or self-deception that they are indeed self-determining. For Günderrode, however, this is not a solution. Indeed, this possibility is closed down in 'Magie und Schicksal', to the extent that the dramatic effects of this play depend on the horrors of a fatalistic version of Spinozism.

The Dangers of Fatalism: 'Magie und Schicksal'

The title of 'Magie und Schicksal', first published as part of Carl Daub and Friedrich Creuzer's *Studien* (1805), betrays the dramatic subgenre to which it belongs. This necessarily makes the play a good example of Spinozist fatalism: it is a fate drama, and the dramatic momentum relies on a concept of fate that necessarily undermines the human freedom of self-determination. The fate drama, or what Saskia Schottelius calls the 'fatalistisches Schauerdrama' [fatalistic Gothic drama],[10] became a popular dramatic genre in the early nineteenth century and drew on tropes from Gothic fiction.[11] Günderrode's drama precedes this specific form but is certainly analogous to it. It is constructed according to classical norms of an exposition, followed by the dramatic climax and the denouement.[12] The thematic models are also drawn from classicist sources. Günderrode draws on tropes and motifs such as astrology from Schiller's *Wallenstein* (1798–99) — contrary to Schiller, in 'Magie und Schicksal', astrology does yield epistemological insights[13] — and fratricide, from the same author's attempt to write a Greek tragedy, *Die Braut von Messina* [The Bride of Messina] (1803).[14] Among its trappings of prophetic dreams, the hint of a family

---

9   George di Giovanni, *Freedom and Religion in Kant and his Immediate Successors: The Vocation of Humankind, 1774–1800* (Cambridge: Cambridge University Press, 2005), pp. 2–3.
10 Saskia Schottelius, *Fatum, Fluch und Ironie: Zur Idee des Schicksals in der Literatur von der Aufklärung bis zur Romantik*, Europäische Hochschulschriften, 1: Deutsche Sprache und Literatur, 1505 (Frankfurt a.M.: Peter Lang, 1995), p. 17.
11 Michael Neumann, '"Das Fatum als Gegensatz der freien Selbstbestimmung" in der Schauerliteratur', in *Inevitabilis Vis Fatorum: Der Triumph des Schicksalsdramas auf der europäischen Bühne um 1800*, ed. by Roger Bauer and others (= *Jahrbuch für internationale Germanistik*, Reihe A, Kongressberichte, 27 (1990)), pp. 210–20 (p. 211).
12 Kastinger-Riley, p. 105.
13 See Daniele Vecchiato, 'Eine "lächerliche Fratze"? Zur Bedeutung und Funktion des astrologischen Motivs in literarischen Wallenstein-Darstellungen des späten achtzehnten Jahrhunderts', *Jahrbuch der deutschen Schillergesellschaft*, 59 (2015), 87–107 (p. 92).
14 A contemporary review of *Magie und Schicksal* noted the similarities to both *Wallenstein* and *Die Braut von Messina*: Heinrich Luden, 'Frankfurt u. Heidelberg, b. Mohr: *Studien*. Herausgegeben von Carl Daub u. Friedrich Creuzer, etc. (Beschluss der im vorigen Stücke abgebrochenen Recension.)', *Jenaer Allgemeine Literaturzeitung*, 260, 31 October 1805, pp. 209–16 (p. 215). Both *Wallenstein* and *Die Braut von Messina*, as well as the reception of Aristotele's *Poetics*, influenced the later popular form of *Schicksalsdrama*: see Rosmarie Zeller, 'Das Schicksalsdrama: Zacharias Werners "Der

curse, and a homage to esoteric practices in the shape of a magical staff powered by a magnetic needle, the drama explores the problem that comes from denying autonomy and the consequent loss of any form of moral orientation altogether. This brings Günderrode's play superficially close to *Die Braut von Messina*. Schiller's dramatic experiment was intended to revive Greek tragedy and met with criticism when first performed in early 1803 precisely because it revived a Greek notion of fate. Whilst this Greek notion of fate served to generate tragic fear, it also had the effect of reducing the characters to puppets that are defenceless against its operations.[15]

The plot of 'Magie und Schicksal' stems from a recurrent theme in Günderrode: the epistemological quest. The innovation in the play lies in combining these epistemological motifs with claims of human agency and self-determination. The plot concerns Alkmenes, an ailing hierophant inducted into the secrets of nature, including astrology, and his son, Ligares. Ligares attempts to convince his father to initiate him into these mysteries, to no avail. Ligares is infatuated with Ladikä, who has rejected him for his rival Timandras. He resolves to remove Timandras in a duel as a ploy to win Ladikä's affections. After Alkmenes' death, Ligares comes across his father's magical staff by accident, which he then uses to kill Timandras. Ladikä rejects Ligares, which leaves him in despair. He happens to meet Cassandra, who has been encountered at intervals in the preceding action. To his horror, he comes to realise that Timandras is his half-brother, and Cassandra the mother who abandoned his father for another man.

The tensions between freedom and necessity are present from the very first scene of the play. Günderrode juxtaposes the hierophant Alkmenes with Ligares as binary forms of human behaviour that correspond roughly to her notes on earthly versus heavenly life: 'Es giebt nur zwei Arten recht zu leben irrdisch, oder himlisch; man kann der Welt dienen, u nüzen […] Oder man lebt himlisch in der Betrachtung des Ewigen' [There are only two ways to live properly: earthly, or heavenly: one can serve the world and use it […] or one lives in a heavenly fashion in the contemplation of the Eternal] (*SW* I, 437). Günderrode sharpens this thought in the play. A life of beholding nature and the heavens necessarily involves acknowledging one's own impotence, since the individual is entirely conditioned by the forces of nature. The active life in society rests, conversely, on an untenable form of self-deception.

Günderrode stresses the significance of metaphysics for understanding human agency in the play's opening. Alkmenes heralds the coming of dawn, since sunlight brings with it the illusion of harmony in nature. As one initiated in the mysteries of nature, Alkmenes is instead privy to the horrific sublimity that lies behind such purported harmony:

---

vierundzwanzigste Februar", seine Imitationen und Variationen', in *Dynamik und Dialektik von Hoch- und Trivialliteratur im deutschsprachigen Raum im 18. und 19. Jahrhundert*, ed. by Anne Feler and others, 2 vols (Würzburg: Königshausen & Neumann, 2015), I, 125–42 (pp. 127–28).

15 Franziska Rehlinghaus, *Die Semantik des Schicksals: Zur Relevanz des Unverfügbaren zwischen Aufklärung und Erstem Weltkrieg*, Historische Semantik, 22 (Göttingen: Vandenhoeck & Ruprecht, 2015), pp. 161–63.

> Da regen sich und dehnen sich die Kräfte,
> Und brausen, heben und bekämpfen sich,
> Als wollte sich der Dinge Ordnung lösen,
> So ringen sie chaotisch wider sich.
> Als sey im Todeskampfe alles Leben,
> So sträubt sich's zwischen Daseyn und Vergehn.
> Entsetzlich so ist Nachts der Dinge Schwanken,
> Daß Lebende den Todten ähnlich sind,
> Und Todte gleich Lebend'gen irdisch wallen. —
> Drum wohl dem der an allen Sinnen blind
> Der Kräfte innre Feindschaft nie gesehen.
> Es hüllt die Nacht in Schatten weislich sich,
> Und senkt sich schwer auf aller Menschen Augen,
> Daß keiner ihre Schrecken je belauscht:
> Da kommt der Morgen, da gießt süßes Leben
> Und Eintracht hin sich über die Natur
>
> [There forces stir and expand
> And roar, rise, and antagonise one another,
> As if the order of things wanted to dissolve,
> So do they struggle in a chaos against one other.
> As if all life were engaged in a deadly struggle,
> So it was caught resisting both existence and decay.
> Horrific is the way that all things fluctuate at night,
> That the living become alike the dead,
> And the dead wander the Earth just like the living. —
> Therefore: praised be those who are stripped of all senses
> And have never espied the forces' internal enmity.
> Night cloaks itself wisely in shadows,
> And hangs heavily on the eyes of all mankind,
> So that no one ever listens in on its terrors:
> So the morning comes and pours sweet life
> And harmony over nature] (*SW* I, 233, ll. 5–20)

Harmony conceals internal and constant discord: the generative forces of nature consist in a violent dialectic, hence the binary patterning of life and death as well as night and day. Nature is allegorised, as in 'Buonaparte in Egypten' (1799) and 'Geschichte eines Braminen', in the trope of the veiled Isis. Günderrode also makes use of the conventional mapping of Isis onto Artemis to emphasise the inviolable and austere force behind nature: should the veil be lifted, the individual is punished for their erotic curiosity as violently as Actaeon (*SW* I, 234, ll. 54–62) was by Artemis.

Nature is conceived of in 'Magie und Schicksal' as hierarchical. This forms the nub of the problem for human agency. Man is part of nature but subsumed into it, and this submissive position is exemplified by Alkmenes' status as a hierophant. Serving Isis, the goddess of nature, may grant access to otherwise inaccessible knowledge, but this comes at the cost of one's self. To discourage Ligares from his fleetingly articulated desire to become a hierophant, Alkmenes warns that greater knowledge is paradoxically disempowering for the individual:

> Es drängen viele sich zum Heiligthume
> Und alle geitzen nach der Göttinn Gunst;
> Doch von den Tausenden, die zu ihr wollen,
> Hebt Einer wohl den dichten Schleier kaum;
> Denn es erheischt ein ungetheiltes Leben
> Die strenge Isis; wer mit fremdem Dienst
> Und andern Wünschen ihrem Tempel nahet,
> Den straft sie für den Frevel fürchterlich. –
> Und doch ist's schwer sich gänzlich hinzugeben.
> Die Priesterinn Apolls zu Delphi selbst
> Wird oft zum Dreifuß mit Gewalt gerissen,
> Gezwungen dann verkündiget ihr Mund
> Was ihr Apoll der Bebenden vertrauet;
> Und wie die Welt auch ihre Weisheit ehrt,
> So zagt sie doch dem Gotte sich zu geben. —
>
> [Many rush towards the shrine,
> And all desire the goddess's favour;
> But of the thousands that wish to see her,
> Barely a single one can in fact lift her dense veil;
> For strict Isis demands
> A whole life; whoever approaches
> Her temple in another's service or with other desires,
> She punishes them dreadfully for their crime. —
> But it is difficult to give oneself completely over to her.
> The priestess of Apollo at Delphi herself
> Is often violently dragged to the sacrificial tripod;
> Under duress she then declares
> What Apollo has imparted to her, trembling;
> And however much the world even honours her wisdom,
> She still hesitates to surrender to the god.] (*SW* I, 235, ll. 67–81)

Any form of self-interest has to be abandoned: knowledge comes at the cost of surrendering one's agency entirely to becoming a conduit for a god. Günderrode's use of the reference to the Delphic oracle helps to convey the inherent tensions in giving oneself over to a god: this state of enthusiasm, of being possessed by a god, is by nature a violent process ('Wird oft zum Dreifuß mit Gewalt gerissen, | Gezwungen dann verkündiget ihr Mund'), which finds physical manifestation in the oracle's trembling. The oracle's alleged reluctance to allow herself to be possessed is based on having to empty oneself completely and sacrifice one's own agency: she cannot claim ownership of the wisdom ascribed to her because it is not her own, rather it passes through her, and there is a suggestion of rape in the violence that is visited upon her ('Wird oft zum Dreifuß mit Gewalt gerissen'). The sum of Alkmenes' knowledge is the realisation of the individual's insignificance and impotence. So great is this constant psychic pressure that, when approaching death, Alkmenes argues that it is better to live in ignorance and act in complete accordance with fate, rather than to be initiated into the mysteries and to be eternally suspended between the Earth and the heavens (*SW* I, 248, ll. 421–34).

This hierarchical model of agency also applies to those who are not initiated into mysteries. Man is not just part of nature on Earth, but rather is perceived as part of the entire system of the cosmos. Günderrode appears to draw on the esoteric principle of universal interdependence, which also exists in the Hermetic tradition as the microcosm and the macrocosm.[16] This interdependence has a distinct vertical hierarchy. The entire cosmos is permeated with a series of causal correspondences and unseen forces, such as magnetism. Human action is determined by the movements of stars and other celestial bodies:

> Nicht weil die Menschen handeln, kreisen Sterne:
> Die Menschen wandeln nach der Sterne Lauf.
> Wie Fluth und Ebbe nach dem Mond sich richten
> Und fallen, schwellen, wie er kommt und geht;
> So heben sich Gedanken und versinken
> Gelenket von der Himmelskörper Lauf.
> Des Menschen Brust ist gleich des Meeres Spiegel,
> Der widerstrahlet von der Sonne Bild
> Und dunkel ist und glanzlos, wenn sie sinket.
>
> [Stars do not follow an orbit because of human action:
> Humans move according to the stars' orbit
> As tides become high and ebb with the moon,
> And fall and swell, just as the moon nears and becomes distant,
> So do thoughts rise and fall
> Guided by the course of heavenly bodies.
> The human breast is like the mirror of the sea,
> Which reflects the image of the sun
> And becomes dark and wan when it sets.] (*SW* I, 235, ll. 89–97)

The analogy that Günderrode draws between the individual and the surface of the sea adapts a metaphor used in 'Des Wandrers Niederfahrt' to describe the individual: 'Des Weltalls seh'nder Spiegel bist du nur' [You are but the sighted mirror of the universe] (*SW* I, 73, l. 126). The image of the mirror in the two passages refers both to the trope in the mystical tradition that the individual is the reflective mirror of God and to an understanding of the individual as a Leibnizian monad. This analogy draws upon the imagery present at the beginning of the scene. If nature is conceptualised as a binary, where daylight brings harmony, and night the violence of generative chaos, it holds that the same is true for the individual. On one level, this is an epistemological claim: there are unconscious and inscrutable depths of the self. But the subtext here pushes this point further: that the individual may also be defenceless against inscrutable passions within.

---

16   Antoine Faivre, 'Renaissance Hermeticism and the Concept of Western Esotericism', in *Gnosis and Hermeticism from Antiquity to Modern Times*, ed. by Roelof van den Broek and Wouter J. Hanegraaff (Albany: SUNY Press, 1998), pp. 109–23 (p. 119). See also Hans-Georg Kemper, '"Eins im All! Und all in Eins!": "Christliche Hermetik" als trojanisches Pferd der Aufklärung', in *Aufklärung und Esoterik: Rezeption — Integration — Konfrontation*, ed. by Monika Neugebauer-Wölk (Tübingen: Niemeyer, 2008), pp. 29–52 (p. 34).

To Alkmenes' son Ligares, this naturalistic conception of the individual is untenable. Not only does he question the astrological predetermination of individual actions, but he also dismisses outright the supine position that this entails. Ligares' own inner sense of freedom, he claims, confirms *a priori* that there is a separate realm of individual will and freedom untouched by the influence of celestial bodies:

> Ich fühle frei mich ganz in meinem Herzen,
> Von der Gestirne Einfluß unberührt;
> Es zieht mich vieles an im bunten Leben,
> Und vieles werd' ich können, weil ich will;
> In diesem stolzen Glauben will ich bleiben,
> Mich selber fühlen als des Schicksals Herr;
> Mich nicht entnerven durch ein feiges Wähnen,
> Als sey ich fremden Mächten unterthan.
>
> [I feel myself to be free in my heart,
> Untouched by the influence of the stars;
> Many things attract me in the bustle of life,
> And I will do many things because I will them to be;
> I will hold on to this proud thought,
> To feel myself to be the lord over fate;
> And not to become weak through a coward's false belief,
> As if I were subject to other powers.] (*SW* I, 236, ll. 107–14)

Ligares makes bold claims about how to justify his actions or rather his unquenchable desire for action: his capacity to act is based on the belief that his will alone translates directly into acts, and he imagines himself as an absolute subject whose will cannot be resisted. Ligares has to feel that he himself is in command of fate, and, since for metrical reasons Günderrode substitutes the unstressed 'des' for the stressed 'meines', this suggests that he is not just in command of his own: 'Mich selber fühlen als des Schicksals Herr'. The precondition of being able to act freely in the world is to avoid the kind of ascetic resignation to which his father subscribes ('Mich nicht entnerven durch ein feiges Wähnen, | Als sey ich fremden Mächten unterthan.').

Ligares goes on to dismiss any correspondence between the processes of the natural world and the individual, believing his father to be oblivious to his desires. Yet Ligares's actions are not drawn from the promptings of feeling that grant him his sense of autonomy, but from the passions within him whose potential he readily acknowledges to be dangerous:

> Doch meinen Busen hat er [Alkmenes] nie durchschauet;
> Wenn er beschwört, gehorcht der Geist ihm nicht,
> Der böse Dämon, der in meinem Herzen,
> Ein gierig Raubthier, sich und mich verzehrt.
> Gleich einem Tieger, der in Libyens Wüste
> Im heißen Sand sich durstig brüllend wälzt,
> So wüthet Leidenschaft in meiner Seele
> Von keinem Tropfen Hoffnung mehr erquickt.
>
> [But Alkmenes never saw through to my heart;
> When he conjures, the spirit does not obey him,

> The vicious demon in my heart,
> A voracious predator, consumes itself and me.
> Just like the tiger, which in the Libyan desert
> Rolls about in the hot sands, both thirsty and roaring,
> So does passion rage in my soul
> No longer satiated by a single drop of hope.]
>
> (SW I, 236–37, ll. 125–32)

Although 'Dämon' did carry positive associations to Herder and Goethe on account of its roots in ancient philosophy,[17] Günderrode's use of 'böse[r] Dämon' is expressly Christian and negative. It refers to the irrational forces within Ligares which threaten to consume him entirely. This finds expression not in the Faustian thirst for knowledge that afflicts other figures in Günderrode's *oeuvre*, but rather — following the patterning of the imagery — in insatiable desire to act. The object of this desire is a domestic love-plot: that Ligares believes that eliminating his love rival Timandras would force Ladikä — who had already rejected him — to accept him.

This fraternal rivalry is subsidiary to the generational conflict between Alkmenes and Ligares.[18] What becomes manifest in this conflict is the central philosophical concern of the play: the question of whether the individual is subject to fate, and therefore all actions are predetermined, against a belief in a form of freedom that permits autonomy.[19] In spite of Ligares' proclaimed autonomy — which he himself undercuts — the characters are conscious of how they are conditioned by fate or chance, or by the invisible hand of plot machinations. Günderrode carefully frames the chance meeting between the love rivals and — unbeknownst to both of them — half-brothers Ligares and Timandras in these terms:

> LIGARES. Gewaltsam hat mich's, mächtig hergezogen,
> Und wie mein Wille immer vorwärts drang,
> Ward ich gezwungen doch zurück zu kehren
> Mit Widerstreben, halb und halb erwünscht.
>
> [LIGARES. Forcibly I've been drawn here, powerfully so,
> And however much my will always pushed on,
> I was nonetheless forced to come back,
> Half reluctantly, but partly I desired it.]
>
> (SW I, 253, ll. 555–58)
>
> TIMANDRAS. Wer du auch seyst, zu dem mich hat geleitet
> Der güt'ge Zufall, o gewähre mir,
> Daß ich die Nacht hier darf bei dir verweilen

---

17 See Angus Nicholls, *Goethe's Concept of the Daemonic: After the Ancients* (Rochester, NY: Camden House, 2006).
18 As Barbara Becker-Cantarino also observes: Barbara Becker-Cantarino, *Schriftstellerinnen der Romantik: Epoche — Werke — Wirkung* (Munich: Beck, 2000), p. 216.
19 Susanne Kord also identifies this as the central conflict of the play: Susanne Kord, *Ein Blick hinter die Kulissen: Deutschsprachige Dramatikerinnen im 18. und 19. Jahrhundert*, Ergebnisse der Frauenforschung, 27 (Stuttgart: Metzler, 1992), pp. 109–10.

> [TIMANDRAS. Whoever you may be, to whom benevolent chance
> Has led me, o bestow upon me my wish
> To spend the night here beside you.] (*SW* I, 254, ll. 583–85)

Where Timandras's reference to chance is a conventional invocation that expresses his hope of receiving hospitality, Ligares's reference exposes the limits of his own alleged autonomy, and it also moves towards the metaphysical understanding of the individual that Alkmenes outlined at the play's opening. Alongside his daemonic passions, there is some form of external, overpowering force that both counteracts and interacts with his will ('Mit Widerstreben, halb und halb erwünscht').

Ligares's further invocations of fate are less nuanced. Fuelled by the sense of being 'des Schicksals Herr', or at the very least that fate is particularly beneficent towards him, Ligares conflates contingent events with the validation of his own desires. He interprets his father's magical sceptre falling into his hands — which Alkmenes expressly did not wish to happen — as confirmation that he must challenge Timandras to a duel and kill him:

> O Schicksal! Schicksal! ich verstehe dich.
> Zu rechter Zeit spielst du mir in die Hände,
> Was Rache mir und Rettung noch verspricht.
> Der Zufall mahnt mich an geschworne Eide,
> Die ich feigherzig fliehend fast vergaß.
> Er oder ich! hab ich das nicht geschworen? –
> O Glück! noch ganz abgünstig bist du nicht,
> Gezwungen hast du dieses Stromes Tiefe,
> Daß er sein Eingeweide spenden muß.
>
> [Oh fate! Fate! I understand you.
> At the right time you play into my hands,
> That which promises me vengeance and salvation still.
> Chance reminds me of sworn oaths,
> Which I, fleeing with a cowardly heart, almost forgot.
> He or I! Is that not what I have sworn?
> O Fortune! You are not yet completely unfavourable towards me,
> You compelled the depths of this current
> So that he must part with his entrails.] (*SW* I, 261, ll. 756–64)

This biased interpretation of contingency leads to Ligares fusing fate with his own will entirely. After having murdered Timandras by using his father's sceptre, Ligares lays a claim on Ladikä, although she has already rebuffed him:

> Du bist nun wieder und für immer mein;
> Der Götter Wille hat dich mir gegeben,
> Denn Gottes Stimme spricht im Schicksal auch.
>
> [Now you are again and forever mine;
> The will of gods granted you to me,
> For the voice of God speaks through fate too.]
> (*SW* I, 268, ll. 948–50)

Here is where Ligares's unbridled egotism comes to an end: Ligares's belief that removing Timandras is misguided because, from his perspective, it constitutes the only physical obstacle between him and Ladikä. Ligares fails to anticipate that imposing his will on Ladikä could result in her objecting to his advances. Instead, when she repeatedly rejects him, he turns to a final and desperate attempt at coercion: he threatens to kill her or kill himself. In short, Ligares's egotism undermines his ability to appreciate that the desires and the will of others exist.

With this conclusion to the plot, alongside the revelation that Ligares has inadvertently slaughtered his half-brother, it may appear that Günderrode's concerns are not so much metaphysical as social, exposing Ligares's failure to appreciate interpersonal and communal aspects of human action. Ligares's single-minded obsession with pursuing Ladikä leaves the character bereft, experiencing a death of sorts in finding that he derives value from nothing else in existence: 'Ich habe nichts, und nichts als sie besessen; | Jedweden Anspruch gab ich willig auf' [I have possessed nothing, nothing other than her; | All other claims I freely forfeited] (*SW* I, 271, ll. 1031–32).

Yet Günderrode also hints at the implications that Ligares's egotism has for morality: namely, that it eliminates morality altogether. Furthermore, this dissolution of morality is also connected with the play's fatalism. After Timandras's murder, Ligares muses on his lack of remorse for the act:

> Es hebt die Brust sich heiter mir und freier,
> Des Mordgefährten Reue fühl' ich nicht.
> Ist's so entsetzlich denn sich Rache nehmen?
> Besteht im ew'gem Kampfe nicht die Welt?
> Muß Leben raubend Leben sich nicht nähren?
> Ich habe was Gemeines nur gethan –
> Es wird die That den Schlummer mir nicht rauben;
> Gespenster quälen den nur, der verzagt;
> Doch sie erschrecket der, der sie nicht scheuet,
> Der keck in ihre tiefste Wohnung dringt.
>
> [My chest rises and falls serenely, and more freely;
> I do not feel a murder-companion's remorse.
> Is it so hideous to take revenge?
> Is not the world just an eternal struggle?
> Does life not have to nourish itself by stealing other life?
> I have only done something commonplace —
> The deed will not rob me of sleep;
> Spirits only torment those who lose heart
> But they fear those who do not recoil from them,
> Those who reach the spirits' deepest abode.] (*SW* I, 262–63, ll. 791–800)

Ligares makes use of a naturalist analogy to justify carrying out his will: that no higher morality can be found than in nature. Therefore, in a move that seems to anticipate forms of Darwinism, Ligares's vengeance is simply an expression of the same eternal strife found in nature.[20] The murder can thus be relativised as something

---

20 There are parallels here with Franz Moor's soliloquy in the first scene of *Die Räuber*: 'Das Recht wohnt beym Ueberwältiger, und die Schranken unserer Kraft sind unsere Gesetze' [Those in power determine what is right, and the limits of our strength make our laws], Friedrich Schiller, *Schillers Werke: Nationalausgabe*, ed. by Julius Petersen and others, 43 vols (Weimar: Böhlaus Nachfolger,

commonplace and justifiable ('Ich habe was Gemeines nur gethan'). Moral pangs of guilt only afflict those weak enough to succumb to despair: 'Gespenster quälen den nur, der verzagt'. Ligares extends this thought to an individual who is audacious enough to dispense entirely with the kind of moral doubts that would make up one's conscience: 'Doch sie erschrecket der, der sie nicht scheuet, | Der keck in ihre tiefste Wohnung dringt.' Such an absence of conscience is prefigured by one of Ligares's first programmatic statements in 'Magie und Schicksal': 'Und vieles werd' ich können, weil ich will' [And I will do many things because I will them to be] (*SW* I, 236, l. 110). The implications of this pithy maxim are played out here: once the will becomes an all-encompassing principle, then all forms of action are justified, at the expense of any moral system that would regulate them.

How can this rejection of morality be reconciled with the dangers inherent in Spinozism? If placing primacy on the will necessarily results in the dissolution of morality, then so does negating the will altogether and acknowledging fatalism, for then the individual becomes a passive vessel through which external forces act. Ligares's previous belief to be 'des Schicksals Herr' [the master of fate] alters at the conclusion of the play. The combination of Ladikä's rejection and the revelation that Timandras is his brother and Cassandra his mother leaves Ligares in a state of despair. Instead of acknowledging his previously much-vaunted agency, he instead portrays himself as the victim of both internal forces and external forces, that is, a victim of fate:

LIGARES.	[...]
	So denke, daß Verzweiflung mich getrieben,
	Und fluche mir nicht, was ich auch gethan.
CASSANDRA.	Was ist geschehen? sprich, was ist geschehen?
	Um aller Götter willen bleib, und sprich.
LIGARES.	Nein! nein! ich darf dein Antlitz nicht mehr sehen,
	Ein Ungeheuer würd' ich scheinen dir. —
	Doch fluch mir nicht; es hat mich zum Verbrechen
	Des Schicksals Wille deutlich selbst geführt,
	Und seine Winke hab' ich nur vollzogen:
	Drum denke, daß ichs nur gezwungen that.
[LIGARES.	[...]
	Please consider that it was desperation that drove me,
	And do not curse me for what I have done.
CASSANDRA.	What has happened? Speak, what has happened?
	Stay, for the sake of the gods, and speak.
LIGARES.	No! No! I must not see your countenance again,
	I would seem a monstrosity to you. —
	But do not curse me; the will of fate clearly
	Led me to the crime,
	And I only carried out what it suggested:
	So think that I acted only because I was forced to.]

(*SW* I, 275, ll. 1143–52)

1943–2010), III: *Die Räuber*, ed. by Herbert Stubenrauch (1953), pp. 18–19.

On one level, portraying oneself as the victim of external forces is a convenient form of self-exculpation to find favour with his mother — 'fluche mir nicht, was ich auch gethan'; 'Drum denke, daß ichs nur gezwungen that.' But the metaphysical underpinnings of the play, as laid out by Alkmenes in the first scene, give his words a broader significance. The horror of fatalism lies in the fact that the individual cannot claim ownership of their actions, cannot make sense of these, or indeed have a point of moral orientation by which to judge them.[21] No individual development, let alone autonomy, is possible.

This has ramifications for how to conceive of the operations of nature or fate as a proxy for divine providence. Fate acts as an independent force in the play, and the term could easily be substituted for that of necessity. To take the thought further: conflating fate and necessity can lead to an implicit denial of God, since God's function is unhappily usurped by fate.[22] This negative Spinozism, precisely the kind that Jacobi found so abhorrent, has nihilistic implications. If the individual is given over to the blind necessity of nature, this eliminates human freedom *and* morality, since there is no moral authority to which the individual can be held accountable. What 'Magie und Schicksal' represents is, in extreme form, a tension inherent within Spinozist panentheism: accepting that the individual is one with nature can come at the cost of negating the individual and human autonomy altogether.

Ambivalences about Revolution: Günderrode's heroic *Tatmenschen*

The negative example of Ligares in 'Magie und Schicksal' only serves to point to how important human agency and the possibility of autonomy are for Günderrode, particularly with reference to individual agency.[23] What Ligares aspires to be is the heroic type of the *Tatmensch* [person of action]. Günderrode's protagonists in her dramas are, more often than not, cut from the same cloth: the revolutionary figures of Mahomed, Hildgund, and Nikator all embody the ideal of a *Tatmensch*, and her poems to Napoleon and Brutus are paeans to the ability of the individual to have world-historical agency. In short, Günderrode's *oeuvre* repeatedly invokes an idealised concept of heroic greatness in these *Tatmenschen*.[24] There is a recurring point of tension in these texts: the individual protagonist's feverish hopes to bring about a new order are undercut by reflexive moments of elegiac melancholy, or by the text cutting off altogether before these hopes can be fulfilled.

This ambivalence, in part, responds to the continued disappointment of revolutionary ideals. It is, in short, a problem of historical contingency. Napoleon's

---

21 Margarete Lazarowicz rightly points to the oppressive function of fate in the play: Lazarowicz, p. 169.
22 Marianne Wünsch, 'Schicksal am Ende der Romantik: Das Beispiel von Grabbes „Herzog Theodor von Gothland"', in *Inevitabilis Vis Fatorum*, pp. 130–50 (p. 141).
23 As Anna C. Ezekiel has noted in the context of *Poetische Fragmente*: Günderrode, *Poetic Fragments*, p. 16.
24 Heroic greatness is itself an ambivalent concept: for an overview of eighteenth-century perspectives on the subject, see Martin Disselkamp, *Barockheroismus: Konzeptionen 'politischer' Größe in Literatur und Traktatistik des 17. Jahrhunderts*, Frühe Neuzeit, 65 (Tübingen: Niemeyer, 2002), pp. 1–15.

imperial ambitions after 1800 represented a second betrayal of republican hopes, after the horror aroused by the Terror of 1792–94.[25] In general, German responses to the French Revolution among public figures and intellectuals were sympathetic to revolutionary ideals until the Revolution descended into bloodshed and violence, and to an extent this can be applied to Günderrode as well.[26] Around 1800, whilst sympathies for the Revolution were diffuse, they remained present across all social strata.[27]

What underpins this ambivalence is also the hope that history embodies some sort of linear, progressivist teleology: the idea that political and social advancement may be possible. But this also has a more abstract dimension to it for Günderrode. The end point of the *telos* is framed as perfection. As soon as the idea of perfection takes on a temporal or historical dimension in this manner, it recalls the concept of perfectibility. Perfectibility is important for Günderrode, and it enjoyed popularity in the debates about anthropology and the philosophy of history in English, French, and German contexts in the eighteenth century. Originally a loan word from French, perfectibility first had an ontogenetic function and referred to the ability of the individual to achieve perfection by developing innate and God-given abilities and faculties.[28] Later it became more malleable, but from Leibniz onward it proved an influential concept for the Enlightenment.[29]

Perfectibility recurs across Günderrode's literary work as 'Vollkommenheit' [perfection] or 'Vervollkommnung' [bringing to perfection].[30] That the latter is used more frequently than the former suggests that perfectibility is a dynamic process that at points defies its own completion. 'Vollkommenheit' recalls both religious or metaphysical meanings, but also has aesthetic weight.[31] These specific uses in Günderrode are philosophical in nature. Indeed, perfection and perfectibility are important ingredients of her panentheistic metaphysics. As Günderrode's studies demonstrate, there is some slippage between philosophical, theological, and historical argument. Her *Studienbuch* from 1799 to 1800 features a section from Herder's *Briefe zur Beförderung der Humanität* [Letters on the Advancement of Humanity] (1793) that outlines a historical teleology. Herder invokes perfectibility as the motor for the development of *Humanität*, which assumes the role of the vocation of humankind:

---

25 Rudolf Vierhaus, *Deutschland im 18. Jahrhundert: Politische Verfassung, soziales Gefüge, geistige Bewegungen* (Göttingen: Vandenhoeck & Ruprecht, 1987), p. 215.
26 Birgit Tautz, 'Revolution, Abolition, Aesthetic Sublimation: German Responses to News from France in the 1790s', in *(Re-)Writing the Radical: Enlightenment, Revolution and Cultural Transfer in 1790s Germany, Britain and France*, ed. by Maike Oergel, Spectrum Literaturwissenschaft, 32 (Berlin: De Gruyter, 2012), pp. 72–87 (p. 72).
27 Wolfgang Kaschuba, 'Revolution als Spiegel: Reflexe der Französischen Revolution in deutscher Öffentlichkeit und Alltagskultur um 1800', in *Französische Revolution und deutsche Öffentlichkeit: Wandlungen in Presse*, ed. by Helger Böning (Munich: Saur, 1991), pp. 381–98 (p. 381).
28 Aaron Garrett, 'Human Nature', in *The Cambridge History of Eighteenth-Century Philosophy*, ed. by Knud Haakonssen, 2 vols (New York: Cambridge University Press, 2006), I, 160–233 (p. 177).
29 Gottfried Hornig, 'Perfektibilität', *Archiv für Begriffsgeschichte*, 24 (1979), 221–57 (pp. 221–22).
30 Most prominently in 'Geschichte eines Braminen' or 'Briefe zweier Freunde'.
31 There is some slippage in the terminology. Günderrode's use of 'Vortrefflichkeit' as a form of perfection maps onto a Platonist idea of aligning aesthetic perfection with a divine principle.

> wie physisch, so ist auch moralisch und politisch die Menschheit im ewigen Fortgang und Streben. Die Perfectibilität ist also keine Täuschung, sie ist Mittel und Endzwek zur Ausbildung alles dessen, was der Charakter unsers Geschlechts Humanität verlangt und gewährt.
>
> [physically, as well as morally and politically, humanity finds itself in eternal progress and striving. Perfectibility is, then, no illusion, it is the means and final purpose for the development of everything that the character of our species demands of humanity and grants.][32]

Herder's concept of perfectibility is complemented by an entry in the pastor Diefenbach's hand, whose argument is more theological in nature:

> Das höchste Ideal moralischer Vollkommenheit ist der große Angebetete. — Im gemilderten Glanz, anziehend und erhebend erscheint das Ideal vollendeter Menschheit. [...] Ewiges Gedräng, ewiges Streben und Fehlen, und nie Vollendung. Zu kühn ist der Gedanke, das Ideal der Menschheit in sich zu realisieren, hätten wir es erreicht, so wäre es nicht Ideal mehr, wir müßten uns nach einem Höhern umsehn.
>
> [The highest ideal of moral perfection is the Most Worshipful. — The ideal of perfected humanity manifests with a lesser radiance, yet it is appealing and elevating. [...] Humanity is eternally urging onward, eternal striving and failing, and never is perfection achieved. The thought of realising the ideal of humanity in oneself is too bold: if we had attained it, then it would no longer be an ideal, and we would have to search for something higher to strive for.][33]

There are structural and linguistic similarities between Herder and Diefenbach, in particular in the notion of perpetual attempts at human development. Diefenbach is more cautious, since the highest form of moral perfection is found only in Christ. The model behind Diefenbach's statement is Platonic: the 'Ewiges Gedräng, ewiges Streben und Fehlen' correspond to *eros*, the desire or longing that drives human activity. Diefenbach is drawing on a notion from classical ontology and natural theology: that God, as the highest being, epitomises ontological and moral perfection.[34] The analogous form of human perfection cannot be attained, because it, like the perfection of God, cannot be exceeded. Instead, it operates as a regulative idea.

At first glance, these examples would suggest that perfectibility endorses a linear teleology of progress, albeit with an eternally deferred endpoint. Yet perfectibility is by no means indebted to progressivist conceptions of human history or the development of human character. As Konstanze Baron and Christian Soboth note, perfectibility must be distinguished from Enlightenment notions of progress.[35]

---

32   Preitz/Hopp III, p. 276.
33   Ibid., p. 277.
34   Stephan Lorenz, 'Leibniz als Denker der Vollkommenheit und der Vervollkommnung: Mit Hinweisen zur Rezeption', in *Perfektionismus und Perfektibilität: Theorien und Praktiken der Vervollkommnung in Pietismus und Aufklärung*, ed. by Konstanze Baron and Christian Soboth, Studien zum achtzehnten Jahrhundert, 35 (Hamburg: Meiner, 2018), pp. 75–96 (p. 76).
35   Konstanze Baron and Chistian Soboth, 'Einleitung', in *Perfektionismus und Perfektibilität*, pp. 9–28 (pp. 14–15).

Within the concept of perfectibility is space for critique and criticism; indeed, in Rousseau's provocative exploration of perfectibility, it can also evoke the potential degeneration of man.[36]

This idea of perfectibility can therefore assume an ambivalent function. Ernst Behler has taken up the notion of perfectibility as an organising principle of his comparative study of the Romantic period. Behler adapts Condorcet's term 'la perfectibilité indéfinie' to make use of 'unendliche Perfektibilität' [endless perfectibility] as a conceptual tool to examine the ambivalences specific to the historical moment of Romanticism. This also stems from the acknowledgement of the problematic nature of the Revolution among the Jena Romantic circle:[37]

> Unendliche Perfektibilität ist auch Ausdruck der kritischen Reaktion dieser frühen Romantiker auf die französische Revolution. In diesem Sinne erscheint die Perfektibilitätsidee in ihren Schriften als ein noch unsicherer Erklärungsversuch, als eine Art Rechtfertigung, als apologetische Reaktion auf eine Folge von Ereignissen, die ihrem Glauben an die Vervollkommnung der Menschheit zu widersprechen schienen. In seltsamer Verschiebung wird die Perfektibilität, die eine motivierende Kraft im revolutionären Bewußtsein gewesen war, als Rechtfertigung der Revolution ans Ende der begonnenen Umwälzung oder in eine unbestimmte Zukunft verschoben. [...]
>
> Diese ambivalente Fassung der Perfektibilitätsidee, charakteristisch für die romantische Mentalität, bekundet sich in den Gegenbewegungen von Enthusiasmus und Melancholie, Affirmation und Skepsis, Billigung und Ablehnung, die sich gegenseitig aufzuheben scheinen, sich aber in Wirklichkeit wechselseitig erzeugen und tragen. Dieser neue Denkstil ist deutlich durch die Erfahrung der französischen Revolution geprägt und vielleicht das wichtigste Merkmal, das von ihr ausgegangen ist.
>
> [Endless perfectibility is also the expression of how the Early Romantics critically responded to the French Revolution. In this sense, the idea of perfectibility appears in their writings as an attempt, itself still uncertain, to provide clarity, a type of justification, an apologetic reaction to a series of events that seemed to contradict their belief in the perfectibility of humankind. In this curious displacement, perfectibility, which had been the motivating force among those with a revolutionary consciousness, becomes deferred as a justification of the revolution to the end of the upheaval that had begun, or is deferred to an undefined point in the future.
>
> This ambivalent conception of perfectibility, which is characteristic of the Romantic mentality, manifests itself in the oscillations between enthusiasm and melancholy, affirmation and scepticism, approval and rejection, which seem to nullify one another, but in reality generate and sustain one another. This new style of thought is clearly shaped by the experience of the French Revolution and perhaps the most important feature that emerged from it.][38]

---

36 For an investigation of this kind of paradox within the concept of perfectibility, see Bertrand Binoche, *L'homme perfectible* (Seyssel: Éditions Champs Villon, 2004), pp. 13–35.
37 Helmut Koopmann, *Freiheitssonne und Revolutionsgewitter: Reflexe der Französischen Revolution im literarischen Deutschland zwischen 1789 und 1840*, Untersuchungen zur deutschen Literaturgeschichte, 50 (Tübingen: Niemeyer, 1989), pp. 62–64.
38 Ernst Behler, *Unendliche Perfektibilität: Europäische Romantik und Französische Revolution* (Paderborn: Schöningh, 1989), pp. 15–16.

For Behler, these ambivalences find expression in the fragmentary poetics and uses of irony among the Jena Romantic circle. This new form of poetics, however, had little bearing on Günderrode's work. Thematically, however, these specific ambivalences of perfectibility can be made productive for interpreting Günderrode's *oeuvre*. Firstly, Günderrode utilises a teleological narrative of human development, which is understood in terms of perfectibility, and is linked to the development of individual agency. Secondly, Günderrode is indebted to republican ideals of freedom and equality, where the former is more explicit and the latter more implicit in her literary work.

It would be tempting to align Günderrode's allegiance to the idea of perfectibility with an understanding of the role of art and literature in early German Romanticism. This had its roots in Schiller's *Über die ästhetische Erziehung des Menschen* [On the Aesthetic Education of Man] (1795), with its claim that art and literature were to be the primary instrument for cultivating the individual and instigating moral and political renewal.[39] What was framed by Schiller as a response to Kantian ethics was turned by Friedrich Schlegel and Novalis into a more comprehensive aesthetic and poetic project. The French Revolution had failed. But it presaged a greater, singular upheaval that would encompass all areas of existence, including poetry and philosophy.[40] Whilst Günderrode does come close at points to endowing the experience of art and literature with a Messianic function, the works I am considering here have more limited aims. Here Günderrode is not offering her readers a redemptive escape from history. The ambivalences about individual agency she explores are a way, rather, of probing political concepts such as freedom and equality, and suggest that perfectibility has limits in political reality and human nature. If these are to be overcome, the solution will lie, not in art, but in metaphysics. What literature can do, however, is to involve the reader in acts of commemoration and anticipation that give body to political hopes. In that respect, at least, Günderrode shares Novalis's belief in the transformative power of 'Erinnerung' [remembrance] and 'Ahnung' [anticipation].[41]

Examining Günderrode's revolutionary texts such as 'Nikator', 'Hildgund', and the two poems on Brutus, reveals ambivalences about what may otherwise appear to be a triumph of individual agency and autonomy. For this, Brutus is a prototype, and the ambivalences about these ideals find semantic expression in both poems. In 'Nikator' and 'Hildgund', the ambivalences become displaced to the dramatic structure: both plays fail to reach a point of narrative closure, which raises questions about the very kind of autonomy that both protagonists develop.

Even Günderrode's most full-blooded panegyric of a revolutionary figure is undercut by the paradoxes of mood that Behler outlines. Whilst Günderrode's two poems dedicated to Brutus may appear to proclaim a quasi-religious ideal

---

39 Beiser, *The Romantic Imperative*, p. 93.
40 Ernst Behler, *German Romantic Literary Theory* (Cambridge: Cambridge University Press, 1993), pp. 59–60.
41 See K. F. Hilliard, *Freethinkers, Libertines and Schwärmer: Heterodoxy in German Literature, 1750–1800*, igrs books, 1 (London: Institute of Germanic and Romance Studies, 2011), pp. 232–34.

of freedom,[42] the heroic quality of this idealised Brutus rests, paradoxically, on historical failure. Brutus is a heroic victim of history.[43] Günderrode was aware of this wealth of associations and projected ideals that had accrued around him. These associations can be traced through the varied reception of Brutus in her *Nachlass*.

In Revolutionary France, republican Rome served as a point of identification for French revolutionaries, and invoking Brutus (Marcus Junius Brutus, the conspirator against Caesar) appealed to the authority of antiquity and demonstrated anti-monarchical intentions.[44] The eighteenth century in general, not just the revolutionary period, saw a proliferation of texts idealising Brutus and vilifying Caesar as a tyrant. Klopstock, Herder, Lessing and Schiller made use of Brutus as a literary figure. So popular was the Brutus topic in the eighteenth century that Friedrich Gundelfinger comments, with use of hyperbole: 'F. L. Stolberg konnte kein B sehen, ohne an Brutus zu denken.' [F. L. Stolberg could not see a 'B' without thinking of Brutus].[45]

Günderrode's Brutus is partly indebted to Shakespeare's portrayal of Brutus as a hero-sage who is, as Geoffrey Miles notes, 'courageous, passionless, immovably enduring in adversity, demonstrating his superiority to fortune by resolute death or suicide'.[46] This aligns the predominant image of Brutus in the eighteenth century as a Stoic as well as a Republican, an image which was established by the popularity of Plutarch's biography.[47] A copy of the 'Römergesang' [The Romans' Song] from Schiller's *Die Räuber* [The Robbers] (1779), where Karl Moor identifies himself with Brutus, is in part of Günderrode's *Nachlass*.[48] Schiller lifts the incident of Brutus meeting Caesar's ghost at the battle of Philippi directly from Plutarch's biography.[49] This song may well be the thematic basis for Günderrode's two poems.

---

42 Lucia Licher interprets the poems as declaring 'ein neues Evangelium' of freedom, in a synthesising reading that points towards Günderrode's treatment of Muhammad as a legitimate prophet of a new religion: Lucia Licher, '"Der Völker Schicksal ruht in meinem Busen": Karoline von Günderrode als Dichterin der Revolution', in *Der Menschheit Hälfte blieb noch ohne Recht': Frauen und die französische Revolution*, ed. by Helga Brandes (Wiesbaden: Deutscher Universitätsverlag, 1991), pp. 113–32 (p. 122).
43 Brutus corresponds to the heroic type of the 'Opferheld' in the typology of heroes whose heroism depends on their noble death: see Michael Gratzke, *Feuer und Blut: Heldentum bei Lessing, Fontane, Jünger und Heiner Müller* (Würzburg: Königshausen & Neumann, 2011), p. 16.
44 Catharine Edwards, 'Introduction: Shadow and Fragments', in *Roman Presences: Receptions of Rome in European Culture, 1789–1945*, ed. by Catharine Edwards (Cambridge: Cambridge University Press, 1999), pp. 1–18 (pp. 8–9). Lucius Junius Brutus, founder of the Roman Republic, could serve the same purpose.
45 Friedrich Gundelfinger, *Caesar in der deutschen Literatur* (Berlin: Mayer & Müller, 1904), p. 108.
46 Geoffrey Miles, *Shakespeare and the Constant Romans* (Oxford: Clarendon Press, 1996), p. 39.
47 Paul Michael Lützeler, '"Die grosse Linie zu einem Brutuskopfe": Republikanismus und Cäsarismus in Schillers *Fiesco*', *Monatshefte*, 70.1 (1978), 15–28 (p. 15).
48 As Morgenthaler notes: *SW* III, 216. The excerpt is part of the collectanea and is written in Günderrode's mother's hand.
49 Jochen Schmidt, 'Grundlagen, Kontinuität und geschichtlicher Wandel des Stoizismus', in *Stoizismus in der europäischen Philosophie, Literatur, Kunst und Politik: Eine Kulturgeschichte von der Antike bis zur Moderne*, ed. by Barbara Neymeyr and others, 2 vols (Berlin: De Gruyter, 2008), I, 3–133 (pp. 110–11).

Another text in the *Nachlass* presents another aspect of the contemporary idealisation of Brutus, and one that does not initially fall into Stoic or republican categories. It is an extract, written in Wilhelmine von Günderrode's hand, from a two-part article in *Zeitung für die elegante Welt* [Journal for the Elegant World] from 1803,[50] entitled 'Nachrichten für die Kunst; in einem Briefe aus Weimar' [Notices on Art; in a letter from Weimar], and was presumably used as part of sociable reading practices for discussion within the family and among friends and acquaintances.[51] The actual topic is androgyny in sculpture and art: how 'jedes einzel [Mann u Weib] nur eine halbe Erscheinung der Menschheit ausdrükken, so stellen beide vereint ein Ganzes im Leben wie in der Kunst' [every individual [man and woman] creates only half of the impression of humanity, when united they both are a whole in life as they are in art] (*SW* I, 469). The initial examples of androgyny are drawn from the classical Greek pantheon and represent 'ein Ganzes — [...] den Gipfel der Kunst' [a whole — [...] the pinnacle of art] (ibid.). Artists, it follows, must themselves be androgynous to generate this ideal of holistic perfection: 'alle Künstler sind gewissermaßen Mittelnaturen schwanken zwischen Mann u Weib' [all artists are to a certain extent medial beings, oscillating between man and woman] (ibid.).[52]

What, the article asks, makes Shakespeare's Brutus androgynous? The answer lies in his character traits, which operate between the poles of (passive) female and (active) male forms of behaviour: 'Unter neuern Kunstwerken will ich nur an den herrlichen, sanften stürmischen, weiblich männlichen Brutus erinnern' [among the more recent works of art, I would like to think of the gentle but fierce and feminine yet masculine Brutus] (ibid.). Brutus therefore offers a holistic ideal of human behaviour. This observation allows the author to make a topical political point. The complete lack of this ideal temperament among the French is used to explain the negative reception of the Revolution and its aftermath:

> Beiläufig bemerkt, ist es der Mangel eben dieser gemilderten Gesinnung mit einem Worte, die gänzliche Abwesenheit des Gemüths, was den Heroismus oder die Vernichtungslust der Franzosen im Leben und in der Kunst, für uns Andern so drückend macht.
>
> [A note in passing: is it the lack of precisely this mild disposition, in a word, the complete absence of any disposition, which makes the heroism or the delight

---

50 Compare 'Nachrichten für die Kunst; in einem Briefe aus Weimar. An den Herausgeber', *Zeitung für die elegante Welt*, 36, 24 March 1803, pp. 279–80 and 'Nachrichten für die Kunst. (Beschluß.)', *Zeitung für die elegante Welt*, 37, 26 March 1803, pp. 287–88.
51 Helga Brandes notes the development of sociable reading practices among women in eighteenth-century German lands, which led to the establishment of reading societies and salons: Helga Brandes, 'Die Entstehung eines weiblichen Lesepublikums im 18. Jahrhundert: Von den Frauenzimmerbibliotheken zu den literarischen Damengesellschaften', in *Lesen und Schreiben im 17. und 18. Jahrhundert: Studien zu ihrer Bewertung in Deutschland, England, Frankreich*, ed. by Paul Goetsch, ScripOralia, 65 (Tübingen: Narr, 1994), pp. 125–33 (p. 130).
52 On androgyny more generally in classical art, see Catriona MacLeod, *Embodying Ambiguity: Androgyny and Aesthetics from Winckelmann to Keller* (Detroit: Wayne State University Press, 1998), p. 27.

in destruction among the French — in life and in art — so oppressive for us others].⁵³

This political aside is left out of the extract in Günderrode's *Studienbuch*. Nevertheless, she was certainly aware of the allure of ancient Republicanism as a device to criticise political events. Appealing to an idealised republican hero appears to be something of a rhetorical reflex. In Günderrode's *Studienbuch* is an entry that summarises Luc-Antoine Champagnaux's account of his time spent in prison with Achille François du Chastellet, a highly educated French general during the Revolutionary wars. Chastellet is represented as something of a modern and equally idealised Brutus: he embodied republican ideals and committed suicide in prison when his situation appeared hopeless. His companion Champagnaux eulogised Chastellet as a virtuous military leader worthy of association with the greatness of classical Greece and Rome, which is also an implied criticism of the political situation in France during the Terror.⁵⁴ Günderrode's condensed summary of the source text omits the Greek reference, which — whether intentional or not — strengthens Chastellet's association with Roman forms of Republicanism: 'Er war [...] eines besseren Jahrhunderts würdig, und würde durch seine Einsichten und Talente den schönsten Zeiten Roms Ehre gemacht haben' [He was [...] worthy of a better century, and on account of his acuity and talents he would have achieved honour in the finest times in Ancient Rome].⁵⁵

Chastellet, like Brutus, is cast as a hero figure not just because of his ideals but also because of the refusal to allow these ideals to be compromised on the cusp of historical disaster for Republicanism. Chastellet is lauded as an ideal Republican, unsullied by associations with the revolutionary terror. Günderrode's poems, which date from the same time as the notes on Chastellet, both idealise Brutus, but problematise Brutus's agency by focusing on the moment of his suicide.⁵⁶ To be sure, Brutus's choice to commit suicide can be brought in line with Stoic values, such as the contempt for death that Günderrode mentions in the first poem: for Seneca, suicide can be a form of moral freedom if life would lead to the loss of liberty.⁵⁷ This choice of liberty, of moral freedom, lends itself to a republican reading as a form of freedom over servitude, by echoing the revolutionary slogan

---

53 'Nachrichten für die Kunst. (Beschluß)'.
54 'Telle fut la fin de ce brave et vertueux militaire, dont ma plume n'a epuissé que foiblement les grandes qualités. Ce siècle n'étoit pas digne de lui: ses lumières, ses talens, ses vertus eussent honoré les plus beaux jours d'Athènes et de Rome' [Such was the end of this brave and virtuous soldier, whose great qualities I can only insufficiently describe with my pen. This century was not worthy of him: his brilliant qualities, talents, and virtues would have honoured the most glorious days of Athens and Rome]. L. A. Champagneux, 'Notices de l'éditeur, sur quelques circonstances de sa détention dans les années 1793 et 1794, pour servir de supplément aux Notices historiques de J. M. Ph. Roland', in Marie-Jeanne Roland de la Platière, *Œuvres de J. M. Ph. Roland, Femme de l'ex-ministre de l'intérieur*, ed. by L. A. Champagneux, 3 vols (Paris: Bidault, 1799), II, 389–440 (p. 413).
55 Preitz/Hopp III, p. 282.
56 Morgenthaler dates them to 1799–1801: *SW* III, 216–17.
57 Marcia L. Colish, *The Stoic Tradition from Antiquity to the Early Middle Ages*, 2 vols (Leiden: Brill, 1990), I, 49.

of 'la liberté ou la mort' [freedom or death].⁵⁸ It is the character's very constancy and ideologically purity — those qualities that imbue Brutus with the sense of the heroic — that become problematic.

The first poem, a sonnet entitled 'Brutus' (c. 1799–1801), starts from the assassination of Julius Caesar, which was the event marking the pinnacle of Brutus's republican endeavours, and Günderrode neatly negotiates this tension by modifying the connotations of 'Freiheit':

> Der Freiheit ward einst Cäsar hingeschlachtet
> Jn seines Ruhmes seines Lebens Fülle.
> Und Brutus schreitet zu dem hohen Ziele
> Das zu erfassen er so sehnlich trachtet;
>
> Doch bald wird es von Dunkel ihm umnachtet
> Es schwankt sein Glük in solchem kühnen Spiele,
> Doch ringt er muthig noch nach seinem Ziele
> Bis zu dem Tode den er stolz verachtet,
>
> Denn freudiger als einst in Cäsars Seite
> Senkt Brutus Dolch in Brutus Busen sich⁵⁹
> Und sterbend erst wird Freiheit seine Beute.
>
> So opferte der Freiheit seinem Gotte,
> Ein wahrer Priester, Brutus selber sich,
> Doch wer ihm stirbt, der lebt in seinem Gotte.
>
> [For the sake of freedom was Caesar slaughtered,
> At the height of his fame and life.
> And Brutus marched toward this high goal,
> Which he so ardently strove to achieve;
>
> But soon he was surrounded by darkness,
> His fortune wavered in such a dauntless game,
> Yet he fought valiantly for his goal,
> Until death, which he proudly scorned,
>
> For — with more joy than once he had in Caesar —
> Brutus plunged the dagger in his own breast
> And in death, freedom became his prize.
>
> So did a true priest of freedom, Brutus himself,
> Sacrifice his life for his God,
> But those who die for their god, live in them.] (*SW* I, 374)

The first freedom is one that Günderrode highlights by allowing the first iambic stress to fall upon it: it is the freedom of Republicanism. That is, Brutus's plot to kill Caesar at the height of his powers was motivated by a desire to preserve

---

58   Thomas Würtenberger, *Symbole der Freiheit: Zu den Wurzeln westlicher politischer Kultur* (Cologne: Böhlau, 2017), p. 181.
59   This reflects Brutus's last words in *Julius Caesar*: 'Farewell, good *Strato*. ----- *Cæsar*, now be still. | I kill'd not thee with halfe so good a will' (V.v, ll. 50–51), in William Shakespeare, *Julius Caesar*, ed. by Sarah Neville, *The New Oxford Shakespeare: Critical Reference Edition*, ed. by Gary Taylor and others, 2 vols (Oxford: Oxford University Press, 2017–), II, 2931–97 (p. 2997).

the republican tradition of Rome, although achieving this goal, as clarified by the second stanza, is made more fraught by the vicissitudes of contingency ('Es schwankt sein Glük in solchem kühnen Spiele').

The second form of freedom is more limited: it is Brutus's personal freedom to escape servitude in death. It is both an act of defiance and a paradoxical form of freedom: 'Und sterbend erst wird Freiheit seine Beute'. It is through death that this personal freedom can be achieved, which Günderrode emphasises with the modifying particle 'erst': never before had Brutus achieved the freedom that he sought. On one level, achieving freedom through suicide is an expression of Brutus's autonomy. On another, Günderrode closes down the possibility that the longed-for republican freedom, or even personal freedom from servitude, can be recovered in political reality.

What is achieved by Brutus's suicide, if read as an act of autonomy? Günderrode introduces a series of religious connotations in the final tercet that associates Brutus's sacrifice with that of Christ, where Brutus dies for deified freedom: 'So opferte der Freiheit seinem Gotte, | Ein wahrer Priester, Brutus selber sich'. Whilst Brutus is idealised, the programmatic *sentencia* encapsulates the sonnet's central paradox: 'Doch wer ihm stirbt, der lebt in seinem Gotte'. Brutus's constancy and absolute adherence to his ideals elevate him to the level of a republican archetype that transcends the historical moment of his lifetime. Implicit here is also the reflexive function of the poem — and a function that is explored further in Günderrode's second poem to Brutus: Brutus lives on and is preserved in the form of *literary* afterlives. Whilst the sonnet roughly confirms Brutus's status as a literary hero, Günderrode's focus on the moment of suicide is not merely a valorisation of Brutus's Stoic and republican values. It contains within it the potential to undermine this fashioning of Brutus as a hero in moments that oscillate between enthusiasm and melancholy, without either mood neutralising the other.

These ambivalences about Brutus as a literary hero are more thoroughly articulated in Günderrode's longer ballad 'Die Sonne taugte sich' [The sun dipped] (*c.* 1799). Its eleven strophes follow the same narrative schema as the sonnet, from the moment of Cassius's death that gives Brutus the resolve to die for freedom to the act of suicide. But Günderrode imbues the poem with heavier tragic pathos. Brutus's sorrow is so great that, on the battlefield at Philippi, he metaphorically occupies an Archimedean point from which he sees, feels, and hears the suffering caused by his defeat:

> Mit einem großen Blik der eine Erd' umfasset
> Mit einem Schmerz zu schwer für diese kleine Welt
> Mit dem Gefühl vor dem die Menschheit scheu erblasset
> Verweilet Brutus noch im Blutgetränktem Feld
> Er fühlt der Sterbenden weitaufgerißne Wunden
> Und hört im Geiste schon von Rom die trauer [*sic*] Kunden.

> [With one great look that encompassed the breadth of the Earth
> With sorrow too deep for this trivial world
> With a strength of feeling that would make humanity turn pale with awe
> Brutus still lingers in the blood-soaked field.

> He feels the wounds, torn asunder, of the dying
> And already hears, in his mind, the news of mourning from Rome.]
> (SW I, 371, ll. 19–24)

With the tricolon, Günderrode hyperbolically elevates Brutus to the point where his capacity for feeling is supra-human: he becomes a metaphor for the suffering of the republican body politic, and this also allows him an appreciation of the world-historical processes to which he must succumb.[60] Symbolically, Brutus asks his remaining loyal troops to flee elsewhere, though he selflessly remains: 'Entflieht der Sclaverei, sucht euch ein Vaterland | Allein nur kan ich mich der Schiksalsgöttin weihen' [flee slavery, find a homeland for yourselves, | Only I can surrender to the goddess of fate] (SW I, 372, ll. 26–27). Beset by pangs of conscience that manifest themselves in the form of the vengeful Erinnyes, Brutus's sorrow stems from the knowledge that his imminent death confirms his inability to prevent the fall of the Republic and with it its ideal of freedom:

> Daß was so zehrend ihm im starken Busen bebet
> Jst, daß er nimmer nun der Römer Ketten bricht
> Auf seinem Grabe wird die Tiranei regieren
> Der Freiheit Genius auf ihrer Trümmer irren.
>
> [What causes his strong breast to shudder
> Is that he will never now be able to break the Romans' chains.
> Tyranny will reign over his grave
> And the genius of freedom will wander among its own ruins]
> (SW I, 372, ll. 45–48)

Günderrode grants him a final speech where Brutus laments the victory of tyranny over justice and the destruction of his value system. But his sorrow does not solely encompass the failure of his political ideology and the regressive politics that Brutus foresees in the wake of Caesar's death. It also addresses the problem of human agency within historical contingency, which is given visceral form in the image of the wounds of sorrow that Brutus carries:

> Jezt bricht sein tiefer Schmerz das lange düstere Schweigen
> Und tausend Wunden bluten in der müden Brust
> 'Ha ruft er! muß den[n] stets das Recht dem Unrecht weichen
> Die Tiranei erringt des Sieges Götterlust;
> Gefühl das mich erdrükt! die Freiheit sinkt zum Staube
> Der Ungerechtigkeit geschlachtet iezt zum Raube.
>
> Die Tugend nante ich ein unabhängig Wesen
> Und Heil verspendent, siegreich ihre schöne Bahn
> Zum reinsten Menschen-Glük von Götter selbst erlesen
> Wähnt ich sie sclavisch nicht dem Schiksal unterthan
>
> [Now does his deep sorrow break the long, sombre silence
> And a thousand wounds bleed in his weary breast

---

60 Irmela Marei Krüger-Fürhoff, *Der versehrte Körper: Revisionen des klassizistischen Schönheitsideals* (Göttingen: Wallstein, 2001), p. 189.

> 'Ha!', he cries, 'must justice always yield to injustice?
> Tyranny wins the divine joy of victory;
> That feeling that overwhelms me! Freedom falls into dust
> Slaughtered to iniquity, now becomes its plunder.
>
> I thought virtue was an independent being,
> Granting salvation, and its lovely path was triumphant,
> Chosen by the gods themselves for the purest happiness of mankind
> I foolishly thought that it was not slavishly subject to fate.]
> (*SW* I, 372–73, ll. 49–58)

Brutus's value system was predicated on an ideal of Stoic virtue that led to human happiness. Whilst the historical Brutus was concerned with the retention of republican values, Günderrode's heightened imagery also suggests an ideal of historical progress that takes on eschatological connotations, with happiness as salvation: 'Und Heil verspendent, siegreich ihre schön Bahn | Zum reinsten Menschen-Glük von Götter selbst erlesen'. For Brutus, this belief is dismissed in a moment of mortal despair as something of a fatal flaw: 'Unseelg'er Jrrtum! könt ich nur allein ihn büsen' [Deplorable error! If only I alone could atone for it] (*SW* I, 373, ll. 59). The irony here lies in the fact that it was necessary for Brutus to delude himself about virtue and to believe that it would inevitably bring about historical change, since this legitimised his own agency in the first place in the plot to assassinate Caesar.

At the same time, this speech pulls in another direction: in the moment of failure — couched here in more despairing and elegiac terms than the first Brutus poem — the speech also assumes a proleptic function. It points towards a possible future in which Brutus's ideals could be realised. But this possibility remains at best subtextual. Günderrode ends the poem with a more expressly reflexive moment than the first poem. It is the ideological descendants of Brutus who ensure that the memory of Brutus persists:

> Doch ewig schweigt sein Ruhm nicht auf der weiten Erde
> Der späte Enkel ehrt noch seinen hohen Sinn
> Und in des Ruhmes weitgewölbten Tempelhallen
> Wird Brutus großer Name nimermehr verhallen.
>
> [But his renown does not remain unknown for eternity on the vast Earth
> Later generations still honour his lofty mind
> And in the wide-arched halls of the temple of renown
> Will Brutus's great name nevermore fade away.] (*SW* I, 373, ll. 63–66)

Here, Günderrode alludes to the Roman concept of *fama*, of reputation and renown, which is etymologically related to what is said about an individual.[61] With its greater focus on an elegiac tone, this poem participates in disseminating Brutus's reputation in a positive sense: this final reflexive gesture is both iterative and performative. It is a eulogy to the ideal of Brutus.

But this final stanza does not fully contain the melancholy that precedes it: it poses the question of how betterment of the individual and society are at all possible

---

[61] Gianni Guastella, *Word of Mouth: Fama and its Personifications in Art and Literature from Ancient Rome to the Middle Ages* (Oxford: Oxford University Press, 2017), p. 58.

in the face of contingency and the limitations of human agency. This semantic tension between hope and melancholy is one that marks both of Günderrode's poems to Brutus, and is a necessary result of Brutus's status as a purified literary hero. His ideological purity allows the ideals he propagated to be upheld, but he also remains a victim of historical contingency; succumbing to contingency also constitutes Brutus's status as a tragic hero.

The performative aspects of both poems do little to resolve this tension. In a positive sense, reading both poems could ensure the continuation of dormant republican ideals, that they may be reactivated simply through the phenomenological act of reading, which would cultivate an appreciation of Brutus's selfless heroism. This act of remembrance is also a veiled criticism of contemporary political circumstances. Brutus's noble failure lends itself to being symbolically mapped onto the descent of the Revolution into tyranny.

What lies behind this performative call to remembrance is an attempt to universalise and immortalise the kind of Republicanism represented by Brutus. Whilst Günderrode may invoke, particularly in her metaphysical texts, a putatively optimistic narrative of human history that rests on a notion of providence, there is also a countervailing tendency towards historical scepticism in other texts. In her correspondence, Günderrode tends towards making generalised statements about perceived cultural decline, where, without elaborating further, she dismisses the present 'pygmäisches Zeitalter' [pygmy age] and 'pygmäisches Geschlecht' [pygmy race].[62]

Günderrode also turns to heroic liberator figures to make a statement about cultural decline. In the Socratic dialogue 'Die Manen' [The Manes] (1804), Günderrode focuses on the deeds of a heroic liberator figure whose sudden death occurred on the battlefield: Gustavus Adolphus, the King of Sweden and devout Protestant, whose interventions in the Thirty Years War came to be a focal point of a memory cult among Protestant Germans in the nineteenth century, since he was considered to have liberated the Germans from Catholic imperial aggression and rule.[63] Gustavus Adolphus had already acquired similar connotations around 1800: Schiller's *Geschichte des dreißigjährigen Krieges* [History of the Thirty Years' War] (1790) portrayed him in an overwhelmingly positive light.[64]

Such strong resonances would help explain why the pupil, the first interlocutor of Günderrode's dialogue, is so distraught upon reading a historical biography of the Swedish king, his deeds, and his death. The premise of the dialogue is a problem of historicising: if all historical phenomena and actors can only be read as a product of a specific context, then the values that they represent are equally transient and cannot be hypostasised to have any meaning outside their context. For the pupil of the dialogue, this realisation necessarily empties Gustavus Adolphus of meaning, and the heroism he represents has disappeared in history. The current

---

62 Günderrode, *Briefe*, p. 82.
63 Kevin Cramer, *The Thirty Years' War and German Memory in the Nineteenth Century* (Lincoln, NB: University of Nebraska Press, 2007), pp. 51–52.
64 Steffan Davies, *The Wallenstein Figure in German Literature and Historiography 1790–1920*, Bithell Series of Dissertations, 36 (Leeds: Maney, 2010), p. 28.

age is therefore bereft. The pupil's emotional sensitivities allow for an intense identification that resolves into melancholic despair and grief: 'Ich weinte um seinen Tod mit heissen Thränen, als sey er heute erst gefallen [...] O möchte ich mit vergangen seyn! und diese schlechte Zeit nicht gesehen haben, in der die Vorwelt vergeht, an der ihre Größe verlohren ist.' [I wept hot tears when I learned of his death, as if he had only fallen today [...] O if I only I could have perished with him! And not seen this dreadful age, in which the world of the past decays and which has lost its greatness] (*SW* I, 30–31). The term 'Vorwelt', like 'Vorzeit', is rich with meaning for Günderrode. It generally refers to a period in the pre-modern world, perhaps in antiquity or the Middle Ages, where human experience was more holistic, and the relationship with nature and religion more harmonious.[65] In 'Der Franke in Egypten', it is also synonymous with the bygone age of heroes (*SW* I, 81, l. 6). Yearning for a heroic age of greater agency is also a reflex in Günderrode's correspondence: the lamentations over Brutus and Gustavus Adolphus follow a similar pattern to Günderrode's use of Ossian. The term 'Vorzeit' had even entered the German language through the reception of Ossian.[66] The attraction of the alleged Bardic songs rested, like 'Die Manen', on the evocation of a melancholic and nostalgic mood.[67]

Whilst 'Die Manen' gains its rhetorical weight through the melancholic despair of the opening, something of the heroic spirit of the deceased can be recovered through active remembrance, so that something of the greatness can be appropriated by future generations: 'So lebt und wirkt aber ein großer Mensch nicht nach seiner Weise in mir fort, sondern nach meiner, nach der Art wie ich ihn aufnehme, wie ich mich und ob ich mich seiner erinnern will' [In this manner, a great individual continues to live and have an effect in me, not according to the way they were, but according to mine, according to how I receive them, how and whether I wish to remember them] (*SW* I, 31). The dialogue proceeds into a metaphysical narrative of Stoic cosmic sympathies that transcend the conventional bounds of temporality, but the active remembrance here is significant in itself. It is qualitatively distinct from the grief from which the pupil originally suffered, since it offers a conciliatory narrative that immortalises Gustavus Adolphus — and therefore makes the same narrative move as Günderrode's self-reflexive immortalisation of Brutus.

Günderrode's treatment of both Brutus and Gustavus Adolphus attempts to universalise and preserve the heroic qualities of these liberator figures. The melancholic edge to Günderrode's use of Brutus connects with narratives of perfectibility. Underpinning the pathos around Brutus is not only an idealised portrayal that almost traps Brutus in literary discourse, but also a hope for historical progress, a hope that is displaced onto practices of remembrance that also act as an eternal deferral of the very progress that is longed for.

---

65   See Dormann, p. 99.
66   Wolf Gerhard Schmidt, *'Homer des Nordens' und 'Mutter der Romantik': James Macphersons 'Ossian' und seine Rezeption in der deutschsprachigen Literatur*, 4 vols (Berlin: De Gruyter, 2003–04), I: *James Macphersons Ossian, zeitgenössische Diskurse und die Frühphase der deutschen Rezeption* (2003), p. 465.
67   Theo Jung, *Zeichen des Verfalls: Semantische Studien zur Entstehung der Kulturkritik im 18. und frühen 19. Jahrhunderts*, Historische Semantik, 18 (Göttingen: Vandenhoeck & Ruprecht, 2012), p. 310.

The idealised figure of Brutus is a heroic archetype that anticipates the protagonists of 'Hildgund' and 'Nikator', both of whom are tyrant-slaying liberator figures. In both cases, Günderrode removes the reflexive element that relativises Brutus within historical processes. Rather, the focus moves from the macro-level to an individual one: to a narrative of self-cultivation and autonomy that is still in accordance with ideas of perfectibility. The shift in focus means that the metaphysical element of perfectibility retreats into the subtext of both 'Nikator' and Hildgund', but its traces can nonetheless be detected in the language of moral universalism, as is elucidated below. The focus in both plays is, therefore, more overtly political. Self-liberation and the discovery of individual autonomy prefigure and act as proxies for political liberation on a grander scale — a liberation that can be roughly described as the collapse of absolutist, monarchical and patriarchal order. By limiting the scope of the dramas to the preconditions of political revolution within individual development, Günderrode allows the tension between melancholy and hope present in the Brutus poems to persist. Rather than existing on a semantic level, as in the Brutus poems, this ambivalence is displaced onto dramatic structure in both 'Hildgund' and 'Nikator'.

Whilst few of Günderrode's dramas are formally complete, all of the dramas that concern political revolution end on a moment of prolepsis. What distinguishes 'Hildgund' and 'Nikator' from 'Mahomed, der Prophet von Mekka', which also ends proleptically, is the lack of millenarian or eschatological hope. In both 'Hildgund' and 'Nikator', the narrative is closed — inasmuch as it concerns the development of the protagonists' autonomy — but the plot remains open-ended and projects into a future beyond the end of the narrative itself. One useful concept to describe this structure in the context of early German Romanticism would be the term non-closure, as defined by Alice Kuzniar in the monograph *Delayed Endings: Nonclosure in Novalis and Hölderlin* (1987). Kuzniar in turn develops this concept from Derrida's 'la clôture';[68] but I wish to avoid the associations of Derrida's terminology and rather adopt Kuzniar's definition of non-closure: as the continual deferral of an ending and ultimate meaning to a narrative.[69] Whilst Kuzniar is keen to point to non-closure with reference to the endless process of writing itself, Susanne Kord has usefully adapted this concept and made it productive for eighteenth-century women's drama:

> Formal nonclosure [...] entails nonresolution and the prolongation of tension, causing the reader or viewer aesthetic discomfort and encouraging speculation and extrapolation in the reader; it displays a mistrust of completed artifice [...] Nonclosure is not to be confused with mere unresolvability, ambiguity, equivocality of meaning [...] it is a deferral of decision.[70]

---

68   See Clare Kennedy, *Paradox, Aphorism and Desire in Novalis and Derrida*, Texts and Dissertations, 71 (London: Maney, 2008), p. 73.
69   Alice Kuzniar, *Delayed Endings: Nonclosure in Novalis and Hölderlin* (Athens: University of Georgia Press, 1987), pp. 3–5.
70   Susanne Kord, 'All's Well That Ends Well? Marriage, Madness, and Other Happy Endings in Eighteenth-Century Women's Comedies', *Lessing Yearbook*, 28 (1996), 181–97 (p. 183).

Both 'Hildgund' and 'Nikator' exemplify this notion of formal non-closure: each ending is sufficiently disruptive to provoke aesthetic discomfort in the reader (both are conceived of as dramas intended to be read, or *Lesedramen*). This deferral of plot is most egregious in 'Hildgund'.

The Question of Female Agency in 'Hildgund'

In the title character of 'Hildgund', Günderrode makes recourse to the trope of the warrior woman, or the cross-dressing masculine heroine that recalls her Ossianic ballad 'Darthula nach Ossian' [Darthula after Ossian] as well as the dramatic sketch 'Mora' and 'Timur' from *Gedichte und Phantasien*.[71] Günderrode derived her material for this short dramatic work, first published in *Poetische Fragmente*, primarily from Ignaz Aurelius Feßler's *Attila, König der Hunnen* [Attila, King of the Huns] (1794), which combined elements of the Latin *Waltharius* poem, concerning Walther of Aquitaine, with material about Attila the Hun, mostly notably that Walther's betrothed Hildgunde is the same woman who is alleged to have murdered Attila.[72]

The play charts Hildgund's return to her Burgundian fatherland,[73] having fled years of captivity under Attila. Her escape had been facilitated by Walther of Aquitaine, who had declared his love for her, — although at no point do we learn if Hildgund reciprocates. Whilst Attila expresses sorrow at Hildgund's betrayal, he sympathises with her since he recognises that Hildgund by nature detests servitude. Attila requests instead Hildgund's hand in marriage; if she does not accept, he will attack Burgundy. Hildgund agrees, which Walther interprets as a betrayal caused by typically feminine 'Wankelmuth' [fickleness] (*SW* I, 97, l. 233), so that her pride is readily flattered by the glory that Attila is offering.[74] Hildgund then goes to Attila's camp and is welcomed: the play ends with Attila and Hildgund going to their wedding celebration, and with an aside from Hildgund that Attila's life will soon end.

Contemporary counterparts for Attila and Hildgund could be found respectively in Napoleon and Charlotte Corday.[75] Like Napoleon, Attila harbours grand ambitions to conquer, and indeed the problematic aspect of Attila's character in the

---

71 See Elisabeth Krimmer's readings of these texts: Elisabeth Krimmer, *In the Company of Men: Cross-Dressed Women around 1800* (Detroit: Wayne State University Press, 2004), pp. 134–39.
72 Erich Regen, *Die Dramen Karolinens von Günderode* (Berlin: Ebering, 1910), p. 13. Feßler uses the account of Attila's death given by the Roman chronicler Marcellinus Comes, since this account was written closest to Attila's own lifetime: Ignaz Aurelius Feßler, *Attila: König der Hunnen* (Breslau: Korn, 1794), pp. 279–80.
73 Burgundy refers to the Germanic peoples who populated parts of Switzerland in the fifth century, and whose kingdom was sacked by Attila. The region of France named as such is a remnant of this Germanic kingdom: see Christopher Cope, *Phoenix Frustrated: The Lost Kingdom of Burgundy* (London: Constable, 1986), pp. 36–37.
74 Günderrode, *Poetic Fragments*, p. 76.
75 This parallel with Corday has been noted by critics commenting on 'Hildgund': Carola Hilmes, 'Unbotmäßig: Karoline von Günderrodes literarische Inszenierungen der "Jungfrau in Waffen"', *Jahrbuch des freien deutschen Hochstifts* (2017), 147–68 (p. 161). Christine Westphalen's drama *Charlotte Corday* was published anonymously in 1804, which portrays Marat's death indirectly.

play lies in his desire to subjugate the remnants of the Roman Empire to his will alongside the other kingdoms over which he already has control. Attila casts himself as a liberating figure and frames his ambition as a violent but necessary act of lifting Roman oppression: 'Wenn meiner Hunnen Schwerdt den Raub der Welt gerächt | Und jenes Römer Volk [...] Dahin geschlachtet hat, dann erst hab ich gesiegt' [When my Huns' sword has avenged the rape of the world | And thoroughly slaughtered that Roman people [...] then only have I won] (SW I, 93, ll. 154–56).[76] Napoleon's invasion of the German states of the moribund Holy Roman Empire lends itself as a parallel to Attila's invasion of both West and East portions of the disintegrating Roman Empire in the fifth century, and so the figure of Attila became one means of discussing Napoleonic incursions around 1800.[77] Like Charlotte Corday, who was stylised by commentators as a female Brutus,[78] and indeed like the biblical figure of Judith,[79] Hildgund intends to catch Attila off guard and kill him in an intimate setting, in the hope of freeing Burgundy from Hunnic rule.

Where Günderrode deviates from the Corday parallel is in the construction of the alleged tyrant: Hildgund does not perceive Attila as unambiguously villainous, as Corday did Marat.[80] Rather, Attila is portrayed as a model of measured leadership rather than a tyrannical stereotype. Hildgund gives a sympathetic account of Attila to her father Herrich, as embodying an ascetic ideal of rulership: he despised the luxury and sensual indulgences he granted to others, since Attila's ideals revolve around conquest of further lands, not the possession of luxurious goods. Attila is also receptive to pleas for mercy. The driving force of the play's action is Attila's magnanimity, when he shows Hildgund clemency in exchange for her hand. This canny political move, not without self-interest on Attila's part — 'Ich fodere sie zurück, Verzeihung soll ihr werden | Und meines Herzens Wahl heischt sie als Königin' [I will reclaim her, she shall have forgiveness | And my heart's choice demands her as Queen] (SW I, 95, ll. 195–96)[81] — paves the way, unbeknownst to him.

In Hildgund, Attila appears to have met his match: she is an equally canny political actor, keen to use dissimulation to achieve her ends. Whilst Hildgund may be an armed warrior who discovered her innate autonomy by escaping Attila's

---

76 Günderrode, *Poetic Fragments*, p. 68.
77 Dagmar von Hoff, *Dramen des Weiblichen: Deutsche Dramatikerinnen um 1800* (Opladen: Westdeutscher Verlag, 1989), p. 97.
78 Wendy C. Nielsen, *Women Warriors in Romantic Drama* (Newark: University of Delaware Press, 2013), p. xxviii.
79 Charlotte Corday was interpreted through the lens of Judith in the 1790s: see Margarita Stocker, *Judith: Sexual Warrior: Women and Power in Western Culture* (New Haven: Yale University Press, 1998), pp. 111–19.
80 The contemporary reception of Corday among Germans was positive: she was a 'Lichtgestalt' [figure of light] compared to Marat, who was seen as exemplifying the worst excesses of the Terror: see Inge Stephan, 'Gewalt, Eros und Tod: Metamorphosen der Charlotte Corday-Figur vom 18. Jahrhundert bis in die Gegenwart', in *Die Marseillaise der Weiber: Frauen, die Französische Revolution und ihre Rezeption*, ed. by Inge Stephan and Sigrid Weigel, Literatur im historischen Prozeß, 26 (Hamburg: Argument, 1989), pp. 128–53 (p. 129).
81 Günderrode, *Poetic Fragments*, p. 72.

camp ('Der Gott, der mich befreit, wohnt in dem eigenen Herzen, | Wer seiner Stimme traut, dem ist die Rettung nah' [The god who freed me dwells in my own heart, | Whoever trusts its voice, to him rescue is near] (*SW* I, 91, ll. 104–05)),[82] her external agency is grounded in the submissive position accorded to her by her sex. To explain to Walther why she has chosen to accept Attila's offer of marriage, Hildgund outlines the fundamental disparity between the sexes:

> Wie herrlich ist der Mann, sein Schicksal bildet er,
> Nur eigener Kräfte Maas ist sein Gesetz am Ziele,
> Des Weibes Schicksal, ach! ruht nicht in eigner Hand!
> Bald folgt sie der Noth, bald strenger Sitte Wille,
> Kann man sich dem entziehn, was Uebermacht befiehlt?
>
> [How lordly is the man, he shapes his destiny,
> By his own powers alone has his law achieved its goal.
> Woman's destiny, ah! does not rest in her own hand!
> Now she follows need, now strict custom's will,
> Can one revoke what superior power commands?]
> (*SW* I, 98, ll. 252–56)[83]

Hildgund's lament about the female state of dependency and the focus on the narrow scope of female agency has a specific dramatic function in the scene: it placates Walther, who was initially incensed at her apparent betrayal, by assuring him of the political logic of her actions. It is expedient to accept the offer, since resisting would likely lead to the destruction of Burgundy. Indeed, this commentary points to the limitations in Walther's understanding of his own agency as a warrior ('Nur eigener Kräfte Maas ist sein Gesetz am Ziele'). Walther's protestations rest on the vain assumption that he can resist Attila through physical force to protect Hildgund, which would in turn negate Hildgund's capacity to act independently.[84]

Yet Hildgund's recognition of her state of dependency should not be taken at face value: it is more a pragmatic than a programmatic statement. What Hildgund does not articulate to Walther is how the marriage proposal allows her to pursue her own ends. In fact, Hildgund tells no one of her plan to assassinate Attila.[85] At best, the plan is vaguely alluded to in Hildgund's last exchange with Walther, but what Walther infers from Hildgund's proclamation of 'In meines Herzens tiefsten

---

82 Ibid., p. 66 (translation adapted).
83 Ibid., p. 76 (translation adapted). This echoes the opening of Goethe's *Iphigenie auf Tauris* (1779–86), where Iphigenie laments: 'Der Frauen Zustand ist beklagenswert. [...] | Wie eng-gebunden ist des Weibes Glück!' [The condition of women is pitiable [...] How tightly bound is women's fortune!], in Johann Wolfgang Goethe, *Sämtliche Werke, Briefe, Tagebücher und Gespräche*, ed. by Dieter Borchmeyer and others, 40 vols (Frankfurt a.M.: Deutscher Klassiker Verlag, 1985–2013), I.5: *Dramen 1776–1790*, ed. by Dieter Borchmeyer (1988), p. 555.
84 As Anna Ezekiel observes: Anna Ezekiel, 'Metamorphosis, Personhood, and Power in Karoline von Günderrode', *European Romantic Review*, 25.6 (2014), 773–91 (pp. 785–86).
85 This important point has only been noted by one critic in a brief discussion of Hildgund: Iris Hermann, 'Theater ist schöner als Krieg: Kleists *Hermannsschlacht* auf der Bühne', in *Hermanns Schlachten: Zur Literaturgeschichte eines nationalen Mythos*, ed. by Martina Wagner-Egelhaaf, Veröffentlichungen der Literaturkommission für Westfalen, 32 (Bielefeld: Aisthesis, 2008), pp. 239–60 (p. 253).

Gründen reifet | Die größte Tat, die je ein Weib gethan' [In my heart's deepest foundations ripens | The greatest deed that ever a woman has done] (*SW* I, 97, ll. 240–41)[86] is left ambiguous. With 'In meines Herzen tiefsten Gründen', Günderrode echoes Hildgund's earlier statement of her autonomy: that she recognises no authority other than the inner voice that commands her to act. Hildgund's self-aggrandising tone and awareness of her position in historical processes ('Die größte Tat, die je ein Weib gethan') is part of her attempt to motivate herself to commit murder. Indeed, one of Günderrode's concerns in the play consists of how Hildgund motivates herself.[87] Hildgund exhorts herself to action, empowering herself through rhetoric to establish the alleged greatness of the deed she will commit, and, after Walther has taken his leave of her, casts herself in the masculine role of a great warrior:

> Was zag ich noch, ists denn zu ungeheuer,
> Als daß die scheue, blasse Lipp' es nennen mag?
> Mord! Ha der Name nur entsetzet,
> Die That ist recht, und kühn und groß,
> Der Völker Schicksal ruht in meinem Busen,
> Ich werde sie, ich werde mich befrein.
> Verbannt sey Furcht und kindisch Zagen,
> Ein kühner Kämpfer nur ersiegt ein großes Ziel.
>
> [Why do I hesitate, is it, then, too monstrous,
> For shy, pale lips to name it?
> Murder! Ha, the name alone appals,
> The deed is just, and bold and great,
> The peoples' destiny rests in my breast;
> I will free them, free me.
> Banished are fear and childish hesitation,
> Only a bold warrior wins a great goal.] (*SW* I, 99, ll. 275–82)[88]

Hildgund's reluctance to divulge her plan to Walther lies in the boldness of murder, which Hildgund rationalises and justifies as 'recht, und kühn und groß'. This rhetorically contains the destructive potency of 'Mord' itself, just as Hildgund counteracts the childish stirrings of fear and hesitation with her self-presentation as an ideal, de-sexed warrior.[89] Hildgund's concerns are not only for the Burgundians. She perceives herself as the universal saviour, as a liberator of all the peoples under Attila's control, and this grandiose thought supports her other desire to liberate herself: 'Ich werde sie, ich werde mich befrein'.

---

86 Günderrode, *Poetic Fragments*, p. 76.
87 Patricia Anne Simpson, *The Erotics of War in German Romanticism* (Lewisburg, PA: Bucknell University Press, 2006), p. 122; Ruth Christmann, *Zwischen Identitätsgewinn und Bewußtseinsverlust: Das philosophisch-literarische Werk der Karoline von Günderrode (1780–1806)*, Trierer Studien zur Literatur, 44 (Frankfurt a.M.: Peter Lang, 2005), p. 196.
88 Günderrode, *Poetic Fragments*, p. 78.
89 As Barbara Becker-Cantarino notes, Hildgund's name is a composite of two Old High German terms for battle, which underpins this self-presentation as a warrior: see Becker-Cantarino, *Schriftstellerinnen der Romantik*, p. 212.

Hildgund's second exhortation to herself, immediately prior to her meeting with Attila at his palace in Pannonia, derives its rhetorical effects from juxtaposing the greatness of Attila's unbridled agency with the agency of an apparently subjugated woman:

> Schon zuckt mein Dolch, bald wird das große Opfer bluten,
> Das, Herrscher einer Welt, ein schwaches Weib besiegt.
> Die starke Kette reißt, die Millionen bindet,
> Die mächtige Feder springt, die einen Erdball drückt;
> Italien zage nicht! ich werde dich befreien,
> Der Völker Geisel fällt durch Hildegundens Hand.
>
> [Already my dagger twitches, soon the great victim will bleed,
> That, ruler of a world, a weak woman conquers.
> The strong chain that binds millions tears,
> The mighty spring that oppresses a globe is released;
> Italy, do not fear! I will free you,
> The peoples' scourge falls by Hildgund's hand.] (*SW* I, 101, ll. 304–09)[90]

Günderrode conveys Hildgund's almost breathless excitement in anticipation of Attila's death through contrasting the metaphorical scale of Attila's might ('Die starke Kette reißt, die Millionen bindet, | Die mächtige Feder springt, die einen Erdball drückt') with the perceived insignificance of Hildgund's agency — 'Das, Herrscher einer Welt, ein schwaches Weib besiegt'. Günderrode also makes reference here to an epithet commonly applied to Attila: *flagellum dei*, or scourge of God.[91] Günderrode secularises this epithet as 'Der Völker Geisel' and shifts the emphasis onto Attila's impingement upon and devastation of the freedoms of individual peoples.

For all of Hildgund's rhetorical triumphalism, Günderrode withholds the very moment that Hildgund fervently hopes for and that the reader must anticipate: Attila's death. The play ends with Hildgund's portentous statement that sharply illustrates her ability to use dissimulation: 'Ich folge meinem Herrn! (für sich) Ha feire nur, Tirann, | Des letzten Tages schnell entflohne Stunden' [I follow my lord! (to herself) Ha, only celebrate, tyrant, | The last day's fast fled hours] (*SW* I, 102, ll. 326–27).[92] The abruptness of the ending has proved troubling for commentators on the play. Such a textual lacuna has given rise to a variety of interpretations, whether it points to the inability of women to act in the political sphere, or to its opposite.[93] Günderrode's refusal to stage Hildgund's longed-for act of killing Attila cannot be dismissed as a form of gender censorship, based on the idea that women cannot act as political agents in the public sphere. The myths around Attila were familiar enough around 1800 that one can safely presume that readers would know of the account of Attila's death at the hand of his new bride.[94]

---

90 Günderrode, *Poetic Fragments*, p. 82 (translation adapted).
91 J. Otto Maenchen-Helfen, *The World of the Huns: Studies in Their History and Culture*, ed. by Max Knight (Berkeley: University of California Press, 1973), p. 141.
92 Günderrode, *Poetic Fragments*, p. 84.
93 Dagmar von Hoff, 'Aspects of Censorship in the Work of Karoline von Günderrode', *Women in German Yearbook*, 11 (1995), 99–112 (p. 108); Kastinger-Riley, p. 119.
94 Christmann, p. 197.

What makes the ending so jarring is the tension between its semantic closure — that Hildgund kills Attila — and its formal non-closure — the refusal to portray what the reader is led to expect to be the logical resolution of the drama. This tension also has the effect of questioning the possibility of any thematic resolution of Hildgund's dramatic arc. Whilst the play focuses on Hildgund coming to realise that her autonomy in grounded within herself and portrays her successfully negotiating her position around the other male political actors, the ending leaves Hildgund suspended in a virtuous fantasy of glorious liberation. On one level, the ending preserves Hildgund's autonomy, inasmuch as she does not have to suffer the consequences of the chaos unleashed by Attila's death, which would draw her back into the state of dependency. On another level, by fusing, in her monologues, Hildgund's desire for liberation from patriarchal social bonds, — which derives from her sense of autonomy, — with a heroic narrative of liberation of peoples, Günderrode shifts these concepts of autonomy, the ability to self-determine, and liberation into an unreal subjunctive mood. Their symbolic confirmation in Attila's death is denied. What remains is merely the desire for autonomy and liberation, which finds expression in the intensity of unconsummated hope, with the conditions of its possibility being unknown.

'Nikator': The Reluctant Revolutionary

The classicising play 'Nikator' — or, in Günderrode terminology, a dramatic sketch or 'dramatische Skizze' — is a companion piece to 'Hildgund'. It was first published in Friedrych Wilmans' *Taschenbuch auf das Jahr 1805* [Pocketbook for the Year 1805]. It similarly charts a narrative of the protagonist's state of dependence shifting into the realisation of his own agency and autonomy. This narrative is anticipated by the protagonist's name, which can be read as a portmanteau of the Greek for victory, *nike*, and the Latin for killer or assassin, *necator*. The notable difference is that Nikator's antagonist, King Egestis, fulfils all the villainous stereotypes expected of a tyrant, to the point of embodying the trope of the Oriental despot.[95] He is prone to irrational actions driven by his passions, such as arbitrary rulership, sexual rapaciousness, and, in a moment of hubris, conflating the divine right of kings with the notion that he himself is the creator God: 'Ich spende Glück und Gunst nach Wohlgefallen | Denn mein Geschöpf ist alles um mich her' [I bestow fortune and favour according to my good will | For my creatures are all around me] (*SW* I, 285, ll. 207–08). Egestis also disregards sexual taboos and succumbs to lust for his niece — 'Ich hungere nach Dir, ich durst' und rase | Nach Deiner Schönheit seligem Beschau'n' [I hunger for you, I thirst and rage | and for the blissful sight of your beauty] (*SW* I, 293, ll. 361–62). Egestis conspires to have Nikator convicted of high treason so that the rival for his niece's affections can be executed. Faced with these abuses of power by Egestis, the reader's sympathies would therefore lie more readily with Nikator. But this raises the question of what form of agency Nikator

---

[95] The association of the Orient with despotism is a negative trope that goes back to the sixteenth century: see Noel Malcolm, *Useful Enemies: Islam and the Ottoman Empire in Western Political Thought, 1450–1750* (Oxford: Oxford University Press, 2019), pp. 201–28.

develops to counteract this despotism, since unlike Hildgund, Nikator does not harbour expressly political desires to liberate himself or his people.

The play opens with the military achievements of Nikator, the king's highest general, being lauded in a public triumph, which Nikator rejects since he has become dissociated from his deeds. In fact, these actions were never under Nikator's ownership, since they were committed in a state of Dionysiac ecstasy that presupposes displaced agency: 'Es ekelt mir den Thyrsus tobend schwingen, | Wenn man nicht voll des Rebengottes ist' [It disgusts me to brandish the thyrsus in a rage | When not completely possessed by the Wine-God] (*SW* I, 277, ll. 5–6). What Nikator suffers from in this curious state of self-estrangement are the fruits of misdirected and misidentified longing that drive him to act without its object being clear: 'Ein tiefes Sehnen ist in meinem Herzen, | Das hungrig stets nach neuem Raube hascht' [a deep longing is in my heart, | which always hungers for new plunder] (*SW* I, 277–78, ll. 15–16). A precursor for this dramatic problem can be found in Günderrode's earlier poem 'Der Franke in Egypten', where primal longing drives the Frenchman to enter into battle, to pursue scientific expeditions, and eventually to realise that the object of this longing is love, found in the bond he forms with a young girl. This is a variant of the narrative of how the individual comes to self-knowledge through knowledge of another, a narrative given paradigmatic form in Novalis's tale of Hyazinth and Rosenblüte in *Die Lehrlinge zu Sais* [The Novices at Sais] (1798–99). But Nikator finds himself in a double bind at the beginning of the play: entrapped not just by his inability to take ownership of his military achievements, but paralysed by his love for Adonia, the daughter of the king's brother, who is now held captive after his campaign. Günderrode neatly summarises Nikator's despair at this romantic entrapment in lines that recall Petrarchan paradoxes: 'Ja, die Gefangene hat mich gefangen, | Die Ueberwundene hat mich besiegt' [Yes, the prisoner has captured me, | The vanquished woman has defeated me] (*SW* I, 278, ll. 29–30).

Even more significant is how Günderrode formulates the terms of Nikator's agency, which brings the play close to the terminology employed in 'Magie und Schicksal'. Günderrode inverts the latter's dramatic narrative of the declaration of free will that ends in fatalist resignation.[96] Nikator outlines his resignation in a speech to King Egestis, which runs counter to the norms of gratitude expected of royal subjects:

> Ein rascher Wunsch treibt mich ins Kriegsgetümmel
> Das launenhafte Glück zeigt sich mir hold,
> Der Zufall will sich mir gewogen stellen,
> Und ich weiß selber nicht, wie mir geschieht;
> Von Schlacht zu Schlacht werd' ich fortgezogen,
> Zum Tapferseyn zwingt die Nothwendigkeit;
> Das Schicksal treibt mich fort in seinen Kreisen
> Und ihm befehlend dien' ich ihm als Knecht.
> Wir möchten gern uns Herrn des Zufalls stellen,
> Doch er gewinnt und er verliert die Schlacht.

---

96 A parallel that Susanne Kord notes: *Ein Blick hinter die Kulissen*, p. 111.

> Der Steuermann beherrschet nicht die Woge,
> Sie reißt ihn fort in ihrem wilden Drang.
>
> [Rash desire drove me into the tumult of war,
> Inconstant fortune proved kind to me,
> Chance, it seems, was propitious towards me,
> And I do not know how it happened;
> I was drawn from battle to battle,
> Necessity forced a stance of bravery;
> Fate propelled me forward in its cycles
> And, obedient, I became its servant.
> We would like to think ourselves as masters of chance,
> But it is chance that wins and loses the battle.
> The helmsman does not control the wave,
> It wrenches him forward with its wild force.]
> (SW I, 279–80, ll. 59–70)

Nikator's lack of agency finds grammatical expression. Nikator is acted upon by the various metaphorical agents of fate and fortune, entirely subject to the vicissitudes of chance, to the extent that he cannot make sense of the events and his actions ('Und ich weiß selber nicht, wie mir geschieht'), even bravery is nullified in its reduction to a necessary reaction rather than a quality he possesses ('Zum Tapferseyn zwingt die Nothwendigkeit'). The belief that the individual can control fate resolves itself into the realisation that this is little more than self-delusion. This insight is encapsulated in the apparent paradox of the following line, where the syntax underscores the semantic juxtaposition: 'Und ihm [dem Schicksal] befehlend dien' ich ihm als Knecht'. Günderrode proceeds to adopt the topos of life as *navigatio* to crystallise Nikator's sense of impotence: 'Der Steuermann beherrscht nicht die Woge, | Sie reißt ihn fort in ihrem wilden Drang'. Chance, or more specifically *fortuna*, has a long tradition of being associated with seafaring, since the Roman goddess Fortuna had mastery over the sea and storms, and became identified with Tyche, the Greek goddess of chance, hence Nikator's suggestion that he is subject to its potentially capricious machinations.[97]

What Nikator is chafing against, it emerges, is his subjection to the king. This becomes manifest in the central conflict of the play. Nikator requests Adonia as the reward for his triumph, which Egestis rejects on the ostensible grounds of the difference in station between the two. Nikator resents the king's decision, which is based on self-interest, and openly resents his subordinate position as well: 'Fluchwürd'ger Irrthum einem König dienen, | Die Krone macht dem Undank stets vertraut' [Serving a king is an error to be cursed | The crown is only too well acquainted with ingratitude] (SW I, 283, ll. 159–60). When the courtier Esla informs Nikator of the king's true intention to keep Adonia for himself, Nikator rhetorically challenges the legitimacy of the king's power: 'Nun, Laune mag bei ihm für Laune gelten, | Ist seine mehr, ist meine minder werth?' [Now, though a whim may be a whim for him, | Is his worth more than mine?] (SW I, 287, ll. 231–32). The

---

[97] Ehrengard Meyer-Landrut, *Fortuna: Die Göttin des Glücks im Wandel der Zeiten* (Munich: Deutscher Kunstverlag, 1997), p. 179.

implication that Nikator is Egestis's equal is expanded upon in the defiant words that close the play's first act. Günderrode is careful to reuse the imagery that served to mark Nikator's lack of agency at beginning of the play, and to modify both the sea imagery and the idea of necessity to convey Nikator's staunch willpower:

> Ist er der Fels? Wohlan! ich bin die Welle,
> Die brandend sich an seiner Stärke reibt;
> Schwer soll ihm diesmal seine Dauer werden,
> Denn ich bin fest, wie die Nothwendigkeit.
> [...]
> Er wird sich hüten, fürchten vor dem Heere,
> Das seinem Feldherrn mehr als ihm gehorcht.
>
> [Is he the rock? Well! I am the wave,
> That, surging, abrades his strength.
> Now his persistence will prove difficult for him,
> For I am as firm as necessity.
> [...]
> He will protect himself, and fear the army,
> That sooner obeys his general than him. (*SW* I, 287, ll. 235–44)

Nikator does indeed present an existential threat to Egestis in political terms: the loyalty of the army would be sufficient to depose the king and brings with it the threat of civil war. Günderrode goes on to demonstrate that Nikator's motivation does not just stem from the desire to recover Adonia, who reciprocates his affections, but also from an ideological rejection of all forms of authority other than that which he finds within himself:

> Ich habe nichts, und gar nichts zu bedenken,
> Als meines Busens heiliges Gebot.
> Eh' mag ich Königen die Treue brechen,
> Als der Natur, die mir im Herzen spricht.
> Wer sie verräth, um eines Königs willen,
> Um Ehre, Ruhm und falscher Pflicht Gebot,
> Der ist nicht werth, daß sie ihm je gesprochen,
> Er ist ein Sklave, der sich selbst verliert.
>
> [I have nothing and nothing else to consider
> Than the sacred commandment from my breast.
> I would sooner break my fealty to kings
> Than to nature that speaks in my heart.
> Whoever betrays that, for the sake of a king,
> For honour, fame, and false duty's command,
> They are not worthy of ever hearing nature's voice
> They are a slave who has lost themselves.] (*SW* I, 290, ll. 305–12)

Nikator makes an absolute claim to his own agency, in a form of Promethean defiance that recalls the rebellion against authority in the *Sturm und Drang*.[98] Any external influence on the individual is tantamount to the loss of the self in

---

98 Christmann, p. 216.

subjugation ('Er ist ein Sklave, der sich selbst verliert'). This raises the question of whether any legitimate form of authority is at all possible outside the individual, since Nikator's statement would rule this out entirely.

What qualifies Nikator's claim to absolute agency is the fact that, unlike Hildgund's, his motivations are of a private nature, and only take on a revolutionary dynamic by force of circumstance. Günderrode also does not portray Nikator as succumbing to the kind of egotism that drives Ligares in 'Magie und Schicksal', since Nikator's will happens to align with those of other characters. He is moved by the plight of Egestis's banished consort, who implores him to remove Egestis. Adonia does, however, object to Nikator's rash attempt to keep her in safety away from the king, and instead insists on speaking to Egestis herself: 'Ich dulde nicht, daß Du mich so behauptest, | Denn hassenswerth soll unser Bund nicht seyn' [I will not tolerate that you lay a claim to me like this, | For our bond should not be hateful] (*SW* I, 291, ll. 319–20).

The play's climax encapsulates the irreconcilable positions of Egestis and Nikator: as a ruse to eliminate Nikator, Egestis accuses him of high treason for offering his loyalty and services to Egestis's brother, Adonia's father, in exchange, in turn, for her hand. Nikator rejects this unsubstantiated charge and insists on his right to court her. Upon realising that Egestis will not yield, Nikator stabs him to death. What is intriguing is how Nikator justifies his act to the royal guards who immediately rush onto the scene:

> Ich bin bereit zu sterben,
> Denn was ich wollte, hab' ich nun erreicht.
> [...]
> Ich wollte nicht durch Mord dem Tod' entgehn,
> Ein größ'res Unheil mußt ich von mir wenden,
> Das dieser Todte frevelnd auf mich lud.
>
> [I am prepared to die,
> For I have now achieved what I wanted.
> [...]
> I did not want to evade death through murder,
> I had to prevent a greater evil,
> That the deceased, in an act of iniquity, forced upon me.]
> (*SW* I, 301, ll. 502–07)

This is partly a matter of Nikator knowing what appeals to his interlocutors: he refers to military codes of honour to deny any cowardice. The 'größ'res Unheil' refers not to Egestis's designs on Adonia, or the plight of his banished queen, but to the king's act of passing Nikator's death sentence to demonstrate the arbitrary power of the despot. In this more abstract sense, Nikator is concerned with self-preservation and asserts his own agency as an equal to Egestis.

The conclusion of 'Nikator' features a milder variant of the non-closure in 'Hildgund'. Although Nikator closes his own dramatic arc by murdering Egestis, the play ends on a note of legal ambiguity about his own eventual fate:

TOTILA.	Er lebe! bis wir ihn vernommen haben.
	[...]
DIE SOLDATEN.	Er lebe! wenn er sich rechtfert'gen kann.
[TOTILA.	May he live! Until we have interrogated him.
	[...]
THE SOLDIERS.	May he live! If he can justify himself.]

(SW I, 301–02, ll. 508–09)

This is the second instance of a legal framework being invoked in 'Nikator' and whether the act of regicide can be justified or not before the law is itself left ambiguous. To use another grammatical analogy: the conclusion of 'Nikator' is imperfective, and not just because it consigns the fate of the protagonist to unknown processes. Although what drives the play is more of a domestic love-plot, like 'Magie und Schicksal', rather than matters of state, the implications of Nikator's agency remain unexplored.

Nikator grounds his agency within the promptings of his heart: 'Ich habe nichts, und gar nichts zu bedenken, | Als meines Busens heiliges Gebot' [I have nothing and nothing else to consider | Than the sacred commandment from my breast] (SW I, 290, ll. 305–06). This is identical to the claim that 'Hildgund' makes for her own agency. Günderrode constructs 'Nikator' in a manner that does not allow this claim to become problematic, since the villainous despotism of Egestis allows for a sense of moral urgency to justify Nikator's actions. But the implications of this are radical: it makes a claim for individual autonomy and equality among individuals that would necessarily collapse social hierarchical structures.

The function of this claim about agency in both 'Nikator' and 'Hildgund' is on one level simply a matter of dramatic expediency. It allows them to break out of conventional social and political bonds and therefore to justify their revolutionary actions. But Günderrode's focus on individual autonomy runs at the expense of considering the function of community: if both Nikator and Hildgund conceive of their freedom as being one free from any external influence, then there can be no legitimate moral, social, or political authority outside that of the individual. Or, that authority itself becomes atomised: there would be as many authorities as there are individuals.

To cut through this potentially anarchic knot, the very phrasing of Hildgund's and Nikator's declarations of agency offers a way out of this impasse: and this is a route that leads back into metaphysics. Both characters use language that happens to point to the possibility of a universal, shared ground of agency. For Günderrode, it is possible to reconcile the self-determining individual with a higher source of agency. This can be demonstrated by comparison with Günderrode's studies in her *Studienbuch* and one of her metaphysical texts. Creating a positive narrative out of historical events is problematic in some of Günderrode's works, most notably in 'Die Manen', where its opening threatens to dissolve into nihilism, and to a lesser extent in the poems on Brutus. The terminology of 'Nikator' and 'Hildgund' points to a metaphysical framework that would inject an element of optimistic teleology to justify individual agency and self-determination.

Moral Universalism in Günderrode

Firstly, some caveats: Günderrode's *Studienbuch* offers a laboratory of thoughts — not necessarily reflecting her own — where the process of excerpting and ordering indicates the topics that interest her as the compiler.[99] These notes are fragmentary and not fully representative of her reading practices, since she only excerpted from texts that she did not own personally.[100]

The notes on ethics, moral freedom, and reason in Günderrode's *Studienbuch* demonstrate a series of overlapping points about how individual agency can be justified. These notes are all lifted from a compendium of contemporary and ancient philosophy and appear to be part of an autodidactic attempt on Günderrode's part to familiarise herself with contemporary philosophy. There are three main points that could summarise these notes, which indicate areas that were of interest to Günderrode. Firstly, the individual will is tied to, or should be conceived of *as if it were* aligned with some sort of law-giving authority, whether it be reason or morality, with reference either to the Kantian categorical imperative, or to Fichte's notion of the absolute will, in which the individual will is subsumed.[101] Or, in quotations from Rousseau, the individual has the innate ability to determine morally justified action, and moral freedom consists in being able to withstand the external impulses of nature ('Im Innern der Seele liegt ein angebohrnes Princip für Recht und Tugend' [In the depths of the soul there is an innate principle of justice and virtue]; 'Die moralische Freiheit macht allein den Menschen zum Herrn seiner selbst: die Herrschaft des Instinkts ist Knechtschaft' [Moral freedom alone makes the individual into their own master: the rule of instinct is servitude]).[102] Secondly, that the individual, conceived of in a naturalistic sense, has the capacity to develop the innate faculties and abilities that lie dormant within it. Thirdly, that the end point of this development is the individual being in complete unison with themselves ('eine völlige Übereinstimmung mit sich selbst [nennt man] Vollkomenheit' [Complete concordance with oneself [is called] perfection]).[103]

Günderrode does adopt a form of moral universalism, but it is not of Kantian origin. As the notes and excerpts show, she was interested in grasping the central tenets of Kantian moral philosophy. But her own moral universalism is not Kantian. Rather, morality, for Günderrode, owes something both to sensibility, also known as *Empfindsamkeit*, and to an innate morality that may be an amalgamation of

---

99 It is not only texts that are excerpted: Günderrode's conversation partners feature too, on occasion writing an entry in their own hand, which suggests that these notes were integrated parts of reading, note-taking, and discussions with acquaintances and family.

100 As was common with authors under financial constraints, such as Herder, Jean Paul, and Winckelmann. See Elisabeth Décultot, 'Einleitung: Die Kunst des Exzerpierens. Geschichte, Probleme, Perspektiven', in *Lesen, Kopieren, Schreiben: Lese- und Exzerpierkunst in der europäischen Literatur des 18. Jahrhunderts*, ed. by Elisabeth Décultot (Berlin: Ripperger & Kremers, 2014), pp. 7–47 (p. 34). Günderrode was known to read more trivial forms of literature, was fond of Goethe and owned a first edition of Schiller's poetry: see Preitz/Hopp III, pp. 226–28.

101 Preitz/Hopp III, p. 265; the most extensive studies of Fichte are from *Die Bestimmung des Menschen* (1799): here, *SW* II, 297–98.

102 Ibid., p. 265.

103 Ibid., p. 266.

Rousseau and Platonism. Both protagonists in 'Nikator' and 'Hildgund' find no higher authority than the promptings and commandments of their own heart.[104] This leads to the idea of innate morality, which has a lineage from Shaftesbury, via Leibniz, through to Rousseau. The preconditions of this idea are metaphysical: that the individual is part of a larger, pre-established, providential order, and that their moral inclinations and resolutions ought to be in harmony with it.[105] As in Rousseau, there is an innate principle at work that allows the individual to distinguish what is right and what is virtuous, and it is through inward reflection that the basis of moral action is disclosed to the individual.

Traces of this moral universalism can be found in Günderrode's other studies, and specifically in her study of Frans Hemsterhuis's *Simon ou des facultés de l'âme* [Simon or the Faculties of the Soul] (1792). Hemsterhuis, known as a Platonist philosopher, draws on a line of thought derived from moral sense theory, specifically from Shaftesbury and taken up by Hutcheson. That is, the individual is endowed with a moral organ, in addition to the five exterior senses. This moral organ serves a metacritical function: it analyses the internal sensations and emotions and determines what is or is not morally justifiable. Hemsterhuis includes in the account the idea of balance and development of internal faculties. The will, intellect, and moral organ are all internal faculties within the individual's soul that require careful application and nurturing to ensure that the individual's will, for example, corresponds to an ethical course of action:

> oder wie er der Wollenskraft eine Richtung vorschreibt vermöge welcher das Wollen verständig u konsequent wird, eben so urtheilt das moralische Organ ob das Wollen mit dem Rechten u sittlichen uebereinstimmt, den[n] wie der Wiederspruch dem Verstand zuwieder ist, eben so ist das unrechtmäßige dem moralischen Gefühl zuwieder.
>
> [or how the individual prescribes an orientation for willpower, and through this orientation, that which is willed becomes intelligible and logical, and just in this manner, the moral organ judges whether is the act of willing corresponds to what is just and ethical, for just as contradiction is anathema to the intellect, so is injustice anathema to moral feeling.] (*SW* II, 301)

In Hemsterhuis's account, and in Günderrode's notes, it is entirely possible that the moral organ remains underdeveloped, which would explain human vice. Hemsterhuis's concept of the moral organ provides at the very least a model to help explicate the otherwise inscrutable mental processes that drive the actions of both Nikator and Hildgund.

To turn back to 'Nikator' and 'Hildgund': in light of Günderrode's interest in

---

104 Matthew Bell, *Goethe's Naturalistic Anthropology: Man and Other Plants* (Oxford: Oxford University Press, 1994), p. 125.
105 Charles Taylor, *Sources of the Self: The Making of the Modern Identity* (Cambridge: Cambridge University Press, 1989), p. 369. See also: Alexander J. B. Hampton, *Romanticism and the Re-invention of Modern Religion: The Reconciliation of German Idealism and Platonic Realism* (Cambridge: Cambridge University Press, 2019), pp. 125–32; Max Wundt, 'Die Wiederentdeckung Platons im 18. Jahrhundert', *Blätter für deutsche Philosophie*, 15 (1941), 149–58; Werner Beierwaltes, *Platonismus und Idealismus* (Frankfurt a.M.: Klostermann, 1972).

Platonist moral universalism, the language of Nikator's and Hildgund's rationale for their actions can suggest how it can merge with a metaphysical framework. The proclamations that Nikator and Hildgund make are so similar that each appears to be modelled after the other:

ESLA.	Gedenk' an Pflicht, an Eid und Treue,
	Ja! an der Götter Rache denke auch.
NIKATOR.	Ich habe nichts, und gar nichts zu bedenken,
	Als meines Busens heiliges Gebot.
	Eh' mag ich Königen die Treue brechen,
	Als der Natur, die mir im Herzen spricht.
[ESLA.	Consider duty, consider your oath and loyalty
	Indeed! Think too of the vengeance of the gods.
NIKATOR.	I have nothing and nothing else to consider
	Than the sacred commandment from my breast.
	I would sooner break my fealty to kings
	Than to nature that speaks in my heart.] (*SW* I, 290, ll. 303–08)
HERRICH.	Und wie entkamet ihr der Szyten wilde Horden,
	Hat dich der Götter Hülf', hast du dich selbst befreit?
HILDGUND.	Der Gott, der mich befreit, wohnt in dem eigenen Herzen,
	Wer seiner Stimme traut, dem ist die Rettung nah
[HERRICH.	And how did you escape the Scythians' wild hordes,
	Did you have the gods' help, did you free yourself?
HILDGUND.	The god who frees me dwells in my own heart
	Whoever trusts his voice, to him rescue is near.]
	(*SW* I, 91, ll. 102–05)[106]

For Nikator and Hildgund, there is no external force that guides or prompts their actions. Hence the rejection of earthly forms of loyalty to one's king and that of any authority of pagan gods, whether it be in the form of fate or chance. Both Nikator and Hildgund assert a form of autonomy so strong that, through the biblical patterning and weight of 'Gebot' and 'Rettung', it is metaphorically elevated to a godlike status. What both Nikator and Hildgund advocate is more extreme than the political concepts of freedom that were advanced in the late Enlightenment, which, in the German context, consisted of the freedom from undue intervention into the individual's private life and their intellectual and religious autonomy.[107] Rather, their understanding of freedom, one that rebels against monarchical or external forms of authority, originates from the period of the French Revolution. As Gerald N. N. Izenberg argues, this declaration amounts to an 'ideological rebellion against fundamental general principles of external authority in favour of a new source of autonomy in the self'.[108] The focus lies on the inward act of heeding

---

106 Günderrode, *Poetic Fragments*, pp. 64–66.
107 Fania Oz-Salzberger, 'Scots, Germans, Republic and Commerce', in *Republicanism: A Shared European Heritage*, ed. by Martin van Gelderen and Quentin Skinner, 2 vols (Cambridge: Cambridge University Press, 2002), II: *The Values of Republicanism in Early Modern Europe*, pp. 197–226 (p. 217).
108 Gerald N. N. Izenberg, *Impossible Individuality: Romanticism, Revolution, and the Origins of Modern*

one's own heart or voice: 'meines Busens heiliges Gebot'; 'Wer seiner Stimme traut, dem ist die Rettung nah'.

How does metaphysics come into play here, and specifically Spinozist panentheism? Günderrode presents an inner voice, conceptually not too far from Rousseau's voice of nature, which resides within, is presumed to be good, and prompts each protagonist to undertake radical political action in tyrannicide. Neither play is expressly metaphysical. The language that Günderrode adopts here holds the potential to extend into more philosophical territory. It heralds a process of internalisation that circumvents the problem that haunted Spinozism: that, as in 'Magie und Schicksal', a fatalist variant of it empties the individual of meaning, who becomes a passive being that responds to external forces. This internalisation also corresponds to Herder's notion that the individual is enlivened with the spirit of nature, which Günderrode takes up in her *Studienbuch*: 'Der Mensch ist nicht ein mechanisches Glied in der Naturkette; sondern der Geist der die Natur beherscht ist theilweise in ihm' [The individual is not a mechanical link in the chain of nature; rather the spirit that rules nature is also partly in them].[109] This offers one way in which panentheism can be reconciled with the underlying ideas in 'Nikator' and 'Hildgund': its aforementioned egalitarianism. In metaphysical terms, the individual relates to the whole as an equal, rather than as its disempowered subject.

The inner voice in Günderrode is both the voice of one's self and the voice of nature, and the framing of Nikator's and Hildgund's agency brings both characters to the point of conflating the individual voice and the voice of nature. Günderrode creates precisely this semantic expansion of the voice of the self into the voice of nature in the confessional prose text 'Geschichte eines Braminen'. The narrator, Almor, finds himself prompted by 'eine innere Stimme' [an inner voice] (*SW* I, 305), just as Hildgund and Nikator are, and this is the catalyst for Almor's own self-development. What distinguishes this voice is that it becomes revelatory. It speaks of the Spinozist panentheism that underpins existence:

> In dieser Sehnsucht, in dieser Liebe sprach der Naturgeist zu mir, ich hörte seine Stimme wohl, aber ich wußte noch nicht, wo sie herkäme; je mehr ich aber darauf lauschte, desto deutlicher war es mir, daß es eine Grundkraft gäbe, in welcher Alle, Sichtbare und Unsichtbare, verbunden seyen.
>
> [With this longing, with this love did the spirit of nature speak to me, I hear its voice well, but I did not know where it came from; the more I listened closely to it, the clearer it became to me that there is a fundamental force which connects everything, all that is visible and invisible.] (*SW* I, 308)

This dual identity of the inner voice as the voice of nature, of a teleological order within and beyond the individual, appears to work against the kind of autonomy central to 'Nikator' and 'Hildgund'. But something of this autonomy can still be preserved in Günderrode's positive formulation of panentheism, when it does not manifest as fatalism, as in 'Magie und Schicksal'. This rests on the idea of compatibilist determinism: that is, the idea that individuals are conditioned, but

Selfhood (Princeton: Princeton University Press, 1992), p. 13.
109 Preitz/Hopp III, p. 265.

have the ability to exercise their will, and their will happens to align with the design of the providential order.[110] This is the case with Almor in 'Geschichte eines Braminen'. Both plays feature a series of premises that make the construction of agency compatible with the metaphysical framework found in 'Geschichte eines Braminen': both imply that the individual is good and can innately determine what is morally justifiable.

The ambivalences of the political narratives 'Nikator' and 'Hildgund' lie in how they reach their climax and exhaust themselves in the near-eschatological moment of potential revolution through tyrannicide. Nikator and Hildgund symbolically become the liberated, autonomous individual, but the texts are imperfective and resist developing this thought fully. Part of the reason for this is pragmatic: the consequences of the plot necessarily mean that the autonomy of both Nikator and Hildgund becomes compromised, and they become subject to another authority. In this reading, the kind of autonomy that Nikator and Hildgund proclaim can only be achieved negatively. Günderrode's understanding of panentheism succumbs at times to a similar kind of non-closure as in 'Hildgund' and 'Nikator'. Panentheism offers a consolation narrative, a flight into the linear progression of metaphysics with the dim hope of spiritual perfection at an undetermined, ever deferred point in the future.

---

110 This is a term used to discuss Schleiermacher's determinism: see Andrew C. Dole, *Schleiermacher on Religion and the Natural Order* (Oxford: Oxford University Press, 2009), pp. 35–70.

CHAPTER 4

❖

From Political to Religious Revolution: The Rise of Muhammad and the Fall of Napoleon

Like many of her contemporaries, Günderrode greeted the news of Napoleon's military and scientific expedition to Egypt in 1798 with great enthusiasm. The trajectory of Napoleon in Günderrode's own work deserves special attention: it may appear that Napoleon belongs to the long line of heroic characters of action, although Napoleon lacks the mythic purity of a Brutus figure and becomes sullied by his imperial ambitions. This is certainly true. What becomes of Napoleon as a literary figure in Günderrode's work is significant because it points to a development in the conceptualisation of political revolution. As has been outlined in the previous chapter, the agency of Günderrode's revolutionary figures rests on moral universalism that presupposes a metaphysical grounding. Revolutionary action, therefore, necessarily extends beyond phenomenal reality.

To push the logic further: political revolution, as exemplified by Napoleon, becomes, in Günderrode, transfigured into political and religious revolution. The desire for political renewal becomes conjoined with a larger, more radical project: a desire for religious renewal. As I will show, this is why the historical disappointment of Napoleon's imperial ambitions leads to a displacement of Bonaparte in favour of the prophet Muhammad,[1] the protagonist of Günderrode's longest play and indeed longest work overall, 'Mahomed, der Prophet von Mekka'. This play is no less than an attempt to rethink religion at the turn of the nineteenth century — and in the form of Spinozist panentheism.

---

1   When referring to the historical figure, I will use 'Muhammad', and 'Mahomed' and 'Mahomet' when discussing Günderrode's texts, depending on the respective orthography.

Günderrode's Napoleon: A Fall through Literary Genre

In the early poem, 'Buonaparte in Egypten',[2] written in December 1799, following Napoleon's elevation to first Consul of the French Republic, Günderrode portrays Bonaparte as an idealised figure with world-historical agency and quasi-Messianic qualities, a hero of mythic grandeur who harks back to the heroic past and heralds the coming of a republican age. Napoleon's expedition to Egypt in 1798 and 1799 was lauded among contemporaries not so much as a display of military prowess, but rather as a cultural and scientific event, where the colonial might of Napoleon would uncover the dormant knowledge of a country in decay, one that had been held in bondage by the Ottomans.[3] What becomes clear in Günderrode's poem is how she accepts the mythical image that Napoleon consciously crafted of himself, and one that was eagerly transmitted in hyperbolic terms in the German-language press.[4]

In the poem, Napoleon is the light-bringer, who will not only revive Egypt, but will bring liberation and revolution to German-speaking lands too. The series of rhetorical questions that mark the poem create a mood of breathless anticipation:

> Alte Bande der Knechtschaft löset die Freiheit,
> Der Begeisterung Funke erwekt die Söhne Egyptens. —
> Wer bewirkt die Erscheinung? Wer ruft der Vorwelt
> Tage zurük? Wer reiset Hüll' und Ketten vom Bilde
> Jener Jsis, die der Vergangenheit Räthsel
> Dasteht, ein Denkmal vergessener Weisheit der Urwelt?
> Bonaparte ist's, Jtaliens Eroberer,
> Frankreichs Liebling, die Säule der würdigeren Freiheit
> Rufet er der Vorzeit Begeisterung zurüke
> Zeiget dem erschlaften Jahrhunderte römische Kraft.
>
> [Freedom loosens the old bonds of servitude
> Enthusiasm's spark awakes the sons of Egypt. —
> Who has caused this phenomenon? Who is bringing back
> The days of old? Who is tearing the veil and chains from the image
> Of Isis, who represents the riddle of the past,
> A monument to forgotten wisdom of the ancient world?
> It is Bonaparte, the conqueror of Italy,
> The darling of France; the upholder of the more worthy kind of freedom,
> He brings back the enthusiasm of the distant past,
> Displays Roman strength to this century of weakness.] (*SW* I, 369, ll. 11–20)

The physiological imagery of force underpins Napoleon's republican associations ('Zeiget dem erschlaften Jahrhunderte römische Kraft'), and his mythic potency

---

2 'Buonaparte in Egypten' functions as part of a series of related poems in the *Studien* and *Nachlass* that hail Napoleon: Karl Wolfart's 'An den Genius des scheidenden Jahrhunderts im August 1799', Preitz/Hopp III, pp. 269–73. In the *Nachlass* is a copy of Friedrich Lehne's 'Dem Consul Napoleon Bonaparte', in Wolfart's hand: see Morgenthaler, *SW* III, 214.
3 Alan J. Bewell, 'The Political Implication of Keats's Classicist Aesthetics', *Studies in Romanticism*, 25 (1986), 220–29 (p. 225).
4 Gerhart von Graevenitz, *Mythos: Zur Geschichte einer Denkgewohnheit* (Stuttgart: Metzler, 1987), pp. 171–78.

is legitimised by his conquest of Italy in 1797. The textual weight of Egypt is significant, and it is a reflexive historical gesture that Günderrode also uses in 'Mahomed, der Prophet von Mekka': it marks a return to a purported origin point for the development of mankind, to the prelapsarian state of the 'Vorwelt' (also synonymous with 'Vorzeit'). Here Günderrode draws on notions of the development of mankind, specifically Herder, who was inspired in part by Winckelmann's organic notion of the growth, peak and decay of Greek art. Herder fashioned his theory of history according to similar biological lines,[5] tracing the development of man from the origins in the East, through Egypt, Greece, Rome, and to contemporary northern Europe.[6] Recuperating this primordial knowledge through liberation, it is hoped, will serve as a means to return Egypt to its cultural peak and further political progress ('die Säule der würdigeren Freiheit | Rufet er der Vorzeit Begeisterung zurüke').

What precisely this knowledge may be is not given further explanation — the cult of Isis functions here as a metonym for the vast repository of potentially revitalising knowledge, religious or otherwise, that awaits discovery and decipherment. The poem performs a form of poetic archaeology through the idealised figure of Napoleon. Günderrode's layering of different images of Egypt also contains *in nuce* the potential for another, metaphysical reading of this arcane knowledge — one that can be further supported by the associations of Egypt with the origins of Judaeo-Christian religions. This subtextual potential helps prepare the ground for 'Mahomed'.

'Buonaparte in Egypten' marks the pinnacle of idealising fervour around Napoleon for Günderrode. What follows is a fall from grace. Firstly, in the early satirical play *Der Kanonenschlag oder das Gastmahl des Tantalus* [The Cannon-shot or Tantalus's Banquet] (1800–1801), Napoleon features as one of the rulers in press reports whose petty desires, such as arrogance and a penchant for luxury, make them subjects ripe for mockery (*SW* I, 413, ll. 6–18). More significant is Günderrode's literary reckoning with Napoleon in the poem 'Der Franke in Egypten'. What the poem neatly performs is Napoleon's fall as a fall through literary genre: no longer is Napoleon fit for the heroic or epic genre, but instead is consigned to the more banal mode of the romance, of the love-plot.

The Frenchman recounts his Napoleonic deeds in a mood of Faustian frustration: in a parallel to the dilemma that Nikator faces, military and scientific prowess in uncovering the secrets of the 'Vorwelt' provide no emotional succour. It appears that nothing can satiate his existential longing: 'Was geb ich ihr [der alten Sehnsucht]? Wohin soll ich mich stürzen? | Was wird des Lebens lange Oede würzen?' [What can I give to it [to this old longing]? Where shall I cast myself | What will add zest to the long desolation of life?] (*SW* I, 82, ll. 32–33). Instead, the object of his longing turns out to be nothing more than love and the self-knowledge that love brings, as well as the love of the girl Lastrata he encounters: 'Wohl mir! dich und mich

---

5   See Robert Cowan, *The Indo-German Identification: Reconciling South Asian Origins and European Destinies 1765–1885* (Rochester, NY: Camden House, 2010), p. 54.
6   See Todd Kontje, *German Orientalisms* (Ann Arbor: University of Michigan Press, 2004), p. 72.

hab' ich gefunden | Liebe hat dem Chaos sich entwunden' [Happy am I! I have found you and myself | Love has wrested itself from chaos] (*SW* I, 84, ll. 92–93). Love functions metaphorically as a cosmic force, as that which makes order out of the raw chaos of matter,[7] but it also functions as a more mundane yet profound interpersonal connection.

The narrative hinges on an idea that Günderrode shares with Friedrich Schlegel: that self-knowledge is predicated on knowledge of another,[8] and there are parallels here to the narrative structure of the *Märchen* [fairy tale] in Novalis's *Die Lehrlinge zu Sais*. But this epistemological point has an ironic ring to it in 'Der Franke in Egypten', since it has the effect of trivialising the entirety of Napoleon's Egyptian campaign.[9] There is no need to mention Napoleon's tyranny to clarify Günderrode's disappointment: literary disillusionment is enacted in an oblique manner, by having a love-conquest become more meaningful than conventional heroic feats of military conquest and empirical investigation.

'Das Licht nur werde!': Mahomet as a Transfiguration of Napoleon

Where Napoleon becomes problematic and is cast aside through this fall in literary genre, Günderrode reassigns these qualities of a political saviour to a less immediate figure: the prophet Muhammad. Indeed, Napoleon and Muhammad stand side by side in *Gedichte und Phantasien*, which also features 'Mahomets Traum in der Wüste' [Mahomet's Dream in the Desert]. This move to Muhammad can be read as a self-critique about processes of literary mythologising, and it is true that Günderrode resists idealising any other contemporary figure. But there is also much to gain by turning to Muhammad, who is not just a political revolutionary, but a founder of a new religion, which is what takes primacy for Günderrode.

There are also contextual and textual reasons for Napoleon and Muhammad to act as parallels. In the broader context, during the Egyptian campaign, Napoleon had identified with Muhammad as a reformer and visionary,[10] and had even characterised himself as a worldly version of Muhammad.[11] Within the textual

---

7   Love as a metaphysical or cosmogonic principle in this sense has a genealogy that goes back to Hesiod's *Theogony* and to forms of Orphism: see Claude Calame, *The Poetics of Eros in Ancient Greece*, trans. by Janet Lloyd (Princeton: Princeton University Press, 1999), pp. 178–81.
8   'Ganz und im strengsten Sinn kennt man niemand sich selbst. [...] denn niemand kennt sich, insofern er nur er selbst und nicht auch zugleich ein andrer ist. Je mehr Vielseitigkeit also, desto mehr Selbstkenntnis' [No one knows themselves completely and in the strictest sense. [...] for no one knows themselves, insofar as they are themselves and not another at the same time. The greater the multiplicity, the more self-knowledge there is] (Friedrich Schlegel, 'Über Lessing', in Friedrich Schlegel, *Kritische Friedrich-Schlegel-Ausgabe*, ed. by Ernst Behler and others, 31 vols (Munich: Schöningh, 1958–) I.II: *Charakteristiken und Kritiken I*, ed. by Hans Eichner (1967), pp. 115–16).
9   Kelly Barry, '1804, May 18: The Subject and Object of Mythology', in *A New History of German Literature*, ed. by David Wellbery and others (Cambridge, MA: Belknap Press, 2004), pp. 494–500 (p. 499).
10 John V. Tolan, *Faces of Muhammad: Western Perceptions of the Prophet of Islam from the Middle Ages to Today* (Princeton: Princeton University Press, 2019), p. 190.
11 Lucia M. Licher, 'A Sceptical Mohammedan: Aesthetics as a Theory of Life's Practice in the Writings of Caroline von Günderrode', in *Transactions of the Ninth International Congress on the Enlightenment, Münster, 23–29 July 1995*, Studies on Voltaire and the Eighteenth Century, 346–48, 3

logic of Günderrode's works, there is a peculiar detail in the draft of 'Mahomed, der Prophet von Mekka': the antiphonic chorus sympathetic to Mahomed is revealed to be composed of former Egyptian slaves. Mahomed, in his role as a merchant, had liberated them (*SW* II, 103, ll. 71–75).[12] At first glance, this is an oddity since it has no basis in the historical biographies of the prophet. On one level, it creates a parallel between Mahomed and Moses, but on another, it also acts as an inheritance from 'Buonaparte in Egypten': Mahomed retains a textual trace of Napoleon's biography.

Why would the values and hopes projected onto Napoleon be easily transposed onto Muhammad? The advantage that Muhammad offers over Napoleon is the potentially selfless aspect of a prophet following a divine calling. This would help circumvent the problem of Napoleon's self-serving tyranny. The use of Muhammad is not merely a retreat into malleable historical sources to present a purified ideal of a political leader. The introduction of a religious element to a political revolutionary makes Günderrode's use of Muhammad potentially contentious, given how intensely debated the reception of Muhammad was in the eighteenth century, where Islam was used as a self-reflexive prism through which internal conflicts within Christianity were carried out.[13]

The introduction of a religious element in Muhammad's calling is, however, significant and attests to Günderrode's literary and intellectual ambition. There is also an internal logic in Günderrode to the merging of the political and the religious. If all human agency is grounded in a form of moral universalism, one that suggests a metaphysical underpinning to human action, then it follows that political revolution necessitates a religious revolution too, to bring these metaphysical underpinnings to light. This is the task of Günderrode's Mahomed.

There is a long history of negative portrayals of Muhammad throughout the medieval and early modern period, where Muhammad was dismissed as an imposter, heretic, and an epileptic.[14] Eighteenth-century portrayals were more nuanced, with the awakening of scholarly interest in Islam.[15] Shorn of its pre-modern stigma,

---

vols (Oxford: Voltaire Foundation, 1996), III, 1450–52 (p. 1451).

12 A trace of this remains in the published version since both choruses are dressed in Egyptian slave clothing (*SW* I, 110, l. 21).

13 Thierry Hentschel, *Imagining the Middle East* (Montreal: Black Rose, 1992), p. 113. A good example of this would be Humphrey Prideaux's *The True Nature of Imposture, Fully Display'd in the Life of Mahomet* (1695): Prideaux, an Anglican, casts Islam as proto-deism, and criticises the deist reduction of Christianity that is founded on natural religion and reason alone.

14 For more detail on these earlier accounts of Muhammad, see John V. Tolan, 'European Accounts of Muhammad's Life' in *The Cambridge Companion to Muhammad*, ed. by Jonathan E. Brockopp (Cambridge: Cambridge University Press, 2010), pp. 226–50 (pp. 226–28). The implication that discussions of Muhammad tended towards the negative in the eighteenth-century would be misleading. Muhammad was admired as a proficient law-maker and -enforcer. In Emmanuel Pastoret's *Zoroastre, Confucius et Mahomet* (1787), Muhammad is portrayed as a paragon of legal and moral virtue. In Jean-Jacques Rousseau's *Du contrat social* (1762), Muhammad is praised as being able to successfully combine political and religious powers in the state.

15 Frederick Quinn, *The Sum of All Heresies: The Image of Islam in Western Thought* (Oxford: Oxford University Press, 2008), p. 57. For a useful survey of competing images of Muhammad in the eighteenth century, see Daniel Cyranka, *Mahomet: Repräsentationen des Propheten in deutschsprachigen Texten des*

Islam became refashioned as a form of natural theology or deism, and served as a counter-image to Christianity for both Lessing and Leibniz.[16] Muhammad became a sympathetic figure for Herder and Goethe as a self-deceiving deceiver with noble intentions, but one seized by mental delirium. According to this view, Muhammad is, in short, an enthusiast, in the negative sense of *Schwärmer* in the eighteenth century, which is a state of self-deluding enthusiasm and referred to those who conflated fictions with real knowledge.[17]

One of the central tensions in the reception of Muhammad is that between the political and the religious: to what extent Muhammad's spiritual calling is a matter of political expediency and dissimulation, where the core of religious revelation — necessarily inaccessible to others — becomes compromised for self-serving ends. In Voltaire's *Le fanatisme ou Mahomet le Prophète* [Fanaticism or Mahomet the Prophet] (1741), for example, Muhammad is a self-aggrandising, bloodthirsty and false prophet who is fully aware of the centrality of deception to his political machinations.

Günderrode's depiction of Muhammad is determined in such a manner to avoid the charges both of enthusiasm and of being a false prophet. This is partly to avoid a regression into the disillusionment associated with Napoleon. Instead, Muhammad remains for Günderrode an idealised, purified figure who is indeed the true prophet. At the same time, the poem 'Mahomets Traum in der Wüste' stages the tension in the dual identity of Mahomet as a political and religious leader. The poem's narrative concerns Mahomet's dream-vision, an attempt to clarify the nature of his divine calling, where this God-given mission corresponds to the promptings of his heart: 'Des eignen Herzens Stimme hören, | Und folgen seiner Eingebung' [To hear the voice of my own heart | And follow its dictates] (*SW* I, 75, ll. 11–12). What proves emotionally problematic about this vision is that it features Mahomet's own death, which provokes despair: 'Von Zweifeln, ruft er, nur umgeben! | Verhauchet der Entschluß sein Leben!' [But surrounded just by doubts, he cries! | That decision makes him breathe his last!] (*SW* I, 76, ll. 28–29). The spiritual vision that follows acts as a means for Mahomet to overcome the fear of his own death and submit to his role as a conduit of the divine will.

It seems, though, that Mahomet's desires may be more worldly and self-serving;[18]

---

18. Jahrhunderts, Beiträge zur Europäischen Religionsgeschichte, 6 (Göttingen: Vandenhoeck & Ruprecht, 2018).

16 Silvia Horsch, '"Was findest Du darinne, das nicht mit der allerstrengsten Vernunft übereinkomme?": Islam as Natural Theology in Lessing's Writings and in the Enlightenment', in *Cultural Exchange in German Literature*, ed. by Eleoma Joshua and Robert Vilain (Rochester, NY: Camden House, 2007), pp. 45–62 (pp. 45–50).

17 Anthony J. La Vopa, 'The Philosopher and the "Schwärmer": On the Career of a German Epithet from Luther to Kant', *Huntingdon Library Quarterly*, 60 (1997), 85–115 (pp. 85–86).

18 Minou Reeves reads Günderrode's Mahomet as being cut from the same cloth as the Mahomet in Voltaire's play, which Goethe had translated into German in 1800: Minou Reeves, 'Pantheism, Heroism, Sensualism, Mysticism: Muhammed and Islam in German Literature from Goethe to Rilke', in *Traces of Transcendency/Spuren des Transzendenten: Religious Motifs in German Literature and Thought*, ed. by Rüdiger Görner, Publications of the Institute of Germanic Studies, 77 (Munich: Iudicium, 2001), pp. 89–103 (p. 94).

to neutralise his mortal despair, he pleads for assurance of his future military and political success: 'Ob meine Fahnen siegreich wehen? | Ob mein Gesetz die Welt regiert?' [Whether my banners will fly in victory? | Whether my law will rule the world?] (*SW* I, 76, ll. 35–36). Whilst the extent of self-interest in Mahomet's motivations remains ambiguous, the poem's narrative logic suggests the primacy of the spiritual calling over the political. For what concludes the poem is a vision indebted in part to the mystical tradition. Günderrode repurposes the visual imagery from 'Buonaparte in Egypten': where Napoleon is the light-bringer in the form of political freedom and progress, Mahomet is the spiritual light-bringer. Mahomet is subject to an overwhelming vision of the course of world history that is eschatological in nature: he witnesses an awesome vision of fermenting chaos, where the heaving elements of the world violently disintegrate in a purifying conflagration. It is also a symbolic death for Mahomed ('Und staunend fühlt er sich leben, | Erwachet aus dem Tod der Schrecken' [And, astonished, he feels his life stir | Awakening from the death of terror] (*SW* I, 77, ll. 63–64)), forcing spiritual purification upon him.

Mahomet's spiritual mission, proclaimed to him by his God, rests on a form of emanationism and perfectibility. The divine is the primordial light ('Urlicht'), a term that is associated with the theosophical and Christian cabbalistic tradition.[19] The course of world history, as the divine voice elucidates, consists of the endless productivity of forces in nature that will cause all impurities, in the fullness of time, to be burned away, leaving that which is pure and divine to return to its point of origin: 'Das Reine nur, der Lichtstoff, währet | Und fließt dem ew'gen Urlicht zu"' [Only what is pure, the matter of light, endures | And flows back to the eternal, primordial light"] (*SW* I, 77, ll. 77–78). As a result, Mahomet's resolve and faith in his mission are restored; his purpose is as a second creator, in a neat biblical quotation: 'Das Licht nur werde! sey mein Ringen, | Dann wird mein Thun unsterblich seyn' [That there be light! should be my endeavour | For then my deeds will be immortal] (*SW* I, 77, ll. 83–84). This anticipates, in part, the participatory metaphysics of 'Briefe zweier Freunde', which is discussed in the sixth chapter, where human agency necessarily contributes to the realisation of the divine.

'Mahomed': An *Apologia* for Religion

Whereas 'Mahomets Traum in der Wüste' does not resolve the tension between Mahomet's religious and political interests, the poem's endpoint, which privileges the religious aspects of Mahomet's calling, points to Günderrode's portrayal of Mahomed in the play published the following year. The portrayal of Mahomed in the play is overwhelmingly positive, although not without complication. Mahomed is the true prophet not just of Islam, but of a universal religion. What purpose does such an idealised portrayal of Mahomed as a true prophet serve? It is not only a way to prevent Mahomed becoming a second Napoleon: Mahomed is not just a

---

19 Klaus Reichert, 'Zur Geschichte der christlichen Kabbala', in *Kabbala und die Literatur der Romantik: Zwischen Magie und Trope*, ed. by Eveline Goodman-Thau and others, Conditio Judaica, 27 (Tübingen: Niemeyer, 1999), pp. 1–16 (p. 2).

purified political revolutionary, but also a purified religious leader. The addition of this religious element is important. The play acts as an *apologia* for religion, and it is worth considering the broader historical context. The German Enlightenment was marked by a crisis of religious orthodoxy.[20] The Romantic generation very much inherited and bore the burden of these problems.[21] Read in this context, the play becomes a narrative about not just political, but religious revolution, and acts as a response to this crisis of orthodoxy and the problem of religious legitimacy.

The play was written in the latter half of 1804 but was not published until 1805 in the collection *Poetische Fragmente*. An earlier, incomplete version of the play, which contains textual variants from the published version, is preserved in a manuscript. In a series of five 'Zeiträume' [periods of time], punctuated by choral odes from an antiphonic chorus, 'Mahomed' charts the ascendancy of the prophet of Islam as a political and religious leader, and is structured around a series of tests of his legitimacy alongside conversion scenes of new followers to Islam.

The play opens with Mahomed proclaiming his double life, caught between the demands of earthly life and those of heaven, and the first 'Zeitraum' ends with Mahomed proclaiming his new religion to the people of Mekka, which sows the seeds of conflict with the elders of Mekka, Sofian, the emir of the Quraysh tribe (given as 'Koreschiten' in the play). The second 'Zeitraum' features scenes of conversion and challenge: the warrior Omar intends to kill Mahomed for having led his sister into the new faith, but Omar's knife fatefully fails to find its target, which causes him to start to believe in the truth of Mahomed's religion. Sofian tests Mahomed but is determined to have the prophet's power quashed since he is a threat to Mekka's stability. Mahomed is banished, but before his departure, his enemies, Sofian and Abu-Johl, conspire to have him killed, and so Mahomed leaves the city with his followers, including Halima, a new convert who is also Sofian's daughter. Mahomed experiences a brief moment of doubt in his mission, but soon recovers, although his followers are puzzled by how he lacks any clear plan for his return to Mekka. Nahlid falls in love with Halima. Omar betrays the Quraysh tribe to join Mahomed's forces. Halima begs Nahlid, one of Mahomed's followers, to spare Sofian's life, who then returns to Mekka. Mahomed is brought to trial before the Grand Emir Habib, accused of high treason, blasphemy, rebellion, and murder by Abu-Johl and Sofian, and is required to perform a miracle to prove the divinity of his mission. Mahomed reluctantly complies and Habib, satisfied with Mahomed's legitimacy as a prophet, throws out the charges brought against Mahomed. Mahomed and Sofian reach a peace agreement, a condition of which is for Halima to be returned to her father. When Nahlid learns of her return to Sofian, he commits suicide. Mahomed and his forces enter Mekka peacefully, and Mahomed prophesises the spread of Islam across Arabia and beyond.

Günderrode's 'Mahomed' is the ambitious attempt to purify and resurrect

---

20 Hans Erich Bödeker, 'Die Religiosität der Gebildeten', in *Religionskritik und Religiosität in der deutschen Aufklärung*, ed. by Karlfried Gründer and Karl Heinrich Rengstorf, Wolfenbütteler Studien zur Aufklärung, 11 (Heidelberg: Schneider, 1989), pp. 145–95 (p. 145).
21 Dirk von Petersdorff, *Mysterienrede: Zum Selbstverständnis romantischer Intellektueller*, Studien zur deutschen Literatur, 139 (Tübingen: Niemeyer, 1996), p. 54.

religion, and functions as a heterodox *apologia* for a positive, revealed and universal religion. Central to this purified faith in 'Mahomed' is the idea of enthusiasm, which remains unsullied by the negative connotations of *Schwärmerei*. Günderrode thus returns enthusiasm to its neutral etymological root, to the meaning of one who is possessed by a god — one of the epithets applied to Mahomed is 'Der Gotterfüllte' [One suffused with God] (*SW* I, 136, l. 798).[22] The divine superstructure of providence, divine will and teleology is firmly in place in the play. Mahomed, therefore, is the true prophet with unmediated access to divine truth and functions as a conduit, but not as a blind instrument, of divine will.

Like Novalis's *Die Christenheit oder Europa* [Christendom or Europe] (1799), or parts of Hölderlin's *Hyperion*, Günderrode's 'Mahomed' is pregnant with hope — hope for revolutionary renewal and hope for a purified political and religious world order. Through detailing the ascendancy of Mahomed as a political and religious leader, it promotes the promise of a soteriological religion, one that is poised on the cusp of realisation. Indeed, its dramatic propulsion stems from eschatological hope. The hope is voiced primarily by the chorus. It is, at times, positively feverish with eschatological anticipation: 'Ein bunt Gewühl wird nun die Erde werden, | Das Mahoms Traumgesichten gleicht' [The Earth will now become a colourful bustle, | That resembles Muhammad's dream vision] (*SW* I, 131, ll. 647–48);[23] 'Von ihm [Mahomed] erzeugt, wird neu die Welt gebohren, | Der Tempel Gottes aus dem Schutt erstehn' [Produced by him, the world will be born anew, | The temple of God shall arise from the rubble] (*SW* I, 180, ll. 2086–87).[24]

This hope is bolstered by a universalising approach to religion, which harmonises religions through syncretism. Günderrode moves beyond a position of Enlightenment humanism, such as that supported by Herder, where religions act as distinct expressions of the experience of God.[25] She also goes beyond the purified image of Islam as a form of deism, and beyond religious toleration; Günderrode posits a form of absolute truth. In 'Mahomed', esoteric forms of divining knowledge — magic, Kabbalic mysticism, ancient mysteries — are given equal credence alongside the three Western monotheisms. This reinvigorates the Neoplatonist and Hermetic notion of perennial philosophy and *prisca theologia*: all religions and secular knowledge systems are, at their core, expressions of the same stable divine truth given to man in antiquity.

What results from this syncretism is an essentially heterodox approach to religion. Heterodoxy does not, as orthodox theologians may fear, inherently threaten to destroy religion altogether.[26] As Gottfried Arnold had radically argued in

22 Günderrode, *Poetic Fragments*, p. 196.
23 Ibid., p. 186.
24 Ibid., p. 266 (translation adapted).
25 Anne Löchte, *Johann Gottfried Herder: Kulturtheorie und Humanitätsidee der Ideen, Humanitätsbriefe und Adrastea*, Epistemata: Würzburger Wissenschaftliche Schriften, 540 (Würzburg: Königshausen & Neumann, 2005), p. 174.
26 As Sarah Mortimer and John Robertson argue, it is false to equate heterodoxy with the move towards modern materialist secularism. Such an association would be a reductively teleological reading. See Sarah Mortimer and John Robertson, 'Nature, Revelation, History: The Intellectual Consequences of Religious Heterodoxy 1600–1750', in *Intellectual Consequences of Religious Heterodoxy,*

Unparteyische Kirchen-und Ketzer-Historie/Vom Anfang des Neuen Testaments Biß auff das Jahr Christi 1688 [Impartial History of the Church and of Heretics, from the Beginning of the New Testament to anno domini 1688] (1699–1700), it was not established church dogma that propagated true belief, but rather free-thinking heretics and dissidents.[27] A heterodox approach, therefore, has the potential to be a liberating means to defend religion.

But adopting a heterodox approach does not avoid the problems associated with establishing religious legitimacy. In 'Mahomed', the question of religious legitimacy is addressed on two levels. On the diegetic level, Mahomed is compelled to defend himself against his religious and political adversaries as the true prophet. On the extradiegetic level, 'Mahomed' offers a general defence of problems associated with religion. Günderrode displays both a critical awareness of these problems and even attempts to circumvent them by retelling the Messiah narrative, in displaced form through the founding of Islam.

The first problem of religious legitimacy is the authority of scripture itself. Anxieties over the continued validity of the biblical narrative, which supports supernatural revelation, appeared confirmed in H. S. Reimarus's radically deist *Apologie oder Schutzschrift für die vernünftigen Verehrer Gottes* [An Apologia and a Defence of the Rational Worshippers of God], published in part by Lessing in the *Wolfenbüttler Fragmente* [Wolfenbüttel Fragments] from 1774 onward. The resulting *Fragmentenstreit* [Fragments Controversy], which consisted of a flurry of pamphlets between Lessing and the orthodox Hamburg pastor Melchior Goeze, garnered the rapt attention of the intellectual public.[28] In the published fragments, the series of *Fragmente eines Unbekannten* [Fragments by an Anonymous Writer], Reimarus reveals the disparity between Christ as portrayed in the scriptures, subsequent Church doctrines of reincarnation and the second coming, and his portrayal in the historical record,[29] as well as questioning the authority of reported accounts of revelation, on the grounds that divine revelation is incompatible with reason.[30]

Reimarus was tapping into an older vein of radical scepticism about scriptural authority, as well as drawing on the biblical philology of theologians such as Johann Salomo Semler and Sigmund Jacob Baumgarten.[31] In the late seventeenth century, the publication of Spinoza's *Tractatus theologio-politicus* (1670), as Ulrich Groetsch observes, had the effect that 'theologians and exegetes felt increasingly pressured to prove not only that the [biblical] event had taken place, but that the description in the Bible was completely credible and accurate.'[32] This should not suggest a

---

1600–1750, ed. by Sarah Mortimer and John Robertson, Brill's Studies in Intellectual History, 211 (Leiden: Brill, 2012), pp. 1–46 (p. 2).
27 Martin Bollacher, *Der junge Goethe und Spinoza: Studien zur Geschichte des Spinozismus in der Epoche des Sturms und Drangs*, Studien zur deutschen Literatur, 18 (Niemeyer: Tübingen, 1969), p. 56.
28 Frederick C. Beiser, *The German Historicist Tradition* (Oxford: Oxford University Press, 2011), p. 144.
29 Ibid., pp. 143–44.
30 Thomas P. Saine, *The Problem of Being Modern or the German Pursuit of Enlightenment from Leibniz to the French Revolution* (Detroit: Wayne State University Press, 1997), p. 202.
31 Ibid.
32 Ulrich Groetsch, 'The Miraculous Crossing of the Red Sea: What Lessing and his Opponents

declinist narrative, an inexorable process of scripture being discredited. Theologians such as Baumgarten, who advocated theological Wolffianism, sought to reconcile theology with Enlightenment thought.[33]

Günderrode cuts through the intricate problems of the legitimacy of scripture — which would include the question of scripture being divorced from historical foundation of religion, the problem of textual transmission and the painstaking historical study of scripture that occupied biblical scholars. The Qu'ran is not entirely analogous to the Bible, and it had never been subject to the kind of sceptical critique among Islamic scholars or philosophers from which the Bible had suffered.[34] It was still considered among Muslims to be the authoritative word of God.[35] But Günderrode, in a boldly ahistorical move, goes one step further to overcome the problem of legitimising scripture. In 'Mahomed', the Qu'ran has already been written.[36] Günderrode thus nips several problems in the bud. Gone is the problem of translation of the Bible from its original languages; gone is the question of how the text was collated and standardised, or whether it is an accurate depiction of historical events. In the play, the Qu'ran, it is implied, is the word of God as mediated through Mahomed and is intimately connected to the immediate historical foundation of Islam.

Structured as a series of revelations given to Mahomed by God, the Qu'ran thus serves as irrefutable evidence for legitimising Mahomed as the true prophet and, by extension, for legitimising the God of Islam. In the trial scene before the Emir Habib, when the elders of Mekka formally accuse Mahomed of blasphemy, Mahomed's first line of defence is recourse to the Qu'ran: 'Hast du den Koran gelesen, und bedarfst du noch eines andern Beweises? Kannst du noch zweifeln, daß Gott durch den Koran spricht? Oder kann ein Sterblicher Worte des Himmels reden?' [Have you read the Quran, and you still require another proof? Can you still doubt that God speaks through the Quran? Or can a mortal speak words of heaven?] (*SW* I, 180, ll. 2102–05).[37] Indeed, Mahomed's consummate proficiency in rhetoric and the word of the Qu'ran mutually reinforce each other. Omar, the warrior whose attempt to slay Mahomed is thwarted by the intervention of providence, is palpably moved after hearing a verse from the Qu'ran: 'Sollte Mahomed so reden können? Ich erstaune! — Laß mich dies Blatt mitnehmen, Nahlid!' [Should Muhammad be able to speak like that? I am astonished! — Let me take this page with me, Nahlid!] (*SW* I, 136, ll. 778–79).[38] The military leader Tarrik, a political ally to Mahomed, succumbs to the appeal of the Qu'ran as well and converts: 'da sah ich Othmann, er verkündigte mir, du seyest der Prophet des einzigen Gottes,

---

during the *Fragmentenstreit* Did Not See', in *Lessings Religionphilosophie im Kontext: Hamburger Fragmente und Wolfenbütteler Axiomata*, ed. by Christoph Bultmann and Friedrich Vollhardt, Frühe Neuzeit, 159 (Berlin: De Gruyter, 2011), pp. 181–99 (p. 184).

33 David Sorkin, 'Reclaiming Theology for the Enlightenment: The Case of Siegmund Jacob Baumgarten (1706–1757)', *Central European History*, 36.4 (2003), 503–30 (p. 505).
34 Katharina Mommsen, *Goethe und die arabische Welt* (Frankfurt a.M.: Insel, 1988), p. 445.
35 Ibid.
36 The Qu'ran was actually collated after Muhammad's death.
37 Günderrode, *Poetic Fragments*, p. 268.
38 Ibid., p. 194.

er las mir den Koran, ich erkannte die Göttlichkeit deiner Sendung und wurde ein Moslem' [There I saw Uthman, he announced to me you were the prophet of the only God, he read the Quran to me, I recognized the divinity of your mission and became a Muslim] (*SW* I, 184, ll. 2207–11).³⁹

But the religion of the play is not wholly Islamic. True, Günderrode makes careful use of the source material. References to 'der große Ueberwinder' [a great conqueror] (*SW* I, 137–38, ll. 830–62),⁴⁰ to the allegory of the seven brothers (*SW* I, 139, ll. 872–91) are all derived from the Qu'ran, and the biblical examples of Hagar and Moses also feature there.⁴¹ But the religious content of the play remains more a displaced form of Christianity than Islamic doctrine.⁴² The play is suffused with a wealth of biblical allusions and parallels: Mahomed's triumphant and peaceful entry into Mekka functions as a parallel to Christ's entry into Jerusalem; the Kabbalic magician, who prophesises that the Qu'ran's time — and therefore Mahomed's — has come, is a proxy for John the Baptist as the messenger for Jesus' mission;⁴³ Mahomed is even declared 'der Verheißene' [the promised one] (*SW* I, 173, l. 1904)⁴⁴ by elderly Arab Jewish rabbis from Yatreb, who are moved by bearing witness to Mahomed praying. Stephanie M. Hilger reads these allusions as familiarising the Christian readers with Mahomed as the foreign and religious Other.⁴⁵

Yet reading 'Mahomed' as an *apologia* reveals the inverse to be also the case. Presenting biblical allusions embedded within an unfamiliar narrative is a form of defamiliarisation. That is to say: for the Christian reader who may be overly familiar with biblical language, Günderrode's decontextualised use of these quotations has the effect of renewing the Word. The density of biblical allusions becomes prominent in Mahomed's central doctrine of eternal life. When describing man's dual nature, which rests on Cartesian dualism and the Christian devaluation of the body, Mahomed depicts this promise of eternal life in lyrical terms inflected with biblical parallels: 'ich bin zwar nur ein Mensch, ein Gefäß von Staub und Asche, wir ihr, aber ein Tropfen aus dem Brunn des ewigen Lebens ist in mir aufbewahrt' [I am indeed only a man, a vessel of dust and ashes, like you, but a drop from the fountain of eternal life is preserved in me] (*SW* I, 157, ll. 1409–11).⁴⁶ This

---

39   Ibid., p. 274.
40   Ibid., pp. 196–98.
41   Regen, p. 30.
42   Ingeborg Solbrig makes a similar observation with regard to the poem 'Mahomets Traum in der Wüste' from *Gedichte und Phantasien* (1804), in Ingeborg Solbrig, 'The Contemplative Muse: Karoline von Günderode's Religious Works', *Germanic Notes*, 18 (1987), 18–20 (p. 18).
43   See John 1. 29–34. James Hodkinson has also provided a discussion of the biblical parallels in the play, reading Mahomed as a parallel to Christ and embodying in part Christian doctrine: see James Hodkinson, 'Der Islam im Dichten und Denken der deutschen Romantik: zwischen Kosmopolitismus und Orientalismus', in *Islam in der deutschen und türkischen* Literatur, ed. by Michael Hofmann and Klaus von Stosch, Beiträge zur komparativen Theologie, 4 (Paderborn: Schöningh, 2012), pp. 60–79 (p. 75).
44   Günderrode, *Poetic Fragments*, p. 256.
45   Stephanie M. Hilger, *Women Write Back: Strategies of Response and the Dynamics of European Literary Culture, 1790–1805*, Internationale Forschungen zur Allgemeinen und Vergleichenden Literaturwissenschaft, 124 (Amsterdam: Rodopi, 2009), p. 113.
46   Günderrode, *Poetic Fragments*, p. 228. For parallels of 'Brunn des ewigen Lebens', see John 4. 14;

reinvigorates a core aspect of Christian salvation history by syncretising it with the Islamic context — the doctrine of eternal life is shared by the two religions — and thus enlivens it by granting it universal validity.

Whilst Günderrode resolves problems associated with scripture, a second problem of religious legitimacy is that of scepticism towards miracles. This falls in line with the attempt throughout the Enlightenment period to eradicate superstitious aspects from religious belief, such as the indiscriminate belief in spirits. The Dutch scholars Van Dale and Balthasar Bekker had done much to root out belief in the Devil, magic and witchcraft,[47] and, in the German context, the rationalist philosopher Christian Thomasius railed against superstition.[48] Spinoza devotes the sixth chapter of *Tractatus theologio-politicus* to a discussion of miracles and argues that, in Scripture, 'miracles do not give a true knowledge of God or teach his providence clearly'.[49] David Hume's section 'Of Miracles' in *An Enquiry Concerning Human Understanding* (1748) points to the unreliability of evidence for them, which is never sufficient for them to be believed.[50]

Whilst miracles do indeed exist in 'Mahomed', they are presented in a sceptical light. When the elders of Mekka and Emir Habib exhort Mahomed to perform a miracle as proof of his divine calling, Günderrode expressly frames the episode in terms which reflect suspicion about a miracle's claim to reflect religious truth. In the 'erster Zeitraum' [first period of time], Mahomed is challenged by Sofian, one of his fiercest adversaries, to perform a miracle. Mahomed's response points to how ill-suited a miracle is for this purpose. A miracle is little more than a charlatan's vacuous confidence trick:

> Was würde es euch helfen, wenn ich dem Thaur Quellen sprudeln hieße, oder der Wüste geböte, sich grün zu bekleiden, würde darum die Wahrheit wahrer, oder das Schlimme gut werden? Ein böser Geist könnte mir die Macht gegeben haben, solches zu thun.
>
> [What would it help you if I ordered the Jabal Thawr to bubble springs, or bade the desert to clothe itself in green? Would the truth thereby become truer, or the wicked become good? An evil spirit could have given me the power to do so.] (*SW* I, 137, ll. 820–24)[51]

Mahomed's reluctance reflects Günderrode's overall approach to the source material, which reduces the fantastical excesses of Mahomed's biography.[52]

Psalm 36. 10; Jeremiah 2. 13 and 17. For Biblical parallels with 'Staub und Asche', see I Moses. 18, 27; Job 30. 19; Psalm 103. 14, I Moses 2. 7.
47   Jonathan Israel, *Radical Enlightenment: Philosophy and the Making of Modernity 1650–1750* (Oxford: Oxford University Press, 2001), p. 633.
48   Martin Pott, *Aufklärung und Aberglaube: Die deutsche Frühaufklärung im Spiegel ihrer Aberglaubenskritik*, Studien zur deutschen Literatur, 119 (Tübingen: Niemeyer, 1992), pp. 123–24.
49   Benedictus de Spinoza, *Theological-Political Treatise*, in *The Collected Works of Spinoza*, ed. and trans. by Edwin Curley, 2 vols (Princeton: Princeton University Press, 1985–2016), II, 65–354 (p. 160).
50   David Hume, *An Enquiry Concerning Human Understanding*, ed. by Peter Millican (Oxford: Oxford University Press, 2007), pp. 79–95.
51   Günderrode, *Poetic Fragments*, p. 196 (translation adapted).
52   For a discussion of how Günderrode reduces the excesses of the trial scene from the accounts in Gagnier and Boulainvilliers, see Regen, p. 48.

Yet this early criticism of miracles as elaborate trickery frames the later, parallel scene in trial before the Emir Habib. Mahomed is hesitant to acquiesce to the demands to perform a miracle, and only does so under duress — although he is aware of divine beneficence towards him: 'O ihr Bethörten! Ihr wollt mich zu Schanden machen, aber der Gott des Sieges ist mit mir! Wohlan, ich will das Wunder thun' [Oh you deceived ones! You would bring me to ruin, but the God of victory is with me! Well then, I will do the miracle] (*SW* I, 181, ll. 2118–20).[53] A miracle — the darkening and then lightening of the moon — is performed and recognised as evidence of divine approval. To be sure, Günderrode does not support the Enlightenment scepticism about miracles. But the miracle itself, as is clear from Mahomed's doubts, has little to do with the core of religion.

With these caveats about religious proofs present in 'Mahomed', this raises the attendant question of how the Mahomed material is useful as an *apologia* to legitimise religion. Günderrode's primary sources consist of two French biographies, Jean Gagnier's *La vie de Mahomet* (1732) and Comte Henri de Boulainvilliers' *La vie de Mahomed* (1730) and possibly an available translation of the Qu'ran.[54] What this material creates is a religious *tabula rasa*. The play returns to a heady period in the past to chart the ascent of Islam, and returns the religion to its prelapsarian state prior to its historical disintegration into factionalism. Capturing these foundational political and religious events returns to a time of a unified and stable religious truth. This brings with it the advantage of avoiding the problem of denominational strife and fragmentation in Christianity. Mahomed's speech to Nahlid about the religious corruption and fragmentation rife in the seventh century has to be read anagogically, and stimulates parallels with the contemporary factionalism within Christianity:

> Das Christenthum hat sich von seinem Erzeuger, dem Judenthum, losgerissen, es hat das elterliche Haus verlassen und ist hinausgewandert nach allen vier Winden, es sendet aus der Ferne die giftigen Pfeile der Verfolgung nach seines Vaters heiligem Haupte; zugleich ist es uneins mit sich selbst, seine Theile bestreiten sich in grimmigen [*sic*] Zwist und sein sonst wohlgebauter Körper ist voll wilder, gräulicher Auswüchse.
>
> [Christendom has torn itself away from its begetter, Judaism, it abandoned its parental house and wandered out to all four winds, it sends out of the distance the poisoned arrows of persecution against its father's holy head; at the same time it is at odds with itself, its parts dispute in grim strife and its otherwise well-built body is full of wild, ghoulish excesses.] (*SW* I, 162–63, ll. 1590–97)[55]

---

53 Günderrode, *Poetic Fragments*, p. 268.
54 The question of whether Günderrode read the Qu'ran is vexed. The only quotation purported to be from Qu'ran given in the play is, according to Erich Regen's thorough study of the source material, most likely Günderrode glossing a section of Boulainvilliers (see Regen, p. 40). Annelore Naumann argues that Mahomed's first speech to the people of Mekka is influenced by the language of the Qu'ran, resulting in a curious mixture of Old Testament and Qu'ranic language, but fails to substantiate this intriguing claim. See Annelore Naumann, *Caroline von Günderrode* (Berlin: Freie Universität, 1957), p. 124.
55 Günderrode, *Poetic Fragments*, p. 238.

On one level, Mahomed's legitimacy as the founder of a new religion is partially justified by claiming to eradicate the corruption of existing religions. But this equally carries weight as commentary on the state of Christianity. The problem is one of religious parochialism. In Mahomed's analysis, Christians stubbornly refuse to acknowledge the debt owed to Christianity's immediate antecedent, Judaism, therefore falsely eliding the commonalities between them.

'Mahomed' constructs a salvatory origin narrative for religion as a solution to this problem of religious desiccation. What Mahomed's doctrine proposes is a universal church, an Islam seen through the prism of religious universalism, which acts as a panacea to religious discord. Mahomed proposes to syncretise all these religious systems: 'das Christenthum soll zurückkehren zu dem Judenthum und sich in meiner Lehre mit ihm versöhnen und vereinigen' [Christendom shall turn back to Judaism and in my teachings reconcile and unite with it] (*SW* I, 163, ll. 1603–05).[56] This harmonising move goes beyond the scope of the historical Mahomed's admiration for Abraham:[57] the opening of the Qu'ran features a strong polemic condemning both Judaism and Christianity and an invocation to God to teach the Muslims the original religion of Abraham.[58] Syncretising these religious systems elevates religion to a universal constant, which builds upon the idea of a universal religion first proposed by Nicholas of Cusa.[59]

Since Mahomed is partially a conflation of the main prophets of Judaism and Christianity, this idea of universal religion becomes intertwined with the narrative of religious origins. In a parallel to a heretical reading of Moses, not supported by the Old Testament, Mahomed is familiar with the Egyptian mysteries — the primal form of natural religion which Moses adopted as a model for his doctrine,[60] and one that, according to Schiller in *Die Sendung Moses* [Moses' Mission] (1790), also formed the basis for Islam.[61] The chorus reports Mahomed's ritual descent into the depths of a pyramid, which is a symbol for the initiation into arcane, hidden knowledge (*SW* I, 121, ll. 353–55).[62]

---

56 Ibid., p. 240.
57 Solbrig, 'Die Orientalische Muse', p. 318.
58 *Der Koran, oder das Gesetz für die Muselmänner [...] Nebst einigen feyerlichen koranischen Gebeten [...] mit Anm. und einem Register vers., und auf Verlangen hrsg. von Friedrich Eberhard Boysen*, trans. by Friedrich Eberhard Boysen (Halle: Gebauer, 1773), p. 17.
59 Franz-Xaver Kaufmann, *Religion und Modernität: Sozialwissenschaftliche Perspektiven* (Tübingen: Mohr, 1989), p. 58. For Cusa, Christianity was the legitimate *religio una*.
60 Accounts of Moses' life from antiquity by Josephus and Philo of Alexandria depict Moses as having been initiated into the Egyptian mysteries: see Marsha Keith Schuchard, *Restoring the Temple of Vision: Cabalistic Freemasonry and Stuart Culture* (Leiden: Brill, 2002), p. 15. For Jan Assmann, there is a Mosaic distinction between Egyptian idolatry and Mosaic monotheism. This distinction was reinterpreted as a continuity from Egyptian cosmotheism to Spinozist Christianity. See Jan Assmann, *Moses the Egyptian: The Memory of Egypt in Western Monotheism* (Cambridge, MA: Harvard University Press, 1997), p. 8.
61 Schiller, *Schillers Werke: Nationalausgabe*, XVII: *Historische Schriften, Erster Teil*, ed. by Karl-Heinz Hahn (1970), p. 377.
62 This is also a textual link back to Napoleon, whose role is to reveal the secrets of Isis in 'Buonaparte in Egypten' and explicitly descends into a pyramid in 'Der Franke in Egypten'.

Mahomed, however, embodies a unique position as the last of the prophets in Near Eastern monotheism: the opportunity to purify the true, historical religious practices which only exist in decayed, diminished form. In a parallel to the Qu'ranic account of Abraham, and one which is lacking in the Bible, Mahomed castigates the people of Mekka for their false idolatry. Mahomed explicitly identifies himself as an admirer of Abraham when he admonishes the people of Mekka. This serves two functions. On one level, the identification with Abraham strengthens Mahomed's claim to legitimacy, and endorses Mahomed as an advocate of Abrahamic religion: 'ein höh'rer Geist spricht durch mich zu euch [...], den ihr nicht kennt, der dem Abraham verhieß [...] von dem Gott ist euer Herz gewichen' [a higher spirit speaks through me to you [...] that you do not know, who promised Abraham [...] from that God your heart has slipped away] (*SW* I, 127, ll. 532–39).[63] But this also performs the act of *anamnesis*: Mahomed reminds the people of the true doctrine that they and their ancestors had abandoned in favour of false idol worship; the people's ecstatic response to Mahomed is not only a mark of his rhetorical skill, but how Mahomed has tapped into their collective preconscious religious intuition.

Along with this layering of prophets, Günderrode attempts to resacralise the priest figure in 'Mahomed'. This runs counter to the anticlericalism of the eighteenth century: to Enlightenment intellectuals, priestcraft was associated with a mystificatory approach to Christianity and despotic obscurantism, which rendered the sacred inaccessible to reason.[64] The priesthood met with criticism from Bayle, Mandeville, Voltaire, Helvétius, Holbach, as well as Hume and Hobbes, for having conspired to oppress the general population through maintaining ignorance and superstition.[65] In the tract *Die Religion innerhalb der Grenzen der bloßen Vernunft* [Religion within the Bounds of Bare Reason] (1793), Kant voices suspicion towards the dogmatic political and legal power falsely wielded by the clergy, which is an abuse of power.[66]

An antidote to this strand of anticlericalism can be found in Schiller's account of Moses in *Die Sendung Moses*, which openly culls material from Karl Leonhard Reinhold's Masonic *Die Hebräischen Mysterien oder die älteste religiöse Freymaurerey* [The Hebraic Mysteries or the Oldest Religious Freemasonry] (1788). Schiller presents Mosaic doctrine as a pious fraud and depicts Moses as a political actor who liberates the Hebrew people through this deception: '*seinen wahren Gott auf eine fabelhafte Art zu verkündigen*' [to declare his [Moses's] true God in the manner of a fable].[67] This is a matter of political expediency and self-interest: a means to gain absolute authority over the Hebrew people to lead them to freedom. The true religion of the

---

63 Günderrode, *Poetic Fragments*, p. 180.
64 Jon Mee, 'Millenarian Visions and Utopian Speculations', in *The Enlightenment World*, ed. by Martin Fitzpatrick, Peter Jones, Christa Knellwolf and Iain McCalman (Abingdon: Routledge, 2004), pp. 536–50 (p. 536).
65 John Stroup, *The Struggle for Identity in the Clerical Estate: Northwest German Opposition to Absolutist Policy in the Eighteenth Century* (Leiden: Brill, 1984), p. 44.
66 Immanuel Kant, *Kant's Gesammelte Schriften: Akademieausgabe*, ed. by Königlich-Preussische Akademie der Wissenschaften zu Berlin and others, 29 vols (Berlin: Reimer; De Gruyter, 1900–), I.VI: *Die Religion innerhalb der Grenzen der blossen Vernunft, Die Metaphysik der Sitten*, p. 180.
67 Schiller, *Schillers Werke. Nationalausgabe*, XVII, 392.

Egyptian mysteries is sympathetically portrayed as a kind of pantheistic Spinozism *avant la lettre*. But this true religion is essentially dispiriting for the subjugated Hebrew people, since it rules out a personal God who would favour the Hebrew people above all others. Instead, Moses creates the elaborate, if inventive deception of monotheism, where the Hebrews are the chosen people of God.

While Schiller consistently attacked organised religion, the depiction of Moses shows parallels to Günderrode's 'Mahomed'.[68] *Die Sendung Moses* and 'Mahomed' share the strict vertical hierarchy between the priest, as the mediator of arcane divine knowledge, and the people, as passive recipients of this message. In the context of universal religion in 'Mahomed', this priestly authority is not problematic dogmatism but is, in fact, a necessity — particularly with regard to how God is conceptualised, and Mahomed's specific role as the sole mediator between man and the divine.

The Problem of the Hidden God

If Mahomed's mission is to proclaim the God of Islam, then this runs against the problem of whether and to what extent it is possible to have knowledge about God. It is one of the central tensions of Christianity, and specifically between apophatic and rationalist branches of theology, that God cannot be directly known or perceived, yet dogma insists that God *can* be known.[69] In the Qu'ran, too, God is hidden.[70] But 'Mahomed' also bears the traces of the fallout from Kantian philosophy. Kant, in three critiques, famously contests the three traditional theistic proofs for the existence of God. Additionally, Kant argues for the hiddenness of God on the basis of the limitations of human cognition.[71] In the *Kritik der reinen Vernunft*, Kant elucidates that it cannot be known that a God does not exist beyond spatio-temporal limits.[72] According to Kant, God cannot be grasped conceptually, which in turn triggers the aesthetic problem of giving representation to what is, essentially, beyond representation.[73]

Negotiating the relationship between the unconditioned and the conditioned — or between the finite and the infinite — was also a central pursuit of early Romantic and Idealist philosophy. For Friedrich Heinrich Jacobi, who influenced the Jena Romantics and Idealist philosophers, any knowledge of the absolute or unconditioned remains necessarily mediated, since the finite and infinite are

---

68   Jeffrey L. High, 'Clever Priests and the Missions of Moses and Schiller: From Monotheism to the Aesthetic Civilization of the Individual', in *Religion, Reason, and Culture in the Age of Goethe*, ed. by Elisabeth Krimmer and Patricia Anne Simpson (Rochester, NY: Camden House, 2014), pp. 79–98 (pp. 79–83).
69   Thomas Merrill, *Christian Criticism: A Study of Literary God-talk* (Amsterdam: Rodopi, 1976), p. 41.
70   Ruqayya Yasmine Khan, *Self and Secrecy in Early Islam* (Columbia, SC: University of South Carolina Press, 2008), p. 26.
71   Eric Watkins, 'Kant on the Hiddenness of God', *Kantian Review*, 14.1 (2009), 81–122.
72   Ian Cooper, *The Near and Distant God: Poetry, Idealism and Religious Thought from Hölderlin to Eliot* (London: Legenda, 2008), p. 5.
73   Thums, p. 19.

dependent on each other.⁷⁴ All attempts to explicate the unconditioned remains in the limited, finite realm.

If, following Jacobi's argument, the true nature of the unconditioned remains beyond comprehension, since all human concepts are limited,⁷⁵ then this could lead an *aporia* about the human capacity for knowledge, or at worst disintegrate into radical scepticism about the subjective capacity for empirically reliable knowledge. This is a problem that Günderrode herself grapples with following her studies of Kantian philosophy, as will be seen in Chapter 5. Jacobi is more indebted to the tradition of humility about the kind of knowledge about nature, God, or even humanity, than any individual can discern. This is prevalent not just in Kant and critical philosophy but in Enlightenment thought more generally.⁷⁶ One approach to this co-dependence between the infinite and the finite, and by extension to that between man and God, is to posit a medial figure. This medial figure can indirectly gain access to the unconditioned but is still limited to a finite framework. Both Novalis in 'Blüthenstaub' [Pollen] (1798) and Friedrich Schlegel in 'Ideen' [Ideas] (1800), in their idiosyncratic conception of religion, highlight the need for a mediator between mankind and the divine.

In 'Mahomed', a narrative of religious origins and revival, priestcraft is neutralised. Mahomed is a self-proclaimed priest with exclusive access to divine providence — 'ich bin der Priester, der das Menschliche dem Göttlichen vermählt' [I am the priest who weds the human to the divine] (SW I, 127, ll. 520–21).⁷⁷ It therefore follows that Mahomed has a didactic function: to unlock the sense of true religion within the individual. This falls very much in line with Schleiermacher's advocacy of a medial figure between man and the divine, to awaken the dormant religious impulse in an individual.⁷⁸

The priest figure refers to another — if partially debunked — origin narrative for religion: the Egyptian mysteries and their Hermetic origins. The *Corpus hermeticum*, upon its rediscovery in the Renaissance, was falsely considered, for instance by Marsilio Ficino, to be evidence of the primordial, pre-Mosaic revelation. Isaac Casaubon's famous rebuttal of this claim is often considered to be a foundational moment in the development of philology.⁷⁹ Whilst Casaubon and other critics were

---

74 Manfred Frank and Elizabeth Millán-Zaibert, *The Philosophical Foundations of Early German Romanticism* (Albany: SUNY Press, 2004), p. 57.
75 Jacobi, *Werke: Gesamtausgabe*, I.I, 260.
76 Peter Hanns Reill discusses this tradition of 'epistemological modesty' with regard to Johann Salomo Semler: Peter Hanns Reill, 'Between Theosophy and Orthodox Christianity: Johann Salomo Semler's Hermetic Religion', in *Polemical Encounters: Esoteric Discourse and its Others*, ed. by Olav Hammer and Kocku von Stuckrad, Aries Book Series, 7 (Boston: Brill, 2007), pp. 157–79 (pp. 162–63).
77 Günderrode, *Poetic Fragments*, p. 180.
78 Schleiermacher, *Kritische Gesamtausgabe*, I.XII, 116.
79 Denis J. J. Robichaud, 'Competing Claims on the Legacies of Renaissance Humanism in Histories of Philology', *Erudition and the Republic of Letters*, 3 (2018), 177–222 (p. 184). For an account of Casaubon's debunking of the *Corpus hermeticum*, see Anthony Grafton, *Defenders of the Text: The Traditions of Scholarship in an Age of Science, 1450–1800* (Cambridge, MA: Harvard University Press, 1991), pp. 145–61.

vindicated — the Hermetic sources dated from the Christian era, not beforehand — this did not spell the end of the appeal of the *Corpus hermeticum* and the overarching ancient theology, a tranche of pagan texts that contained vestiges of the true religion.[80] A tradition of Christian Hermeticism that was not dependent on the attribution of antiquity to Hermetic sources persisted, such as in the Cambridge Platonism of the seventeenth century.[81]

The association of the Egyptian mysteries with a form of ancient wisdom and theology could still be made productive in the eighteenth century. The literary trope of the veiled Isis, lifted from Plutarch's description of the temple inscription at Saïs, helped to inspire renewed interest in the mysteries.[82] Recourse to this notion of the veiled Isis acted as one way to express Spinozist sympathies at the end of the eighteenth century,[83] as it involves an equation of the veiled Isis, an anonymous divinity, with the Hebrew Tetragrammaton 'I am who I am': this identification allows Yahweh and the cosmic god, or *deus siva natura*, to become one.[84] A veritable wave of texts made use of this material, including Schiller's poem 'Das verschleierte Bild zu Sais' [The Veiled Image at Sais] (1795), Novalis's *Die Lehrlinge zu Sais*, and even Kant, who, in *Kritik der Urteilskraft* [Critique of Judgment] (1790), quotes Plutarch's inscription from the Temple of Isis at Saïs with admiration.[85]

These mysteries, located at Eleusis and Saïs, foreground the hidden truth of the divine through elaborate initiation rituals into ever more esoteric fields of knowledge, as well as the metaphorical descent into the underworld.[86] Mahomed has in the play glimpsed the hidden core of religion and survived unscathed. In the closing scene of the play, upon Mahomed's triumphant entry into Mekka, the chorus ecstatically praises Mahomed — in terms which recall the tripartite motif of the Saïs temple inscription in Plutarch: 'Du siehst, was wird, was ist, und was gewesen, | Und ahndend sahst du diese große Stunde' [You see what will be, what is, and what has been, | and through intuition you saw the coming of this great hour] (*SW* I, 199, ll. 2643–44).[87] This resonance with Plutarch not only supports Mahomed's legitimacy, but also forms part of a reconstruction of Western religious

---

80 See the seminal study: D. P. Walker, *The Ancient Theology: Studies in Christian Platonism from the Fifteenth to the Eighteenth Century* (London: Duckworth, 1972).
81 Douglas Hedley, 'God and Giants: Cudworth's Platonic Metaphysics and his Ancient Theology', *British Journal of the History of Philosophy*, 25.5 (2017), 932–53 (p. 934).
82 Norbert Klatt, '". . . des Wissens heißer Durst": ein literarischer Beitrag zu Schillers Gedicht "Das verschleierte Bild zu Sais"', *Jahrbuch der deutschen Schillergesellschaft*, 29 (1985), 98–112.
83 Simonis, p. 261.
84 Karl Leonhard Reinhold made this equation, as Jan Assmann has illustrated: Assmann, *Moses the Egyptian*, pp. 120–21.
85 Kant, *Kant's Gesammelte Schriften*, I.V: *Kritik der praktischen Vernunft. Kritik der Urtheilskraft*, p. 316.
86 *Ägyptische Mysterien: Reisen in die Unterwelt in Aufklärung und Romantik*, ed. by Jan Assmann and Florian Ebeling (Munich: Beck, 2011), pp. 7–27.
87 Günderrode, *Poetic Fragments*, p. 298 (translation adapted). Günderrode here alters the order of the tenses given in Plutarch's version. In other texts the inscription is more precisely reproduced. The conception of the religion and the divine as outlined in 'Geschichte eines Braminen' (1804) includes an accurate rendering of the motif: 'Es ist eine unendliche Kraft, ein ewiges Leben, das da Alles ist, was ist, was war und werden wird' [It is an endless force, an eternal life, which is everything that is, that was, and that will be] (*SW* I, 309).

history, by excavating the primal cosmotheism of the Egyptian mysteries and conjoining it with the roots of Western monotheism.[88]

Whilst the invocation of the Egyptian mysteries can help explain the return to a vertical priestly hierarchy, it does little to solve the problem of divining knowledge of God. If sense perception cannot yield any insight into God, then a simple solution to this is to postulate internal sense perception — a form of perception that is not marred by the unreliability of external sense data. It is not that plumbing the inner depths of the self unlocks divine insight, but rather that forms of inner sense perception — which function by analogy with and in contrast to the external senses — offer a more reliable, suprasensory form of perception.

Mahomed receives spontaneous divine revelations through the faculty of 'der innere Sinn', a recurrent theme throughout Günderrode's work, and one which most prominently features in the Socratic dialogue 'Die Manen'.[89] Caught as Mahomed is between the phenomenal world and the divine, this internal, suprasensory perception is fundamental to Mahomed's position as a mediator. Mahomed concisely expresses his 'doppeltes Leben', or 'zweifaches Leben', in the play's opening monologue:

> Das Gestirn der Zwillinge, das auf dieser ganzen Reise mich stets begleitet, auf das ich hoffend stets geblickt, erlischt im Morgenstrahl. Zweifaches Leben floß aus diesem Gestirn auf mich herab, und ein Sinnbild war es mir, meines doppelten Lebens, das mich theilweise an die Erde und die Geschäfte der Welt knüpft, und mich theilweise zu dem Ueberirrdischen und zu seltsamen Offenbarungen führt. Wenn die Gestirne um Mitternacht hoch über meinem Scheitel steh'n, so fallen mit ihren senkrechten Strahlen allerlei wunderliche Lichter in meine Seele, die dann verschwinden, wenn die Sterne vom Sonnenlicht verschlungen werden.
>
> [The star of Gemini, which ever escorts me on this whole journey, to which I ever gazed hopefully, expires in the morning rays. Twofold life flowed down to me from this star, and it was to me a symbol of my double life, that partly joins me to the earth and the affairs of the world, and partly leads me to the unearthly and to strange revelations. When the stars at midnight stand high over my head, then with their vertical rays all sorts of fantastical lights fall into my soul, which then disappear when the stars are devoured by sunlight.] (*SW* I, 111, ll. 30–40)[90]

When engulfed by divine insight, Mahomed is, as in 'Mahomets Traum in der Wüste', paralysed in a state of ecstatic rapture, similar to the *unio mystica*, where Mahomed's physical awareness is suspended: 'es ist ein Zustand der Verzückung, sein äußeres Auge ist todt, aber sein inneres betrachtet die Tiefen der Dinge' [In a state of rapture, his outer eye is dead, but his inner [eye] observes the depths of things] (*SW* I, 155, ll. 1355–56).[91] Mahomed's first experience of 'der innere Sinn' is an immediate, and temporally jarring, glimpse into providence (*SW* I, 116, ll. 194–

---

88 Jan Assmann, *Religio Duplex: How the Enlightenment Reinvented Egyptian Religion*, trans. by Robert Savage (Cambridge: Polity, 2014), p. 15.
89 See Dormann for a study of this concept in Günderrode's work.
90 Günderrode, *Poetic Fragments*, p. 154.
91 Ibid., p. 226.

98). What will become an ecstatic *unio mystica* is, upon the onset of the prophetic gift, unsettling to the point of mental distress.

This distress carries implications for discerning knowledge of what lies beyond the phenomenal world. Mahomed's intellectual and rational attempts to decode the visions prove to be futile, and it is the lack of comprehension which is particularly troubling: 'aber ich wußte sie [die Eingebungen] damals noch nicht zu ordnen und mir zu eigen zu machen, sie beherrschten mich vielmehr und quälten mich' [back then I did not know how to order them [the images] and make them my own; far more they ruled me and plagued me] (*SW* I, 117, ll. 208–10).[92] What underpins this passage is an absolute disjuncture between human and divine truth. When attempting to comprehend divine truth, human reason is liable to error. It therefore requires the intervention of the divine to divest it of this capacity for error. This takes place in an act of revelation — in the sense of stripping away the impurities innate to human cognition.

This is precisely the process that Mahomed undergoes at the hands of the angel. Here Günderrode conflates two vital episodes in Muhammad's biography: the visitation of the angel Gabriel, which constitutes Muhammad's conversion to Islam, and the realisation of his prophetic calling. Günderrode depicts this act of spiritual purging of Mahomed's doubt with a deeply visceral image:

> Da nahm der Engel das Herz aus meiner Brust und drückte es gewaltig, bis ihn ein dunkler Tropfen entquoll, es war die irrdische Angst und der Zweifel; und als er das Herz wieder in meine Brust gefügt hatte, war es mir sehr wohl und leicht, denn die enge Schranke der Sterblichkeit war von mir abgefallen.
>
> [Then the angel took the heart out of my breast and pressed it forcefully, until a dark drop sprung from it: it was earthly fear and doubt; and when he had joined my heart again in my breast, I felt very well and light, for the narrow limit of mortality had fallen away from me.] (*SW* I, 117–18, ll. 241–46)[93]

The pragmatic function of the passage is to remove Mahomed's doubt, so that he can proselytise for the God of Islam. But this passage is also the logical culmination of Mahomed's account of his development as a prophet, and the final obstacle to this is unlocking the divine impetus and meaning behind the visions. The implicit function of this epiphany is therefore that God, whose will is manifest as the angel, furnishes Mahomed with the correct interpretative apparatus to understand the visions. This experience is so profound that it is ineffable. Mahomed cannot fall back on any familiar sensory concepts to relate the experience: 'Der Engel ergriff hierauf meine Hand und führte mich in Räume, die noch kein Auge gesehen, ich vernahm Dinge, die noch kein Ohr gehöret hat' [The angel thereupon gripped my hand and led me in spaces that no eye had yet seen, I heard things that no ear has yet heard.] (*SW* I, 118, ll. 246–48).[94] Mahomed may finally be able to grasp the visions, but the divine still remains beyond the limits of human conceptualisation.

This problem of determining divine knowledge even finds embodiment in

---

92 Ibid., p. 162.
93 Ibid., p. 164 (translation adapted).
94 Ibid. See Isaiah 64. 4.

Mahomed himself. Mahomed, too, is rendered essentially unknowable. Redefining the prophet as a humanised enthusiast is problematic: it describes a protagonist whose agency is displaced, since all his actions are ostensibly manifestations of divine will. This is complicated by the question of Mahomed's own will. Mahomed abandons all human consideration and thought for resignation and faith in God's will. In both his religious function and political agency, therefore, Mahomed's actions are potentially unintelligible to both acolytes and political and religious adversaries alike.

Mahomed's response to divine will is concisely formulated in the angel's tripartite maxim: 'siehe! glaube! thue!' [see! believe! act!] (*SW* I, 117, l. 239).[95] This signifies a return to a faith-based, revealed religion. The core through which religiosity, faith, and Mahomed's mission is channelled is feeling: 'Er thut, wie der Moment ihm eingegeben, | Und Gottes Wille ist ihm sein Gefühl' [He does as the moment prompts him | And God's will is to him his feeling] (*SW* I, 136, ll. 802–03).[96] Mahomed's religiosity is therefore rooted in emotion-based intuition. Whilst this marks a continuation of Günderrode's language from 'Hildgund' and 'Nikator', the religious inflection here brings Mahomed close to being a manifestation of the kind of religion of feeling, or *Gefühlsreligion*, propounded not only by Schleiermacher but also by Jacobi. Jacobi's theological agenda places primacy on an expansive and tenuous concept of faith,[97] and on revelation. It is the act of absolute obedience and faith that allows Mahomed to act. Günderrode's reliance on revelation is part and parcel of the overarching narrative of religious origins. As Lessing argues in *Die Erziehung des Menschengeschlechts* [The Education of Humankind] (1780), in a curious dialectic between reason and revelation, divine revelation stands at the earliest phase of religious formation and fulfils an essentially didactic function in spurring on human development.[98] Mahomed becomes, therefore, the literary embodiment of this primordial, historical revelation.

Günderrode reduces Mahomed's prophetic gift to circumvent the latent problem that prophet characters in drama may have the benefit of complete foresight. The visions do not allow Mahomed to entirely perceive the preordained course of events. When the visions are genuinely prophetic, it is only to a limited degree: 'aber oft fand ich zwischen ihnen und den Begebenheiten der folgenden Tage einen dunklen Zusammenhang' [but often I found between them and the incidents of the following days a dark connection] (*SW* I, 116, ll. 205–06).[99] The insights Mahomed receives into providence are also spontaneous and restricted to the immediate moment: 'In jedem Augenblicke Gottes Willen erspähen, ihn in den Begebenheiten und dem, was man Zufälle nennt, lesen, das ist meine Weisheit' [In each moment

---

95 Ibid.
96 Ibid., p. 196.
97 See Beiser, *The Fate of Reason*, pp. 89–91, for a discussion of the philosophical problems associated with Jacobi's concept of faith.
98 Gotthold Ephraim Lessing, *Werke und Briefe in zwölf Bänden*, ed. by Wilfried Barner and others, 12 vols (Frankfurt a.M.: Deutscher Klassiker Verlag, 1985–2003), x: *Werke 1778–1781*, ed. by Arno Schilson and Axel Schmitt (2001), 73–99 (p. 75).
99 Günderrode, *Poetic Fragments*, p. 162.

to espy God's will, to read him in the incidents and in that which one calls chance, that is my wisdom] (*SW* I, 161, ll. 1556–59).¹⁰⁰

But these insights are problematic, since they demand total resignation to the promptings of divine providence. Therefore Mahomed cannot formulate any independent plan for his prophesied conquest of Arabia. As a result, his agency as a political figure becomes displaced: 'ich habe nicht mit irrdischer Klugheit einen Plan für die ferne Zukunft ersonnen und jeden Umstand bedacht, der kommen könnte' [I have not with earthly cleverness devised a plan for the far future and considered each circumstance that could come] (*SW* I, 161, ll. 1554–56);¹⁰¹ 'Ich habe sie [die That] gar nicht bedacht, sie ist über mich gekommen; über den Zeiten hat sie geschwebt wie eine Wolke über der Erde, nun aber ist sie reif geworden und träufelt wie Himmelsthau auf mich herab' [I have not considered it [the deed] at all; it came over me; it hovered over the times like a cloud over the earth, but now it has become ripe and trickles down over me like heaven's dew] (*SW* I, 125, ll. 471–74).¹⁰² Mahomed's will, or so he claims, becomes entirely sublimated by divine will: 'werdet ihr denn nie begreifen, daß von meinem Wollen gar nicht die Rede ist?' [will you never grasp that it is not at all a matter of my will?] (*SW* I, 126, ll. 491–92).¹⁰³ Abject submission to divine will is at the core of Islamic teaching: the double etymological meaning of Islam refers to the peace derived from the individual's complete surrender to providence.¹⁰⁴

There is, however, a more pragmatic, politically shrewd element to this rhetoric. By declaring himself the mouthpiece of God and appealing to a higher authority which cannot be accessed, Mahomed both justifies his actions and renders himself partially immune to his adversaries' attempts to discredit him. This is why, in the judgement scene before Habib, the last and most significant of the scenes which test Mahomed's legitimacy as a prophet, Mahomed claims: 'Gott spricht durch meinen Mund, der Sprecher Gottes kann nicht irren' [God speaks through my mouth, the speaker of God cannot err] (*SW* I, 180, ll. 2096–98).¹⁰⁵

Politically shrewd this may be, it has the effect of alienating Mahomed from his followers. Omar, who is gradually drawn to Islam upon hearing the recitation of a verse of the Qu'ran, is sceptical about Mahomed's spontaneous prophecies and his absolute resignation to God's plan. For a political, religious and military leader, it runs counter to prudence not to formulate plans: 'Es ist eine frevelhafte Verwegenheit in dieser Art zu handeln' [It is outrageous audacity to act in this way] (*SW* I, 162, ll. 1572–73).¹⁰⁶ Abu-Taleb, Mahomed's uncle, decries Mahomed's single-minded adherence to pursuing a religious cause as foolhardy obstinacy. Abu-Taleb also laments his feeling of emotional betrayal on account of Mahomed's — to

---

100 Ibid., p. 236 (translation adapted).
101 Ibid.
102 Ibid., p. 178.
103 Ibid.
104 S. A. Nigosian, *Islam: Its History, Teaching, and Practices* (Bloomington: Indiana University Press, 2004), p. xv.
105 Günderrode, *Poetic Fragments*, p. 266.
106 Ibid., p. 238.

Abu-Taleb's mind — false elevation of his mission:

> du zerreißest alle Bande der Menschheit, trittst aus ihrem Verein, um dich auf eine Höhe zu stellen, wo keine Freundschaft, keine Liebe dich erreichen kann, wirst ein Fremdling unter den deinen, verlassen bin ich nun, abgerissen von dir, das ist der Lohn meiner Liebe.
>
> [you tear apart all bands of humanity, leave their society, in order to set yourself on a height where no friendship, no love can reach you, become a stranger among your own. I am now abandoned, torn away from you: that is the reward of my love.] (*SW* I, 126, ll. 497–501)[107]

The problem, therefore, of Mahomed's self-imposed estrangement from others is that their loyalty is not free from self-interest. It has to be based on some degree of reciprocity, which Mahomed cannot provide since he disavows political and earthly endeavours: 'nur meine Füße wandeln auf Erden, mein Haupt berührt die Himmel, seht in diesem Sinne ist alles Irrdische mir sehr gering' [Only my feet wander on earth; my head touches the heavens. See, in this sense everything earthly is very narrow to me] (ibid., ll. 505–07).[108]

Whilst Mahomed can yield to divine will, the legitimacy of his own authority as a human prophet is not beyond question. Variations of the elusive phrase 'was mir zu sagen noch übrig bleibt, wirst du und ganz Mekka von mir hören, wann die Stunde gekommen ist, bis dahin schweige und gehorche' [what remains for me to say you and all Mecca will hear from me when the hour has come; until then be silent and obey] (*SW* I, 118, ll. 249–50)[109] run as a leitmotif throughout the play. Yet this demand for absolute loyalty cannot be met. Even Mahomed's most enthusiastic admirer, Halima, who falls in love with the prophet, is thrown into disarray when she believes that Mahomed wishes to sacrifice her to further his mission. Halima is torn between loyalty to the Muslim cause and the horror that Mahomed's bloated ambition amounts to succeeding at any human cost: 'Er will nur herrschen, mag auch die Welt darüber zu Grunde gehen, das kümmert ihn nicht. — O Himmel, verzeih, daß ich den Propheten lästere!' [He only wants to rule, may the world perish over it, that does not concern him. — Oh heaven! forgive that I blaspheme the prophet] (*SW* I, 187, ll. 2295–97).[110] Halima's analysis indicates a problem in Mahomed's claim to religious legitimacy. In her emotional turmoil, Halima does not recognise Mahomed as the conduit of divine will, but rather can only perceive what she believes to be Mahomed's total self-interest.

The question this raises is to what extent Mahomed makes use of dissimulation when he claims that his will is entirely sublimated in that of God. To be sure, Mahomed is an agent of divine providence. But this does not preclude Mahomed from acting out of self-interest. Indeed, given Mahomed's limited prophetic gift, his professed desire not to fight alongside his forces to take Mekka appears motivated by self-interest — especially when it is preceded by a rousing speech urging his

---

107 Ibid., p. 178.
108 Ibid., pp. 178–80.
109 Ibid., p. 164.
110 Ibid., p. 278.

men into combat, since they lack his absolute conviction (*SW* I, 191, ll. 2392–2402): 'Ich begleite euch nicht, denn ich will nicht mit dem Schwerdt in der Hand die heilige Mekka betreten, mich soll nicht das Gewinsel der Sterbenden empfangen, friedlich will ich einziehen, so geziemet mirs' [I will not accompany you, for I will not enter the holy Mecca with my sword in my hand, the whimpering of the dying shall not receive me, I want to move in peacefully, that befits me] (*SW* I, 191–92, ll. 2417–20).[111] This does come to pass: Mahomed enters Mekka as a prince of peace. But unless Mahomed is withholding prescient information from his followers about Mekka's peaceful surrender, this passage remains morally dubious. Mahomed refrains from participating in the offensive, whitewashes the potential suffering it will cause, and indulges in conscious self-deception by feigning that the action is not a military or violent campaign. In particular, the casual and impersonal mode of 'so geziemet mirs' points to Mahomed's cynical self-stylisation as a bringer of peace.

This question of whether Mahomed's will remains sublimated in order to embrace divine providence is, however, never fully resolved. Nor does it resolve the question of how Mahomed establishes his irrefutable legitimacy as the one true prophet. What lies beyond doubt is Mahomed's remarkable capacity to induce enthusiasm in others for the true religion. At the very least, Mahomed's rhetorical skill and eloquence as an orator dispel any doubt about his calling:

> Wenn ich an jenen Tag zurückdenke, an dem er [...] den ungeheuren Einfall hatte, Arabien zu erobern, mein Geist widerstrebte damals diesen abenteuerlichen Gedanken, aber seine Beredtsamkeit hielt meine Zweifel gefangen
>
> [If I think back to that day when he [...] had the monstrous idea to conquer Arabia, my spirit then resisted this adventurous thought, but his eloquence held my doubts captive] (*SW* I, 189, ll. 2348–52)[112]

This is more than specious sophistry. Adopting the topos of *humilitas*, Mahomed professes: 'nicht versteh ich der Rede Künste noch Schmeichelei, die die Herzen gewinnt, wie der Geist mir gebietet, so thue ich' [I do not understand the arts of speech nor flattery that wins hearts; as the spirit commands so I do] (*SW* I, 127, ll. 533–35).[113] Mahomed's rhetoric is therefore a form of a expressivism, one of the only means to make otherwise hidden religious truths perceived in the depths of the self manifest.[114] Classical rhetorical practice determines that the speaker can only arouse emotions in the audience if the speaker is possessed by those very emotions.[115] Mahomed generates his own enthusiasm by instilling in himself the absolute conviction that the people of Mekka will be receptive to his religious message (*SW* I, 127, ll. 514–21). The effect that Mahomed, as the enthused orator, exerts on the people of Mekka is rapturous: the inspired crowd follows him from the scene (*SW* I, 130, ll. 623), an event which is partially repeated following Mahomed's interrogation by the elders of Mekka (*SW* I, 141, l. 953). Even when Mahomed does

---

111 Ibid., p. 284.
112 Günderrode, *Poetic Fragments*, pp. 280–82.
113 Ibid., p. 180.
114 Taylor, *Sources of the Self*, p. 374.
115 Brian Vickers, *In Defence of Rhetoric* (Oxford: Clarendon Press, 1988), p. 75.

not assume the public role of the orator, an innate germ of religious enthusiasm remains within his speech. Halima is converted to Mahomed's Islamic doctrine by eavesdropping on Mahomed's private conversations (*SW* I, 149, ll. 1189–92). Halima intuitively identifies 'die göttlichen Wahrheiten' [the divine truths] (*SW* I, 149, l. 1190) in Mahomed's speech.

Religion in 'Mahomed'

But what is this doctrine that Mahomed is charged with propagating? The core of religion in the play has been identified as pantheism, specifically Spinozist pantheism.[116] This is, however, both a misleading and an imprecise definition. To be sure, Günderrode draws on the association of Islam with natural religion, whereby nature and God become one and the same — an association that pervaded the contemporary understanding of Islam.[117] When Mahomed himself declares the terms of the *shahada*, the Muslim declaration of faith and allegiance to the one Prophet and God, it assumes startling monist form: 'Es ist ein einziger Gott, in dem Himmel und Erde und alle Dinge sind, und Mahomed ist sein Prophet' [There is a single God, in whom heaven and earth and all things are, and Muhammad is his prophet] (*SW* I, 133, ll. 692–94).[118] The expansion is clear: all aspects of creation are subsumed into the divine — thus corresponding to the Spinozist tenet of *deus sive natura*.

Günderrode's 'Mahomed' draws on both Leibniz-Wolffian optimism in addition to Herder's mediating forces for the reading of religion in 'Mahomed'. From these elements Günderrode crafts an eclectic panentheism. At the core of Mahomed's teaching is that the divine is the active and dynamic life principle: 'Taub blieben jene falschen Götter. Wo keine That ist, da ist keine Kraft, wo keine Wirkung ist, da fehlt das Wirkende' [Deaf remained those false gods. Where there is no deed, there is no force, and where there is no effect, then there is no agent at work behind

---

116 Lazarowicz, pp. 153–54; Lucia Maria Licher even reads religion in the play as a proxy for Schelling's identity philosophy and *Naturphilosophie*: see Licher, p. 172.
117 Katharina Mommsen (p. 183) notes: 'Nie verschmelzen im Islam Gott und Natur miteinander wie in Spinozas *divina natura* [...] Schöpfer und Schöpfung bleiben im Islam wie im mosaisch-christlichen Monotheismus stets voneinander getrennt' [In Islam, God and nature never merge with one another as they do in Spinoza's *divina natura* [...] In Islam as in the monotheism of Moses and Christianity, creator and creation remain separate from one another at all times].
118 Günderrode, *Poetic Fragments*, p. 190. A productive point of comparison here is the extant manuscript version of the play. The manuscript offers an orthodox reading of Islamic monotheism. When Mahomed castigates the people of Mekka for their idol worship, their crime is misguided veneration of creation, rather than of the Creator: 'da ihr das einzlne, das Geschöpf, zu eurem Gott e(r-)hobt verlohret ihr das ewige Leben im Ganzen' [since you elevated the individual or what has been created as your God, so you have wholly lost eternal life] (*SW* II, 100, ll. 35–36). In the published version of the play, Günderrode breaks with this monotheism. The people of Mekka denigrate God by idolising individual parts of the divine and thus subdivide the divine totality: 'Und diesen Gott habt ihr verlassen? habt ihn zersplittert in eure Götzen, Feuer, Sonne, Mond und Thiere? [...] Da ihr seine Glieder anbetetet, da entwich sein Geist von euch' [And you abandoned this God? You fragmented Him in your idols, in fire, sun, moon, and animals? [...] Since you worshipped his limbs, so did His Spirit flee from you] (*SW* I, 128, ll. 553–56).

it] (*SW* I, 115, ll. 161–63).[119] It is God from which all flows, and is the source from which all emanates: 'Er ist ein Gott des Lebens, sein ewiges Seyn strömt in frischen Quellen durch den ganzen Weltkreis, durch alle Räume und alle Himmel' [He is a God of life, his eternal being streams in fresh wellsprings through the whole circle of the world, through all spaces and all heavens] (*SW* I, 128, ll. 551–52).[120] The core principle of Mahomed's teaching, therefore, is indebted to Herder's vitalist reading of Spinoza.

This also marks a turn towards the philosophy of nature, where nature is the external manifestation from which divine will and action can be discerned. Here lurks the danger of conflating nature and the divine. In 'Mahomed', there is a firm distinction between *natura naturans* and *natura naturata*. This distinction lies at the heart of Mahomed's impassioned castigation of the people of Mekka. Whilst Mahomed promotes a distinctly Protestant iconoclasm, he also identifies the grave error of idol worship as the veneration of *natura naturata*, the moribund products of divine activity:

> Da ihr seine Glieder anbetetet, da entwich sein Geist von euch, darum ist seine Kraft in euch erloschen, darum seyd ihr versunken in dumpfe Thierheit, gefangen in der Zeit, und habt kein ewiges Leben, keinen Himmel und keine Seligkeit; darum habt ihr keine Thatkraft, weil nur Leben ausgeht vom Leben, eure Götzen aber sind todt, ohne Wirkung, ohne Heil für euch
>
> [Since you worshipped His limbs, so did His spirit escape from you, for that reason His power in you is extinguished, for that reason you have descended into dull animality, imprisoned in time, and have no eternal life, no heaven and no blessedness; that is why you have no vitality, for life only emanates from life but your idols are dead, without effect, without salvation for you] (*SW* I, 128, ll. 555–61)[121]

Mahomed's polemical vision of idol worship is bleak: it is tantamount to being entrapped in transient materiality, which both rejects and reveals an underlying anxiety about the radical, atheist materialism of the mid-eighteenth century. Worship of *natura naturans* not only offers the possibility for salvation, but it equally leads to a radical form of human agency and autonomy which is wholly dependent on a transcendent referent ('darum habt ihr keine Thatkraft'), since human agency acts by analogy with infinite divine productivity.

Identifying the divine with infinite productivity leads to the question of religion as a whole in the play. The central image for the divine is lyrically biological, the majestic tree of life, an image perhaps influenced by Herder's *Gott. Einige Gespräche*:[122] 'da verwandelte er sich plötzlich in einen Baum, der hinaufreichte bis an den Mond,

---

119 Günderrode, *Poetic Fragments*, p. 160 (translation adapted).
120 Ibid., p. 182.
121 Ibid., p. 182 (translation adapted).
122 Herder described God as 'Gott, die ewige Wurzel vom unermeßlichen Baum des Lebens, der durch das Weltall verschlungen ist: Er die unendliche Quelle des Daseyns, des größesten Geschenks, das nur Er mitteilen konnte' [God, the eternal root of the endless tree of life, which is entwined through the cosmos: He is the eternal source of being, that greatest of gifts, that He could impart], in Herder, *Werke in zehn Bänden*, IV, 770.

er überschattete die ganze Ebne und Völker und unermeßliche Reiche bargen sich unter seinen Zweigen' [there it transformed itself suddenly into a tree which reached up to the moon, it overshadowed the whole plain, and peoples and immeasurable realms harboured themselves under its branches] (*SW* I, 117, ll. 236–39).[123] This is clearly a poetic vision of an all-encompassing divine force, immanent within the world and one that gives rise to life. At the same time, Günderrode retains elements of salvation history. The doctrine of eternal life jettisons the material imperfections of the body for an aethereal body that encases the soul: 'so steigt [die Seele des Frommen] in den Raum der Gestirne und bildet sich einen Körper aus Luft' [it climbs aloft [the soul of the pious person] in the space of the stars and creates itself a body out of air] (*SW* I, 139, ll. 900–02).[124] Transcendence is also integral to Mahomed's visions, where the compressed intensity of his experience extends beyond the spatial and temporal bounds of the phenomenal world: 'Ich habe, seit ich von dir entfernt war, mehr denn hundert Jahre verlebt, denn ich war nicht in der Zeit, nein! über ihr, und sah, wie sie in ihren Strudeln das sterbliche Geschlecht dahin reißt' [While I was away from you I spent more than a hundred years, for I was not within time, no! over it, and saw how it drags the mortal race along in its whirl] (*SW* I, 114, ll. 117–20).[125] What emerges, therefore, is a panentheistic conflation of transcendence and immanence,[126] one that eliminates mechanistic explanations for the universe through Spinozist dynamism, avoids slipping into radical materialism, and moves away from the radically transcendent creator God, the quintessential *deus absconditus*, of deism.

But are these theoretical distinctions any more than dry, metaphysical ruminations? This harmonising, holistic and lyrical model in 'Mahomed' carries greater significance for how man is conceptualised. Religion does not denote mere theological concerns devoid of political implications: indeed, the two interpenetrate in 'Mahomed'. If religion was commonly understood in the eighteenth century as an anthropomorphic projection,[127] then it follows that it is also the medium for which questions are articulated about the position of man in relation to the world. Johann Joachim Spalding's influential *Betrachtung über die Bestimmung des Menschen* illustrates this point.[128] Through this salvation history, Günderrode attempts to salvage concepts in the play through Mahomed, the mouthpiece of divine truth.

---

123 Günderrode, *Poetic Fragments*, p. 164.
124 Ibid., p. 200.
125 Ibid., p. 158.
126 Transcendence and immanence are not mutually exclusive — it is transience which would contradict transcendence.
127 T. J. Reed, *Light in Germany: Scenes from an Unknown Enlightenment* (Chicago: University of Chicago Press, 2015), p. 97.
128 The question of 'Bestimmung des Menschen' became, in Norbert Hinske's words, a 'Standardformel' for the second half of the eighteenth century. See Norbert Hinske, 'Das stillschweigende Gespräch: Prinzipien der Anthropologie und Geschichtsphilosophie bei Mendelssohn und Kant', in *Moses Mendelssohn und die Kreise seiner Wirksamkeit*, ed. by Michael Albrecht and others, Wolfenbütteler Studien zur Aufklärung, 19 (Tübingen: Niemeyer, 1994), pp. 135–56 (p. 141).

Firstly, Günderrode attempts to resurrect human progress: the concept of divine productivity reinvigorates teleology and the Enlightenment optimism in an open-ended, provisional form of human progress. This finds expression not only in the salvatory doctrine of eternal life. Mahomed, the embodiment of providential will, does establish a new political order, but the play culminates in a moment of prolepsis. The prayer of thanks to Allah (*SW* I, 200, ll. 2647–57) both demarcates a moment of triumphant political victory — the surrender of Mekka — and the direct invocation of the divine, which points to the religious work still to be done. At its core, this is a doctrine of hope, which is exposed in one of the final choral odes. For the chorus, perceiving the fulfilment of long-held hopes is paradoxically disheartening:

> Seh' ich das Ziel nun
> Meines Beginnens,
> Muthigen Strebens
> Ende vor mir. —
> Jegliches Ende
> Schrecket die Seele,
> Scheucht des Gedankens
> Ringen und Streben
> Rückwärts. [...]
> Endlichkeit redet
> Wehmuth zum Herzen,
> Lähmet das Leben
> Muthiger Lust.
>
> [I see the goal now
> Of my endeavours,
> Brave striving's
> End before me. —
> Any ending
> Frightens the soul,
> Shoos the mind's
> Wrestling and striving
> Backward. [...]
> Finitude speaks
> Woe to the heart,
> Lames life's
> Brave desire.] (*SW* I, 195–96, ll. 2526–40)[129]

Perceiving a definite endpoint of hope threatens to nullify hope entirely, and indeed the vigorous drive to fulfil that hope ('Lähmet das Leben | Muthiger Lust'), not just to the point of inertia but to despair ('Endlichkeit redet | Wehmuth zum Herzen'). The shock that the chorus undergo is linked with their conception of hope. Before this final, disillusioning awakening, the chorus had engaged in an act of conscious self-deception, keeping hope alive by keeping the moment of fulfilment out of sight. Whilst all hope is transient, it becomes animated only when it is provisional.

---

129 Günderrode, *Poetic Fragments*, p. 292 (translation adapted).

In 'Mahomed', Günderrode restores religious belief as a prism through which to apprehend the world and holds the transcendent and immanent realms in a delicate, co-dependent balance. This organic cohesion of the phenomenal and noumenal realms does raise the question of the status of the individual. For the kind of immanent dispossession that Mahomed undergoes, the self-emptying — or in Christological terms, *kenosis* — in order to be inhabited by divine will is more than the ambiguous sublimation of individual will. It is a radical critique of individual autonomy.

In the presence of an immanent and transcendent God, Mahomed submits so that his will coincides with that of God:

> Ist nicht Gott der Urborn alles Wissens und aller Erkenntniß? Und ist es nicht höhere Weisheit, sich seinen Fügungen hingeben, als sich von ihm losreißen und seinen eignen Plan haben wollen, der vielleicht dem Willen Gottes zuwider ist?
>
> [Is not God the original spring of all knowledge and all cognition? And is it not highest wisdom to abandon oneself to his providence than to rip oneself free of him and want to have a plan of one's own that is perhaps contrary to the will of God?] (*SW* I, 162, ll. 1574–78)[130]

What underpins this assertion of submission is an essential optimism in the benevolence and omniscience of God: that God's will is in all things and determines the chain of causation. It follows, then, that any agency that deviates from this surrender to divine will is hubristic and misguided. When taken by surprise at the appearance of the Emir Habib, Mahomed allays a surge of anxiety by reaffirming his belief in divine benevolence: 'O Himmel! Welche Gefahr umgiebt mich? Doch stille, meine Seele! es muß ja Rettung kommen' [Oh heaven! what danger surrounds me? But silence, my soul! certainly rescue must come] (*SW* I, 171, ll. 1831–32).[131] Here, the omnipresence of the divine renders the philosophical or ethical question of free will null and void. What emerges, instead, is religious determinism that functions along Spinozist lines: for Spinoza, the core of religion is absolute submission to God.[132]

This form of autonomy leads to one further way in which Günderrode draws immanence and transcendence together and re-evaluates the distinction between the sacred and the secular. Mahomed occupies an exceptional position among prophets precisely because he combines spectacularly successful political and religious action. Yet in Goethe's planned but unfinished *Mahomet* play, the worldly and the religious would have been treated as discrete entities. The principal tension in Goethe's play would have been that Mahomet's self-created religious conviction — Mahomet's yearning, hymnic invocation of a divine, transcendent force functions as an act of self-conversion[133] — recedes before worldly corruption:

---

130 Ibid., p. 238.
131 Ibid., p. 252.
132 This has parallels with Madame Guyon's notorious theology of self-annihilation in addition to Schleiermacher's notion of 'schlechthinnige Abhängigkeit' [total subjection] to God: see Charly Coleman, 'Resacralizing the World: The Fate of Secularization in Enlightenment Historiography', *The Journal of Modern History*, 82.2 (2010), 368–95 (p. 388).
133 Goethe describes this act of self-conversion as 'Nachdem sich also Mahomet selbst bekehrt'

'Das Irdische wächst und breitet sich aus, das Göttliche tritt zurück und wird getrübt' [the earthly element grows and spreads, the divine element retreats and becomes obscured].¹³⁴ Although Mahomet would have eventually been ennobled in the final act, the intended targets of Goethe's *Mahomet*, so Goethe himself claims, were Johann Caspar Lavater and Johann Bernhard Basedow, who misused religious claims as a means to pursue more mundane and self-serving ends.¹³⁵ Günderrode herself operates within this binary between religious fervour and secular interests in a more critical approach towards Mahomed in 'Geschichte eines Braminen', where the narrator, Almor, traces the corruption of Mahomed's original religious inspiration: '[ich] sah endlich, wie Ehrgeiz, eine zügellose Einbildungskraft, und die Gewalt der Umstände ihn verführt hatten, unheilige Mittel und Zwecke mit dem Heiligen zu verbinden' [I finally saw how ambition, unrestrained imagination, and the power of circumstance seduced him to fuse unholy means and ends with what is sacred] (*SW* I, 309).

Günderrode's 'Mahomed', however, synthesises the sacred and the secular. This marks a move away from a fundamentally Christian binary, for, as Anthony Pagden observes, 'Christ has specifically repudiated any link between the secular and the sacred, as had generations of Christian theologians.'¹³⁶ To be sure, Mahomed necessarily inflates the religious aspect of his mission — 'Doch das alles ist nun anders, ein Höheres liegt mir ob und andere Sorgen' [But all that is different now. Something higher rests on me, and other worries] (*SW* I, 113, ll. 105–06).¹³⁷ This becomes qualified following Mahomed's realisation that physical conflict is a pragmatic necessity to propagate his doctrine: 'Dem irrdischen Trotz müssen wir eine irrdische Gewalt entgegensetzen' [To earthly defiance we must oppose an earthly force] (*SW* I, 157, ll. 1425–26).¹³⁸ Indeed, this realisation falls at the midpoint of the play and forms the nexus for Mahomed's dual missions: the secular, as foretold in the prophecy of Mahomed's conquest of Arabia by the Christian monk Bahira at Bosra (*SW* I, 116, ll. 180–86)¹³⁹ is henceforth combined with the sacred, the dissemination of his religious doctrine.

Günderrode delineates this attempt at synthesising the sacred and the secular in Mahomed's allegory of the three founder prophets of Western monotheisms. Christ fulfils a purpose in redeeming mankind: to preserve the transcendent realm for man's salvation: 'Aber der Gott gebot, da erwuchs ihm ein Sohn, der hatte nur ein Auge, da er immer gen Himmel richtete und die Erde nicht sehen konnte' [But

[After Muhammad has converted himself in this way], in Goethe, *Sämtliche Werke, Briefe, Tagebücher und Gespräche*, I.14: *Aus meinem Leben. Dichtung und Wahrheit*, ed. by Klaus-Detlef Müller (1986), p. 686.
134 Ibid.
135 Ibid., p. 685.
136 Anthony Pagden, 'The Immobility of China: Orientalism and Occidentalism in the Enlightenment', in *The Anthropology of the Enlightenment*, ed. by Marco Cipollini and Larry Wolff (Stanford: Stanford University Press, 2007), pp. 50–64 (p. 63).
137 Günderrode, *Poetic Fragments*, p. 158.
138 Ibid., p. 230.
139 In Muslim tradition, this is one of the non-Muslim affirmations of Muhammad's exalted status. See Kecia Ali, *The Lives of Muhammad* (Cambridge, MA: Harvard University Press, 2014), p. 42.

God commanded, there arose to him a son who had only one eye, which he always directed toward heaven and which could not see the earth] (*SW* I, 138, ll. 845–47).[140] The allegory implies a teleological development from Christ to Mahomed:

> Und Gott gebot abermals, da erwuchs dem Greise noch ein Sohn, der ist groß und stark, er hat zwei Augen, das eine richtet er gen Himmel, das andere zur Erde [...] in der einen Hand trägt er ein Buch, in der andern ein Schwerdt
>
> [And again God commanded, there arose to the old man another son, who is great and strong, he has two eyes, the one he directs toward heaven, the other to earth [...] in the one hand he carries a book, in the other a sword] (*SW* I, 138, ll. 851–56)[141]

What Mahomed therefore represents is more than a revolutionary political leader.[142] He embodies the process of embedding religion within a series of secular ethical, legal, and indeed military codes.[143] Religion does not enjoy rarefied status divorced from these spheres. Rather, it includes an engaged form of constant, invigorated agency — hence the maxim of 'siehe! glaube! thue!' [see! believe! act!]. This agency operates in the individual by analogy with infinite divine productivity — the animating force of the cosmos. On one level, this operates as the self-realisation of divine providence: 'Herr, überall war das heilige Wort des Koran lebendig in That und Wirkung' [Lord, everywhere the holy word of the Quran was living in deed and effect] (*SW* I, 184, ll. 2216–17).[144] The proleptic prayer that ends the play encapsulates this marriage of sacred and secular interests: Mahomed envisages the total expansion of this universal religion to enclose the western Mediterranean and the Far East (*SW* I, 200, ll. 2652–55).

With this ending, 'Mahomed' bears parallels with the dramatic non-closure of 'Nikator' and 'Hildgund'. In the case of 'Mahomed', the marriage of the sacred and secular is, at best, uneasy, and there is a certain logical pragmatism to the narrative stopping short. If the institutionalisation and factionalism are, to a degree, inevitable and problematic, then Günderrode eliminates a known historical problem in the development of religion by not portraying the development of Islam. Instead, what remains preserved as an ideal in 'Mahomed', is religion in its pure, prelapsarian state, yet to be realised or established as a social or political institution. Mahomed's unbridled agency — like Bonaparte in 'Buonaparte in Egypten' — heralds a new age that resists textual realisation, an age that can only manifest itself in anticipation, never in actuality.

---

140 Günderrode, *Poetic Fragments*, p. 198.
141 Ibid.
142 See Nina Berman's reading of 'Mahomed', in Nina Berman, *German Literature on the Middle East: Discourses and Practices, 1000–1989* (Ann Arbor: University of Michigan Press, 2011), p. 183.
143 'Buch' refers to the Qu'ran as both a religious text and as the basis for Islamic law.
144 Günderrode, *Poetic Fragments*, p. 274.

'Geschichte eines Braminen': Spinozist Panentheism and the *vita contemplativa*

The prolepsis and non-closure that 'Mahomed' ends with rests on ambivalences about the efficacy of revolutionary agency — here, with an expressly religious purpose. Mahomed's displaced but vigorous agency can also not be brought to a halt. Mahomed embodies, in this sense, a *vita activa*. There is a companion text to 'Mahomed' that probes the metaphysical aspects of Spinozist panentheism and helps to clarify the function of this panentheism.[145] It also pulls in a different direction on the topic of human agency. As opposed to Mahomed's displaced agency, necessarily brought about by *kenosis*, the prose text 'Geschichte eines Braminen' presents a narrative of self-determination in the form of a *vita contemplativa*. Written by the middle of 1804 and published in 1805 in Sophie von La Roche's journal *Herbsttage* [Autumn Days],[146] it is a confessional narrative that charts the personal development of its narrator Almor. Almor is an embodiment of the intermingling of Occident and Orient: half-French, born in Smyrna, he was raised a Muslim in a historically Christian family. The narrative is told retrospectively: Almor leaves Smyrna for an unspecified major city in Europe at fourteen to stay with his father's business partner, associates with louche young men, and indulges in women and the theatre. Through self-reflection, Almor discovers an inner, moral world, and is moved to leave Europe for the Persian Gulf, and then travels towards Tibet, follows the course of the Ganges to the Bay of Bengal, before meeting a wise brahmin just outside Delhi. The brahmin tells Almor of the truths of religion, palingenesis, and metempsychosis, and Almor is initiated into the brahmin caste. Upon the old brahmin's death, Almor assumes responsibility for his young daughter, Lasida, and resides, he claims, peacefully within the brahmin's hut.

Before attending to the text itself, it is important to consider its narrative precursors. The vocabulary of 'Geschichte eines Braminen' draws on Günderrode's autodidactic studies. It contains Günderrode's only reference to Herder's notion of 'Humanität', the descriptions of the nature of religion draw on Günderrode's studies of Schleiermacher's *Reden über die Religion: Reden an die Gebildeten unter ihren Verächtern* [Speeches on Religion: Speeches to its Cultured Despisers] (1799) and *Monologen* [Monologues] (1800).[147] Yet there is an important and hitherto unacknowledged intertext for 'Geschichte eines Braminen': Johann Joachim Spalding's *Betrachtung über die Bestimmung des Menschen*. Spalding's tract, which went through

---

145 There is a textual suggestion that the texts were composed at a similar time: the biological metaphor used to describe Mahomed's mission in both texts is almost identical: in 'Mahomed': 'Wir haben einen köstlichen Zweig vom Baum der göttlichen Seligkeit erhalten, diesen sollen wir der Erde einimpfen; daß er aber gedeihen möge, thut es Noth, daß wir einen guten Stamm erlesen' [We have received a wonderful branch from the tree of divine blessedness, and with this we shall inoculate the earth; so that it may flourish, however, it is necessary that we select a good stem] (*SW* I, 157, ll. 1431–34); in 'Geschichte eines Braminen': 'wie eine mächtige Sehnsucht ihn getrieben, diesen Zweig vom ewigen Lebensbaum dem verwitterten Stamm seines Volkes einzuimpfen' [how a powerful longing had driven him to inoculate the weather-worn stem of his people with the branch from the tree of eternal life] (*SW* I, 308).
146 See Günderrode, *Briefe*, p. 226; pp. 346–47.
147 As Morgenthaler notes: *SW* III, 158; also Regen, pp. 73–75.

eleven official editions between its first publication in 1748 and 1794, was one of the bestselling works of devotional thought in the eighteenth century.

Günderrode was certainly familiar with Fichte's *Die Bestimmung des Menschen*, which drew on Spalding's vocabulary, structure, and style,[148] and served as a means, in part, to popularise his speculative thought after the *Grundlage der gesammten Wissenschaftslehre* [Foundations of the Science of Knowledge] (1794–95).[149] But there are structural hints of an inheritance from Spalding in 'Geschichte eines Braminen'. On one level, the text is almost a confessional monologue, and shares a meditative quality with Spalding's tract; the interlocutor Lubar interrupts Almor once, briefly, so that the text is functionally homodiegetic rather than heterodiegetic. More significantly, the stages of Almor's development recall the stages outlined by Spalding. Almor proceeds from sensory and sensual pleasures, to the life of the mind as the exercise of reason to promote virtue, which he experiences as a destructive form of self-castigation, and then to religion and to the realisation of a doctrine of immortality, in the form of palingenesis and transmigration of the soul.[150] Günderrode also shares an essential eudaemonic optimism with Spalding, which in Spalding's case is indebted to the Leibniz-Wolffian tradition and to the philosophy of the Earl of Shaftesbury.[151]

Why this recourse to Spalding? Spalding's tract, though apologetic in intention, was popular because it forsook conventional forms of theological argumentation and biblical exegesis.[152] Another aspect of its appeal would be the premise that the individual is free to choose their own path, although this might necessarily prove arduous.[153] Schleiermacher, too, sought in his *Reden* to reveal the pulse of religion that had been obscured by layers of dogma.[154] When read in the context of both Spalding and Schleiermacher, Günderrode's text belongs to a tradition of seeking alternatives to ground religious belief, free of antiquated, institutionalised

---

148 Albrecht Beutel, 'Spalding und Goeze und *Die Bestimmung des Menschen*: Frühe Kabalen um ein Erfolgsbuch der Aufklärungstheologie', in *Literatur und Theologie im 18. Jahrhundert: Konfrontationen — Kontroversen — Konkurrenzen*, ed. by Hans-Edwin Friedrich and others, Hallesche Beiträge zur europäischen Aufklärung, 41 (Berlin: De Gruyter, 2011), pp. 108–21 (p. 109).

149 Günter Zöller, '"An Other and Better World": Fichte's *The Vocation of Man* as a Theologico-Political Treatise', in *Fichte's Vocation of Man: New Interpretive and Critical Essays*, ed. by Daniel Breazeale and Tom Rockmore (Albany: SUNY Press, 2013), pp. 19–32 (p. 23).

150 Compare Spalding's stages of 'Sinnlichkeit' [sensuality], 'Vergnügen des Geistes' [pleasure of the mind], 'Tugend' [virtue], 'Religion' [religion], and 'Unsterblichkeit' [immortality], which remain consistent across editions of the text from 1763 onward: see Johann Joachim Spalding, *Kritische Ausgabe*, ed. by Albrecht Beutel, 12 vols (Tübingen: Mohr Siebeck, 2001–13), I.1: *Die Bestimmung des Menschen*, ed. by Albrecht Beutel, Daniela Kirschkowski and Dennis Prause (2006).

151 Clemens Schwaiger, 'Zur Frage nach den Quellen von Spaldings Bestimmung des Menschen: Ein ungelöstes Rätsel der Aufklärungsforschung', in *Die Bestimmung des Menschen*, ed. by Norbert Hinske (= *Aufklärung*, 11.1 (1999)), pp. 7–19 (p. 17).

152 Mark-Georg Dehrmann, *Das 'Orakel der Deisten': Shaftesbury und die deutsche Aufklärung* (Göttingen: Wallstein, 2008), p. 140.

153 Andreas Urs Sommer, 'Sinnstiftung durch Individualgeschichte: Johann Joachim Spaldings *Bestimmung des Menschen*', *Zeitschrift für Neuere Theologiegeschichte*, 8 (2001), 163–200 (p. 167).

154 Richard Crouter, *Friedrich Schleiermacher: Between Enlightenment and Romanticism* (Cambridge: Cambridge University Press, 2005), p. 60.

elements of theological argumentation. This is combined with a narrative of radical individual autonomy that acknowledges no higher authority than the inner promptings of the self. As I shall show, this concept of autonomy is dependent on Günderrode's attempt to find a new basis for religious belief in the form of Spinozist panentheism.

Whilst it is true that *Bestimmung des Menschen* had lost something of its charge by 1800 and had been reduced to a slogan,[155] Günderrode shows an interest in the concept,[156] and it does feature in 'Geschichte eines Braminen': 'Zuerst betrachtete ich meine Natur und Bestimmung abgesondert' [At first I regarded my nature and my vocation as separate] (*SW* I, 305). This phrasing, which gives equal weight to 'Natur' and 'Bestimmung', is telling: what is to be inferred is that the discovery of one's self, of one's nature, necessarily leads to one's 'Bestimmung'.

This is the point where the metaphysical underpinnings of panentheism prove useful: if one's nature is linked to a divine essence or substance, then the development of the self and the development of the entirety of spiritualised nature go hand in hand. Günderrode's aphoristic notes from Fichte's *Einige Vorlesungen über die Bestimmung des Gelehrten* [Some Lectures on the Scholar's Vocation] (1794) virtually provide a prompt for this metaphysical narrative: 'Nent man eine völlige Übereinstimmung mit sich selbst Vollkomenheit, so ist diese Vollkomenheit das höchste unerreichbare Ziel des Menschen; Vervollkomnung aber ins Unendliche ist seine Bestimmung' [If we are to call complete correspondence with oneself perfection, so this perfection is the highest, unachievable goal of the individual human; an endless process of perfectibility is his or her vocation].[157] Fichte's use of the term in context refers to the 'Bestimmung' of the individual in the context of society, not in creation,[158] and specifically with regard to the application of reason. In 'Geschichte eines Braminen', this terminology carries metaphysical weight, in line with Günderrode's general understanding of 'Vollkommenheit' and 'Vervollkommnung'. The idea of divine perfection and perfectibility through purification, present in 'Mahomets Traum in der Wüste', becomes a central element to the religion described in 'Geschichte eines Braminen'.

What of the narrative stages before religion? Günderrode develops a tripartite model of human existence: the animal, the human and the divine. Each stage brings an expansion of an understanding of how the individual relates to and is in embedded in the world. The animal stage, associated with commerce and sensory pleasures, is one of dull, mechanical materialism, where the acquisition of capital serves to satiate Almor's appetite for pleasure and distraction. This is an individualistic state in which Almor is unencumbered and unattached.

---

155 Laura Anna Macor, *Die Bestimmung des Menschen (1748–1800): Eine Begriffsgeschichte*, Monographien zur Philosophie der deutschen Aufklärung, 25 (Stuttgart-Bad Canstatt: frommann-holzboog, 2013), p. 31.
156 Alongside the notes on Fichte's *Die Bestimmung des Menschen* (1800) (*SW* II, 288–98) is also the poem entitled 'Des Menschen Bestimmung', Preitz/Hopp III, p. 268, which is lifted from August Hennings, *Der Musaget: Ein Begleiter des Genius der Zeit. Sechstes Stück* (Altona: Hammerich, 1799), p. 90.
157 Preitz/Hopp III, pp. 266–67.
158 Macor, pp. 313–15.

What follows is how the moral world — the human world — reveals itself to Almor following the death of his father, which awakens his dormant intellectual capacities. Keen to be a 'Bürger des moralischen Reiches' [citizen of the moral realm] (*SW* I, 305), Almor is drawn to a form of moral cosmopolitanism that verges on the utopian, where the free activity of the individual manifests in a duty towards others in this moral community: '[ich trat] in die freye Thätigkeit eines denkenden Wesens, das sich selbst einen Zweck seines Thuns setzt, aus dem beschränkten persönlichen Eigennutz in die große Verbrüderung aller Menschen, zu aller Wohl' [[I entered] into the free activity of a thinking being, who sets a purpose for their own actions, out of limited, personal self-interest into the great fraternity of all people, for the common good] (*SW* I, 305). What is implied, but not further articulated, is that all agents — understood as rational agents — exist in a common moral community, and that the principles of moral action are universal: here Günderrode runs close to Kant's conception of a moral cosmopolis.[159]

The creation of this moral fraternity hinges, though, on the overzealous application of reason that causes profound emotional distress. The torturous application of reason in the pursuit of virtue[160] is a form of self-mortification that denies the essential goodness of human nature:

> Warum ist denn alles gut, was auf Erden ist, nur der Mensch nicht? Warum soll er allein anders werden, als er ist? Ist nur *der* tugendhaft, der auf den Ruinen seines eignen Geistes steht und sagen kann: Seht, diese hatten sich empört, aber sie sind gefallen, ich bin Sieger worden über sie Alle! — Barbar! freue dich nicht deines Siegs, du hast einen Bürgerkrieg geführt, die Ueberwundenen waren Kinder deiner eignen Natur, du hast dich selbst getödtet in deinen Siegen, du bist gefallen in deinen Schlachten.
>
> [Why is then everything good on Earth, but not the individual human? Why should they alone become something other than what they are? Is only that person virtuous who stands upon the ruins of their own spirit and is able to say: Look — these parts of me were outraged, but they have fallen, I have become the victor over them all! — Barbarian! Do not enjoy your victory, you have conducted a civil war, and those who were defeated were the children of your own nature, you have killed yourself in your victories, you are the one to have fallen in your battles.] (*SW* I, 305–06).[161]

---

[159] Pauline Kleingeld, *Kant and Cosmopolitanism: The Philosophical Ideal of World Citizenship* (Cambridge: Cambridge University Press, 2011), p. 17. Günderrode makes a note of the categorical imperative in her *Studienbuch*: Preitz/Hopp III, p. 265.

[160] In Günderrode's *Studienbuch*, virtue, in quotations from John Locke and Hermann Christoph Gottfried Demme, is defined as the application of the laws of reason to determine what is right, and to act against one's own inclinations for the sake of what reason considers to be best: see Preitz/Hopp III, p. 266.

[161] This section has strong parallels with a section from a letter to Claudine Piautaz from 1801–03, where the criticism of this ethic of virtue is even more pronounced: 'Alles war gut was geschaffen war, sagt die heilige Schrift, warum war es den[n] der Mensch nicht? Warum soll er anders sein als er ist? Wunderbar! — dies erfüllt mich mit Trauer. Seine Empfindungen u Wünsche am Altare der Nothwendigkeit, oder der Sitte schlachten, das nent man Tugend. Sich Stükeweise selbst morden, ist also Tugend. Triumphierend auf den Trümmern seines eignen Geistes stehen, sagen können, „seht hier zu meinen Füssen die Erschlagenen, die Gefesselten, die Brandstätten mein Wille ist Sieger

The objection here is twofold. If one proceeds from the premise of the essential goodness of all that is, then the application of virtue appears nonsensical, if not downright dangerous, given the psychic violence it exerts: the very faculty that is meant to civilise is ironically and metaphorically turned into its opposite, barbarism. The second point is that the sacrifice of the self for the sake of the community — 'keine Ertödtung des *Einen*, damit das *Andre* besser gedeihe' [the individual should not be put to death so that the other should better thrive] (*SW* I, 306) — desiccates the individual. If the first, animal stage amounted to the pursuit of self-interest above all, then this second, human stage, to follow the textual logic, is equally unsatisfactory, since it involves the pursuit of the interests of the whole over the individual.

The third stage of religion offers an answer to this conundrum, by allowing for both self-development and the development of the whole cosmos. The religious section of the text is marked by Almor's return to the Orient from France, in accordance with an epistemological principle of *ex oriente lux*. The narrative still rests on Almor's radical conception of autonomy: as with 'Nikator' and 'Hildgund', for Almor there is no higher authority that that found within the self. But this has anarchic implications. The interlocutor Lubar exists solely to provide an important objection to Almor's claims about autonomy. If one finds no higher authority than that within the self and therefore, like Almor, completely withdraws from all social bonds, this is tantamount to the dissolution of society. Almor's retreat from society is framed as a metaphorical death or suicide:

> Ich kann [...] diesen Schritt eben so wenig gut heißen, als den Selbstmord; beyde sind für die menschliche Gesellschaft gleich nachtheilig, und was würde aus ihr werden, wenn sich jeder erlauben wollte, sich für sie zu tödten?
>
> [I can [...] endorse this act as little as I would suicide; both equally produce disadvantages for human society, and what would become of society, if everyone wished to be able to die for its sake?] (*SW* I, 307)

What Almor's self-imposed exile recalls is a negative form of cosmopolitanism that is associated with Cynicism in the eighteenth century. Cynic cosmopolitanism is defined by refusal — by the refusal to participate in and heed human societies and systems of law, in short, a rejection of civic attachment where non-belonging is a condition of independence and freedom.[162] Almor adopts a posture of a radical form

---

worden über sie alle"; dies ist das belohnende Gefühl des Tugendhaften. — Trauriger Triumpf! — Mich dauern die Gemordeten, u die Gefesselten, u ich möchte den Sieger fragen warum hast du das gethan!' [Everything that was created is good, according to scripture, so why not the individual human? Why should they alone become something other than what they are? Strange! — this fills me with sadness. What is called virtue is to slaughter feelings and desires on the altar of necessity, or morals. Virtue, then, is to murder oneself piece by piece. To stand triumphantly on the ruins of one's own spirit and to be able to say: 'Behold at my feet the slain, those thrown in chains, and the sites of conflagrations; my will has become victor over them all!' — this is the feeling that rewards the virtuous. Woeful triumph — I pity those who have been murdered and those cast in chains, and I would like to ask the victor: why did you do it?] (Karoline von Günderrode, letter to Claudine Piautaz, 1801–03, Freies Deutsches Hochstift (FDH), MS 20369, fols 2^v–3^r)

162 Louisa Shea, *The Cynic Enlightenment: Diogenes in the Salon* (Baltimore, MD: Johns Hopkins University Press, 2010), pp. 76–77.

of individualism, and his rebuttal to Lubar brushes aside the issue without providing conceptual resolution: Almor proclaims a universal principle that each individual should follow their 'innere Natur' [inner nature] (*SW* I, 307), whether that may be to engage with society and worldly matters or not.

This conceptual unease indicates where Günderrode's interests lie: in the metaphysical grounding of the individual, not in a philosophical or social theory of how the individual has particular moral or civic duties towards others in a community. This recourse to the universality of 'innere Natur' is only tenable if it is grounded in a Leibnizian idea of pre-established harmony, and that self-development and self-cultivation coincide with the preordained development of the whole.

This perfect reciprocity is the solution presented by Spinozist panentheism in 'Geschichte eines Braminen', which is framed as the highest stage of human development.[163] This move to religion is significant in the narrative, since one of the first pieces of information the reader learns about Almor is his indifference to the external and institutional manifestations of religion: the ceremonial aspects of religion had little hold over him in his youth, and his father thought religion little more than a useful political institution. Almor comes to realise that the internal aspects of religion offer a solution to the problem of instrumentalising reason. In a moment that fuses Christian and Kantian terminology, the function that religion performs is to allow space for the free self-determination of the individual: 'Mir ist jeder Einzelne heilig, er ist Gottes Werk, er ist sich selbst Zweck' [Every individual is sacred to me, they are God's work, and an end in themselves] (*SW* I, 310). This may imply an atomised form of self-determination, but the equation of the individual with creation as 'Gottes Werk' suggests how religion expands the bonds that the individual has: there is an interdependence between the individual and the entirety of the cosmos.

With religion, Günderrode again enacts a form of poetic archaeology. Rather than Egypt being the point of origin for human civilisation and religious traditions, now it is India that represents the most primordial form of human development. Günderrode taps into the notion of India as the seat of an ancient civilisation, which reflects contemporary speculation that Hindu culture stretched back two millennia, and in some estimations, up to four millennia before Christ's birth.[164] This falls in line with the expanding image of the Orient, with the term 'Morgenland' coming to encompass India at the end of the eighteenth century,[165] but also with speculation in the proto-anthropological and ethnographic world histories of the period, where various 'out of the East' origin theories were proposed.[166]

---

163 Whilst Günderrode states that it is necessary to experience all three stages of human development, there is a clear hierarchy established by the narrative progression that privileges the final stage.

164 A. Leslie Willson, *A Mythical Image: The Ideal of India in German Romanticism* (Durham, NC: Duke University Press, 1964), pp. 38–39. For an overview of the Romantic longing for India, see Joanna Neilly, *E.T.A. Hoffmann's Orient: Romantic Aesthetics and the German Imagination* (Cambridge: Legenda, 2016), pp. 3–5.

165 See Nicholas A. Germana, 'Herder's India: The "Morgenland" in Mythology and Anthropology', in *The Anthropology of the Enlightenment*, pp. 118–40 (p. 119).

166 Johann Christian Gatterer suggested that the earliest men, after the Biblical flood, 'lebten,

What is the resonance of this recourse to India? As in 'Mahomed', it is an idealised attempt to reconstitute a primordial, prelapsarian state where the individual is integrated in divinised nature.[167] For Almor, the good life consists of living in accordance with nature, as well as with one's natural wholeness and goodness.[168] The religious syncretism of 'Mahomed' is again deployed to legitimise Spinozist panentheism, with the addition of Hinduism, which, during the surge of Indophilia around 1800, was thought of as a primordial form of monotheism:[169]

> [ich ging] zur Betrachtung seines [Mahomeds] Bildes in den Geistern anderer Religionsdarsteller über; ich durchging Zoroasters, Confutsees, Moses und Christus Lehren, die Ueberbleibsel der ägyptischen Priesterweisheit, und der Hindu heilige Mythen. So verschieden der Geist aus diesen Allen gesprochen hat, habe ich doch nur einen Sinn in diesen Formen gefunden, mit dem sich der Meinige innigst verbunden hat, wodurch er erweitert und verstärkt wurde.
>
> [[I proceeded] to consider his [Mahomed's] image in the minds of other interpreters of religion; I went through the teachings of Zoroaster, Confucius, Moses and Christ, the remnants of wisdom from the priests of ancient Egypt, and the holy myths of the Hindus. Whilst the Spirit spoke in disparate ways from these sources, yet I only found one meaning in these texts, which intimately with my own understanding, explaining and strengthening it.] (SW 1, 309)

Hinduism becomes conceptually useful for Günderrode because it contains the belief of transmigration of the soul and reincarnation. These concepts, alongside metempsychosis and palingenesis, are not historically alien to the Western hemisphere. Pythagoras, Plato, Socrates, Cicero, Ovid and Virgil all considered the idea of rebirth.[170] Friedrich Creuzer produced German translations of Pythagoras's work specifically for Günderrode's reading.[171] Lessing tantalisingly refuses to rule out the possibility of rebirth in *Die Erziehung des Menschengeschlechts*, which ends with a teleological narrative of human development.[172]

[...] im Nordwesten von Indien' [lived, [...] in the north-west of India], Johann Christian Gatterer, *Einleitung in die synchronistische Universalhistorie* (Göttingen: Vandenhoek, 1771), pp. 63–64. Christian Ernst Wünsch writes of 'Asien, wo die Wohnsitze der ersten Menschen gewesen seyn sollen' [Asia, where the first humans are supposed to have lived] (Christian Ernst Wünsch, *Unterhaltungen über den Menschen: Erster Theil: über die Kultur und äußerliche Bildung desselben*, 2nd edn (Leipzig: Breitkopf, 1796), p. 386); Christian Wilhelm Dohm postulates India as the 'wahre Vaterland' [true homeland] and 'Wiege des menschlichen Geschlechts' [cradle of the human race] (Edward Ives, *Reisen nach Indien und Persien*, trans. by Christian Willhelm Dohm, 2 vols (Leipzig: Weidmanns Erben und Reich, 1774), I, 101).

167 Licher notes this conceptual equivalence between nature and origin: Licher, p. 98.
168 There are some parallels here to Rousseau's pure state of nature, although Günderrode is altogether more metaphysical: see Laurence D. Cooper, *Rousseau, Nature, and the Problem of the Good Life* (University Park: Pennsylvania State University Press, 1999), p. 40.
169 Christine Maillard, '"Indomanie" um 1800: ästhetische, religiöse und ideologische Aspekte', in *Der Deutschen Morgenland: Bilder des Orients in der deutschen Literatur und Kultur von 1770 bis 1850*, ed. by Charis Goer and Michael Hofmann (Munich: Wilhelm Fink, 2008), pp. 67–84 (p. 79). See also Friedrich Majer, 'Ueber die mythologischen Dichtungen der Indier: an Alwina', in *Poetisches Journal*, ed. by Ludwig Tieck (Jena: Frommann, 1800), 165–216 (pp. 172–73).
170 See Lieselotte E. Kurth-Voigt, 'Existence after Death in Eighteenth-Century Literature: Prolegomena to a Study of Poetic Visions of the Beyond and Imaginative Speculations about Continued Life in a Future State', *South Atlantic Review*, 52.2 (1987), 3–14 (p. 9).
171 Preisendanz, p. 63.
172 Lessing, *Werke und Briefe*, x, 73–99. Günderrode alludes to Lessing's text in 'Geschichte eines

Günderrode naturalises the Hindu doctrine to suit a Christian context, by refashioning the understanding of rebirth so that the soul is continually purified to be reunited with the divine. This universalising tendency, the absorption and cultural translation of ideas, is paradoxically bound up with the purported authority of ancient theology: the earliest manifestations of a particular concept or doctrine are the most potent because they are unadulterated by later philosophical developments.

Christianising this Hindu notion of palingenesis and metempsychosis has narrative significance. It allows Günderrode to find a solution for the text's central tension of how self-development corresponds with the world around it, without lapsing into atomised individualism. Almor is cosmopolitan on a metaphysical level: he learns from the wise brahmin, who initiates him into their secret rites, that the transmigration of the soul is founded on the dialectical relationship between man and divinity. This is understood in Spinozist, and specifically Herder's, terms as ontological force, as 'Urkraft':

> Er [der Greis] lehrte mich, wie in jedem Theile des unendlichen Naturgeistes die Anlage zu ewiger Vervollkommnung läge, wie die Kräfte wanderten durch alle Formen hindurch, bis sich Bewußtseyn und Gedanke im Menschen entwickelten; wie von dem Menschen an, eine unendliche Reihe von Wanderungen, die immer zu höherer Vollkommenheit führten, der Seelen warteten; wie sie endlich auf geheimnißvolle Weise sich alle vereinigten mit der Urkraft, von der sie ausgegangen, und Eins mit ihr würden, und doch zugleich sie selbst blieben, und so die Göttlichkeit und Universalität des Schöpfers mit der Individualität des Geschöpfes vereinigten.
>
> [He [the old man] taught me, how there is the potential for eternal perfectibility in every part of the unending Spirit of Nature, how the forces would move through all forms, until thought and consciousness had developed in humankind, and how from the individual human onward, there would be an endless series of transmigrations, which would lead to higher perfection, and the souls would await becoming united, at last, in a mysterious way, with the primal force, from which they had first emerged, and became One with it, and yet would remain themselves, and so would fuse the divinity and universality of the Creator with the individuality of that which had been created.] (*SW* I, 312)

What this provides is absolute reciprocity: all that the individual requires is to develop their innate capacities in a narrative of perfectibility; the development of the individual necessarily corresponds to the development of the whole. The highest form of perfection is not perfect oneness, but rather a form of dual-aspect monism. Whilst it rests on a form of emanationism, the return to the divine does not, as will be shown in the following two chapters, become problematic because it demands the dissolution of the individual entirely. Günderrode's vision here instead runs close to Herder's interpretation of freedom as a form of global determinism: acting according to the necessity of one's own nature is how the divine operates in the world. This recalls, in turn, Spinoza's doctrine of *amor dei intellectualis*.

Braminen'. The phrase 'Ja, es muß eine Zeit der Vollendung kommen' [Yes, a time of perfection must come] (*SW*, 310) prefaces a harmonic eschatology: 'Nein; sie wird kommen, sie wird gewiß kommen, die Zeit der Vollendung' [No; it will come, it will certainly come, the time of perfection], in Lessing, *Werke und Briefe*, x, 96.

How can this metaphysical recuperation of religion in 'Geschichte eines Braminen' be reconciled with the revolutionary politics and pronouncement of a new religion in 'Mahomed'? The trajectory of this chapter may suggest a degree of political resignation: that, when political figures fail, the ideals that they came to embody become displaced, to live on in literary form where they persist as regulative ideas. Spinozist metaphysics would be both a retreat from reality and a means to keep the ideals of the Revolution alive in dignified literary and philosophical form. It is true that Günderrode's texts hold on to idealised portraits of revolutionary individuals. Equally, what is revealed by moving from Napoleon to Mahomed, and on to Almor, is how panentheism depends upon revolutionary ideals. Mahomed's displaced agency, his submission to divine will at the expense of his own as *kenosis*, and Almor's autonomy, are two sides of the same coin. They combine in the idea of global determinism, of finding a higher form of freedom by recognising one's own subjugation. Where 'Mahomed' is a careful defence and *apologia* for religion, 'Geschichte eines Braminen' offers a metaphysical variant of Republicanism.

CHAPTER 5

Ascent and Descent: Platonism and Cognition in Günderrode

Both Almor and Mahomed function as idealised figures who have privileged access to the divine, to the ground of being: with Mahomed as a positively inflected *Schwärmer* and political leader and Almor as the initiate into the mysteries, indeed, the *prisca theologia* of the brahmins. Whilst there is a tension between Mahomed's status as a political leader and as a prophet, what is not foregrounded as a difficulty in either text is the cognitive process of how the characters come to achieve their revelations of the divine. Given the metaphysical commitments of panentheism across Günderrode's work, this raises a cognitive and epistemological question: if the world is part of the divine, but the divine extends beyond it, how it is possible to negotiate between phenomenal reality and the noumenal realm that would allow metaphysical truths to be disclosed to an individual?

It is this epistemological question that recurs across Günderrode's poems and prose. Before attending to Günderrode specifically, it is worth considering theories of cognitive or sensory expansion in the late eighteenth century, as these will help to sharpen an understanding of Günderrode's distinctiveness. In an unpublished *Nachlass* fragment entitled 'Daß mehr als fünf Sinne für den Menschen sein können' [That Man May Have More than Five Senses], Gotthold Ephraim Lessing explores the idea that the five physiological senses could be expanded to include senses for the new phenomena of electricity and magnetism respectively. What would follow, Lessing argues, is an expansion of human consciousness:

> Kaum aber werden wir den Sinn der Elektricität oder den Sinn des Magnetismus selbst haben: so wird es uns gehen, wie es Saunderson würde ergangen sein, wenn er auf einmal das Gesicht erhalten hätte. Es wird auf einmal für uns eine ganz neue Welt voll der herrlichsten Phänomene entstehen, von denen wir uns jetzt eben so wenig einen Begriff machen können, als er sich von Licht und Farben machen konnte.

> [But we would hardly have a sense for electricity or a sense for magnetism itself: in that case, we would experience things much as Saunderson [Nicholas Saunderson, the blind mathematician] would have, had he all of a sudden gained the power of sight. At once we would experience an entirely new world replete

with the finest phenomena, which we would barely be able to conceptualise, much as he would barely have been able to conceptualise light or colour.]¹

What Lessing is alluding to here is a thought experiment in philosophy of mind, namely the Molyneux problem, and one that was taken up by John Locke in *An Essay Concerning Human Understanding* (1689). The question it posed was whether a man who was born blind and who had regained his sight would be able to distinguish between a cube and a sphere that he had formerly known by touch. Locke concluded that since the mind was a *tabula rasa* and that the man had no visual experience, the man would therefore not be able to recognise objects through the faculty of sight.² By alluding to Nicholas Saunderson, Lessing draws on Denis Diderot's approach to the Molyneux problem in his *Lettre sur les aveugles* [Letter on the Blind] (1749), where Diderot uses Saunderson as a prominent example.³

The interest in the Molyneux problem was derived not only from how one could relate one sense to another, but also from the question of the adequacy of the senses. By implicitly comparing those endowed with the canonical five senses to Saunderson, Lessing raises the question of whether they are both alike in being devoid of further senses.

Lessing was not alone in this thought about the limitations of the five senses and the potential scope for their expansion. To give just one other example from the eighteenth century: Christoph Martin Wieland's early work *Briefe von Verstorbenen an hinterlassene Freunde* [Letters from the Dead to Friends Left behind] (1753) is a series of eight missives where the dead impart their higher knowledge to the living. At the beginning of the fourth letter, the speaker Theagenes describes the process of sensory expansion he experiences upon death:

> [...] ich schaue die ew'gen Jdeen,
> Sie, die in euere Gruft⁴ durch die engen Ritzen der Sinne
> Gleitende Schatten nur werfen, die ihr für Wesen umfasset.
> Mein erweiterter Geist entfaltet höhere Kräfte,
> Die, auf Erden unbrauchbar, im Grunde der Seele verborgen,
> Schlummerten; innere Sinnen, auch weite Behälter der Wahrheit,
> Augen für hellere Gegenstände, erhabne Begierden,
> Denen die Erde zu leicht, der Cirkel des Menschen zu eng ist.
>
> [[...] I behold the eternal ideas,
> Those that cast but floating shadows into your cave
> through the narrow gaps of the senses, which you comprehend as beings.
> My expanded spirit is open to higher forces,
> Which cannot be used on Earth, lay concealed in the depths of the soul,
> Dormant; inner senses, capacious receptacles of truth,
> Eyes for clearer objects, sublime desires,
> For whom the Earth is too light, and the realm of humankind too narrow.]⁵

1   Lessing, *Werke und Briefe*, x, 229–32 (p. 231).
2   Jessica Riskin, *Science in the Age of Sensibility: The Sentimental Empiricists of the French Enlightenment* (Chicago: University of Chicago Press, 2002), p. 19.
3   Gaukroger, pp. 415–16.
4   A reference to Plato's cave.
5   Christoph Martin Wieland, 'Briefe von Verstorbenen an hinterlassene Freunde', in *C. M. Wieland's Sämmtliche Werke*, 36 vols (Leipzig: Göschen, 1853–58), XXVI: *Vermischte Schriften* (1856), p. 42.

Stripped of the material imperfections of the body, the previously imperceptible faculties of the soul awaken as it ascends into the heavens, and indeed, into a cosmic voyage beyond the Earth. These faculties allow Theagenes to perceive the divine order of the cosmos, which follows the common eighteenth-century principle of the Great Chain of Being, where all the spheres nearer the divine are closer to perfection compared to the more distant, material spheres.[6] What Theagenes can therefore reveal through these expanded senses of the soul is how the cosmos is structured around divine beneficence and perfectibility, in which all creation, by becoming ever more spiritualised, is moving towards its own perfection.

Both Lessing and Wieland outline a teleological narrative in which the senses can be expanded to the point of perfection. For Günderrode, this idea of sensory expansion becomes a tension. The question that preoccupies her is how sensory perception can be expanded to look *beyond* phenomenal reality. What recurs in Günderrode is not just an awareness of the limitations of physiological senses, but also the cognitive limitations of the individuated self, and how these can be overcome.

This process, or at least the attempt to overcome sensory and cognitive limitations, forms a textual movement based around verticality, which is a consistent feature of Günderrode's poetry in particular. As with Wieland, what can be traced in Günderrode is a textual and cognitive movement of ascent — coterminous with the individual desire for greater knowledge. Where tension emerges is how this movement of ascent is thwarted, frustrated, so that the movement of ascent turns into its opposite: the descent into phenomenal reality. Brigitte Peucker has identified this tension between ascent and descent as an essentially Romantic predicament.[7] It derives from the frustrating split between the material world and the sense that there is a metaphysical underpinning to this reality, although this cannot be perceived (much as this experience of greater perception is desired). Indeed, if the movement described above could be termed *anabasis* (the upward movement towards greater knowledge), an inverted movement of *katabasis* also occurs across Günderrode, where it is indeed the descent into the underworld, or understood more figuratively as a descent into the depths of the self. Christine Battersby reads this distinction in Günderrode between transcendence upwards and transcendence into the self (or the body) along gendered lines, with the former being coded as masculine and the latter feminine.[8] At their core, these oscillating vertical movements are complementary sides of an epistemological process. This is a repeated feature across Günderrode's work and is embedded within a general search for the infinite, an idea not exclusive to Romanticism (where it is framed as a search for the ineffable philosophical Absolute) but prevalent throughout the eighteenth century.[9]

---

6   Lieselotte E. Kurth-Voigt, 'Existence after Death: Changing Views in Wieland's Writings', *Lessing Yearbook*, 17 (1985), 153–76 (pp. 156–57).
7   Brigitte Peucker, *Lyric Descent in the German Romantic Tradition* (New Haven: Yale University Press, 1987), p. 1. Peucker selects later Romantic figures, such as Eichendorff, and poetic descendants of Romanticism in the nineteenth and twentieth centuries.
8   Christine Battersby, *The Sublime, Terror and Human Difference* (London: Routledge, 2007), p. 127.
9   Arthur O. Lovejoy, *The Great Chain of Being: A Study in the History of an Idea* (Cambridge, MA: Harvard University Press, 1936), p. 250.

This notion of ascent or descent is not, however, a repetition of a commonplace eighteenth-century idea. To outline what precisely it is in Günderrode, I will first define it negatively, to contrast it with what it responds to. The impetus for this motif can be found in the poem 'Vorzeit, und Neue Zeit' [The Past Era, and the Present Era] (*c.* 1800–1802), which is one of Günderrode's critiques of contemporary society and processes of rationalisation. The central tension of the poem derives from two competing perceptions of the world and means of understanding both nature and humanity:

> Ein schmahler rauher Pfad schien sonst die Erde.
> Und auf den Bergen glänzt der Himmel über ihr,
> Ein Abgrund ihr zur Seite war die Hölle,
> Und Pfade führten in den Himmel, u zur Hölle.
>
> Doch alles ist ganz anders nun geworden,
> Der Himmel ist gestürzt, der Abgrund ausgefüllt,
> Und mit Vernunft bedekt, und sehr bequem zum gehen.
> Des Glaubens Höhen sind nun demolieret.
> Und auf der flachen Erde schreitet der Verstand,
> Und misset alles aus, nach Klafter und nach Schuen.
>
> [The Earth once seemed a narrow, rough path
> And on the mountains would heaven gleam above;
> An abyss to its side was hell,
> And paths led to heaven, and to hell.
>
> Yet now everything has entirely changed:
> Heaven has fallen, the abyss has been filled in,
> And covered with reason, and very comfortable to traverse.
> The heights of faith are now demolished
> And on the flat Earth does intellect stride
> And measures everything, in fathoms and feet] (*SW* I, 375)[10]

'Vorzeit, und Neue Zeit' has been equated with Novalis's poem 'Wenn nicht mehr Zahlen und Figuren' [When Numbers and Figures Cease] because it reflects on the disenchantment of the world brought about by rationalisation and empiricism, which become pernicious when they are dogmatically and universally applied.[11] Yet this does not exhaust the argument of the poem. A Baconian empiricist and rationalist paradigm attaches too much importance to human intellect and reason as faculties to comprehend and categorise natural phenomena. The result of this is that human experience becomes technically easier to manage but also becomes flattened out — '[alles ist] mit Vernunft bedekt, und sehr bequem zum gehen'.

---

10 'Klafter' and 'Schuen' are two units of measurement. Klafter is a measurement of length that varies according to region but roughly corresponds to six feet. As a maritime measurement it is the equivalent of a fathom. A 'Schuh' is an antiquated term for a foot.

11 Astrid Weigert, 'Gender and Genre in the Works of German Romantic Women Writers', in *The Oxford Handbook of European Romanticism*, ed. by Paul Hamilton (Oxford: Oxford University Press, 2016), pp. 240–55 (p. 250); for the poem as a reflection on disenchantment more generally, see Felix Forster, *Dante Gabriel Rossetti und der romantische Desillusionismus* (Göttingen: V&R unipress, 2014), p. 40.

This flattening out of experience is given poetic form by dismantling the holistic image of the first strophe in the second, but also by the shift in metre: from uneven pentameter in the first strophe to pedestrian alexandrines in the sixth, seventh, and tenth lines. Here, the value of all phenomena lies in how they are empirically quantifiable: 'misset alles aus, nach Klafter und nach Schuen'. Quantifying nature in such a manner not only carries the danger of fragmentation by overlooking how it functions as an interlocking whole — which is reflected, by contrast, in the holistic religious world-view. Scientific empiricism can also desiccate nature (in accordance with the Baconian maxim of *dissecare naturam*),[12] because it creates a cleavage between lived experience — represented by a religious world-view — and the data it amasses about nature. Such quantification also objectifies nature and implicitly removes humans from nature, since this process presupposes that human reason and intellect *can* dissect nature.

But this is no call to arms to re-enchant nature. Rather, the tone of the poem is more elegiac: a lament that the religious and holistic world-view that once held sway has lost its legitimacy because it cannot justify itself when faced with inflexible empiricism and rationalism — 'Des Glaubens Höhen sind nun demolieret'. The modern world-view is ironically absorbed into the poem through its language — 'demolieret'; 'bequem zum gehen'. The implication is not that the religious world-view is obsolete. Rather, one of the tensions in the poem is the underlying assumption that religious feeling and individual spiritual aspirations do still exist, but they lack an object towards which they can be directed. What is lacking is an understanding of nature that is innately imbued with theological meaning and represents divine and moral order. What is also lacking, therefore, is the assurance of a singular truth, the unity of experience that was once provided by Christian faith ('des Glaubens Höhen'). But the legitimacy of the Christian world-view has been called into question because the methods by which rationality and empiricism establish truth — especially when applied dogmatically — cannot, according to Günderrode, be reconciled with faith.

Furthermore, there are implications for the objectification of nature, and the removal of man from nature. Whilst the pathos of 'Vorzeit, und Neue Zeit' rests on the impossibility of a return to this holistic experience of nature as the manifestation and guarantor of theological meaning, in philosophical terms, it equally points towards Kant's Copernican turn to the subject. The onus falls upon the individual to construct meaning and to grasp the transcendent ground of existence once provided by institutionalised Christianity.

---

12 Jacques Le Rider, 'War die Klassik farbenfeindlich und die Romantik farbengläubig? Von Lessings *Laokoon* zu Goethes *Farbenlehre* und deren Nachwirkung', in *Goethe und das Zeitalter der Romantik*, ed. by Walter Hinderer (Würzburg: Königshausen & Neumann, 2007), pp. 31–50 (p. 33).

Günderrode and Kantian Epistemology

The disparity between faith and reason in 'Vorzeit, und Neue Zeit' raises a question of epistemology: given the questionable legitimacy of Christian orthodoxy, what would be the valid means to perceive a metaphysical totality that underpins existence? One route that Günderrode uses to approach this problem is through engaging with Immanuel Kant's notion of rational faith. Using Kant to fuel metaphysical speculation may seem misplaced, since Kant limited human knowledge to the objects of experience.[13] For Kant, human reason can neither prove nor disprove the existence of God,[14] and he famously stated in the *Kritik der reinen Vernunft* that knowledge must be denied in order to make room for faith: 'ich mußte also das Wissen aufheben, um zum Glauben Platz zu bekommen' [Thus I had to deny knowledge in order to make room for faith].[15] Positive faith for Kant is pure rational faith or moral faith, based on the subjective conviction of moral certainty:

> Nein, die Überzeugung ist nicht logische, sondern moralische Gewißheit, und, da sie auf subjectiven Gründen (der moralischen Gesinnung) beruht, so muß ich nicht einmal sagen: es ist moralisch gewiß, daß ein Gott sei etc., sondern: ich bin moralisch gewiß etc. Das heißt: der Glaube an einen Gott und eine andere Welt ist mit meiner moralischen Gesinnung so verwebt, daß, so wenig ich Gefahr laufe, die letztere einzubüßen, eben so wenig besorge ich, daß mir der erste jemals entrissen werden könne.
>
> [No, the conviction is not logical but moral certainty, and, since it depends on subjective grounds (of moral disposition) I must not even say 'It is morally certain that there is a God,' etc., but rather 'I am morally certain' etc. That is, the belief in a God and another world is so interwoven with my moral disposition that I am in as little danger of ever surrendering the former as I am worried that the latter can ever be torn away from me.][16]

The essence of religion, for Kant, is morality, and the primary tenets of religious belief, or 'Glaubensartikel', are the belief in God and in immortality. Thus Kant advances an Enlightenment position of equating religion with morality[17] — one that Schleiermacher would vigorously reject in *Reden über die Religion*.

Whilst there is no evidence to suggest that Günderrode read Kant's critiques or *Die Religion innerhalb der Grenzen der bloßen Vernunft*, she certainly had acquired indirect knowledge of Kantian ideas and of the understanding of moral faith from the *Kritik der reinen Vernunft*. In early 1800, Günderrode writes to her friend Karoline von Barkhaus from Butzbach, where she was staying to aid her recently bereaved

---

13   James Krueger and Benjamin Lipscomb, 'Towards a Synoptic Vision: Reading Kant Metaphysically, Reading him Whole', in *Kant's Moral Metaphysics: God, Freedom, and Immortality*, ed. by James Krueger and Benjamin J. Bruxvoort Lipscomb (Berlin: De Gruyter, 2010), pp. 1–19 (p. 14).
14   Cooper, p. 5.
15   Kant, *Kant's Gesammelte Schriften*, I.III: *Kritik der reinen Vernunft* (2. Aufl. 1787), Bxxx/p. 19. Immanuel Kant, *The Critique of Pure Reason*, trans. and ed. by Paul Guyer and Allen W. Wood (Cambridge: Cambridge University Press, 1998), B xxx/p. 117.
16   Kant, *Kant's Gesammelte Schriften*, I.III, B857/pp. 536–37; Kant, *The Critique of Pure Reason*, B857/p. 689.
17   Manfred Kuehn, *Kant: A Biography* (Cambridge: Cambridge University Press, 2001), p. 250.

grandfather, and recounts the meeting with a local pastor, Johann Georg Diefenbach: 'mit Wärme und Offenheit sprach er über Religion, Aufklärung, Vorurtheil, und Völkerwohl. [...] [er] scheint [...] mir von gleichen Religionsmeinungen mit uns, dies allein empfiehlt ihn mir schon sehr' [with warmth and openness he spoke of religion, enlightenment, prejudice, and the welfare of the people [...] [he] seemed [...] to me to share our religion convictions, and this alone is a reason to have confidence in him].[18]

Although Günderrode's initial enthusiasm for Diefenbach appears to have cooled,[19] he was responsible for introducing Günderrode to philosophical logic and therefore to philosophy as a discipline, and also to the tenets of Kantian philosophy. He encouraged her to study Johann Gottfried Kiesewetter's *Grundriss einer reinen allgemeinen Logik nach Kantischen Grundsätzen: Zum Gebrauch für Vorlesungen* [Outline of a Pure General Logic according to Kantian Principles: For Use in Lectures] (1795),[20] and corresponded with Günderrode to help her refine her understanding of Kiesewetter's — and by extension Kant's — concepts.[21] What is now considered the best-known attempt to popularise Kant's critical philosophy is Karl Leonhard Reinhold's *Briefe über die kantische Philosophie*, yet Kiesewetter was himself a popular Kantian. He was a philosopher and professor of philosophy and logic in Berlin, was taught by Kant and ranks as 'der eigentliche *Modephilosoph* des Kantianismus' [the actual *fashionable philosopher* of Kantianism].[22]

In the *Nachlass*, an unpublished manuscript points to the theological importance of Diefenbach for Günderrode. It is a theological tract, presumably written in Diefenbach's own hand,[23] and deals primarily with the question of revelation — understood in propositional terms as something that is rationally demonstrable.[24] It also discusses the shared belief in divine providence between the author and interlocutor, presumed to be Günderrode.

The final two leaves of the manuscript, however, deal with the question of how the existence of God can be inferred. To address this question, Diefenbach proceeds

---

18   Günderrode, *Briefe*, p. 61. Diefenbach had previously made a great impression on Charlotte, Karoline's favourite sister: ibid., p. 60.
19   Ibid., pp. 62–63.
20   These studies are reproduced in truncated form in *SW* II, 302–49. The manuscript of the studies ends at §202, p. 92 of J. G. C. C. Kiesewetter, *Grundriß einer allgemeinen Logik nach Kantischen Grundsätzen zum Gebrauch für Vorlesungen begleitet mit einer weitern Auseinandersetzung für diejenigen die keine Vorlesung darüber hören können. Zweiter Theil welcher die angewandte allgemeine Logik enthält* (Berlin: Lagarde, 1796).
21   The only known letter from Diefenbach to Günderrode discusses the distinction that Kiesewetter draws between 'Verstand' and 'Vernunft', in *SW* III, 335.
22   Karl Rosenkranz, *Geschichte der Kant'schen Philosophie*, ed. by Steffen Dietzsch (Berlin: Akademie, 1987), p. 249.
23   There is circumstantial evidence to support this claim. An extract from one of Diefenbach's sermons in Günderrode's *Studienbuch* is entitled 'Bruchstück aus einer Predigt vor einer Landgemeinde' (Preitz/Hopp III, pp. 273–74) and is written in the same hand as the theological tract, a hand that is, bar the letter from Diefenbach to Günderrode, not present anywhere else in the *Nachlass*.
24   This is a common conception of revelation in the eighteenth century. See Antony N. Perovich Jr., 'Fichte, Hegel, and the Senses of "Revelation"', in *Fichte, German Idealism and Early Romanticism*, ed. by Daniel Breazeale and Tom Rockmore (Amsterdam: Rodopi, 2010), pp. 259–74 (p. 260).

in a quasi-Kantian fashion, since the universal maxims that underpin moral law are equated with the concept of God. To make this argument, Diefenbach, following Kant,[25] debunks both empirical and rational approaches to acquiring knowledge of God. Thus, one basis for the cosmological argument is invoked only to be dismissed, because any form of empirical observation cannot reliably establish a chain of causality that would lead to a creator:

> Wir bemerken z. B. überall Veränderungen in der Natur, die wir aber nie in ihren ganzen Umfang umfassen. Es sind also nur Veränderungen ihrer Theile, wo einer in den anderen wirket. In den meisten Theilsveränderungen welche wir bemerken, sehen wir auch andere in Bewegung gesetzte Naturtheile, die als Ursache entweder jene Veränderungen hervorbrachten oder als Wirkung von derselben abhiengen. Und so greift eins ins andere, und geht in einem ewigen Kreislauf fort ohne daß wir auf eine erste Ursache kommen.
>
> [We notice, for example, alterations in nature everywhere, which we, however, never grasp in their full scope. So these are only alterations of its parts, where one part acts in the others. When we notice the majority of these partial alterations, we can also see other parts of nature that have been set in motion, which either, as a cause, brought about those alterations or, as an effect, depended on them. And so one interacts with another, and continues in an eternal cycle without us coming to a first cause.][26]

The complexity of natural phenomena could lead the observer to mistake interdependent processes for a linear chain of causality. It follows that any pattern of cause and effects cannot lead to the first principle. What cannot be empirically perceived is the Aristotelian unmoved mover, 'eine erste Ursache', the *prima summa*. Diefenbach then moves on to discuss the limitations of reason in pursuit of the creator:

> Aus den Gesetzen des Denkens (und dem unmittelbaren Bewußtsein) bring ich aber ebensowenig einen Schöpfer hervor. Jenes heiligen Wesens bin ich mir nicht als Schöpfer, sondern als Gesetzgeber in mir bewußt worden. Daß die Natur nichts gegen ihn vermöge, muß ich annehmen, weil sonst seine Gebote in mir Thorheit seyn mussten, das sie aber doch nicht seyn können, weil sie der Vernunft nothwendig angehören. [...] Aber auch nur soweit führet mich die Vernunft mit Gewißheit, nicht bis zu einer Schöpfung — welche zwar wahr seyn kann, aber weder aus der Natur noch aus der Vernunft erkannt wird, und, wenn sie geglaubt wird, nur auf der Autorität einer unmittelbaren göttlichen Benachrichtigung geglaubt werden kann.
>
> [But nor do I produce a creator from the laws of thought (and from immediate consciousness). I have become aware of that holy being not as a creator, but as a law-giver in me. I must assume that nature has no power over him, because otherwise his commands in me would be folly, but they cannot be that, because they are necessarily part of reason [...] But reason only leads me this far with certainty, not to a concept of the creation — which may admittedly be true, but cannot be perceived from nature or from reason, and, if creation

---

25 Kant critiques the three main arguments for the existence of God — the cosmological, ontological and physico-theological, in the third *Hauptstück* of the *Kritik der reinen Vernunft*.
26 MS Ff. K. v. Günderrode Abt. 2 A2, fol. 87ʳ.

is to be believed, this can only be on the authority of immediate divine communication.]²⁷

Here, Diefenbach wants to make space for revealed religion, for the aspect of revelation that does transcend the laws of nature and therefore, even if it were rationally demonstrable, could not be inferred by reason. Belief in the creator and creation can be established 'nur auf der Autorität einer unmittelbaren göttlichen Benachrichtigung'. Faced with the limitations of subjective perception and inquiry, Diefenbach falls back onto the notion that the internal, rational moral law alone proves the existence of God. The moral imperative is apodictic, and has a source beyond the individual's nature, as the 'Gesetzgeber'. The individual possesses the freedom to obey the moral imperative, since if an individual's natural inclinations could not be overcome, then they would be useless ('Daß die Natur nichts gegen ihn vermöge, muß ich annehmen, weil sonst seine Gebote in mir Thorheit seyn mussten').

This theological tract is only indicative of the kinds of questions that interested Günderrode. Yet traces of Kantianism can be found in Günderrode's letters. In a letter to Gunda Brentano in 1802, Günderrode explores an epistemological *aporia* that is close to Diefenbach's statement of 'Wir bemerken z. B. überall Veränderungen in der Natur, die wir aber nie in ihren ganzen Umfang fassen' [We notice, for example, alterations in nature everywhere, which we, however, never grasp in their full scope]. Günderrode examines a Spinozist or Leibnizian problem: how can one establish a first cause if only the chain of events is perceptible?

> Überhaupt ist mirs ganz unbegreiflich daß wir kein anders Bewustsein haben, als Wahrnehmungen von Wirkungen, nirgends von Ursachen. Alles andere Wissen scheint mir (sobald ich dies bedenke) nicht wissenswürdig, solang ich des Wissens Ursache, mein Wissensvermögen, nicht kenne. Diese Unwissenheit ist mir der unerträglichste Mangel, der gröste Widerspruch. Und ich meine wenn wir die Gränze eines zweiten Lebens wirklich betretten, so müßte es eine unsrer ersten innern Erscheinungen sein, daß sich unser Bewustsein vergrösere und verdeutlichere; den[n] es wäre unerträglich, diese Schranke in ein zweites Leben zu schleppen.

> [In any case, it is completely incomprehensible to me that we have no other consciousness than perceptions of effects, never of causes. All other knowledge — as soon as I consider this — seems not worthy of knowing to me, as long as I do not know the cause of this knowledge, my capacity for knowledge. This ignorance is the most unbearable deficiency, the greatest contradiction. And I think if we do indeed cross a boundary into a second life, so one of the first internal phenomena that occurs must be that our consciousness expands and becomes clearer; for to drag this limitation into a second life would be unbearable.]²⁸

The epistemological problem here is twofold: perceiving only effects, rather than causes, could lead to an infinite regress of effects — that is, never being in the position to establish the underlying cause and therefore to extract the causal

27 Ibid., fols 87ᵛ–88ʳ.
28 Preitz, 'Karoline von Günderrode in ihrer Umwelt. II', p. 168.

structure that would lead to an underlying truth. But this also takes a Kantian turn for Günderrode — indeed, it takes Kant's Copernican turn. The missing cause is not the *prima summa* as with Diefenbach's theological tract, but rather a subjective faculty. The individual understanding generates knowledge in the first place: 'solang ich des Wissens Ursache, mein Wissensvermögen, nicht kenne'. The danger here is that this thought could develop into radical scepticism that tips into all-encompassing doubt about any conscious experience, since experience could be dismissed as subjectively constructed to the extent that no 'objective' knowledge can be discerned. And this is what underpins Günderrode's lament of 'Diese Unwissenheit ist mir der unerträglichste Mangel, der gröste Widerspruch': the individual capacity for knowledge is self-defeating if it cannot reliably yield any knowledge at all.

The culmination of this thought contains *in nuce* a paradoxical tension that defines the movement of ascent and descent. To counter this potential for scepticism, Günderrode concludes with an intriguing thought about sensory expansion after death, about how consciousness can be heightened in order to circumvent this epistemological problem: 'Und ich meine wenn wir die Gränze eines zweiten Lebens wirklich betreten, so müßte es eine unsrer ersten innern Erscheinungen sein, daß sich unser Bewustsein vergrösere und verdeutlichere'. The paradox is that sensory expansion can only occur *in* and *through* death, rather than through any other cognitive and perceptual leaps. This is tantamount to a failure of the movement of ascent or descent, since there is an absolute limit set on what the individual can know, given the limitations of their faculty of understanding. Whilst there is the potential expansion of consciousness, in this case it is understood as an impossibility within life itself.

Yet this is far from Günderrode's last word on the limits of individual consciousness. The movement of ascent and descent throughout Günderrode's works is marked by a desire to expand individual consciousness and perception to attain absolute knowledge. However, it is held in check by the idea of limit, in the sense that the attempt to overcome the limitations of the self will fail.

Ascent, Descent, and the Inner Sense

A running theme throughout Günderrode's *oeuvre* is a turn towards the subject — in particular towards a divided subject, trapped within the phenomenal world and yet with an innate awareness of transcendence — whose task it is to attain a holistic world-view. This can be achieved through non-rational forms of perception, and thus the movement of ascent or descent has an innately cognitive or perceptual aspect to it. Indeed, this perceptual aspect links directly back to Kant's epistemology, and not just because of the desire to expand individual consciousness laid out in the letter to Gunda Brentano. In a letter of between 1801 and 1803 presumably addressed to Claudine Piautaz, Günderrode is happy to concede that the individual cannot extricate itself from spatiotemporal bounds. But this is with the exception of the inner senses, which exist outside space:

> Ich habe oft darüber nachgedacht, aber ich glaube nicht daß man zwei Zustände zugleich haben kann; ich glaube sie folgen (mögen auch die Zeitabschnitte noch so klein sein) auf einander. Wie wunderbar sind wir doch mit der Zeit verflochten — in der Logik lernte ich, <u>es lassen sich keine Anschauungen der äusseren Sinne ohne die Merkmale Zeit u Raum gedenken, u keine Anschauung des inneren Sinnes ohne das Merkmal Zeit</u>. Sehr sonderbar das mir das eben erst zum recht deutlichen Begriff wird.
>
> [I have often given thought to this matter, but I do not believe that one can have two states at the same time; I believe that they follow one another (as small as the periods of time themselves may be). How wonderful it is that we are woven into time — in logic I learned <u>that no perceptions of the external senses can be thought of without the properties of time and space, and no perception of the inner sense can be thought of without the property of time</u>. How curious that this has only just become a completely clear concept to me.][29]

This distinction falls in line with Günderrode's study of Kantianism:[30] here, 'der innere Sinn' is merely the subject's ability to perceive its own concepts as objects of thought. But the concept of 'der innere Sinn' is one that Günderrode extends into the notion of a legitimate, reliable, and internalised version of physical sight, also known as the spiritual eye, or 'das Auge des Geistes'.

The early poem 'Der Dom zu Cölln' [The Cathedral at Cologne] (c. 1800–1802) features an ascending movement which functions as sensory expansion. This is bound up with a thought that is analogous to that of Lessing's in 'Daß mehr als fünf Sinne für den Menschen sein können': new senses can be developed to perceive particular phenomena or stimuli. It is through this expansion of sense perception brought about by 'der innere Sinn' that Günderrode moves beyond Kantianism. Given that rationality and empiricism cannot produce absolute knowledge, there must be some means of discerning the truths that underpin reality, without there being an insuperable dualism between the phenomenal world and the infinite totality.

As laid out by the Lehrer in 'Die Manen', 'der innere Sinn' facilitates the apprehension of spiritual forces that give rise to religion:

> Blos geistige Kräfte können unsern äussern Sinnen nicht offenbar werden; sie wirken nicht durch unsere Augen und Ohren auf uns, sondern durch das Organ, durch das allein eine Verbindung mit ihnen möglich ist, durch den inneren Sinn, auf ihn wirken sie unmittelbar. [...]
>
> Wem also der innere Sinn, das Auge des Geistes, aufgegangen ist, der sieht dem Andern unsichtbare mit ihm verbundene Dinge. Aus diesem innern Sinn sind die Religionen hervorgegangen, und so manche Apokalipsen der alten und neuen Zeit.

---

29 Karoline von Günderrode, letter to Claudine Piautaz, 1801–03, Freies Deutsches Hochstift (FDH), Frankfurt a.M., MS 20369, fols 1^r–1^v (underlining present in the manuscript).
30 Kiesewetter, ad. § 53, p. 67: 'jede Anschauung eines Gegenstandes muß schlechterdings die Formen derselben, wenn sie eine äußere ist, Raum und Zeit, und wenn sie eine innere ist, die Form der Zeit an sich tragen' [every perception of an object must absolutely include the forms of space and time, if it is an external perception, and the form of time, if it is an internal perception].

[Mere spiritual forces cannot be revealed to our external senses; they do not affect us through our eyes and ears, but rather via an organ that is the only one to permit a connection with these forces, it is the internal sense that they directly affect. [...]

Whoever has developed an internal sense, the spiritual eye, they are capable of seeing that which is invisible but connected with them. It is out of the internal sense that religions developed, and thereby many of the revelations from the past and the present.] (*SW* I, 34–35)

The Lehrer is quick to point out that 'der innere Sinn' is conventionally understood as 'überspannte Einbildung' [overactive imagination] (*SW* I, 35), and therefore is part and parcel of *Schwärmerei*. At the same time, the Lehrer avoids associating 'der innere Sinn' with all manner of visions of spirits, since this would amount to the kind of Swedenborgian communion with spirits that Kant satirically attacked in *Träume eines Geistersehers, erläutert durch Träume der Metaphysik* [Dreams of a Spirit-Seer, Explained through Dreams of Metaphysics] (1766). As a concept across the eighteenth century, 'der innere Sinn' is not confined to mysticism but can refer to an aesthetic sense for Hutcheson and for Winckelmann, or to the moral organ that allows an individual to perceive both the divine and the self for Hemsterhuis.[31]

In 'Der Dom zu Cölln', Günderrode adopts 'der innere Sinn' as a form of aesthetic insight brought about by synaesthesia, since it is the interactions between different senses that disclose truths that could not otherwise be discerned. Therefore, these sensory experiences counter and expand upon the hierarchical Enlightenment model of sense perception which, following Platonic thought, gave primacy to sight.[32] Whilst Novalis emphasises the importance of poetry, and specifically, the *Märchen* as a means to expand sensory experience,[33] the importance of aesthetics in Günderrode's 'Der Dom zu Cölln' is likely to derive from her reading of Schiller's philosophical poems, such 'Das Reich der Schatten' [The Realm of Shadows] and 'Die Künstler'.[34]

> Fünffach wölbt sich die Dekke auf Gruppen gothischer Säulen,
> Höher hebt sich der Chor, stolzer getragen empor,
> Schön ist das Jnnre geziert mit Erzen u Marmor und Teppchen
> Und ein purpurner Tag bricht durch die farbigen Fenster. –
> Aber dort wo die Dunkelheit dichter sich webt durch die Säulen!
> Hauchet ein Modergeruch dumpf aus der Tiefe herauf,
> Alda schlafen die Helden der Kirche im hüllenden Sarge
> Und ihr Bildniß ruht drauf, sie falten die Hände zum Beten
> Und ihr starrender Blick hat sich zum Himmel gewand.
> Staunend seh ich sie an, mir ist als müßten sie reden
> Aber sie starren noch fort wie sie es Jahrhunderte thaten
> Und mich schauert so tief daß also stumm sind die Toden.

---

31   Dormann, pp. 111–27.
32   Peter Utz, *Das Auge und das Ohr im Text: Literarische Sinneswahrnehmung in der Goethezeit* (Munich: Fink, 1990), p. 8.
33   Novalis, *Schriften*, ed. by Paul Kluckhohn and others, 3rd edn, 5 vols (Stuttgart: Kohlhammer, 1960–88), II: *Das philosophische Werk I*, ed. by Richard Samuel (1965), p. 564.
34   See Walter Morgenthaler's notes in *SW* III, 221–22.

Doch da hebt sich Gesang, u Orgeltöne, sie schweben
Feiernd die Dome hinauf, wo glänzende Heilige beten
Und es wandeln die Töne sich um in Fittche der Engel
Und umrauschen melodisch woogend die heiligen Bilder.
Und zum Himmel verkläret sich alles Musik, und Farben, u Formen,
Aus dem entzükten Auge verschwinden die Gräber, und Toden,
Und den stummen Grüften entsteiget ein freudiges Jauchzen. –
Ja ich habe die Auferstehung gesehen im Auge des Geistes.
Und das Leben der Kunst, es führte die Seele zum Himel.
Dichtkunst! Du Seele der Künste, du die sie alle gebohren,
Du beseelest das Grab steigest zum Himel empor.

[The ceiling's arches are spread fivefold on groups of Gothic columns
The quire is raised higher, carried more proudly upward;
The interior is beautifully decorated with bronzes, and marble, and tapestries
And a crimson day bursts through the coloured windows. —
But below, where darkness densely weaves through the columns!
From the depths, a musty, dull odour emanates,
The church's heroes slumber there, cloaked in their coffins
And their likenesses lie in repose upon them, they clasp their hands in prayer
And their petrified gaze is turned towards heaven.
I look upon them, astonished, it is almost as if they were to speak
But their gaze continues just as they had for centuries
And it caused a deep shudder to know that the dead are mute in such a way.
Yet then arises song, and the sounds of the organ, they float
Upwards, jubilant through the cathedrals, to where shimmering saints pray
And the notes are transformed into angels' wings
And rush around the holy images, surging with melody
Towards heaven everything is transfigured: all music, and colours, and shapes;
Before my ecstatic eye, the graves and the dead disappear
And from the silent crypts rises a joyful exultation. —
Yes! I saw the resurrection in my mind's eye.
And the vitality of art, it led souls to heaven.
Poetry! You soul of the arts, you who bore them all,
You ensoul the grave, rise to heaven above.] (*SW* I, 379)

The primary problem with which the speaker is faced is an existential one: how one can commune with the dead, and by extension, receive assurances about the core Christian doctrine of eternal life. The upper reaches of the cathedral represent architectural splendour, but this opulence is distinct from the gloom on the ground level: 'Aber dort wo die Dunkelheit dichter sich webt durch die Säulen! | Hauchet ein Modergeruch dumpf aus der Tiefe herauf'. The speaker struggles to assign meaning to the 'Helden der Kirche' interred in the cathedral. Their lifelike effigies foster the hope that some form of communication can be established with them. But this is thwarted at every turn: 'Staunend seh ich sie an, mir ist als müßten sie reden | Aber sie starren noch fort wie sie es Jahrhunderte thaten'. The speaker is aware that this is a foolhardy endeavour — hence 'wie sie es Jahrhunderte thaten'. Yet this does not diminish the fear caused by alienation from the dead: 'mich schauert so tief daß also stumm sind die Toden'. These existential concerns, with their emphasis on mortality, contain a self-reflexive element — the horror at the silent dead could turn into a *horror vacui* and despair at one's own mortality. From the perspective of the Christian poet, such despair could dismantle faith in Christian salvation history.

But this potential problem does not develop beyond nascent doubt. Rather, the swell of liturgical music triggers a potent response in the speaker: the notes break this sense of dislocation and open up an alternative experience of time focused on the absolute intensity of the moment. As a result, the disjuncture between the lower and upper reaches of the cathedral begins to dissolve alongside the non-communication between the speaker and the dead. This shift is not only structurally emphasised by the *volta*, but also through the first instance of enjambement, which creates a spatial suspension between the lines: 'Doch da hebt sich Gesang, u Orgeltöne, sie schweben | Feiernd die Dome hinauf'. Music interacts with the imagination of the speaker and provokes synaesthesia so that sight and hearing become entwined: 'es wandlen die Töne sich um in Fittche der Engel'. All sense perception then dissolves into purifying ascension: 'zum Himmel verkläret sich alles Musik, und Farben, u Formen'.

Yet this is no absolute surrender to ecstatic sensory rapture. The speaker retains the awareness that this is an aesthetic illusion: 'Aus dem entzükten Auge verschwinden die Gräber, und Toden'. But this does not devalue the intensity of the experience. Quite the opposite: the visions induced by the liturgy become so profound that they culminate in ineffability — hence the temporal lacuna indicated by a dash. Although the vision of the resurrection of the dead does take place, this is recounted after the fact: 'Ja ich habe die Auferstehung gesehen im Auge des Geistes'. These revelatory visions are generated by 'der innere Sinn', which, as in 'Die Manen', has religious import: the speaker is seized by the vision of the joyous resurrection and salvation of mankind, and thus their Christian faith is restored.

Curiously, the last three lines of 'Der Dom zu Cölln' shift away from the veneration of music and ascribe a Messianic function to the poetic impulse: 'Dichtkunst! Du Seele der Künste, du die sie alle gebohren, | Du beseelest das Grab steigest zum Himel empor'. This inverts the historical narrative in which lyrical poetry is a derivative form of music. By assigning 'Dichtkunst' the role of mediator between immanence and transcendence, Günderrode signals a return to the conception of the poet in antiquity, where poetic inspiration originates in divine intervention, as Socrates states in Plato's *Ion*.[35] Whilst the poetic impulse revives and redeems the soul from bodily decay, it is poetry that is the ascending force alongside the visionary resurrection of the dead. What Günderrode advocates here is a positive form of art understood as religion, or *Kunstreligion*: it is poetry, through the operations of 'der innere Sinn' or 'das Auge des Geistes', which creates jubilant glimpses into transcendent limitlessness.[36] This ecstatic vision of spatial

---

35 'For all good poets utter all those fine poems of theirs not through skill, but when inspired and possessed, and good lyric poets do the same. [...] For a poet is a light and winged and sacred thing, and is unable to compose until he is inspired and out of his mind', in Plato, *Ion*, in *Classical Literary Criticism*, ed. by T. S. Dorsch and Penelope Murray (London: Penguin, 2004), pp. 1–14 (p. 5).

36 See also the *Nachlass* fragment, 'Herrlicher Sänger es schloß ein Gott dir die sterblichen Augen | Aber mit den Augen des Sinns siehst du die Fülle der Welt' [Wondrous singer, a god closed your

and sensory unity temporarily allows the transcendent and immanent realms to overlap.

'Der Dom zu Cölln' is one of the more orthodox Christian of Günderrode's works, but in broad terms it features a successful form of cognitive ascent: the speaker overcomes its initial dislocation through a series of perceptual leaps that culminate in a revelation. As such it bears comparison in its narrative structure with 'Ein apokaliptisches Fragment'. What is omitted from 'Der Dom zu Cölln', however, is any attempt to work against the destructive objectification of nature as lamented in 'Vorzeit, und Neue Zeit'. Rather than providing affirmation for central tenets of Christian doctrine, the emphasis of this movement of ascent or descent in general across Günderrode lies on the textual movement towards a potential unification of the individual and nature — but nature understood as the manifestation of divine order.[37] Any successful attempt at unification both legitimises spiritual longings and regains the assurance of interdependence between the individual and divine order, which anticipates Schleiermacher's 'schlechthinnige Abhängigkeit' [absolute dependence] of the individual on the divine.[38]

But in Günderrode, this movement of ascent or descent is also both prone to failure and treated with scepticism. The propensity for failure is connected to the question of individual agency and of the human capacity for (self-)knowledge. The successful ascent seen in 'Der Dom zu Cölln' finds its counterpart in failure that takes the form of enforced descent. 'Der Luftschiffer' [The Aeronaut] (c. 1802–04), a poem from the *Nachlass*, is presumably inspired by fashion for flight following the first manned hot-air balloon flight in Paris in November 1783. The poem encapsulates the problems involved with ascent and how it can be thwarted:

> Gefahren bin ich in schwankendem Kahne
> Auf dem blauligten Ozeane
> Der die leuchtenden Sterne umfließt,
> Habe die Himlischen Mächte gekrüßt.
> War in ihrer Betrachtung versunken
> Habe den ewigen Äther getrunken
> Habe dem Jrrdischen ganz mich entwand
> Droben die Schriften der Sterne erkant
> Und in ihren Kreißen u Drehen
> Bildlich den heiligen Rythmus gesehen
> Der gewaltig auch jeglichen Klang
> Reißt zu des Wohllautes wogendem Drang
>
> Aber ach! es ziehet mich hernieder
> Nebel überschleiert meinen Blick
> Und der Erde Gränzen seh ich wieder
> Wolken treiben mich zu ihr zurük

mortal eyes | but with the eyes of a higher sense you see the plenitude of the world] (*SW* I, 398).

37   The attempt to reunify self and nature is also present in Novalis and Hölderlin. See Jane E. Kneller, 'Romantic Conceptions of the Self in Novalis and Hölderlin', in *Figuring the Self: Subject, Absolute, and Others in Classical German Philosophy*, ed. by David E. Klemm and Günter Zöller (Albany: SUNY Press, 1997), pp. 134–48 (p. 135).

38   Schleiermacher coined this phrase in *Der christliche Glaube* (1821–22).

> Wehe! das Gesez der Schwere
> Es behauptet neu sein Recht
> Keiner darf sich ihm entziehen
> Von dem irrdischen Geschlecht.
>
> [I travelled in the swaying barge
> On the blue ocean
> That flows around the radiant stars,
> Greeted the heavenly powers,
> Was rapt in contemplation of them,
> Drank the eternal ether
> Have freed myself from all that is Earthly.
> Above I discerned the writing of the stars
> And saw in their circles and turns
> The image of holy rhythm
> Which powerfully wrests every tone
> to the surging pulse of harmonious sound.
>
> But oh! Downwards it pulls me,
> Mists veil my gaze,
> I see the earth's limits once more,
> Clouds drive me back.
>
> O! The law of gravity,
> It claims its right anew,
> No one can escape it
> Of the Earthly race.] (*SW* I, 390)

Of particular importance here is the deixis of both time and place. The double or split perspective[39] of the speaker, who, in recounting the technological wonder of flight and the perception of heavenly phenomena, reveals its earthbound position — 'Droben die Schriften der Sterne erkant'; 'es ziehet mich hernieder' — thus proleptically alluding to the eventual return to the earth's surface. Thus the act of transcending human limitations is undercut by an awareness of its brevity. Even flight is understood only by poetic analogy to the more familiar experience of sailing — an analogy which is present in a potential source of inspiration for the poem, Jean Paul's 'Des Luftschiffers Giannozzo Seebuch' [The Diary of the Aeronaut Giannozzo] (1801), included as part of *Titan* (1800–1803).

What comes to the fore in the first strophe is how Günderrode establishes the assertion of human agency — the repeated 'Habe' takes precedence at the beginning of the lines, as well as 'War'. This confident tone then culminates in the bold claim 'Habe dem Jrrdischen ganz mich entwand'. The desire of the speaker is not merely to observe, but also to partake of, and to absorb 'den ewigen Äther', which establishes this flight as a search for transcendence. But this is equally a search for order, as revealed in the last quartet of this first strophe, in which the speaker begins to sense the harmonic resonance of the cosmos in the movement of celestial

---

39 Sabine Eickenrodt helpfully discusses this 'Doppelperspektive' in her reading of the poem. See Sabine Eickenrodt, *Augen-Spiel: Jean Pauls optische Metaphorik der Unsterblichkeit* (Göttingen: Wallstein, 2006), pp. 256–64.

bodies — 'Bildlich den heiligen Rythmus gesehen' [saw the image of holy rhythm] — that is, the Pythagorean harmony of the spheres. The musical consonance of the cosmos is therefore proof of divine order. In sensing this harmony, the speaker's excitement becomes aurally perceptible through the quality of long, open vowels and diphthongs, ending with the tantalising open vowels of 'des Wohllautes wogendem Drang'.

Yet this harmony remains out of reach. What follows is the *volta* and the inevitable descent, which Günderrode marks metrically as a contraction, by the shift from loose dactyls to tighter trochees, which are compressed over the course of the two strophes from pentameter to clipped tetrameter. With this comes the persona's loss of unbridled agency: it is exposed to the forces of nature — 'es ziehet mich hernieder', and the claim to have surpassed earthly limits has to be repudiated on account of Newtonian physics — 'das Gesetz der Schwere | Es behauptet neu sein Recht'. The didactic epigram that concludes the poem, 'Keiner darf sich ihm entziehen | Von dem irrdischen Geschlecht', a counterpoint to 'Habe dem Jrrdischen ganz mich entwand', summarises the tension generated by the desire for ascent. For man suffers from dual nature: he is tied to materiality, but has spiritual aspirations and a desire for divine order that allow temporary elevation — aspirations that are, in this case, dashed. Mere will does not suffice, since human agency is subject to and limited by the laws of nature.

The *Nachlass* poem 'Einstens lebt' ich süßes Leben' [Once a Dulcet Life was Mine] (*c.* 1802–03) follows a similar pattern of ascent and descent, but significantly includes a substratum of Platonic thought that generates this movement. The speaker imagines itself suspended at the threshold between the Earth and the heavens and is driven by the desire to commune with the heavenly forces of the constellations. These are both personified and encrypted representatives of cosmic order ruled over, in a touch of Catholicism, by a virgin. The speaker is then caught by the sudden remembrance of its own origins, which is marked by a metrical break from the clipped Adonic line to an uneven trochaic tetrameter:

> Und es hielt ein tiefes Sehnen
> Jn mir selber mich gefangen
> Und mir war als hab ich einstens
> Mich von einem süßen Leibe
> los gerissen, und nun blute
> Erst die Wunde alter Schmerzen.
>
> [But a deep-down longing held me
> Prisoner within myself;
> And I felt as if I had at one time
> Wrenched myself from a sweet body,
> And were feeling only now
> The bleeding wound of pain gone by.] (*SW* I, 385, ll. 80–85)[40]

By echoing the language that opens the poem, this forms an emphatic narrative

---

40 Jeannine Blackwell and Susanne Zantop (eds.), *Bitter Healing: German Women Writers 1700–1800. An Anthology* (Lincoln: University of Nebraska Press, 1990), p. 433.

turn. This intuitive realisation is Platonic *anamnesis*: through remembrance, the speaker learns of its earthbound origins. The trauma of birth is recalled as the primal split from the Earth-as-mother: 'Da ward mir als sey ich entsprungen | Dem innersten Leben der Mutter' [Then I felt that I was sprung | From the Mother's innermost life] (ibid., ll. 93–94).⁴¹ So traumatic is this *anamnesis*, coupled with the speaker lamenting its error in straying beyond the limits of the Earth, that the speaker descends and returns — an act of self-dissolution and death — to the maternal womb: '[zu] der verhülleten | Quelle des Lebens' [[to] the shrouded | Wellspring of life] (*SW* I, 386, ll. 111–12).⁴² The use of Platonic *anamnesis* here is significant. *Anamnesis* and Platonic *eros* recur across Günderrode's *oeuvre*, often in the form of a dialectic, and are even an integral part of the movement of ascent. But the use of *anamnesis* and *eros* as means of recovering intuitive, forgotten knowledge raises the question of what constitutes Günderrode's reception of Plato, and how this may influence textual occurrences of ascent and descent.

Ascent and Platonism: *eros* and *anamnesis*

There are no documentary indications that Günderrode was familiar with the works of Plato. The only direct reference to Plato's works is in an unpublished letter to Günderrode of early 1805, when Lisette Nees von Esenbeck, a friend of Günderrode and the wife of Christian Nees von Esenbeck, exhorts Günderrode to read the first two volumes of Schleiermacher's translation of Plato — 'Suche doch ja Schleyermachers Übersezung des Plato zu bekommen' [Try to obtain a copy of Schleiermacher's translation of Plato].⁴³ Nees von Esenbeck contrasts Schleiermacher's sound philosophical interpretation of Platonic philosophy with Friedrich Stolberg's three-volume translation *Auserlesene Gespräche des Platon* [Selected Platonic Dialogues] (1796–97), and thus echoes Goethe's critical review in the essay *Plato als Mitgenosse einer christlichen Offenbarung* [Plato as Party to a Christian Revelation] (1796). Goethe considered Stolberg to have distorted Plato by Christianising the source material. This reading recommendation is one of many that Nees von Esenbeck offered to Günderrode.⁴⁴ What is significant, however, is that it neatly points to the juncture in Plato reception around 1800. Schleiermacher's rigorous translation made possible a new interpretation of Plato, which was itself inspired in part by Friedrich Schlegel's reading of him.⁴⁵

Before Schleiermacher there was a resurgence of interest in Plato in the second half of the eighteenth century, indeed what Michael Franz has called the discovery

---

41   Ibid., pp. 433–35.
42   Ibid., p. 435.
43   Lisette Nees von Esenbeck, letter to Karoline von Günderrode, 28 February 1805, Freies Deutsches Hochstift (FDH), Frankfurt a.M., MS 8345, 3ᵛ.
44   Others include Friedrich Schlegel, Goethe, Tieck, and Novalis, as a bid to wean Günderrode off Schiller — whom she favoured — and, in particular, the declamatory rhetoric of Schiller's dramas.
45   Christoph Asmuth, *Interpretation — Transformation: Das Platonbild bei Fichte, Schelling, Hegel, Schleiermacher und Schopenhauer und das Legitimationsproblem der Philosophiegeschichte* (Göttingen: Vandenhoeck & Ruprecht, 2006), p. 19.

of Plato in the spirit of sensibility.[46] Of particular interest, therefore, were the dialogues concerned with love — *Phaedrus* and the *Symposium*. The latter was accorded special status as the most poetic of Plato's works,[47] and together they were the most frequently published, translated and imitated Platonic dialogues in the latter half of the eighteenth century.[48] The popular success of Moses Mendelssohn's *Phädon oder über die Unsterblichkeit der Seele* [Phaedon or On the Immortality of the Soul] (1767) ushered in a period of Platonising essays and dialogues, promoted by Friedrich Heinrich Jacobi. One mediator for this resurgence of interest in Platonic ideas, alongside Rousseau and Shaftesbury, was the Dutch philosopher Hemsterhuis, whose writings drew particular attention to the Platonic conceptions of the soul and *eros*.[49] Whilst Günderrode did make excerpts from Hemsterhuis's *Simon ou des facultés de l'âme*, Platonic ideas were so widespread around 1800 that this is only one of many sources of Platonic ideas. Hölderlin's *Hyperion*, too, builds on the cult of Diotima and alludes to the myths recounted in the *Symposium*.[50]

On the whole, Günderrode's engagement with Platonic ideas accords with their reception during the period of sensibility, for the simple reason that the texts that adopt Platonic *eros* and *anamnesis* fall in line with the general reception of Plato in the latter half of the eighteenth century. Also, there is a Platonic imprint to relatively early texts, dating from around and prior to 1804, which eliminates the possibility that Günderrode's engagement with Schleiermacher's edition of Plato was her primary source of Platonic ideas.

In Diotima's speech in Plato's *Symposium*, *eros* is a *daimon*, a mediating spirit between the earthly and the divine:

> He [*eros*] occupies middle ground [...] he lies between mortality and immortality [...] Divinity and humanity cannot meet directly; the gods only ever communicate and converse with men [...] by means of spirits. [...] There are a great many spirits, and one of them is love (202d–203a).[51]

As the progeny of the god of plenty and the goddess of poverty, *eros* is naturally attracted to the beautiful (203b), and precisely because of this parentage, *eros* strives to be godlike but forever remains the almost-god, and forever lacks that which it desires (204a). That Günderrode was aware of this understanding of *eros* is shown by the opening of the poem 'Liebe' (1804), which is structured around a series of Petrarchan oppositions: 'O reiche Armuth!' [O rich poverty!] (*SW* I, 79, l. 1).

---

46 Michael Franz, *Schellings Tübinger Platon-Studien* (Göttingen: Vandenhoeck & Ruprecht, 1996), p. 77.
47 Stefan Matuschek, 'Die Macht des Gastmahls: Schlegels *Gespräch über die Poesie* und Platons *Symposion*', in *Wo das philosophische Gespräch ganz in Dichtung übergeht: Platons Symposion und seine Wirkung in der Renaissance, Romantik und Moderne*, ed. by Stefan Matuschek (Heidelberg: Winter, 2002), pp. 81–96 (p. 85).
48 Bernd Auerochs, 'Platon um 1800: Zu seinem Bild bei Stolberg, Wieland, Schlegel und Schleiermacher', *Wieland-Studien*, 3 (1996), 161–93 (p. 163).
49 Michael Erler, *Die Philosophie der Antike: Platon* (Basel: Schwabe, 2007), p. 542.
50 Stephan Lampenscherf, '"Heiliger Plato, vergieb . . .": Hölderlins "Hyperion" und Die neue Platonische Mythologie', *Hölderlin-Jahrbuch*, 28 (1992–93), 128–51.
51 Plato, *Symposium*, trans. by Robin Waterfield (Oxford: Oxford University Press, 2008), pp. 43–44.

For Günderrode, *eros* is also metaphysical and impersonal. Therefore, it lacks a corporeal or sexual element, and is concerned with the incorporeal — in Platonic terms, the Forms. It is, as laid out in the first of a series of aphoristic notes in the *Nachlass*, the expression of impersonal love and striving for unattainable perfection:

> Die Vortreflichkeit ist ein Ganzes wir haben sie nicht, sie ist gleichsam wie die Bläue des Himels über uns, u unsere Vortreflichkeit, ist nur ein Streben zu ihr, eine Ansicht von ihr; drum ist keine Persöhnliche Liebe, nur Liebe zum Vortreflichen
>
> [Perfection is a whole; we do not possess it, it is, as it were, like the blue of the sky above us, and our perfection is only striving towards it, a visual perception of it; therefore there is no personal love, only love for perfection] (*SW* I, 436)

Whilst perfection cannot be achieved by the individual — which is why *eros* is so well suited to the movement of ascent — it can be perceived, and the introduction of this aesthetic element points to the conflation of perfection and beauty. Yet 'Vortreflichkeit' is not merely a philosophical abstraction for Günderrode: it is a quality by which she habitually judged acquaintances, resulting in Christian Nees von Esenbeck, in a letter to Günderrode, ironically quantifying relative levels of individual 'Vortreflichkeit'.[52]

It is this understanding of *eros* as striving for that which it cannot ever possess that is developed further in the poem 'Liebe und Schönheit' [Love and Beauty]. 'Liebe und Schönheit' belongs to a triad of early poems, including 'Tendenz des Künstlers' and 'Der Dom zu Cölln', all written by 1804, and all of which concern the role of the artist and poet. Up to a point, all three poems valorise the artist. It is in 'Liebe und Schönheit' that the artist is also explicitly the creator, as Prometheus. As in the mythological account,[53] Prometheus crafts and ensouls man with a spark of sunlight: 'Doch dieser [Sonnen]Funke, er entflammt im Bilde | Jn das des Künstlers Weisheit ihn verhüllte' [Yet this spark, it ignites in the image | In which the artist's wisdom cloaked it] (*SW* I, 377, ll. 5–6). Prometheus, it appears, has moulded a perfect synthesis of soul and corporeal form: the artist-as-creator is thus capable of mediating between the divine and the earthly, which reflects the kind of praise bestowed upon the artist (however ironically) by Socrates in Plato's *Ion*.

But the image of the artist-as-creator is not simply one of valorisation. In 'Liebe und Schönheit', this act of creation results in a primordial split, the rupture between individual and totality. This does not assume a moral dimension as in the Christian sense of the fall into sin. Rather, Günderrode interprets the Promethean creation myth through the lens of the narrative of the primordial split, and draws attention to this layering of mythological narratives through a use of a curious transposition to startle the reader: Prometheus ensouls man with both sunlight and a droplet of absolute beauty: 'Bis er [Prometheus] der Sonne Funken hat entwendet; | (Ein Tropfe der der Schönheit Meer enttroff)' [Until he [Prometheus] had stolen a spark from the sun; | (A drop that fell from the sea of beauty)] (*SW* I, 377, ll. 3–4). As a

---

52   Günderrode, *Briefe*, pp. 107–09.
53   For a contemporary account of the myth, see Karl Philipp Moritz's *Götterlehre oder mythologische Dichtungen der Alten* (1791).

consequence of the loss of primordial unity, the individual remains latently aware of the trauma of their birth, and this awareness manifests itself as *eros*:

> Von Schönheit ist das Leben ausgegangen,
> Doch es vergißt den hohen Ursprung nicht;
> Es strebt zu ihm, und Lieb ist dies Verlangen,
> Die ewig ringet nach dem Sonnenlicht.
> Denn Lieb ist Wunsch, Erinerung des Schönen,
> Die Schönheit schauen will der Liebe Sehnen.
> [...]
> Doch ach! unendlich ist das Reich des Schönen,
> So auch unendlich unserer Liebe Sehnen.
>
> [Life sprang forth from beauty
> But it does not forget its high origin;
> It strives towards it, and this longing is love,
> which eternally strives for the sunlight.
> For love is desire, remembrance of the beautiful;
> Love's longing wishes to behold beauty
> [...]
> But oh! endless is the realm of beauty,
> So endless too is our love's longing.] (*SW* I, 377, ll. 7–18)

Here Günderrode combines the Platonic idea of *anamnesis*, the unconscious remembrance of a past state — in this case, the state of absolute beauty — 'Lieb ist [...] Erinerung des Schönen', and *eros*, the desire towards and to behold this beauty — 'Es strebt zu ihm [dem hohen Ursprung]'. What Günderrode develops here is a dialectic between *anamnesis* and *eros*, similar to that which is proposed by Socrates in Plato's *Phaedrus*, where it is exemplified by the man who, by perceiving earthly beauty, seeks hopelessly to strive towards true beauty (249d).[54] For Günderrode, *anamnesis* is simply innate, not provoked by any external stimulus. The tension of the poem stems from the soul's remembrance of the pure beauty in its 'hohen Ursprung', and its inability to ascend to this primal unity. And it is a tension that necessarily remains unresolved, which is exemplified by the elegiac tone of the closing couplet. The syntactic parallels of the couplet underscore the cleavage between the 'Reich des Schönen', which cannot be directly experienced, and 'unserer Liebe Sehnen' — the ever-thwarted erotic desire. With the phrase 'unserer Liebe Sehnen' — a contrast to 'der Liebe Sehnen' at the end of the preceding stanza — *eros* is stripped of a degree of abstraction, and is instead formulated as a universal human affliction. Thus what 'Liebe und Schönheit' presents, *in nuce*, is the tension within the movement of ascent: the desire for transcendence is here grounded in the awareness of absolute beauty, but the individual cannot, in keeping with the concept of *eros*, rise above material reality to perceive anything on the metaphysical plane.

---

54 Plato, *Phaedrus*, trans. by Robin Waterfield (Oxford: Oxford University Press, 2002), p. 33.

'Immortalita': Liebe as the Source of Absolute Agency

What 'Liebe und Schönheit' points towards, but does not realise within the text, is a triadic narrative: of primordial unity, a fall, and an eventual return to unity. This type of narrative has been identified as a feature of Romantic writing by M. H. Abrams in his seminal *Natural Supernaturalism: Tradition and Revolution in Romantic Literature* (1971). For Abrams, this tripartite narrative is part of an inheritance from Christian theology as well as from Neoplatonism.[55] The dramolet 'Immortalita' (1804) both adopts Platonic *eros* and adheres to this triadic narrative. In this respect, 'Immortalita' is unusual in Günderrode's *oeuvre*, because its resolution unambiguously stages the coming of a utopian golden age,[56] 'die goldne Zukunft' [golden future] (*SW* I, 44, ll. 107–08), a state of redemption and reconciliation that has clear resonances with Christian salvation history. Elsewhere, Günderrode alludes to a future perfective state ('Briefe zweier Freunde') or constructs texts to end proleptically, on the cusp of some form of harmony and resolution ('Mahomed, der Prophet von Mekka'; 'Nikator') that cannot be realised, but nonetheless evokes utopian anticipation.[57] By contrast, 'Immortalita' functions as an allegorising counterpart to 'Klingsohrs Märchen' [Klingsor's Fairy Tale] from Novalis's novel *Heinrich von Ofterdingen* (1800), Indeed, of the two sonnets that Günderrode writes in praise of Novalis, 'Novalis deinen heilgen Seherblikken' [To Novalis, your sacred seers' eyes], makes explicit reference to 'Klingsohrs Märchen' as a source of eschatological hope:

> Du [Novalis] siehst das Recht, das Wahre, Schöne siegen
> Die Zeit sich selbst im Ewigen zernichten
> Und Eros ruhend sich dem Weltall fügen
>
> [You [Novalis] see what is right, true, and beautiful triumph,
> Time destroy itself in eternity
> And Eros, quiescent, submit to the cosmos] (*SW* I, 391, ll. 9–11)

For Günderrode, Novalis's writings validate a sense of eschatological anticipation: Novalis is imagined as a visionary poet who possesses the ability to reveal world-historical events that are yet to come (ibid., ll. 12–14). The two elements that Günderrode extracts from 'Klingsohrs Märchen' — the dissolution of historical time into eternity, and Eros yielding to the cosmos — are revealing about Günderrode's own interests, and indeed, address the two primary themes in 'Immortalita'.

---

55 M. H. Abrams, *Natural Supernaturalism: Tradition and Revolution in Romantic Literature* (New York: Norton, 1971), p. 181.
56 Licher, p. 388: 'Das Stück gestaltet die Utopie des Goldenen Zeitalters als Ziel der Natur-Geschichte, die wiederkehrend verheißene Überwindung aller Trennung' [The play fashions the utopia of the golden age as the goal of the history of nature, the promised, and recurrent, triumph over all separation].
57 Some critics, particularly when approaching German Romanticism from a poststructuralist or deconstructionist perspective, have questioned the idea of the golden age as a completive process, and have instead examined how these visions of the future are presented with a strong sense of indeterminacy. See, for example, Alice Kuzniar, *Delayed Endings: Nonclosure in Novalis and Hölderlin* (Athens: University of Georgia Press, 1987).

'Immortalita' is a dramolet, set in a cave at the mouth of the underworld, but this Classicising setting is little more than a veneer for Günderrode to rethink this triadic narrative inherited from Christian theology. Immortalita, the allegorical embodiment of immortality, is a powerless goddess held captive within an enchantment of an *ouroboros*, the ancient symbol of a circular serpent consuming its own tail — an alchemical as well as Masonic symbol whose meanings include the passing of time and eternity, eternal return, and the One and All.[58] In 'Immortalita', the *ouroboros* as a form of imprisonment points to all that is lacking: a holistic understanding of the cosmos where all the elements — mortal and immortal — interact. Rather than the *ouroboros* being a symbol of completeness, it is one of separation, since it operates as part of the enchantment that separates eternal life from the temporal realm. The opening of the dramolet sets out a scene of moribundity, where Immortalita has lost any sense of identity — 'Ich weiß es nicht! warum kenne ich mich nicht?' [I do not know! Why do I not know myself?] (*SW* I, 42, ll. 46–47). Her purpose — as immortality incarnate — has become lost since the very concept has fallen into disrepute. As Immortalita herself laments, she is trapped in a sense of longing for a future that is nostalgia for a past age of unity:

> O Zukunft wirst du der Vergangenheit gleichen! jener seligen fernen Vergangenheit, wo ich mit Göttern in ewiger Klarheit wohnte [...] aber ein finsteres Zeitalter kam, von ihren Thronen wurden die seligen Götter gestoßen, ich wurde von ihnen getrennt, ihr Leben war dahin, sie giengen zurück in die Lebenselemente aus denen sie entsprungen waren, ehe mein Hauch ihnen Dauer verliehen hatte
>
> [O future, will you be akin to the past! To that blessed, distant past, where I resided with the gods in eternal brightness [...] but a dark age came, the blessed gods were cast from their thrones, I was separated from them, their life was gone, they returned to the elements of life from which they had come, before my breath could have granted them permanence] (*SW* I, 43–44, ll. 72–81)

This passage echoes Schiller's despondent vision of 'die entgötterte Natur' [godless nature][59] in the first version of 'Die Götter Griechenlands' [The Gods of Greece] (1788), as well as his famous portrayal of the Greek era in the sixth letter of *Über die ästhetische Erziehung des Menschen* as a period of organic harmony that acts as a powerful counterpoint to what Schiller argues is the fragmentation brought about by a rational, empirical understanding of the world.[60] In Günderrode's version of this Greek ideal, there is a theogony: the gods are a divinised, reified form of 'die Lebenselemente' [the elements of life], and it is the very concept of immortality that causes the 'Lebenselemente' to be understood as divine. The divinised 'Lebenselemente' were once held together and given coherence by Immortalita, and thus the entire cosmos, from the mortal to the immortal, was an interlocking whole. With 'die Herrschaft des Unglaubens' [the rule of unbelief] (*SW* I, 43, l.

---

58 For an account of its various meanings from antiquity to the eighteenth century, see H. B. de Groot, 'The Ouroboros and the Romantic Poets', *English Studies*, 50 (1969), 553–64.
59 Schiller, *Schillers Werke: Nationalausgabe*, I: *Gedichte in der Reihenfolge des Erscheinens*, ed. by Julius Petersen and Friedrich Beißner (1943), p. 194.
60 Ibid., XX: *Philosophische Schriften. Erster Teil*, ed. by Benno von Wiese (1962), pp. 321–28.

69), however, Immortalita had become obsolete, and the cosmos, stripped of its animation, fragments and recedes into its constituent parts. This is precisely the narrative drawn out in 'Vorzeit, und Neue Zeit': the loss of a coherent, holistic world-view through unbelief, although Günderrode then offers a panacea to the atomised world that Immortalita inhabits.

What can liberate Immortalita from this existential desolation? It is love, but in a form that Günderrode adapts from Plato and combines with Christian elements. To this end, Günderrode invents the figure of Erodion as an exemplary, allegorical redeemer:

> Ungern mögt' ich dir von etwas anderm reden, als von meiner Liebe, aber so ich dir mein Leben erzähle, rede ich von meiner Liebe. Höre mich denn: ich bin Eros Sohn und seiner Mutter Aphrodite, diese doppelte Vereinigung, der Liebe und Schönheit, hatte schon in mein Daseyn die Idee eines Genusses gelegt, den ich nirgends finden konnte, und den ich doch überall ahndete und suchte. Lange war ich ein Fremdling auf Erden, und ich mochte von ihren Schattengütern nichts genießen, bis mir durch einen Traum oder Eingebung eine dunkle Vorstellung von dir in die Seele kam.
>
> [I would not like to speak of anything other than my love, but as I tell you of my life, so I will speak of my love. Listen to me then: I am the son of Eros and his mother Aphrodite, this double union of love and beauty imbued my existence with the idea of pleasure that I could not find anywhere, but one that I sensed and sought everywhere. For a long time I was a stranger on Earth, and I could not enjoy any of its shadow-goods, until an obscure idea of you emerged in my soul in a dream or in a moment of inspiration.] (*SW* I, 45, ll. 120–29)

By constructing Erodion as the progeny of the incestuous union of Eros and Aphrodite, Günderrode adapts the origin story of *eros* from Diotima's speech in the *Symposium* to create a form of *eros* that is paradoxically perfective. Erodion's sense of lack and his desire for the highest form of pleasure are so profound that he is compelled — unconsciously — to transcend earthly bounds. His parentage imbues him with a form of unerring, absolute agency that enables him relentlessly to seek out the object of his desire beyond the mortal, physical world: 'denn meine Eltern, die wohl wußten, daß der, aus Lieb' und Schönheit entsprungen, nichts höheres auf Erden finden würde, als sich selbst, hatten mir diesen Glauben gegeben, damit meine Kraft nicht ermüden möge, nach Höherem zu streben ausser mir' [for my parents, who knew well that, having been born of love and beauty, I would find nothing higher on Earth than myself, had given to me the belief, so that my strength would not waver to strive for something higher than myself] (*SW* I, 46, ll. 147–51). What results from this absolute agency is Erodion's Orphic quest to redeem the beloved Immortalita. Günderrode adapts the trope of the descent into the underworld as an act of self-sacrifice. In order to pursue this transcendent goal, Erodion is willing to sacrifice his earthly existence, and, therefore, to risk losing his own mortality: 'fröhlig sagt' ich der Oberwelt das letzte Lebewohl; die Nacht verschlang mich eine gräßliche Pause! und ich fand mich bei dir' [joyfully I said my last farewell to the overworld; the night consumed me a dreadful pause! And then I found myself with you] (*SW* I, 46, ll. 163–65).

Thus, in this moment of sacrifice, Erodion is the embodiment of 'glaubige [sic] Liebe' [love full of belief] (*SW* I, 43, l. 63) and is a proxy for Christ, as Helga Dormann has rightly observed.[61] The redeeming moment is when Erodion liberates Immortalita and ensouls her, allowing her to re-establish her identity by beholding his love: 'du hast mir eine Seele eingehaucht. [...] in deiner Liebe erblicke ich mich selbst verklährt; ich weiß nun wer ich bin' [you have breathed a soul into me [...] in your love I see myself transfigured; I know now who I am] (*SW* I, 46–47, ll. 173–75). This ensoulment revivifies Immortalita, and leads to the symbolic destruction of the barrier between the underworld and the overworld, so that the cosmos once again spans the totality of the immortal and the mortal realms. As a Christ-like figure, Erodion surrenders his mortal life as an act of love to Immortalita and is rewarded with immortality.

But by resurrecting immortality and eternal life as the reconciliation between life and death, Günderrode legitimises the individual longing for spiritual transcendence, because part and parcel of this 'goldne Zukunft' [golden future] is that the immortal realm *can* be accessed: 'von nun an sey es den Gedanken der Liebe, den Träumen der Sehnsucht, und der Begeisterung der Dichter vergönnt, aus dem Lebenslande in das Schattenreich herabzusteigen und wieder zurück zu gehen' [from now on let it be the preserve of thoughts of love, dreams of longing and the enthusiasm of poets to descend from the realm of life into the shadow world and then to return again] (*SW* I, 47, ll. 202–05). The first two elements are present in Erodion, but stress falls upon the third element, on '[die] Begeisterung der Dichter'. Günderrode thereby elevates the poet to the status of a mediating figure between the mortal and the immortal, but also as a mediator between the material world — all that can be empirically analysed — and those experiences that are not immediately accessible to the senses or processed by rational forms of cognition. Indeed, the role ascribed to the poet here has parallels with Günderrode's own thoughts about creativity. In the letter to Claudine Piautaz from between 1801 and 1803, Günderrode argues that any involvement with prosaic reality is antithetical to poetic creativity. Creativity and the operations of the imagination are instead dependent on a kind of asceticism:

> Im Genus ist keine Dichtung, (die Wirklichkeit tödet den Traum) nur in der Sehnsucht, diese ruft ein anders Leben hervor in uns, als das Wirkliche. [...] Das Leben läßt sich nicht theilen; man kan nicht in der Unterwelt mit den Schatten wandeln, u zugleich auf der Oberwelt unter der Sonne u mit den Menschen.
>
> [In pleasure there is no poetry (reality destroys the dream), only in longing, which generates a different life in us than what is real. [...] Life cannot be divided: you cannot wander among the shadows in the underworld and at the same time with people under the sun in the overworld.][62]

This thought is embedded in the typically Platonic idea of the divorce between spirit and matter, but in an aesthetic sense. In addition to the classical topos of the journey into the underworld, Günderrode draws on the imagery of Schiller's

---

61   Dormann, p. 211.
62   Karoline von Günderrode, letter to Claudine Piautaz, 1801–03, Freies Deutsches Hochstift (FDH), Frankfurt a.M., MS 20369, 1[r].

'Das Reich der Schatten' (1795): the underworld is also the aesthetic realm of beauty, from which poets can draw, in the context of 'Immortalita', transcendent inspiration, and which in the letter also designates the depths of the imaginative self. Beyond this aesthetic aspect, Günderrode's privileging of the spiritual over the material is underscored by Erodion's closing comment, 'wohl mir, daß ich den Muth hatte, [...] das Sichtbare dem Unsichtbaren zu opfern' [Happy am I to have had the courage [...] to sacrifice the visible to the invisible] (*SW* 1, 48, ll. 214–16). This has an additional meaning in referring back to how Erodion came to be aware of Immortalita's existence: through a 'dunkle Vorstellung' [obscure idea] (*SW* 1, 45, l. 129), and through afflatus and dreams.

'Der rege Trieb, die Wahrheit zu ergründen!': Ascent and Descent as Part of an Epistemological Process

Whilst Erodion in 'Immortalita' serves as a model for a successful epistemological quest, Günderrode's adoption of Platonic *eros* and *anamnesis* is also focused on the cognitive and perceptual aspects of the processes that the subject uses in order to achieve knowledge of the absolute being. The epistemological quest, as Helene M. Kastinger-Riley highlights, was common in literature around 1800 and is a recurring topic for Günderrode:

> Eines der Themen, das von Günderrode öfters bearbeitet wird, ist der menschliche Drang, der Natur ihre Geheimnisse abzufordern und in das Wesen der Schöpfung einzudringen [...]. In der Literatur sind die vielen Bearbeitungen und Variationen des Faustmotivs, die Wiederentdeckung des Orients als 'Urheimat' und die Symbolik der Isis-Figur Beispiele für die dichterische Einkleidung dieses allenthalben spürbaren Wissensdurstes der Menschheit.
>
> [One of the themes that is frequently dealt with by Günderrode is the human desire to uncover nature's secrets and to delve into the essence of creation [...]. In literature, the many reworkings and variations of the Faust motif, the rediscovery of the Orient as the 'primordial homeland' and the symbolism of the Isis figure function as examples of how the human desire for knowledge, perceptible everywhere, assumes poetic garb.][63]

The end goal of the epistemological quest is to reveal the secrets of a divinised, animate nature, but without falling foul of the desire to objectify and, by extension, control nature. This is founded on Günderrode's panentheistic understanding of the cosmos, which, combined with the epistemological quest, leads to the question of how this can be achieved without artificially elevating man above nature. Such an elevation would amount to a transgression since it would necessarily objectify nature. It also becomes problematic in the context of Spinozist panentheism, which makes a distinction between the productive part of nature, *natura naturans*, and the products of nature, *natura naturata*. Since man belongs to the latter category, and therefore cannot assume the role of *natura naturans* by attempting to control nature, man is instead subject to this divine will.

---

63 Kastinger-Riley, p. 95.

Another limit to the epistemological quest is the question of what man should know. As Lessing famously articulated in *Eine Duplik* [A Rejoinder] (1778), absolute truth can be ascertained by God alone, not by man. For man it is better to seek the truth: 'Ich fiele ihm [Gott] mit Demut in seine Linke [in der er den Trieb nach Wahrheit hält] und sagte: Vater gieb! die reine Wahrheit ist ja doch nur für dich allein!' [I would humbly grasp his left hand (which contains the desire for the truth) and would say: Father, give this one! pure truth is just for You alone!].[64] This is precisely the point of Günderrode's ballad 'Der Adept' (1804): the adept Valus is driven by the Faustian desire for knowledge, 'Ein Weiser, der schon viel erforschet, | Doch nie des Forschens müde war' [A wise man who had explored many topics | But had never tired of his investigations] (*SW* I, 49, ll. 1–2), and becomes initiated into a mystery cult. The first stage allows Valus to distinguish between appearance and reality, to observe the single 'Naturgeist' [nature spirit] (*SW* I, 49, l. 18) that is inherent in and animates all natural phenomena. The third level of initiation, however, allegedly leads to a mastery of nature: 'Denn sie, die alles sonst durchschauten | Beherrschen jetzo die Natur' [For they, who otherwise could see through everything, | Now were in control of nature] (*SW* I, 50, ll. 27–28). Yet this, the highest truth of the mystery cult, is paradoxically disempowering and dislocates Valus from the rest of humanity. It is a false elevation since assuming a godlike role condemns Valus to a life of everlasting sameness, as Valus himself laments in the moralising final stanza: 'Nicht Ew'ges kann der Mensch ertragen, | Und wohl dem, wenn er auch vergeht' [Man cannot endure what is eternal, | And envy him who perishes] (*SW* I, 51, ll. 51–52). Where the arrogant youth in Schiller's 'Das verschleierte Bild zu Sais' — certainly an intertext for Günderrode's ballad — is punished with death for his brashness, the adept in Günderrode is left longing for his own demise, as liberation from intolerable existence. Valus's initial *curiositas* develops into the sin of *acedia*,[65] the state of torpor; the adept is suspended between human and divine life since he can partake neither of human life nor of the promised mastery of nature.

Instead, Valus leads a petrified, presumably immortal, existence, a living death in which existence has been stripped of meaning: 'Geleert hat er des Lebens Becher | Und lebet immer, immer fort' [He has drained the cup of life | And still, still lives on] (*SW* I, 50, ll. 45–46). The tension in the poem derives firstly from a thought articulated in 'Vorzeit, und Neue Zeit': that scientific dogmatism leads to the separation of man and nature by objectifying nature. This is combined with the political implications carried by an initiation into a mystery cult. This recurrent narrative in novels of the late eighteenth century centres on the idea of initiation into hidden knowledge — whether Masonic or not — as being part and parcel of legitimising rulership over a state.[66] Valus's failure, therefore, lies in transposing

---

64 Lessing, *Werke und Briefe*, VIII: *Werke 1774–1778*, ed. by Arno Schilson (1989), p. 510.
65 To continue the Faust motif, for Leonard Forster, the danger in Faust's striving, like Valus's, is that it degenerates into *acedia*, the sin of sloth. See Leonard Forster, 'Faust and the Sin of Sloth', in *The Discontinuous Tradition: Studies in German Literature in Honour of Ernst Ludwig Stahl*, ed. by Peter F. Ganz (Oxford: Clarendon Press, 1971), pp. 54–66.
66 *Ägyptische Mysterien*, p. 22.

this trope of the wisdom required for ruling over a polity onto the wisdom that is allegedly required to master nature.

Whilst 'Der Adept' adopts a moralising tone to underscore the fact that it is impossible for the individual to objectify and control nature, an acceptance of human limitations does not imply that the search for truth is framed, as it is in Lessing, exclusively in terms of a recognition of human limitations. In 'Des Wandrers Niederfahrt' and 'Ein apokaliptisches Fragment', the movement of ascent and descent derives from the attempt to transcend individual and conscious limitations to access metaphysical reality. This echoes Diefenbach's theological tract about how, according to the precepts of Kantianism, one cannot ascertain the existence of a creator through empirical means. The conviction that there *must* be some higher, noumenal form of reality, and also that the individual must be resigned to their inability to experience it, does not suffice. The question that arises in both 'Des Wandrers Niederfahrt' and 'Ein apokaliptisches Fragment' is what form of cognition can be adopted to look beyond contingent, phenomenal reality.

'Des Wandrers Niederfahrt' is a failed attempt to seek out fundamental truth. The Wandrer is driven, like Valus, by the insatiable desire for knowledge, which is expressed through an indirect quotation from Lessing's *Duplik*: 'Der rege Trieb: die Wahrheit zu ergründen!' [The strong desire to uncover the truth] (*SW* I, 72, l. 82). An awareness of the limitations of individual capacities, as well as the unbridled human desire for knowledge, appears to thwart the Wandrer's quest. The poem charts how the Wandrer forsakes the phenomenal world and attempts to seek out the fundamental truth, as with 'Immortalita', through a journey into the underworld. Günderrode embeds this classical topos with an initiation into arcane knowledge; indeed, rather than the descent into the world of the dead, what the Wandrer desires is to experience the origin of life. The Wandrer is a pupil to an absent 'Meister' [master] (*SW* I, 69, l. 1), and requires instruction from the mythologically ambiguous 'Führer' [leader],[67] the progeny of the sun god and the veiled night. This Führer, as 'der Herold der Nacht' [the herald of the night] (*SW* I, 69, l. 9), is akin to Hermes and mediates between the realms of darkness and light and therefore can grant the Wandrer access to the 'Reich der dunklen Mitternacht' [realm of dark midnight] (*SW* I, 70, l. 31), which Kastinger-Riley rightly interprets as a threshold where no oppositions exist.[68] Even with the Führer as a mediator, the poem reads as a failed initiation attempt, in which the most profound mystery remains undisclosed.

The Wandrer's justification for embarking on this descent is similar to that which motivates Valus in 'Der Adept': it stems from the belief that transient phenomena do not correspond with truth:

> Geblendet hat mich, trüg'risch, nur der Flimmer,
> Der Ird'sches nie zur Heimath sich erwählt.
> Vergebens wollt' den Flüchtigen ich fassen,
> Er kann doch nie vom steten Wandel lassen

---

[67] Dormann, p. 170; Lucia Maria Licher speculatively attempts to trace the mythological associations of the 'Führer': see Licher, pp. 284–85.
[68] Kastinger-Riley, p. 97.

> [I was only blinded by the illusion of the shimmering glow,
> Which never chooses the earthly realm as its home.
> In vain I aimed to grasp that fleeting glow,
> Which could never cease its constant change.] (*SW* I, 70, ll. 36–39)

What the Wandrer proclaims here is the damaging split between appearances and reality: the phenomena that can be experienced in the world could be devalued because they are transient and generate a series of sense-impressions that may not in themselves lead to truth. Instead, the Wandrer seeks out the underworld, which exists outside temporal bounds. It also offers a prelapsarian state before 'Schmerz' and 'Jrrsal': 'dies schwankende Gebild | Der Dinge Ordnung, dies Geschlecht der Erde! | Dem Schmerz und Jrrsal ewig bleibt Gefährte' [This capricious shape | of the order of things, this earthly race! | To whom pain and erring are eternal companions] (ibid., ll. 47–49). The Wandrer's underlying conviction draws a distinction between accidental and contingent reality, *natura naturata*, and the generative force that gives rise to nature, *natura naturans*.

But just as Valus is incapable of controlling nature in 'Der Adept', the Wandrer has a false conception of what this profound knowledge may be:

> Die unvermischten Schätze wollt' ich heben
> Die nicht der Schein der Oberwelt berührt
> Die Urkraft, die, der Perle gleich, vom Leben
> Des Daseyns Meer in seinen Tiefen führt.
>
> [I wish to lift the unadulterated treasures
> Which the light of the overworld has not touched,
> The primordial force, which leads, like the pearl, from life,
> The sea of existence, into its depths.] (*SW* I, 72, ll. 88–91)

What the Wandrer envisages in the 'Urkraft' is a tangible, generative force from which all existence derives — the use of 'Urkraft' draws on Herder's vitalist reading of Spinoza's God[69] — or at least a perceptible womb, the incubator for all potential life: 'zum Kreis der stillen Mächte, | In deren tiefem Schoos das Chaos schlief' [In the circle of silent powers | In the depths of their womb did chaos slumber] (*SW* I, 70, ll. 40–41).

The Wandrer descends beyond the ferment of chaos, the nexus where the otherwise opposing elements — of fire and water — intersect, only to find that beyond there is merely absence. Whilst the earth spirits the Wandrer encounters confirm that a ground of being does exist, and gives rise to appearances, this plenitude of life, or 'Lebensfülle', is no active 'Urkraft', but rather functions like a static version of Jakob Böhme's unground or *Ungrund*.[70] It is a negative form of existence that only exists insofar as it contains the potential to exist: 'Das Ungeborne ruhet hier verhüllet | Geheimnißvoll, bis seine Zeit erfüllet' [The unborn rests here, mysteriously | Enshrouded, until its time has come] (*SW* I, 73, ll. 110–11). It is *un*human, whereas the metaphors the Wandrer employs to describe original being

---

69 Timm, *Gott und die Freiheit*, p. 235.
70 Paola Mayer, *Jena Romanticism and its Appropriation of Jakob Böhme: Theosophy, Hagiography, Literature* (Montreal: McGill-Queen's University Press, 1999), pp. 21–22.

reveal the logical fallacy to which he succumbs: 'Wie es [das Leben] sich kindlich an die Mutter schlingt | In ihrer Werkstadt die Natur erschauen' [How it [life] wraps itself around its mother, like a child; | To behold nature at work in its domain] (*SW* I, 72, ll. 93–94).

The Wandrer, therefore, anthropomorphises the ground of being, which presupposes the human capacity to perceive, even to comprehend it. However, this 'Lebensfülle' exists in both an unconscious state — 'Ihr Daseyn ist noch Traum' [Its existence is still a dream] (*SW* I, 73, l. 101) — and a preconscious state, and therefore the Wandrer is barred from accessing it. In a desperate bid to acquire more knowledge, the Wandrer suggests self-sacrifice to return to his previous state, understood in a Neoplatonist sense as a return to the One: 'Laßt wieder mich zum Mutterschoose sinken, | Vergessenheit und neues Daseyn trinken' [Let me return again to the maternal womb | to imbibe oblivion and a new existence] (*SW* I, 73, ll. 116–17). But this is, as the Erdgeister elaborate, a futile strategy, since all existence is determined so that the original separation from the 'Lebensfülle' cannot be reversed:

> Zu spät! du bist dem Tage schon geboren;
> Geschieden aus dem Lebenselement.
> Dem Werden können wir, und nicht dem Seyn gebieten
> Und du bist schon vom Mutterschoos geschieden
> Durch dein Bewußtseyn schon vom Traum getrennt.
>
> [Too late! You have been born to the day,
> Separated from the element of life.
> We dictate Becoming, not Being,
> And you have split from the mother's womb,
> Separated from dreams by your consciousness.] (*SW* I, 73, ll. 119–23)

The Erdgeister make a distinction between being and becoming. As with 'Liebe und Schönheit', birth is a destructive act that fragments primordial unity, and prevents it, in this case, from being reinstated. It is consciousness, and the splitting of unity, in a philosophical sense, between subject and object, that becomes a problem of cognition here. The Erdgeister then tantalise with one cognitive possibility for circumventing the barrier of consciousness:

> Doch schau hinab, in deiner Seele Gründen
> Was du hier suchest wirst du dorten finden,
> Des Weltalls seh'nder Spiegel bist du nur.
>
> [But look down, in the depths of your soul,
> What you seek here you will find there,
> You are but the sighted mirror of the universe.] (ibid., ll. 124–26)

This comment resembles Novalis's famous sixteenth aphorism in 'Blüthenstaub', 'Wir träumen von Reisen durch das Weltall: Ist denn das Weltall nicht in uns? Die Tiefen unsers Geistes kennen wir nicht — Nach Innen geht der geheimnisvolle Weg' [We dream of a journey through the universe. But is the universe then not in us? We do not know the depths of our spirit. Inward goes the mysterious path].⁷¹ There are certainly further parallels between this aphorism and 'Des Wandrers Niederfahrt', such as the reworking of Plato's allegory of the cave, so that phenomenal reality conceals the true form of reality. The Wandrer seeks out the 'Reich der dunklen Mitternacht' [realm of dark midnight] (*SW* I, 70, l. 31) that is untouched by the distortions of light: 'vom frechen Lichte nicht durchdrungen' [not penetrated by brazen light] (ibid., l. 46). For Novalis, the inversion of Plato's metaphor is more explicit: 'Die Außenwelt ist die Schattenwelt, sie wirft ihren Schatten in das Lichtreich' [The external world is the shadow world, casting its shadows into the world of light].⁷²

But Günderrode is less interested than Novalis in exploring the untapped depths of the self. The suggestion is more that dreams and unconscious states form an alternative and fruitful form of cognition, which is grounded on the assumption that the individual, as a microcosm, reflects the macrocosm, as in the Renaissance conception of the world, whose structures are indebted to Aristotle.⁷³ Günderrode neatly sums up the paradox of the Wandrer's position: 'Des Weltalls seh'nder Spiegel bist du nur'. The mirror metaphor draws on a trope in the mystical tradition in which the individual soul is the reflective mirror of God, but also draws on the Leibnizian concept of the monad. Whilst the individual is indeed reflective of the cosmos and thus generates an image of the cosmos, this remains invisible to their physical sense of sight. The task at hand is, therefore, to penetrate beyond the individual's spatial, temporal and sensory limits to the plenitude of life which the Wandrer not only postulates but knows to exist, yet cannot perceive. Thus the text ends at a point of failure for the Wandrer, but simultaneously indicates how an expansion of individual consciousness can occur.

Günderrode takes up this thought of 'des Weltalls seh'nder Spiegel' and develops it to its logical conclusion in the short prose text 'Ein apokaliptisches Fragment', also from *Gedichte und Phantasien*. It is a positive counterpart to 'Des Wandrers Niederfahrt' and is a case in which the movement of ascent and descent is successfully completed. The text traces the expansion of an individual consciousness to the point at which it experiences its inherent connection to the totality: the speaker escapes the limitations of its subjectivity, but without having to surrender its individuality. This reading is supported by the initial review of *Gedichte und Phantasien* by Günderrode's sometime literary mentor Christian Nees von Esenbeck: 'ein Versuch, das Losreisen des Endlichen von dem Absoluten und dessen Rückkehr ins All unter subjectiven Formen des Bewußtseyns auszusprechen' [an attempt to express the splitting of the finite from the absolute and its return to the cosmos through subjective forms of consciousness] (*SW* III, 65).

In 'Ein apokaliptisches Fragment', Günderrode does not suggest that dreams offer a visionary form of cognition, but rather that conscious and unconscious states dialectically interact and generate a higher form of consciousness and insight. In

---

71 Novalis, *Schriften*, II, 417–19; Frederick C. Beiser (ed. and trans.), *The Early Political Writings of the German Romantics* (Cambridge: Cambridge University Press, 1996), p. 11.
72 Novalis, *Schriften*, II, 419; Beiser, *The Early Political Writings of the German Romantics*, p. 11.
73 Allen G. Debus, *Man and Nature in the Renaissance* (Cambridge: Cambridge University Press, 1978), p. 12.

his assessment of *Gedichte und Phantasien*, Clemens Brentano considers the title of 'Ein apokaliptisches Fragment' little more than a claim to erudition that does not sit well with the tenor of the whole collection.[74] But Brentano misses the point: the title points to both the biblical context, since — it is indeed written as a series of scriptural verses, and to the theme of apocalypse — as revelation through cognition and perception.[75] Apocalypse here does not refer to the end times and accompanying millennial anticipation for the dawning of a posited 'goldenes Zeitalter' [golden age] but is simply a revelation, the uncovering of a previously hidden truth.

Contrary to readings such as Sabine Eickenrodt's, which are explicitly biographical, linking 'Ein apokaliptisches Fragment' to Günderrode's relationship with Friedrich Karl von Savigny,[76] the revelation is of an abstract nature. By purging itself of individual consciousness, and therefore undoing the process of individuation, the speaker is able to experience how everything in the ever-gestating universe is interconnected. The question is whether undoing individuation results in the destruction of the self. In a psychoanalytic reading of Günderrode, Olaf Berwald has touched upon the question of how to reconcile the individual with a divine totality:

> das eirenische Ziel harmonischen Einsseins jenseits kognitiver und ontologischer Trennungslinien basiert auf aggressiven Einverleibungs–und Selbstauflösungsphantasien. [...] Das Günderrodesche fiktionale Ich versucht vergeblich, der Unruhezone zwischen narzißtischer Sehwut und euphorisch demütigem, pantheistisch gläubigem Selbstvernichtungsdrang zu entkommen.
>
> [the irenic goal of harmonious oneness that overcomes separation along cognitive and ontological lines is based on aggressive fantasies of assimilation and self-dissolution [...] Günderrode's fictional speaker attempts in vain to break free of the disquieting space that oscillates between narcissistic, voyeuristic rage and the drive to self-destruction, marked by euphoric humility and pantheistic belief.][77]

Berwald's reading, however, goes too far in orchestrating a causal link between the desire for transcendent unity and the desire to dissolve and destroy the self entirely. But Berwald touches upon an interesting problem for 'Ein apokaliptisches

---

74   Günderrode, *Briefe*, p. 144: 'dieses erscheint besonders durch einen hie und da hervorblickenden kleinen gelehrten Anstrich, der oft nicht im Gleichgewicht mit dem Ganzen steht, zum Beispiel Worte wie Adept, Apokalyptische und so weiter als Titel' [this appears especially through the occasional, small pretension to erudition, which does exist in equilibrium with the whole, for example, phrases such as adept, apocalyptic and so forth as titles].

75   The extant manuscript fair copy of 'Ein apokaliptisches Fragment' (MS. Ff. K. v. Günderrode Abt. 2 A3, , fols 171^r–174^v) does not initially distinguish between the sections numerically as biblical verses. Numbering is added from the fifth verse and then retrospectively added to the first four in darker pen.

76   'Das *Apokaliptische Fragment* literarisiert die Vision einer todeserotischen Vereinigung mit Savigny, dem *Freund als dem anderen Ich*' [The *Apocalyptic Fragment* renders, in literary form, the vision of an erotic union in death with Savigny, the *friend understood as the second self*]. Sabine Eickenrodt, '"Die Vergangenheit war mir dahin!" Karoline von Günderrodes apokalyptische Vision', in *Geschriebenes Leben: Autobiographik von Frauen*, ed. by Michaela Holdenried (Berlin: Schmidt, 1995), pp. 185–97 (p. 196).

77   Olaf Berwald, *Visuelle Gewalt und Selbstverlust bei Günderrode, Hölderlin und Fichte* (Ann Arbor: UMI, 2006), pp. 19–21.

Fragment', in which death is both limit and self-dissolution through the overcoming of individuality.

As with 'Des Wandrers Niederfahrt', the point of departure finds the speaker in 'Ein apokaliptisches Fragment' situated in a geographical nodal point — 'Ich stand auf einem hohen Fels im Mittelmeer, und vor mir war der Ost, und hinter mir der West' [I stood on a high rock in the Mediterranean, and before me was the East, and behind me the West] (*SW* I, 52) — just as the Wandrer finds himself at the nexus of geographical and elemental poles. Unlike the Wandrer, the speaker finds itself separated from the totality of nature, but is driven by a desire to unite with this totality: 'Ich wollte mich hinstürzen in das Morgenroth, oder mich tauchen in die Schatten der Nacht' [I wanted to plunge into the red of dawn, or dive into the shadows of the night] (ibid.). And the only means to resolve this frustrating separation is through dream-cognition. The speaker's dream offers a refracted image of its conscious position: a vision of the vast, fermenting sea. This, however, does not give any cognitive insights, but results in the speaker forgetting itself through loss of memory: 'bis meine Erinnerung erlosch' [until my memory was extinguished] (*SW* I, 53). Awakening brings with it self-remembering, albeit through heady disorientation: 'Da ich aber wieder erwachte, und von mir zu wissen anfieng' [Then but as I awoke again and began to know of myself] (ibid.). And these 'dumpfe und verworrene Träume' [dull and confused dreams] (ibid.), although not in themselves revelatory, give rise to a dynamic, conscious and unconscious cognition. From the transition between the dream and conscious states, the speaker becomes aware, however tentatively, of its own hidden origin: '9. Aber es war ein dunkles Gefühl in mir, als habe ich geruht im Schoose dieses Meeres und sey ihm entstiegen, wie die andern Gestalten' [9. But there was a dark feeling in me, as if I had rested in the womb of this sea and had emerged from it, like the other forms] (ibid.). Here the speaker develops a form of Platonic *anamnesis*, coming to the intuitive realisation that it can recall its own origins. But how this realisation coalesces is significant: Günderrode, like Leibniz and Lessing, stresses how emotion, the 'dunkles Gefühl' [dark feeling] that is prerational and pre-conceptual, generates true ideas.[78] The subjunctive 'als habe ich geruht' is not indicative of the unreality of this thought, but rather of the (non-rational) process of cognition at work.

What follows is a dream-like transfiguration of phenomenal reality — whether the remaining verses take place within a dream or not remains ambiguous — in which the speaker appears to itself as a dew-drop and playfully communes with the elements, just as the speaker in the *Nachlass* poem 'Einstens lebt ich süßes Leben' initially perceives itself as dissolved into a nebula and suspended in the heavens. Günderrode's imagery, of the lyrical subject as a dewdrop, is indebted to emblematic images from the tradition of nature mysticism.[79] This state of free play is undercut by the emergence of another Platonic concept — *eros*, the longing for divine perfection or beauty from which the individual derives — although initially

---

78 Henry E. Allison, *Lessing and the Enlightenment: His Philosophy of Religion and its Relation to Eighteenth-Century Thought* (Ann Arbor: University of Michigan Press, 1966), pp. 72–75.
79 Rolf Christian Zimmermann, *Das Weltbild des jungen Goethe: Studien zur hermetischen Tradition des deutschen 18. Jahrhunderts*, 2 vols (Munich: Fink, 1969–79), II, 299.

this lacks an object: 'Aber eine Sehnsucht war in mir, die ihren Gegenstand nicht kannte' [But there was a longing in me that did not know its object] (ibid.). It is immediately conceptualised as the desire to return to the source of life. This return is figured as death; however, it is not death as a loss of self, but rather, death as a transition towards a higher form of consciousness that frees the speaker from its own limitations:

> 12. Einst ward ich gewahr, daß alle die Wesen, die aus dem Meere gestiegen waren, wieder zu ihm zurückkehrten, und sich in wechselnden Formen wieder erzeugten. Mich befremdete diese Erscheinung; denn ich hatte von keinem Ende gewußt. Da dachte ich, meine Sehnsucht sey auch, zurück zu kehren, zu der Quelle des Lebens.
> 13. Und da ich dies dachte, und fast lebendiger fühlte, als all mein Bewußtseyn, ward plötzlich mein Gemüth wie mit betäubenden Nebeln umgeben. Aber sie schwanden bald, ich schien mir nicht mehr ich, und doch mehr als sonst ich, meine Gränzen konnte ich nicht mehr finden, mein Bewußtseyn hatte sie überschritten, es war größer, anders, und doch fühlte ich mich in ihm.
>
> [12. At one point I became aware that all the beings that had arisen from the sea returned to it again and were created again in changing forms. I was disconcerted by this phenomenon, for I had not known of any end. Then I thought that I too longed to return to the source of life.
> 13. And as I thought of this and felt almost more alive than all of my consciousness, my mind was surrounded all of a sudden by benumbing mists. But these soon disappeared, and I seemed no longer myself, and yet more than I otherwise was; I could no longer find the limits of myself, my consciousness had transcended them, it was larger, different, and yet I felt myself in it.] (*SW* I, 53–54)

The speaker expands its consciousness, and indeed beyond itself, which results in a tension within the linguistic structures. No longer can the speaker understand itself as an independent being — it remains grammatically so, and yet is not by having ascended to a higher plane of being beyond conscious limits; this cleaves close to the Neoplatonist notion of *henosis*.[80] Death is not an absolute endpoint, since there is no linear end to time in the text: the speaker was previously liberated from a linear understanding of temporality to a fluid, continuous, indeed timeless, present: 'Die Vergangenheit war mir dahin! ich gehörte nur der Gegenwart' [The past was lost to me! I belonged only to the present] (*SW* I, 53). Death functions as a threshold, that, when passed, generates deeper cognitive insights, since what the subject has achieved is a state of productive reciprocity between itself and the rest of nature: 'Erlöset war ich von den engen Schranken meines Wesens [...] ich war allem wiedergegeben, und alles gehörte mir mit an' [I was released from the narrow limits of my being [...] I was restored to everything, and everything was a part of me] (*SW* I, 54). The implication here is that individuation, as in a Manichean understanding, constitutes the Fall — the lyrical, and increasingly oracular biblical tone of the text

---

80   See Werner Beierwaltes, *Denken des Einen: Studien zur neuplatonischen Philosophie und ihrer Wirkungsgeschichte* (Frankfurt a.M.: Klostermann, 1985), p. 123.

suggests that 'Erlöset' is just as much redemption as it is liberation; or at least that the limitations of individuation have been overcome so that the speaker has returned to the vitalising totality.

The final verse of 'Ein apokaliptisches Fragment' brings with it a change in perspective with an ecstatic declamation and the only explicit allusion in the text to the Book of Revelation:[81]

> Drum, wer Ohren hat zu hören, der höre! Es ist nicht zwei, nicht drei, nicht tausende, es ist Eins und alles; es ist nicht Körper und Geist geschieden, daß das eine der Zeit, das andere der Ewigkeit angehöre, es ist Eins, gehört sich selbst, und ist Zeit und Ewigkeit zugleich, und sichtbar, und unsichtbar, bleibend im Wandel, ein unendliches Leben.
>
> [Therefore, whoever has ears, let them hear! It is not two, not three, nor a thousand, it is one and all; it is not that body and spirit are separated, that one belongs to time, the other to eternity, it is one, belongs to itself, and is both time and eternity, visible and invisible, constant in change, an infinite life.] (ibid.)

What is revealed is not the end of times as the apocalypse, and eternal life is not the preserve of the kingdom of heaven. Rather, there is no eschatology since eternal life is immanent and present, but imperceptible to the external senses. In a riposte to metaphysical dualism, what the speaker proclaims is dual-aspect monism, in which time and eternity, permanence and transience co-exist within the all-encompassing 'unendliches Leben'. What has been previously overlooked by critics is the weight of the rhetorically stressed 'Eins und alles': this is the Spinozist formula *hen kai pan*, which gained prominence following the pantheism controversy,[82] and became a popular maxim among the Early Romantic generation.

But in the context of the tension between the individual and the totality, what Günderrode realises here is an extension of her modification of Schleiermacher's *Reden über die Religion*. As Ruth Christmann has noted,[83] at the end of the second *Rede*, Schleiermacher argues that one can experience the infinite within a moment of reality: 'Mitten in der Endlichkeit Eins werden mit dem Unendlichen [...] das ist die Unsterblichkeit der Religion' [To become one with the infinite in the middle of the finite [...] that is the immortality of religion].[84] Günderrode's study of Schleiermacher's second *Rede*, however, makes a significant alteration: Günderrode rules out the possibility of transcendent experience within life — it occurs only through death and self-dissolution:

> Strebt darnach schon hier eure Jndividualität zu vernichten u zu leben im Einen u Allem, strebt mehr zu sein als ihr selbst, damit ihr wenig verliehrt wenn ihr euch verliehrt; seid ihr so zusamengeflossen mit dem Universum, so ist kein Tod für euch, ihr gehört der Unendlichkeit. Das ist die Unsterblichkeit der Religion.

---

81   'Drum, wer Ohren hat zu hören, der höre!' echoes a refrain from Revelation 2. 7; 2. 11; 3. 6; 3. 13. The formulation here is closer to Matthew 11. 15; 13. 9, and Luke 8. 8.
82   Beiser, *The Romantic Imperative*, p. 175.
83   Christmann, p. 84.
84   Schleiermacher, *Kritische Gesamtausgabe*, I.XII, 128.

[Strive even here to destroy your individuality and to live in the One and All, strive to be more than yourself so that you lose little when you lose yourself; if you have coalesced with the universe in this way, then there is no death for you, you belong to infinity. That is the immortality of religion.] (*SW* II, 285–86)

What emerges, therefore, in 'Ein apokaliptisches Fragment' is the same paradox first highlighted in Günderrode's letter to Gunda Brentano. Any expansion of consciousness, or as in 'Ein apokaliptisches Fragment', any overcoming of the self, only occurs through the cessation of individuation and therefore exemplifies the ultimate form of defeat for the individual's desire to know.

CHAPTER 6

The Practice of Poetry in *Melete*

Of all of Günderrode's works, her third and final collection, *Melete*, is the most intimately connected to her sensational biography. Its publication history is troubled. Günderrode had entrusted Friedrich Creuzer with negotiating its publication in early 1806; he sold it to his publisher Zimmer und Mohr in Heidelberg.[1] After Günderrode's suicide in July the same year, although the collection was complete and had been sent to the printers in Heidelberg, Creuzer withdrew it from publication.[2] Although some studies and drafts of texts related to *Melete* are in Günderrode's *Nachlass*, it was not until the end of the nineteenth century that any substantive trace of the suppressed collection was found. In 1896, quite by chance, the remnants of one copy of *Melete* were found, comprising the first five signatures and some manuscript pages.[3] The collection was first published in this shortened, incomplete form in 1906 to mark the centenary of Günderrode's death. What *Melete* would have been in a complete state is unknown; titles of two now lost plays by Günderrode are mentioned in the correspondence with Creuzer, *Hippolyt* and *Pompejus*, although it is not clear whether they ever were intended to be part of *Melete*.[4] As it stands, *Melete* breaks off in the prose text 'Valorich'.

Given the circumstances of its creation and suppression, *Melete* presents a certain interpretative challenge to commentators: how can an interpretation of it be disentangled from what happened during and after its completion — Günderrode's suicide and Creuzer's move to prevent its publication? Indeed, some commentators have been tempted to read *Melete* as a reflection of Günderrode's relationship with Creuzer.[5] Its themes of mythologised love and death happen to chime with the themes that are used to interpret Günderrode's death, and such readings rest on the assumption that interpretations of literature may grant insights into the psychology

---

1 Preisendanz, p. 234.
2 This was not Creuzer's decision alone: Creuzer's correspondence with his cousin Leonhard suggests that the Heidelberg theologian Carl Daub had been the one to convince Creuzer of the necessity of suppressing publication: see Preisendanz, p. 318.
3 The copy was found in the possession of Freiherr von Bernus at Stift Neuburg and is presumed to have been inherited from Johann Friedrich Heinrich Schlosser (1780–1851), a lawyer based in Frankfurt and former owner of Stift Neuburg, which served as a meeting-place for Romantic writers and intellectuals. See Erwin Rohde, *Friedrich Creuzer und Karoline von Günderrode: Briefe und Dichtungen* (Heidelberg: Winter, 1896), p. 121.
4 Preisendanz, p. 270; p. 274.
5 See Edith Kempf's lexicon article: Edith Kempf, 'Karoline von Günderrode', in *Deutsche Literatur: Aus fünf Jahrhunderten*, ed. by Hermann Korte (Stuttgart: Metzler, 2015), pp. 228–29.

of the author. The sacrificial love portrayed in 'Die Malabarischen Witwen' [The Widows of Malabar], for example, is itself seductive in this context, and can lead to restatements of Goethe's famous claim about the sickness of Romanticism, and a sickness that can pathologise Idealism too.[6]

Whilst reading *Melete* as a biographical or psychological document is doubtless reductive, there are specific points of autobiographical resonance: the interlocutors in 'Briefe zweier Freunde' [Letters between Two Friends], 'der Freund' [the friend] and 'Eusebio', Greek for 'the blessed one', correspond to the epithets that Günderrode and Creuzer used for each other in their letters. Creuzer himself appeared flattered by such a favourable literary portrayal.[7] But although *Melete* is in part the product of a creative and intellectual collaboration, the loss of Günderrode's letters to Creuzer, about a hundred in total, together with the survival of his, has the effect of granting him undue agency in the conception of *Melete* over and above his role in overseeing its publication. *Melete* was composed partially in collaboration with Günderrode's close friend and confidante Susanne von Heyden.[8] It is clear from correspondence with previous male mediators, such as Christian Nees von Esenbeck's in his critique of 'Mahomed, der Prophet von Mekka', that Günderrode did not necessarily heed the advice given to her.[9]

The overlap between *Melete* and the end of Günderrode's life has prevented the collection from being read as evidence of Günderrode's poetic ambition, and in particular as evidence of the intersection between poetics and metaphysics. The concept of practice of poetry is understood here in a double sense. Firstly: that the experience of poetry is a phenomenological performance and has a disclosive function to the reader. The experience of poetry allows the reader to enter into the virtual space of the poem, which can reveal metaphysical truths, as it does in 'Adonis Todtenfeyer' [The Funeral Ceremony of Adonis]. Secondly, I use the term 'practice' to stress how Günderrode develops poetics *through* poetry, through the deployment of a variety of forms and traditions, rather than through theoretical reflection. Poetics and metaphysics, as will be elucidated over the course of the present chapter, go hand in hand. *Melete* places a greater emphasis on what poetry does and how poetry acts on the reader compared with Günderrode's two preceding collections. The idea of *poiesis* links poetics and metaphysics: poetry can bring into being that which would otherwise not exist and can therefore disclose metaphysical truths.

As yet, there has been no concerted critical effort to interpret *Melete* as a discrete corpus. This is curious, since it features Günderrode's programmatic statements about the function and pragmatics of poetry and invites the reader to treat the collection as a coherent whole, whereas the two preceding collections, *Gedichte und*

---

6   See Barbara Becker-Cantarino, 'Liebestod: Goethe "Der Gott und die Bajadere" und Günderrode "Die Malabarischen Witwen"', in *Emotionen in der Romantik: Repräsentation, Ästhetik, Inszenierung*, ed. by Antje Arnold and Walter Pape (Berlin: De Gruyter, 2012), pp. 21–32 (p. 31).
7   Preisendanz, p. 233; p. 262.
8   Creuzer notes Heyden's and Günderrode's collaborative philosophising (Preisendanz, p. 172). Heyden also acted as an amanuensis when Günderrode's eyesight proved too poor for her to write effectively: see Morgenthaler: *SW* III, 375.
9   *SW* III, 126–34.

Phantasien and *Poetische Fragmente*, function more as assemblages of disparate texts. To be sure, the diversity of materials and poetic modes in *Melete* does make the collection resist an overarching interpretation. The variety of subject-matter, verse forms and metres creates, as Helga Dormann has argued, an arabesque-like structure that recalls Friedrich Schlegel's use of irony.[10] A good proportion of *Melete* is also composed of love poetry.[11] For reasons of space, these poems will not be analysed in detail in the present chapter, but those which explicitly connect to Günderrode's metaphysical interests, such as 'Die Malabarischen Witwen', are discussed below.

With this exclusion in mind, my fundamental claim is that the texts in *Melete* are thematically interrelated so that the collection can be read as having a single main thread, one that is both philosophical and poetic. *Melete* takes up the idea of syncretism that is important for the legitimisation of Islam as the completion of the Western monotheisms in 'Mahomed, der Prophet von Mekka'. But Günderrode develops this thought further to an almost global span, ranging from Greek, Zoroastrian, and Norse mythologies to Hindu practices, before producing a Neoplatonist and Schellingian cosmology of her own design in 'Briefe zweier Freunde', her longest philosophical text.

Melete has been recognised as Günderrode's most mature and ambitious collection, distinguished by its lyrical intensity and formal control.[12] The title and the authorial pseudonym of Ion have, however, mostly escaped critical attention.[13] The correspondence between Günderrode and Creuzer indicates that it was chosen with some care. The original title that Günderrode proposed was Mnemosyne, the goddess of memory. For Creuzer, this was an unwise title given the use of Mnemosyne for the title of mnemotechnical handbooks at the time.[14] The name Ion also had drawbacks, according to Creuzer, although Günderrode would later argue for its inclusion first as a title, then as a pseudonym.[15] Not only is the titular rhapsode of Plato's dialogue *Ion* a less than respectable character, but the name had also become associated with August Wilhelm Schlegel's Neoclassical adaptation of Euripides' *Ion*,[16] which had been something of a fiasco when first staged in Weimar in 1802.[17] What becomes clear from these conceptual discussions is an attraction to Neoclassicism, born of Günderrode's and Creuzer's shared antiquarian interests, and also an affinity for Platonism, since the alternative names Creuzer suggests are either the three Boeotian muses — Mneme, Aoede, and Melete, who preceded the Olympian muses — or Platonists from antiquity.[18]

---

10 Dormann, p. 97.
11 There are accompanying texts in the *Nachlass* that ironise the stance of the lovelorn speaker in *Melete*: *SW* I, 392–93.
12 Becker-Cantarino, *Schriftstellerinnen der Romantik*, p. 220; Lazarowicz, p. 208; Naumann, p. 76.
13 The exception is Helga Dormann, who highlights the conceptual discussions between Creuzer and Günderrode as well as the etymology of the name 'Melete': Dormann, pp. 90–92.
14 Preisendanz, p. 216.
15 Ibid., p. 224.
16 Ibid.
17 Roger Paulin, *The Life of August Wilhelm Schlegel: Cosmopolitan of Art and Poetry* (Cambridge: OpenBook, 2016), pp. 186–89.
18 Preisendanz, p. 216.

Naming the collection after one of the three original muses is a mark of poetic ambition since it locates the collection at the point of origin for poetic inspiration and creativity as a sacred practice. But what of the weight of the name Melete itself? If Günderrode wished to indicate a return to the origins of poetic inspiration, then Aoede, the muse of song, might have been a more fitting title. As a term, *melete* has associations with the rhetorical tradition, as an equivalent to *exercitatio*, to the honing of an intellectual skill in oratory.[19] Being in possession of *melete* is inherently relational. In Plato's dialogues, the term 'names a condition [...] in which something *appears or presents itself to me* and *thereby affects me* in a concerning way'.[20] Although Melete is only specifically invoked as a muse in conventional terms at the start of Günderrode's collection, this relational aspect applies also to the 'Zueignung' [Dedication] that follows 'An Melete' [To Melete]. Where the latter is an expression of poetic *humilitas* that looks back to antiquity as a source of plenitude compared to the barren present,[21] the former is a programmatic statement about the function and pragmatics of poetry, and specifically of the role that the reader plays in creating the meaning of the texts.[22] 'Zueignung', then, is about the practice of poetry.

The sonnet 'Zueignung' is structured as a consciously intersubjective act, where the topos of the poet's supplication to the reader[23] in the first and third stanzas is complemented by the phenomenology of reading in the second and fourth:

> Ich habe Dir in ernsten stillen Stunden,
> Betrachtungsvoll in heil'ger Einsamkeit,
> Die Blumen dieser und vergangner Zeit,
> Die mir erblüht, zu einem Kranz gewunden.
>
> Von Dir, ich weiß es, wird der Sinn empfunden,
> Der in des Blüthenkelchs Verschwiegenheit
> Nur sichtbar wird dem Auge, das geweiht
> Im Farbenspiel den stillen Geist gefunden.
>
> Es flechten Mädchen so im Orient
> Den bunten Kranz; daß Vielen er gefalle,
> Wetteifern unter sich die Blumen alle.

---

19   Lucia Calboli Montefusco, 'Exercitatio', in *Der Neue Pauly*, ed. by Hubert Cancik and others. <http://dx.doi.org/10.1163/1574-9347_dnp_e407880> [accessed 3 July 2019].

20   Sean D. Kirkland, *The Ontology of Socratic Questioning in Plato's Early Dialogues* (Albany: SUNY Press, 2012), p. 101.

21   As Luciano Zagari notes as part of a series of familiar poetic tropes (such as botanical metaphors) that Günderrode adopts in the poem: Luciano Zagari, '"Die Leiche der Venus": Griechische Mythologie und Kunst der Deformation in romantischen Gedichten und Erzählungen. 1. Novalis, Karoline von Günderrode', in *Deutsche und italienische Romantik: Referate des Bad Homburger Colloquiums in der Werner-Reimers-Stiftung*, ed. by Enrico de Angelis and Ralph-Rainer Wuthenow (= *Jacques e i suoi quaderni*, 13 (1989)), 249–62 (p. 260).

22   Helga Dormann understands 'Zueignung' as a programmatic statement as well: Dormann, p. 234.

23   It has been argued that this poem is dedicated to Creuzer, which gives it a personal or private meaning, but one that does not exclude more generalised reading of the poem. See Lazarowicz, pp. 210–12.

> Doch Einer ihren tiefern Sinn erkennt,
> Ihm sind Symbole sie nur, äußre Zeichen;
> Sie reden ihm, obgleich sie alle schweigen.
>
> [I have in solemn, quiet hours
> Of contemplation, in sacred solitude,
> Woven into a wreath the flowers of this age
> And of those before, which blossomed in my care.
>
> You, I know, possess the sensitivity
> That, in the calyx's silence,
> Only becomes visible to the anointed eye,
> That senses the quiet spirit in the dance of colour.
>
> In the Orient, maidens each weave in this manner
> A coloured wreath; so that it may please many,
> The flowers vie with one another.
>
> Yet some may discern their deeper meaning:
> They are mere symbols to them, external signs;
> They speak to them, although all are silent.] (*SW* I, 318)

Here Günderrode cultivates a form of hermetic poetics, couched in the language of the mysteries, of initiations into secret rites and truths.[24] The texts themselves are resistant to reading ('des Blüthenkelchs Verschwiegenheit'), and therefore the ideal reader should already be an initiate into a secret mode of reading ('Von Dir, ich weiß es, wird der Sinn empfunden'); the neat rhyme of 'Verschwiegenheit' and 'geweiht' emphasises this logical progression from exoteric silence to esoteric knowledge. What the latter might be is left ambiguous. Thus the poem performs the point that the final stanza makes: 'de[r] stille[] Geist' and 'ihr tief[rer] Sinn' are mere placeholders or signifiers and remain dormant, awaiting the reader who would be capable of disclosing what they signify. Hence the closing *sententia*, which highlights the central paradox of the poem that both communicates and resists communication at the same time: 'Sie reden ihm, obgleich sie alle schweigen'. This embodies the tension of writing: an act that both speaks but remains silent. The act of poetic imagination laid out in the opening stanza, one that led to the creation of *Melete*, should, it is suggested, be replicated by the reader. To follow the logic of the language of the mysteries: the sacred space that the reader, as hierophant, enters, is the experience of the literary texts as texts themselves.

There is also a pragmatic level to the sonnet: the silence of poetry refers not only to the distinction between the exoteric and the esoteric, but also to the silence of not being read. At the same time, this gesture towards hidden meaning is a challenge to the reader. On one level, the poetic voice alludes to the entertaining function of poetry — one part of the Horatian maxim *prodesse et delectare* — to a broader audience ('daß Vielen er gefalle, | Wetteifern unter sich die Blumen alle'). The hidden or esoteric element of the poem is the move beyond the physical text itself, from the visible to the invisible, from the sign to the signified. The body of

---

24 Dirk von Petersdorff has traced *Mysterienrede* as a specific form of self-understanding for German Romantic writers and thinkers: see Petersdorff.

the wreath as a series of flowers also points to the careful construction of *Melete* itself, where the individual poems function as part of the wreath of the whole.

To draw on Wolfgang Iser's terminology from his discussion of phenomenological theories of art, what Günderrode stresses is the reciprocity between the artistic aspect of the text as created by the poet, and the aesthetic aspect of the text that is realised by the reader.[25] The sonnet points to this reciprocity through its alternating structure, but the convergence of text and reader — the act of bringing the text into existence — remains virtual and necessarily beyond poetic representation.

Elsewhere in *Melete*, Günderrode stresses how important this reciprocity between reader and the poet is. The ballad 'Der Gefangene und der Sänger' [The Prisoner and the Singer] takes an archetypal setting of a man imprisoned in a cell beneath a tower that may be inspired by the legend of Richard the Lionheart and the travelling poet Blondel;[26] a travelling singer passes by and his song happens to assuage the prisoner's anguish, so the prisoner begs him to stay. What develops from this is affective interdependence: both poet and prisoner become captive to their communicative situation,[27] with neither being able to perceive the other; nor is the singer, like the prisoner, able to leave. The final quatrain states:

> Und harren dort werd' ich die Jahre hindurch,
> Und sollt' ich drob selber erblassen.
> Es ist mir so weich und so sehnend ums Herz
> Ich kann den Geliebten nicht lassen.
>
> [And over many years I will tarry there,
> And even if I therefore grow pale and old.
> My heart is filled with feeling so tender and longing
> I cannot leave my beloved.] (*SW* I, 337, ll. 29–32)

The singer's sense of unfulfilled longing, one that is both voluntary and involuntary, leads to a self-destructive paralysis ('Und sollt' ich drob selber erblassen'); this insoluble tension is the central idea of the ballad. What Günderrode simulates in this ballad — framed in emotional terms — is the all-consuming need for a poet to have an audience, just as this need is reciprocated by said audience.

---

25 Wolfgang Iser, 'The Reading Process: A Phenomenological Approach', *New Literary History*, 3.2 (1972), 279–99 (p. 279).

26 The legend of Richard the Lionheart and Blondel achieved some popularity in the latter half of the eighteenth century, particularly in opera, the most famous examples being Handel's *Riccardo Primo* (1727) and André Ernest Modest Grétry's *Richard Cœur de Lion* (1784): See Albert Gier, '"O Richard, o mon roi": Richard Löwenherz im Musiktheater', in *Richard Löwenherz, ein europäischer Herrscher im Zeitalter der Konfrontation von Christentum und Islam*, ed. by Ingrid Bennewitz and Klaus von Eickels, Bamberger interdiziplinäre Mittelalterstudien, Vorträge und Vorlesungen, 8 (Bamberg: University of Bamberg Press, 2019), pp. 171–96 (p. 172). There are also literary workings of the narrative in the late eighteenth century, such as Wieland's 'Richard Löwenherz und Blondel: Eine Anekdote aus der Geschichte der provenzalischen Dichter' (1777), published in the *Teutscher Merkur*; also August Friedrich Ernst Langbein's ballad 'Richard Löwenherz und Blondel', included in his collection of *Gedichte* (1800), as well as Friedrich August Müller's verse epic *Richard Löwenherz: Ein Gedicht in Sieben Büchern* (1790).

27 As Karin R. Daubert also remarks: Karin R. Daubert, 'Karoline von Günderrode's "Der Gefangene und der Sänger": New Voices in Romanticism's Desire for Cultural Transcendence', *New German Review*, 8 (1992), 1–17 (p. 7).

To return to 'Zueignung': the poem makes a weighty claim for the function of poetry. That is, poetry serves as an appropriate medium for disclosing higher truths, but to a limited audience of hierophants. To follow the textual logic: the reader has to develop a faculty or sensitivity in order for reading to fulfil this disclosive function. Again, it may be tempting in the present context to align Günderrode with the literary theories of the Jena Romantic circle, such as Schlegelian theories of irony, allegory, fragmentation of meaning and (in)comprehensibility. But there are more illuminating parallels here to Günderrode's earlier work about the cognitive leaps involved in aesthetic or poetic experience. The central idea of 'Der Dom zu Cölln' is that aesthetic and specifically poetic experience has a revelatory function and can reveal higher truths by inducing a state of ecstasy in the mind of the viewer or reader. Equally, interactions between conscious and unconscious forms of cognition in 'Ein apokaliptisches Fragment' yield metaphysical insights — namely, the truth of Spinozist panentheism.

What I would like to suggest is that the 'Zueignung' operates in this line of texts, except that it is not declaratory or declamatory in the manner of Günderrode's previous work. Instead, the onus lies on the reader to train their cognitive faculties to perceive what underpins *Melete* as a whole. What unites the earlier texts by Günderrode is the search for revelatory knowledge. But in *Melete*, reading itself can perform an epistemological function. What distinguishes *Melete*, then, is that Günderrode's metaphysical commitments, with the exception of 'Briefe zweier Freunde', are not proclaimed, but rather have to be inferred. What is common to Günderrode's previous metaphysical texts — from 'Immortalita', 'Die Manen' to 'Mahomed, der Prophet von Mekka', among others — is how to mediate between inner and outer worlds; in Günderrode's notes on the workings of the imagination, complete withdrawal from an outer world is required for the imagination to operate at all.[28] Just as the poet must mediate between the inner world of the imagination and the outer world, so too must the reader.

This, in turn, leads back to how to interpret the title of *Melete*: it is to do with the art of reading itself, a mode of reading that is almost a spiritual exercise or exercise for the soul.[29] In Pierre Hadot's summation, *melete* can be best rendered as meditation: 'the exercise designated by *melete* corresponds, in the last analysis, rather well to what we nowadays term *meditation*: an effort to assimilate an idea, notion, or principle, and make them come alive in the soul'.[30] To build on the notion of meditative reading: the focus in 'Zueignung' lies in how the reader has to withdraw from the external signs of the text (and the external world around them). But what the poem promotes is a specific mode of reading, one that is anagogical, a retreat from the outer to the inner world that grants the act of reading a spiritual or mystical resonance.

---

28 Günderrode, *Briefe*, p. 125.
29 For a stimulating discussion of the function of *askesis*, a term related to *melete* in the rhetorical tradition, and the pragmatics of eighteenth-century poetry, see Gabriel Trop, *Poetry as a Way of Life: Aesthetics and Askesis in the German Eighteenth Century* (Evanston, IL: Northwestern University Press, 2015).
30 Pierre Hadot, *Philosophy as a Way of Life: Spiritual Exercises from Socrates to Foucault*, trans. by Michael Chase (Oxford: Blackwell, 1995), p. 112.

This understanding of reading as a spiritual process is not unique to Günderrode. What the effects of reading may be — intellectual, spiritual, or physiological — were also the topic of debate in the eighteenth century.[31] Reading as a spiritual process fits into a tradition of the *poeta vates* [divinely inspired poet], one that originates in antiquity, but was revived by Klopstock in the eighteenth century.[32] The *poeta vates* is endowed with particular divine inspiration and can proclaim religious truth — meaning that poetry itself is valorised as a medium of salvation. This valorisation of the poet goes hand in hand with the recontextualisation of sacred texts as objects of historicising scholarship.[33]

But Günderrode pushes beyond these common tropes of understanding art or poetry as religion, or *Kunstreligion*. The act of reading is to help make a single metaphysical principle come alive in the soul of the reader, and this should not come at the expense of the kaleidoscopic scope of cultural and poetic traditions on which Günderrode draws. To put it pointedly: *Melete* functions, in part, as a poetic version of the maxim *hen kai pan*, in which all cultural and poetic traditions recall and articulate in manifold form an underlying universal truth.

An example of how poetry can achieve the kind of revelatory and ritualistic quality suggested by 'Zueignung' can be found in Günderrode's hymn to Adonis, which functions as a syncretising act of communion. Of the Adonis poems in *Melete*, the first two sonnets under the heading of 'Adonis Tod' [Adonis' Death] are not from Günderrode's hand, but were penned by Creuzer, with Günderrode having suggested improvements.[34] The Adonis poems, as Helga Dormann has usefully pointed out, act as counterpoints to each other: Creuzer humanises Aphrodite in her suffering, whereas Günderrode deifies Adonis in death.[35] Read side by side, the sonnets lead into Günderrode's elegiac poem, since Creuzer focuses on the palliative quality of Aphrodite's sung lament that helped found the cult of Adonis.

But there is a temporal rift between the two sets of poems. Whilst the speaker could be the mourning goddess of Creuzer's sonnets,[36] there is a textual detail that indicates otherwise: 'Laßt die Klage uns erneuern!' [Let us renew the lament!] (*SW* I, 321, l. 23). This points to a collective, performative act of mourning. What 'Adonis Todtenfeyer' explicitly performs, therefore, are the cultic rites associated

---

31 See Britta Herrmann, 'Von der Macht der Worte und der Gewalttätigkeit des Dichters: Zur Erzeugung virtueller Realität im 18. Jahrhundert', *Annali di Ca' Foscari: Serie occidentale*, 52 (2018), 89–105.

32 Heinrich Detering, 'Was ist Kunstreligion? Systematische und historische Bemerkungen', in *Kunstreligion: Ein ästhetisches Konzept der Moderne in seiner historischen Entfaltung*, ed. by Albert Meier and others, 3 vols (Berlin: De Gruyter, 2011–14), I: *Der Ursprung des Konzepts um 1800* (2011), pp. 11–27 (p. 15).

33 See Jonathan Sheehan, *The Enlightenment Bible: Translation, Scholarship, Culture* (Princeton: Princeton University Press, 2005).

34 As Morgenthaler notes: *SW* III, 165. The fair copy of the Adonis sonnets is in Creuzer's hand. Creuzer also wrote of Adonis in his *Symbolik und Mythologie der alten Völker, besonders der Griechen* (1810–12).

35 Dormann, p. 217.

36 As Roswitha Burwick claims: Roswitha Burwick, 'Liebe und Tod in Leben und Werk der Günderode', *German Studies Review*, 3.2 (1980), 207–23 (pp. 219–20).

with Adonis,[37] that is, the festival of Adonia, a women's festival in ancient Athens.[38] This ritualised event focused on Adonis as the epitome of transience: Adonis, a syncretic vegetation god, originates in Syria and was then translated into Greek religion. As a deity, he represents the process of life, death, and rebirth.[39] Hence the practice of the gardens of Adonis that were associated with the Adonia festival: women would cultivate plants in shallow soil in pots, so the plants would grow and wither quickly as well.[40] This shift from the mythic narrative of Creuzer's sonnets to the religious customs that developed as a result emphasises how social meaning is generated through repeated rituals that reaffirm a central metaphysical idea — here, the idea of eternal life. But there is another, more tangible level: the poem itself enacts and is a sacred ritual that leads the reader to the joyous disclosure of this truth.

For Günderrode the narrative of the Adonia is significant: it involved ritualised mourning of the death of Adonis, followed by ritualised joy over the god's resurrection and immortality.[41] This collective movement from lamentation to joy is the poem's fundamental dynamic. Günderrode's reading privileges Adonis as the epitome of transience rather than focusing on his beauty, which is mentioned only once: 'Daß der süße Leib des Schönen | Muß dem kargen Tode fröhnen' [So that the sweet body of the Beautiful | Must serve austere death] (*SW* I, 321, ll. 21–22).[42]

'Adonis Todtenfeyer', as critics have observed, makes recourse to the Baroque theme of *vanitas*, and is formally close to Lutheran hymns.[43] This formal choice makes the poem inherently syncretic, over and above the fact that Adonis was a god already subject to cultural translation in antiquity. Günderrode opens the poem with a piece of linguistic misdirection. Were it not for the title, the immediate association that the opening would create is with Christ, not Adonis. 'Adonis Todtenfeyer', therefore, is Günderrode's rewriting of the Passion and the Resurrection, in Lutheran form but with a naturalised understanding of resurrection.[44] This is made

---

37   Also noted by Stephanie Galasso, 'Form and Contention: *Sati* as Custom in Günderrode's "Die Malabarischen Witwen"', *Goethe Yearbook*, 24 (2017), 197–220 (pp. 198–99).
38   Robert Parker, *Polytheism and Society at Athens* (Oxford: Oxford University Press, 2007), pp. 283–89.
39   The non-Greek origins of Adonis were known in the eighteenth century: see 'Adonis', in Benjamin Hederich, *Gründliches mythologisches Lexicon*, ed. by Johann Joachim Schwabe (Leipzig: Gleditsch, 1770), pp. 69–70.
40   There is some ambiguity in the Greek accounts about whether these gardens represented fertility or not: see Marcel Detienne, *The Gardens of Adonis: Spices in Greek Mythology*, trans. by Janet Lloyd (Hassocks: Harvester Press, 1977), pp. 101–03.
41   As described by Hederich, pp. 64–65.
42   For a comparison of Günderrode's 'Adonis Todtenfeyer' and more classicist renderings of the Adonis myth, see Robert Blankenship, *Suicide in East German Literature: Fiction, Rhetoric, and the Self-Destruction of Literary Heritage* (Rochester, NY: Camden House, 2017), pp. 85–87.
43   Christmann notes that the poem echoes the well-known seventeenth-century church hymn, 'Ach wie flüchtig, ach wie nichtig ist der Menschen Leben' [Oh, how fleeting, oh, how trivial is human life], with the text by Michael Franck (1609–67), Christmann, pp. 182–83. See also Becker-Cantarino, 'The "New Mythology"', pp. 51–52.
44   There are acknowledged parallels between Adonis and Christ, which may have contributed to aspects of the cult of Adonis being incorporated into Christian rituals: see Joan E. Taylor, *Christians*

clear by the opening, which functions as a *lamentatio*. The familiar parameters of the *vanitas* motif are burst open. Gone is the juxtaposition between the transience of the Earth versus the eternity of heaven. Rather, eternal life is found in this world:

> Wehe! daß der Gott auf Erden
> Sterblich mußt gebohren werden!
> Alles Dasein, alles Leben
> Ist mit ihm dem Tod gegeben.
> Alles wandelt und vergehet,
> Morgen sinkt was heute stehet;
> Was jezt schön und herrlich steiget,
> Bald sich hin zum Staube neiget;
> Dauer ist nicht zu erwerben,
> Wandeln ist unsterblich Sterben.
>
> [Woe! That the God on Earth
> Should be born mortal!
> All existence, all life,
> Is given unto death with him,
> All that is changes and perishes,
> That which stands today shall fall tomorrow;
> What now arises, fair and splendid,
> Will soon sink into dust;
> Permanence cannot be attained,
> Change is undying death.] (*SW* I, 321, ll. 1–10)

The tenth line of the poem turns away from the conventions of lamenting transience and encapsulates its central argument. This argument is a paradox: natural processes turn mortality into an eternal process of transformation. Whilst the mood of the line may itself be one of lamentation, it opens up the possibility that if death is an eternal, cyclical process, so too is life.

The poem goes on to evoke the beginning of the cultic rites surrounding Adonis: the mourning ritual parallels the function of the god, by itself symbolically bringing about resurrection in new life. Here, Günderrode reinterprets the source material: the symbols for Adonis are the anemone flower and the rose. In Ovid's rendering of the myth in *The Metamorphoses*, Adonis, having been gored to death by a boar, was cradled by Aphrodite, and his blood created the fragile anemone flower, while Aphrodite's tears produced the rose.[45] The speaker exhorts her fellow initiates to perform the ritualistic practices that recognise Adonis's status as a god:

> Rufet zu geheimen Feyern,
> Die Adonis heilig nennen,
> Seine Gottheit anerkennen,
> Die die Weihen sich erworben,
> Denen auch der Gott gestorben.

---

and the Holy Places: The Myth of Jewish-Christian Origins (Oxford: Clarendon Press, 1993), pp. 109–10.
45   This is one of differing accounts: Laurialan Reitzammer, *The Athenian Adonia in Context: The Adonis Festival as Cultural Practice* (Madison: University of Wisconsin Press, 2016), p. 118. Günderrode's source appears to be Bion of Smyrna's 'Lament for Adonis': see Morgenthaler, *SW* III, 175.

[Call us to secret rituals,
Which proclaim Adonis as holy,
And acknowledge his divinity,
Which the blessings too have acquired,
For which the God has also died.] (*SW* I, 321, ll. 24–28)

The divinity of Adonis is to be revealed through secret rituals ('geheime Feyern'). The implication here is one of repetition: the collective act of remembrance amounts to a symbolic re-enactment of the death of Adonis through the breaking of the flowers that symbolise Adonis — the anemone flower and the rose. The logic is cyclical: since these flowers were created upon Adonis's death, a further metamorphosis — albeit metaphorical — or even transubstantiation, is required for a resurrection to occur:

> Brecht die dunkle Anemone,
> Sie, die ihre Blätterkrone
> Sinnend still herunter beuget,
> Leise sich zur Tiefe neiget,
> Forschend ob der Gott auf Erden
> Wieder soll gebohren werden!
>
> Brechet Rosen; jede Blume
> Sei verehrt im Heiligthume,
> Forscht in ihren Kindermienen,
> Denn es schläft der Gott in ihnen;
> Uns ist er durch sie erstanden
> Aus des dumpfen Grabes Banden.
> Wie sie leis hervor sich drängen,
> Und des Hügels Decke sprengen,
> Ringet aus des Grabes Engen
> Sich empor verschloßnes Leben;
> Tod den Raub muß wiedergeben,
> Leben wiederkehrt zum Leben.
> Also ist der Gott erstanden
> Aus des dumpfen Grabes Banden.
>
> [Break the dark anemone,
> Whose crown of leaves
> Bows downward in silent contemplation
> Quietly dips into the depths
> Examining if the God on Earth
> Is to be born again!
>
> Break the roses; each flower
> Shall be honoured in the sanctum;
> Examine their child-like countenances,
> For the God slumbers in them:
> To us has he arisen through them
> Out of the dull bonds of the grave,
> How they quietly press outward,
> And break the cover of the hill,
> Hidden life struggles upward

> Out of confines of the grave;
> Death must restore what has been stolen;
> Life returns to life,
> Thus has the God arisen
> Out of the dull bonds of the grave.] (SW I, 322, ll. 29–48)

The anticipation in these verses is palpable: the ritual breaking of the flowers — the anemone here being briefly anthropomorphised — features linguistic repetition, moving from the lightly hypothetical ('Forschend ob der Gott auf Erden | Wieder soll gebohren werden!') into the definite ('Forscht in ihren Kindermienen, | Denn es schläft der Gott in ihnen'). The resurrection occurs as a matter of ritualistic assurance: it is the sight of the flowers sprouting from what appears to be — perhaps only symbolically — the funeral mound of Adonis that delights the neophytes. Günderrode carefully adopts language that not only stresses the liberation of this resurrection ('sprengen', 'Ringet'), but phrases as well that have religious resonance with Christ's Passion ('des dumpfen Grabes Banden'),[46] culminating in the resurrection, rather than rebirth, of Adonis. This revelation of life after death is that life simply exists as a cycle, nullifying death, and any fear of it, altogether ('Leben wiederkehrt zum Leben').

This is a radical reinterpretation of resurrection: Adonis is resurrected *through* nature. Whilst the ritualistic act may generate meaning symbolically, there is also the suggestion here that the distinction between what is symbolic and what is real is blurred. The meaning to be inferred from this ritual is that nothing is lost through death. There is a chain of metamorphoses that stresses the endless (and ritually practised) rebirths and resurrections. The overarching principle of life dissolves any distinction between gods, humans, and nature, insofar as everything is part of nature. This also chimes with a common thought in *Melete*, one that will be found again in 'Die Malabarischen Witwen' and 'Briefe zweier Freunde': that death is only a dissolution into constituent parts — atoms or elements — and that these are simply reconstituted in the endless productivity of nature.

It is this overarching principle of life that shapes *Melete*. Whilst Günderrode's metaphysical commitments tend to be relatively stable, there is also a shift in the understanding of panentheism in the collection. Prior to *Melete*, as discussed in the previous chapter, a consistent tension across Günderrode's *oeuvre* is the attempt of the individual speaker or subject to escape the limitations of individuality and those of phenomenal reality. This is often couched in textual movements of ascent and descent, where the latter takes the form of *katabasis* in 'Des Wandrers Niederfahrt' and the dramolet 'Immortalita'. Where once there was the implication of some form of transcendence, in *Melete* transcendence collapses into immanence. Instead, there is no transcendence of phenomenal reality. Nature is a physical, finite manifestation of a divine and dynamic principle that realises itself through history. This history is universalised and no longer anthropocentric: it is the story, not of the progression of societies, but of the perfection of organic matter. In this manner, Günderrode takes panentheism to its logical end, indeed to the point where it becomes pantheism. Whilst originally conceived of as a means of avoiding the dangers associated

---

46   See Bach's cantata, 'Christ lag in Todesbanden' (BWV 4).

with mechanistic materialism of the Cartesian tradition, panentheism becomes transfigured into a kind of spiritualised materialism. The vertical axis that marked Günderrode's earlier metaphysical texts is flattened out and becomes a horizontal plane and is one of temporal progression rather than vertical, spatial progression.

Such a flattening out of Günderrode's understanding of metaphysics is given visual form in a series of diagrams that Günderrode drew as part of her studies of Schelling's philosophy of nature. The two diagrams make use of the vocabulary of Schellingian philosophy of nature to juxtapose deism with naturalism. In the former, the absolute lies outside of the world as the 'Ewiges oder Absolutes in höchster Potenz' [The eternal or the Absolute in the highest power] (*SW* II, 359), whereas the universe functions as 'Absolutes in zweiter Potenz Oder das Abbild des Ewigen Einen in der Vielheit oder Prinzip des Universums' [the Absolute in the second power or the image of the Eternal One in multiplicity or the principle of the Universe] (ibid.). The naturalistic conception of the universe allows for a synthesis of the universe with the absolute, a fusion of the subject and object, of the ideal and the real, spirit and material (*SW* II, 358).

Of Myth and *Melete*

One topic must be dealt with before the significance of the *Melete* collection for Günderrode's metaphysical thought can be considered: namely, the question of myth, or rather, what myth does for Günderrode. Analysing Günderrode through the lens of myth — through a broad spectrum of traditions, whether it be Persian, Greek, Egyptian, Norse, or the 'inauthentic' Ossianic bardic poetry — has proved to be a rich vein that scholars have tapped into, drawing on texts from the entire *oeuvre* and on specific texts from *Melete*.[47]

But the significance of mythic material for Günderrode is subsidiary to that of poetry and the poetics described above. It is, as was common in the late eighteenth century, a tool of poetic expression and representation.[48] More than any other of Günderrode's collections, and as has already been highlighted above, *Melete* highlights the function of poetry and the poet — indeed, the title refers to one of the pre-Olympian muses. There are also several points in *Melete* where Günderrode cuts against the mythic trappings to expose the core of the metaphysical ideas that gave rise to these mythic narratives. It is the poetic form that acts as a medium of revelation — a point which I will return to below.

It is worth attending to how Günderrode fits into debates around mythology at the turn of the nineteenth century,[49] to prevent her from being pulled into the

---

[47] See Simonis, pp. 254–78; also Barbara Becker-Cantarino, 'Mythos und Symbolik bei Karoline von Günderrode und Friedrich Creuzer', in *200 Jahre Heidelberger Romantik*, ed. by Friedrich Strack and Barbara Becker-Cantarino (Berlin: Springer, 2008), pp. 281–98.
[48] This is in keeping with how mythology was understood before Romanticism, by Winckelmann, Moritz, and Schiller, among others: see Daniel Greineder, *From the Past to the Future: The Role of Mythology from Winckelmann to Schelling* (Oxford: Peter Lang, 2007), p. 14.
[49] Gerhard Schulz, *Geschichte der deutschen Literatur: Die deutsche Literatur zwischen Französischer Revolution und Restauration*, 2 vols, Geschichte der deutschen Literatur, 7 (Munich: Beck, 1983), II, 643.

slipstream of dominant narratives around mythology — whether it is the New Mythology or *Neue Mythologie* propounded by Friedrich Schlegel or the comparative mythology of Friedrich Creuzer — since there are superficial commonalities with both. One important difference is that compared to contemporaries such as Schlegel, Schelling and Creuzer, or even Herder and Winckelmann, Günderrode is neither an aesthetic or philosophical theoretician nor a philologist. Rather, she is a practitioner of poetry and philosophy and therefore there is no conceptual fixity in the deployment of myth. She is more experimental.

As Annette Simonis has argued, Günderrode's approach to myth is indebted to late Enlightenment approaches,[50] which move away from the earlier Enlightenment interest in fable over myth, where myth itself had no metaphysical or psychological import. There is certainly a metaphysical weight to Günderrode's use of myth in *Melete*, and Günderrode's adaptation of material is part and parcel of a mythic and religious syncretism[51] that runs from 'Mahomed, der Prophet von Mekka' and 'Geschichte eines Braminen' to *Melete* itself.[52] Within this syncretism there is a universalising tendency, an idea derived from the notion of a perennial philosophy containing only one single, underlying truth.[53] The structure of *Melete* helps create a series of correspondences that suggest a unity of diverse phenomena and traditions.[54] The internal coherence between some of the poems will be discussed in further detail below. There is some slippage between myth and cultic forms of religion in *Melete*, which can be read as part of a Romantic practice of excavating other cultural traditions to create a repository of potent images and symbols. This is because the attraction towards mythology among figures such as Friedrich Schlegel and Schelling stemmed partly from problems specific to the development of Protestantism at the turn of the nineteenth century, and its perceived stagnation. In mythology, in George S. Williamson's phrase, Schlegel and Schelling, for instance, sought 'a nonbiblical source of sacred symbolism and narrative, which had the potential to rejuvenate aesthetic and religious life'.[55]

In this case: how useful is it to align Günderrode with the *Neue Mythologie*?[56] The 'Rede über die Mythologie' [Speech on Mythology] (1800) in the *Athenaeum* developed the idea that the post-Revolutionary age demands a new form of mythology, so as to provide an alternative form of rationality that would work against the

---

50   Simonis, pp. 270–71.
51   Ibid., p. 258.
52   For a discussion of mythic syncretism at the turn of the nineteenth century, see Graevenitz, pp. 209–60.
53   Maria Cieśla-Korytowska, 'On Romantic Cognition', in *Romantic Poetry*, ed. by. Angela Esterhammer (Amsterdam: John Benjamins, 2002), pp. 39–53 (p. 44).
54   Andrew Bowie, *Aesthetics and Subjectivity*, 2nd edn (Manchester: Manchester University Press, 2003), p. 64.
55   George S. Williamson, *The Longing for Myth in Germany: Religion and Aesthetic Culture from Romanticism to Nietzsche* (Chicago: University of Chicago Press, 2004), p. 24.
56   Lucia Maria Licher is keen to fuse Günderrode's use of myth with the Schlegelian project of *Neue Mythologie*: see Licher, p. 342; Christmann assigns Günderrode's work in *Melete* to the project of the New Mythology without further elaboration of how this can be inferred: Christmann, pp. 182–83.

perceived dogmatism of Enlightenment thought.[57] Another point of reference that has been the subject of lively scholarly debate and interpretation[58] would be *Das älteste Systemprogramm des deutschen Idealismus* [The Oldest Systematic Programme of German Idealism] (1797–98), a prose text in Hegel's hand, written at the Tübingen seminary in collaboration with Hölderlin and Schelling. Since the manuscript was only discovered at the turn of the twentieth century, there can be no genetic link to Günderrode. It proposes a mythology of reason, that ideas must become mythological, as mythology should become a matter of reason, as part of a project of universal education that will lead to the equality and freedom of all.[59] The political implications dormant in this new mythology — immanent rational progress in the world — amount to a dissolution of myth entirely.[60]

The main impediment to bringing Günderrode into a discussion of *Neue Mythologie* is a positivist one: whilst Günderrode certainly was interested in the discussions about founding a new religion in Schlegel's 'Ideen' and Schleiermacher's *Reden über die Religion*, there is no evidence of Günderrode's reception of Schlegel's *Neue Mythologie* or the aesthetic theory of which it is a part.[61] More importantly: Schlegel's conception of mythology or religion rests on, in Ernst Behler's analysis, a form of emancipatory humanism, in which there is no transcendence, and the individual attains the ethical maturity that Lessing presaged at the end of *Die Erziehung des Menschengeschlechts*, and where the world is perceived poetically and symbolically.[62]

Not least because Schlegel's use of the term mythology is quite elastic — as it is in the *Ältestes Systemprogramm* — these aesthetic and utopian projects push in different directions from Günderrode. Where Günderrode may hypothetically have sympathy with the political implications of these aesthetic programmes, she deploys mythic material to subsume or ground the individual metaphysically in the world as a means of emphasising teleological determinism. Furthermore, mythic material is used to intuit the reality of the natural processes and forces that determine the world. This is taken to a radical extreme in *Melete*, where there is little or no ethical distinction between the individual human and the natural world.

The second temptation with regard to myth would be to slot Günderrode's work into the narrative of Friedrich Creuzer's seminal philological work on myth, since the concepts that would feed into Creuzer's later magnum opus *Symbolik*

---

57 Manfred Frank, *Der kommende Gott: Vorlesungen über die Neue Mythologie: 1. Teil* (Frankfurt a.M.: Suhrkamp, 1982). See also Jochen Fried, *Die Symbolik des Realen: Über alte und neue Mythologie in der Frühromantik* (Munich: Fink, 1985).
58 As Rüdiger Bubner notes: Rüdiger Bubner, *The Innovations of Idealism*, trans. by Nicholas Walker (Cambridge: Cambridge University Press, 2003), p. 7.
59 Georg Wilhelm Friedrich Hegel, *Werke in zwanzig Bänden*, ed. by Eva Moldenhauer and Karl Markus Michel, 20 vols (Frankfurt a.M.: Suhrkamp, 1969–71), I: *Frühe Schriften* (1971), pp. 234–36 (p. 236).
60 Nicholas Halmi, *The Genealogy of the Romantic Symbol* (Oxford: Oxford University Press, 2007), pp. 149–50.
61 As Christmann also notes: Christmann, p. 119.
62 Ernst Behler, 'Friedrich Schlegel's "Rede über die Mythologie" im Hinblick auf Nietzsche', *Nietzsche-Studien*, 8.1 (1979), 182–209 (pp. 199–205).

und Mythologie der alten Völker [Symbolism and Mythology of the Ancient Peoples] (1810–12) were being developed throughout the period of his association with Günderrode.[63] Indeed, there are resemblances between the sections on the Osiris and Isis myth in the *Symbolik* and Günderrode's phrasing.[64] Whilst *Melete* testifies to the intimacy of their creative collaboration, and Creuzer provided Günderrode with advice on what to read on the subject, the evidence is that the dialogue with him only confirmed ideas she had already been working with in her earlier works. Creuzer's contention, in the *Symbolik*, that myths are derived from primordial images,[65] and that Greek myths reproduced concepts that had been transmitted from India,[66] for example, would not have been a new idea to Günderrode, as we can see from 'Geschichte eines Braminen'. Whilst it is the case that Creuzer and Günderrode enjoyed a period of intense creative collaboration, what distinguishes Günderrode is how she deploys poetic syncretism to explore a naturalistic understanding of the universe in *Melete*.

Nature as Cure

In *Melete*, this naturalistic understanding of the universe is referred to as a dynamic principle of life that is both cyclical and eternal. The dynamic element derives from the notion of polarity, which was a widespread principle of scientific and literary writing about nature around 1800, from Goethe, Kant, to Schelling, and Johann Wilhelm Ritter.[67]

How do these abstract notions of life and polarity come alive in poetic form? Whereas Adonis served to expose the truth of eternal life, Günderrode turns to polytheistic religious traditions in a series of poems that play with the idea of the polarity of natural forces, by, in part, stripping back the personified veil of deities to expose what lies behind: a deification of nature as *hen kai pan* and the embodiment of the sublime. The poetic narratives, however, also draw on vocabulary that is more familiar from the medical psychology of the eighteenth century. The dynamics of natural forces have curative properties, assuaging both fanaticism and melancholy.

Like 'Adonis Todtenfeyer', the ballad 'Eine persische Erzählung' is syncretic, but in a manner so explicit as to be jarring. It draws on the Zoroastrian tradition, and Günderrode would have found reliable sources about this tradition: the French adventurer and explorer Antequil-Duperron had collected and translated the canonical texts in 1771,[68] which were translated into German by the theologian

---

63 See, for example, Creuzer's influential essay *Idee und Probe alter Symbolik*, first published in the second volume of Creuzer's and Carl Daub's *Studien* (1806).
64 As Morgenthaler notes: *SW* III, 188.
65 Christoph Jamme, ' "Göttersymbole": Friedrich Creuzer als Mythologe und seine philosophische Wirkung', in *200 Jahre Heidelberger Romantik*, pp. 486–98 (p. 487).
66 Friedrich Creuzer, 'Philologie und Mythologie, in ihrem Stufengang und gegenseitigem Verhalten', *Heidelberger Jahrbücher der Literatur für Philologie, Historie, Literatur und Kunst*, 1.1 (1808), 3–24 (p. 21).
67 See Antje Pfannkuchen and Leif Weatherby, 'Writing Polarities: Romanticism and the Dynamic Unity of Poetry and Science', *The Germanic Review*, 92 (2017), 335–39 (p. 336). See also Robert J. Richards, *The Romantic Conception of Life* (Chicago: University of Chicago Press, 2002).
68 Bradley L. Herling, *The German Gita: Hermeneutics and Discipline in the Early German Reception*

and historian Johann Friedrich Kleuker.[69] Günderrode creates a mixture of gods and mythical figures from different traditions: Ormuzd corresponds to the Zoroastrian god of light; Mitra, according to the textual logic of the poem, is the counterpoint to Ormuzd, and is therefore not, as Walter Morgenthaler claims, a misspelling of Mithra, the Avestan god of light (SW III, 190). Rather, Mitra is a telluric god of darkness that is associated with the feminine;[70] Luna refers to the Roman goddess of the moon.[71] But this is not a matter of terminological looseness on Günderrode's part. Her studies of world religions suggest both an interest in and an awareness of discrete traditions that make it unlikely that she would have conflated them unthinkingly.[72] Instead, Günderrode is presenting, through a series of equivalences that suggest universality, an unusually explicit syncretism in the poem. Zoroastrianism's dualistic cosmology is helpful as it maps neatly onto the concept of polarity; what is implicit is that, just as in 'Magie und Schicksal', deified, antagonising forces constitute an underlying unity.[73]

This syncretism is in fact secondary to the narrative of the poem, which tells the story of a cure for fanaticism and religious madness. This becomes clear in the opening and closing lines of the poem. From 'Rasend am Altar des Feuers | Ormuzd Priester war geworden' [The priest of Ormuzd had become | Consumed with rage at the altar of fire] (SW I, 331, ll. 1–2), we move to a gesture towards the successful cure: 'Daß im Arm der Mitternächte | Schweren Wahnsinns er genese' [So that, in midnights' embrace, | He might recover from his severe madness] (SW I, 332, ll. 57–58). The narrative is straightforward. The priest of Ormuzd is driven to deluded madness by his fanatical devotion[74] to the god of light; he is beset by both psychological and physiological symptoms: 'Rasend, zitternd' [Raging, trembling] (SW I, 332, l. 35). The priest cannot accept the impending darkness of nightfall — and this is the core of his delusion — since it would represent the final defeat for Ormuzd in the cosmic struggle between light and darkness. To prevent this, he scales a cliff and shoots an arrow towards Luna as she rises above the sea. The forward momentum of his bowstring snapping back causes him to lose his balance, and he plunges into the depths.

The priest's death reveals the ironic nature of the cure that follows: whilst this

---

of Indian Thought, 1778–1831 (New York: Routledge, 2006), p. 59.

69   Albert F. de Jong, *Traditions of the Magi: Zoroastrianism in Greek and Latin Literature* (Leiden: Brill, 1997), pp. 5–6. Herder also discusses Zoroastrianism as a primarily political religion in his *Ideen zu einer Philosophie der Geschichte der Menschheit*.

70   This may derive in part from Friedrich Creuzer's androgynous concept of Mithra-Mitra; Creuzer's source for Mitra as a telluric, feminine god (related to Persephone and Isis in Creuzer's account) is Herodotus: Friedrich Creuzer, *Friedrich Creuzers Symbolik und Mythologie* (Leipzig: Heyer und Leske, 1819), pp. 733–34.

71   As Morgenthaler notes: SW III, 190.

72   See the studies of different religious traditions: SW II, 413–17.

73   This duality, that the gods are means of describing polarised natural forces that are aspects of a unified nature, is noted upon in the German translation of the *Zend-Avesta*: Johann Friedrich Kleuker, *Anhang zum Zend-Avesta*, II.1 (Leipzig: Hartknoch, 1783), p. 130.

74   For a discussion of fanaticism in the context of melancholy and enthusiasm, see Hans-Jürgen Schings, *Melancholie und Aufklärung: Melancholiker und ihre Kritiker in Erfahrungsseelenkunde und Literatur des 18. Jahrhunderts* (Stuttgart: Metzler, 1977), pp. 185–96.

fatal act is couched in terms of Faustian hubris — 'Sterbend büßt er sein Erkühnen' [Through death he atones for his boldness] (SW I, 332, l. 52) — his rebellion only exposes his impotence. So grave is the priest's fanatical delusion that the only recovery or recuperation occurs through death. Here the poem operates on a double level. In terms of the medical discourse of the eighteenth century, the priest's death is an ironic variant of the water cure, the shock of hydrotherapy that could involve sudden immersion in water.[75] The textual logic of the poem on a religious or mythic level equally dictates that an excessive adherence to one pole in this dualistic cosmology has to be counterbalanced by exposure to its opposite. Günderrode formulates this motif of descending into water as a cyclical return. Just as in 'Einstens lebt' ich süßes Leben', or 'Ein apokaliptisches Fragment', the sea is the fermenting primordial chaos:

> Mitleidsvoll ihm Mitra lächlet;
> Aber gütig nimmt das Dunkel
> Auf in seinem heil'gen Schooße
> Freundlich den verirrten Kranken,
> Daß im Arm der Mitternächte
> Schweren Wahnsinns er genese.
>
> [Mitra smiles upon him with pity,
> Yet the darkness, benevolent,
> Receives with kindness the confused,
> Ailing man in its sacred womb
> So that, in midnights' embrace,
> He might recover from his severe madness.]
> (SW I, 332, ll. 53–58)

The final irony is the lack of antagonism among the forces the priest abhors: note the density of the adjectives 'mitleidsvoll', 'gütig', 'freundlich' and their prominence in their position in the lines, as well as the shift, highlighted by 'Aber', from Mitra's pity to the priest's absorption into the maternal womb. This magnanimous gesture by Mitra undermines the notion of a dualistic cosmic struggle that exerted such psychic pressure on the priest and instead exposes the essential benevolence of nature.

These polarities — between the aridity of heat and the fecundity of water, between the masculine and feminine — also mark the poems 'Aegypten' and 'Der Nil'. The language of the poems, as Kevin Hilliard has argued, allows them to function as a cure for melancholy, by analogy with Goethe's 'Mahomet's Gesang' [Mahomet's Song] (1772–73).[76] Egypt itself was associated with melancholic qualities in the eighteenth century.[77] The rejuvenation of a lethargic and parched land through

---

75 This was a cure proposed by the Dutch physician Herman Boerhaave for melancholy in 1735: see *The Nature of Melancholy: From Aristotle to Kristeva*, ed. by Jennifer Radden (Oxford: Oxford University Press, 2002), pp. 173–80.

76 K. F. Hilliard, 'Orient und Mythos: Karoline von Günderrode', *Frauen: MitSprechen — MitSchreiben: Beiträge zur literatur- und sprachwissenschaftlichen Frauenforschung*, ed. by Marianne Henn and Britta Hufeisen, Stuttgarter Arbeiten zur Germanistik, 349 (Stuttgart: Heinz, 1997), pp. 244–55 (p. 246).

77 K. F. Hilliard, 'Goethe and the Cure for Melancholy: "Mahomets Gesang", Orientalism and the Medical Psychology of the 18th Century', *Oxford German Studies*, 23 (1994), 71–103 (p. 92).

the eroticised flood of the Nile may recall earlier poems such as 'Buonaparte in Egypten' and 'Mahomets Traum in der Wüste', where revolutionary political agency is required to rejuvenate a slumbering polity.[78] Whilst these previous narratives of purification and rejuvenation are steeped in political metaphor, the resonance of 'Aegypten' and 'Der Nil' lies in the manner in which nature is personified.

The two poems are an example of counterpoint, in dialogue with each other. Günderrode neatly marks the shift in tone from one to the other, from deathly torpor to the near-orgasmic effusions of the river's swelling, through the 'Aber' (*SW* I, 330, l. 1) that opens 'Der Nil' ('Aber ich stürze von Bergen hernieder' [But I plunge down from the mountains]). This shift is also manifest in Günderrode's careful metrical juxtaposition. The relative weight of the trochaic lines in 'Aegypten' supports the mood of torpor; this enervation is emphasised in the final stanza with a series of participles that suggest a passive state of almost paralytic *acedia*:

> Schwer entschlummert sind die Kräfte,
> Aufgezehrt die Lebenssäfte;
> Eingelullt im Fieberträum
> Fühl' ich noch mein Dasein kaum.
>
> [The powers are in a deathly sleep,
> All sap of life expended;
> Lulled in the fever-dream
> I can barely sense my existence still.] (*SW* I, 329, ll. 13–16)

'Der Nil' metrically counteracts the torpor of its predecessor partly through the shift into dactylic feet. But there are syntactic changes, too. The short, clipped lines of 'Aegypten', replete with the tension of stasis and enervation, are superseded by longer, looser lines — still in tetrameter — that are full of vigour:

> Jauchzend begrüßen mich alle die Quellen;
> Kühlend umfange ich, Erde, auch dich;
> Leben erschwellt mir die Tropfen, die Wellen,
> Leben dir spendend umarme ich dich.
>
> [All the springs greet me in jubilation;
> I gather you, Earth, too, in a cooling embrace;
> Life swells and surges into me in drops, in waves,
> And I bestow life on you in my embrace.] (*SW* I, 330, ll. 5–8)

What is important here is the state of reciprocity, which is stressed by the patterning of the lines that alternate between the sources of the river and the earth. There is an exchange of an essential force of life, as visually emphasised and foregrounded in 'Leben erschwellt mir die Tropfen, die Wellen | Leben dir spendend umarme ich dich'. That is, as the last stanza goes on to clarify, with a moment that is suggestive of incest, the source of the river (and therefore its energy) lies in the earth itself. The river comes into being from the earth for an erotic release into and embrace with the earth.

Where 'Aegypten' is a poem of stasis and inertia, 'Der Nil' thrives on the

---

78 Nina Berman draws this comparison in a brief discussion of Günderrode: Berman, pp. 174–75.

propulsion of action in the present moment. It is fitting, therefore, that the flooding itself is not perfective in the poem — that would mark a point of exhaustion and dissolution. Instead, Günderrode ends the poem on an apostrophic exhortation, one that wills consummation:

> Theueres Land du! Gebährerin Erde!
> Nimm nun den Sohn auch den liebenden auf,
> Du, die in Klüften gebahr mich und nährte,
> Nimm jezt, o Mutter! den Sehnenden auf.
>
> [You precious land! Earth, our mother!
> Receive now your son, yes, your loving son,
> To whom you gave birth in your chasms, and nourished,
> Receive now, oh mother! your longing son.] (*SW* I, 330, ll. 9–12)

What of the mythic subtexts for these poems? Günderrode is in part drawing on the Egyptian myth of the deities Isis and Osiris, both siblings and spouses, although no explicit reference is made to them in either poem. In her notes on world mythologies, Günderrode references the fact that these dual gods are projections of natural processes, of the annual flooding of the Nile, where Osiris represents 'die [...] wirkende [*sic*] Kräfte' [the active forces of nature] and Isis 'die leidende Natur Kräfte [*sic*]' [the passive, suffering forces of nature] (*SW* II, 413).[79] Here it is worth briefly considering the broader context — and not just the comparative mythology of Creuzer. In the late eighteenth century, fertility cults were interpreted as the earliest form of human religion, one employing symbols and myths to describe the generative forces in nature.[80] This primordial form of nature worship amounted to natural philosophy in symbolic form. As with the ritualised 'Adonis Todtenfeyer', the situation in 'Aegypten' and 'Der Nil' is typological, not least because the mythic subtexts describe natural processes that recur annually.[81] But the former poem made use of the Adonis narrative as a means of conveying a metaphysical truth, acted out as a historical ritual but also in the performative aspects of the text itself.

This distinction raises the question, therefore, of what the specific effect may be of stripping away all mention of a mythic subtext. What 'Adonis Todtenfeyer' and these two poems have in common is a concern with fertility rituals and cults. Shorn of the ritualistic qualities of 'Adonis Todtenfeyer', 'Aegypten' and 'Der Nil' depict a fertility cycle that makes use of poetic means that have curiously hitherto escaped critical attention. This is the rhetorical figure of personification, and one that is shared by the poem 'Der Caucasus', which immediately follows the two in

---

79 Günderrode's source for these notes is a handbook compiled by Julius August Remer, a professor of history and statistics at the University of Helmstedt. Morgenthaler suggests a variety of different possible sources (*SW* III, 348), but Günderrode's notes most closely align with the phrasing of Remer's handbook. What is present in Remer's account but missing in Günderrode's notes is the explicit identification of Osiris with the Nile and Isis with the Egyptian land: see Julius August Remer, *Handbuch der ältern Geschichte von der Schöpfung der Welt bis auf die große Völkerwanderung* (Braunschweig, 1794), p. 152.
80 S. C. Humphreys, *The Strangeness of Gods: Historical Perspectives on the Interpretation of Athenian Religion* (Oxford: Oxford University Press, 2004), pp. 197–222.
81 Westphal, p. 118.

Melete.[82] In 'Der Caucasus', the mountain range combines *natura naturans* (figured in the poetic voice) and *natura naturata* (the transient aspects of the natural world) to represent *hen kai pan*. The Caucasus becomes a majestic embodiment of the sublime, where the reader should be left in awe of the godlike mountain range.[83]

To be sure, personification of nature is a common feature of eighteenth-century nature poetry; this often takes the form of second-person or third-person apostrophising.[84] Whilst apostrophe, for example, conjures an imagined presence of an addressee and is, such as in Günderrode's technically accomplished 'Orphisches Lied' [Orphic Song], essentially concerned with the self-constitution of the speaker,[85] the first-person perspective instead grants agency and a voice to that which cannot speak outside the poetic mode.

This is not a mere mundane point about the possibilities offered by poetic abstraction. It is, rather, one that is loaded with philosophical significance. This poetic figure of personification can be better described by the term prosopopoeia, which, in classical rhetoric, is a mode of imaginary speech,[86] and the poetic act of giving a mask and a voice to that which cannot speak, since it is inanimate or dead.[87] The difference here is the act of giving voice to that which is animate. Prosopopoeia does have a radical effect too, since it carries philosophical resonance. The philosophical effect of the first person is that Günderrode grants natural forces — and by extension, the entirety of the natural world — a poetic self and subjectivity. This move is consistent with a logical extension of Günderrode's aversion to objectifying and ossifying approaches to the natural world in 'Vorzeit, und Neue Zeit'.

Where the motif of the epistemological quest in earlier poetry was marked by a Promethean desire for a fundamental Platonic truth, only to be frustrated by the limitations of human cognition, there is a shift in perspective in these texts from *Melete*. The distinction between the individual subject and nature is poetically dissolved. Rather than being discursively stated, this remains more a subtle grammatical suggestion. This is a peculiarity of the poetic form itself, of *poiesis*, by

---

82 Martina Ölke has noted stylistic and linguistic similarities between 'Der Caucasus' and the two preceding poems, particularly with 'Aegypten', that supports reading the poems together: Martina Ölke, 'Verhinderter Ausbruch? Zur Konzeption des (weiblichen) Genies in Karoline von Günderrodes Gedichten *Aegypten* und *Der Nil*', in *Bei Gefahr des Untergangs: Phantasien des Aufbrechens. Festschrift für Irmgard Roebling*, ed. by Ina Brueckel and others (Würzburg: Königshausen & Neumann, 2000), pp. 117–31 (pp. 124–25).
83 The aesthetic theory of the sublime in the eighteenth century made external aspects of nature a legitimate subject for poetry. See Christian Begemann, 'Erhabene Natur: Zur Übertragung des Begriffs des Erhabenen auf Gegenstände der äußeren Natur in den deutschen Kunsttheorien des 18. Jahrhunderts', *Deutsche Vierteljahrsschrift für Literaturwissenschaft und Geistesgeschichte*, 58 (1984), 74–110.
84 For a survey of personification in nature poetry, with a focus on the Anglophone context, see Bryan L. Moore, *Literature and Ecology: Ecocentric Personification from Antiquity to the Twenty-first Century* (New York: Palgrave Macmillan, 2008).
85 Jonathan Culler, *The Pursuit of Signs: Semiotics, Literature, Deconstruction* (London: Routledge, 2005), pp. 125–26.
86 Quintilian, *The Orator's Education*, ed., trans. by Donald A. Russell, 5 vols (Cambridge, MA: Harvard University Press, 2001), IV, 51.
87 Michael Riffaterre, 'Prosopopoeia', *Yale French Studies*, 69 (1983), 107–23 (p. 104).

bringing into being that — here, connections between the human subject and nature — which would otherwise not exist. To frame it in philosophical terms: the shift that occurs in *Melete* is one between epistemology and ontology. It appears no longer necessary to make the secrets of nature explicable, but rather it is sufficient to express what nature *is* in poetic form.

The Question of Schelling

At this juncture, it would be tempting to unite this insertion of subjectivity in nature with Günderrode's affinity for the philosophy of Schelling. There is good reason to suspect such a connection. Indeed, Schelling had, as Bruce Matthews argues, also propounded the importance of the 'aesthetic act of *poesis*', one that precedes thought, 'whereby the philosopher constructs for himself the intuition of this undetermined oneness'.[88] Although this is an appealing commonality, Schelling's philosophy of art was far less important for Günderrode than his philosophy of nature or *Identitätsphilosophie* [philosophy of identity].[89] One fundamental thought in the philosophy of nature as a whole is to reinsert humankind into nature, and into the history of nature — to realise, in philosophical terms, the original identity between subject and object. For Schelling, the ego and nature existed in a state of pre-reflexive unity.[90]

Before discussing 'Briefe zweier Freunde', establishing why Schelling was important for Günderrode is necessary since the draft for 'Briefe', the short 'Jdee der Erde', is suffused with Schellingian vocabulary. Schelling's influence on Günderrode has been recognised by previous scholarship.[91] In typically effusive language, Günderrode lauds Schelling's work to Friedrich Creuzer as 'göttliche Filosofie' [divine philosophy].[92] There is one fundamental question, however, that has remained unexplored: why should Günderrode have found Schelling's philosophy of nature and philosophy of identity so attractive in the first place? My central contention is that Günderrode's extensive studies of Schelling derive from the fact that his philosophy offers further elaboration of ideas already present in her earlier work and studies.

There are some immediate contextual reasons for Günderrode's familiarity with Schelling. The intellectual environment in Heidelberg was a cradle of Schellingian ideas:[93] the theologian Carl Daub attempted to reconcile Schelling's philosophy

---

88   Bruce Matthews, *Schelling's Organic Form of Philosophy: Life as the Schema of Freedom* (Albany: SUNY Press, 2011), p. 3.
89   Creuzer did have Schelling's 1805 lectures on the philosophy of art copied down for Günderrode, although the extent of these copies is not clear: Preisendanz, p. 133.
90   Sibille Mischer, *Der verschlungene Zug der Seele: Natur, Organismus und Entwicklung bei Schelling, Steffens und Oken* (Würzburg: Königshausen & Neumann, 1997), pp. 32–33.
91   For a thorough study of Günderrode's studies and deviations from Schelling's original texts, see Christmann, pp. 97–119.
92   *SW* III, 344.
93   As Jakob Friedrich Fries — himself the exception as an avowed Neo-Kantian — notes in 1806: as cited in Alfred Kloß, *Die Heidelbergischen Jahrbücher der Literatur in den Jahren 1808–1816* (Leipzig: Voigtländer, 1916), p. 16.

with theology,[94] whilst Creuzer is also clearly taken by Schelling's philosophy for its metaphysical import.[95] It was, however, the botanist Christian Nees von Esenbeck who first introduced Günderrode to Schelling's and Henrik Steffens's work on the philosophy of nature.[96]

What of the appeal of Schelling's ideas for Günderrode? Firstly, Schelling's philosophy of nature offers a means to reconcile the findings of empirical sciences — which, as a form of knowledge production, had not yet separated into the disciplines of science known today — and metaphysics. The promise of the philosophy of nature is that it allows for some middle ground between a holistic religious worldview and the scientific world-view. That is, it is part of a metaphysical project that provides a ground for the results of empirical investigation.

Secondly, one of the most important philosophical influences on Schelling is Spinoza.[97] Schelling's philosophy of nature lends itself to being adopted as one part of Günderrode's panentheistic armoury. There is a clear monist tendency in Schelling, where the complex organisational processes of mind and nature exist in a state of identity ('Die Natur soll der sichtbare Geist, der Geist die unsichtbare Natur sein' [Nature should be visible spirit, spirit should be invisible nature]).[98] Furthermore, in Schelling's philosophy of nature and in Spinoza, nature is not just a product of creation, it is creation itself and is eternal reality, not just the phenomenal appearance of eternal reality.[99] Nature is also the medium through which the divine becomes manifest, through the self-organisation of the organic whole of the world.[100] This also would help to explain why Günderrode was so taken with Schelling's early philosophy of nature and philosophy of identity. Schelling himself, as Daniel Whistler argues, had broken with philosophical tradition by claiming that the ground of reality is not transcendent to reality itself: 'The absolute immanence of the ground of reality to reality itself is a constant defining principle of Schelling's philosophy between 1801 and 1805. [...] Everything is encompassed univocally in one immanent realm.'[101]

Schelling's philosophy of nature and philosophy of identity found favour with Günderrode because they are a metaphysical project and marked an important step towards recuperating metaphysics from the pejorative associations that had come

---

94 Preisendanz, p. 227.
95 See the discussion of critical (Kantian) philosophy opposed to Schelling's philosophy of nature in Preisendanz, pp. 100–01.
96 Max Preitz, 'Karoline von Günderrode in ihrer Umwelt, I: Briefe von Lisette und Christian Gottfried Nees von Esenbeck, Karoline von Günderrode, Friedrich Creuzer, Clemens Brentano und Susanne von Heyden', *Jahrbuch des freien deutschen Hochstifts* (1962), 208–302 (p. 247).
97 Jason M. Wirth, *Conspiracy of Life: Meditations on Schelling and his Time* (Albany: SUNY Press, 2003), p. 33.
98 Friedrich Wilhelm Joseph von Schelling, 'Einleitung zu: Ideen zu einer Philosophie der Natur als Einleitung in das Studium dieser Wissenschaft', in *Ausgewählte Schriften*, ed. by Manfred Frank, 6 vols (Frankfurt: Suhrkamp, 1985), I, 245–94 (p. 294). Günderrode paraphrases this in her *Studienbuch*: 'die Natur also der sichtbare Geist, der Geist die unsichtbare Natur sei', in Preitz/Hopp III, p. 296.
99 Dale E. Snow, *Schelling and the End of Idealism* (Albany: SUNY Press, 1996), p. 85.
100 Matthews, p. 7.
101 Daniel Whistler, *Schelling's Theory of Symbolic Language: Forming the System of Identity* (Oxford: Oxford University Press, 2013), p. 73.

to be attached to it. Kant's critique of knowledge put paid to metaphysics of the kind that would make claims about knowledge of the ultimate nature of the world or the existence of God.[102] But the kind of metaphysics that Kant had criticised was of the Leibniz-Wolffian tradition, and one that was conceived of to support a deistic theology, where a supernatural entity, the absolute, was placed outside the bounds of the phenomenal world.[103] Schelling's metaphysics of nature instead offers a series of naturalistic solutions to the philosophical problems bequeathed to the post-Kantian generation.[104]

Günderrode's notes take a curious turn from discussing the nature of the absolute to an elaboration of the philosophy of chemistry. This shift may appear surprising but is entirely consistent with Schelling. Chemistry is essential to Schelling's earliest works on philosophy of nature, the *Erster Entwurf zu einer Philosophie der Natur* [First Draft of a Philosophy of Nature] (1799), and the *System des transzendentalen Idealismus* [System of Transcendental Idealism] (1800).[105] Günderrode was sufficiently interested in chemical theories that she made excerpts from Joseph Franz von Jacquin's *Lehrbuch der allgemeinen und medicinischen Chymie zum Gebrauche seiner Vorlesungen* [Textbook of General and Medical Chemistry for Use in his Lectures] (1798). Jacquin, a professor of botany and chemistry at the university of Vienna, was a follower of the ideas of Antoine Lavoisier,[106] the influential French chemist whose pneumatic theories had formed part of the so-called Chemical Revolution of the eighteenth century.

What is fundamental to these chemical studies and to Schelling's philosophy of nature are theories of matter. Schelling propounded a theory of matter that moved beyond Newtonian ideas of inert matter upon which forces were extrinsically exerted according to ideas of extension. Instead, Schelling asserted that matter was animated by opposed forces — polarised potencies — that form a dialectic in the self-organisation of nature.[107] In doing so, Schelling builds upon Kant's theory of matter from *Metaphysische Anfangsgründe der Naturwissenschaft* [Metaphysical Foundations of Science] (1786), which determined that matter is constituted by the opposing forces of repulsion and attraction.

---

102 Edward Kanterian, *Kant, God and Metaphysics: The Secret Thorn* (London: Routledge, 2018), pp. vii–viii.
103 Frederick C. Beiser, 'Introduction: Hegel and the Problem of Metaphysics', in *The Cambridge Companion to Hegel*, ed. by Frederick C. Beiser (Cambridge: Cambridge University Press, 1993), pp. 1–24 (p. 8).
104 See Iain Hamilton Grant, *Philosophies of Nature after Schelling* (London: Continuum, 2008), pp. vii–viii. See also Ben Woodard, *Schelling's Naturalism: Motion, Space and the Volition of Thought* (Edinburgh: Edinburgh University Press, 2019).
105 Schelling's sustained interest in the results of the empirical natural sciences — what would come to be known as biology or life sciences as well as physics and chemistry — were prominent in his writings on the philosophy of nature until 1800, after which Schelling's engagement with research in the natural sciences subsided and his work became more metaphysically speculative.
106 Robert Rosner and Rudolf Werner Soukup, 'Die chemischen Institute der Universität Wien', in *Reflexive Innensichten aus der Universität: Disziplinengeschichten zwischen Wissenschaft, Gesellschaft und Politik*, ed. by Karl Anton Fröschl and others (Göttingen: V&R unipress, 2015), pp. 211–24 (p. 212).
107 George di Giovanni, 'Kant's Metaphysics of Nature and Schelling's Ideas for a Philosophy of Nature', *Journal of the History of Philosophy*, 17.2 (1979), 197–215 (p. 208).

This theory of matter based on the polarity of forces, understood in terms of the natural sciences, is attractive because it offers a convenient parallel to the metaphysical theory of matter that Herder developed in *Gott. Einige Gespräche*. To understand matter as having inherent forces in a metaphysical sense, as Herder did with the help of Leibniz, functions, to an extent, as an analogue to matter being constituted by the forces of magnetic repulsion and attraction. The distinction lies in the loss of the idea of substance: instead, in Schelling's organic conception of matter and, by extension, nature, matter is determined by a dynamic balance and play of forces.[108]

There is a certain synthesising element to Schelling's work that makes it appealing to Günderrode. For example, Schelling's hypothesis that magnetic, electrical and chemical processes corresponded to modifications of a single underlying process was given empirical weight through experiments carried out by the scientists Johann Wilhelm Ritter and Hans Christian Ørested.[109] This connection between the empirical and metaphysical has the effect of reciprocally legitimising and dignifying both.

While these theories of the constitution of matter may appear abstruse — and Günderrode's literary work does without the complexity present in her studies of Schelling, which include intricate diagrams — they are also of broader philosophical and poetic significance. In 'Die Malabarischen Witwen', for example, Günderrode interprets the *satī* practice in Hinduism, or the ritual burning of widows on funeral pyres, as the apotheosis of ritualised and sacrificial love.[110] But this apotheosis of love finds expression in the way forces in matter operate. Self-immolation and dissolution of individuals into their constituent elements may build on the Schellingian idea of matter being constituted by opposing forces, but the idea of polarity is dropped in favour of a system of sympathies and affinities.[111] Instead of the tension resulting from polarised forces, in Günderrode it is the force of attraction, on an almost molecular level, between the individuals that brings them back together in an erotic embrace, paradoxically in the moment of the body being vaporised ('Denn die vorhin entzweiten Liebesflammen | In Einer schlagen brünstig sie zusammen' [For now the once divided flames of love | come together ardently in a single flame]; 'Vereinet die getrennten Elemente, | Zum Lebensgipfel wird des Daseins Ende' [United are the separated elements; | The end of

---

108 Richards, p. 295.
109 Marie-Luise Heuser-Keßler, *Die Produktivität der Natur: Schellings Naturphilosophie und das neue Paradigma der Selbstorganisation in den Naturwissenschaften* (Berlin: Duncker & Humblot, 1986), p. 21.
110 This deviates from the negative assessment of the practice, such as in Herder's *Ideen*, see Herder, *Werke in zehn Bänden*, VI: *Ideen zur Philosophie der Geschichte der Menschheit*, ed. by Martin Bollacher (1989), p. 319. Critics have also noted how Günderrode's interpretation deviates from the meaning of the ritual in its original context: Dorothy M. Figueira, 'Die Flambierte Frau: Sati in European Culture', in *Sati: The Blessing and the Curse: The Burning of Wives in India*, ed. by John Stratton Hawley (New York: Oxford University Press, 1994), pp. 55–78 (p. 57).
111 This is an inheritance from the early modern theories of chemistry, but, for Günderrode, may have found confirmation in writings of Plotinus, for whom it has an important metaphysical function: see Jeremy Adler, *'Eine fast magische Anziehungskraft': Goethes 'Wahlverwandtschaften' und die Chemie seiner Zeit* (Munich: Beck, 1987), pp. 37–39.

existence becomes the pinnacle of life] (*SW* I, 325, ll. 10–11; 13–14)). The personal and material becomes fused in 'Vereinet die getrennten Elemente', to the point of depersonalisation entirely; 'Elemente' is a term for Günderrode that refers to matter in general. This idea of love as a unifying or totalising force recalls the poem 'Überall Liebe' [Love Everywhere] in *Melete*, where the force of love as attraction is a universal constant, even in the afterlife and the underworld.[112]

Günderrode makes use of Schelling's Platonic dialogue *Bruno oder über das göttliche und natürliche Prinzip der Dinge* (1802), as a springboard to overcome Cartesian dualism:

> Die wahre Jdee des Materialismus ist früher verlohren gegangen [...] So ist also die Materie das Ewige Eine; u wie sie sich auch trennen mag für die Erscheinung, in das was wir Möglichkeit u Wirklichkeit, Form u Wesen Endliches u Unendliches, Körper u Geist, Repulsion u Attraktion nennen so sind doch in ihr alle diese Gegensätze nicht, diese sind vielmehr ihre verschiedene Offenbahrungen. Der organische Körper aber, die vollkomenste Syntese von Form u Wesen, denken u sein, Geist u Körper ist ihr ähnlichster Abdruk.
>
> [The true idea of materialism was lost early on [...] In this manner, matter is the Eternal One; and however it may become separated in appearances, into what we call possibility and reality, form and essence, the finite and the infinite, body and spirit, repulsion and attraction, it does not contain these oppositions, rather these are its various manifestations. The organic body, however, the most perfect synthesis of form and essence, thought and being, spirit and body, is its closest imitation.] (*SW* II, 404–06)

This is an attempt to vitalise matter, with the concept of the organism as the epitome of a unity of apparently diametrically opposed concepts. The textual logic here reflects a long-standing interest of Günderrode's in dual-aspect monism, which was previously given clearest expression by the ecstatic declaration at the end of 'Ein apokaliptisches Fragment'. The image of the organic body as the highest synthesis of form and being, however, offers a naturalist variant of the panentheism of this work. This spiritualised understanding of matter offers a redeemed form of materialism.

Poetic Creativity as (Self-)Cure: 'Briefe zweier Freunde'

This reframing of panentheism as a spiritualised materialism is important for 'Briefe zweier Freunde'. Its composition suggests an interweaving of poetic and philosophical concerns. Formally, it harks back to Socratic dialogues, but it is a Romantic variant in its formal variety, proceeding from a sonnet to a partly fragmented epistolary correspondence.[113] Another deviation from the structure of the Socratic dialogue is the feature, particular to Günderrode, that the junior interlocutor, as in 'Die

---

112 Peter von Matt has identified this universalising understanding of love as a cosmic force as part of pantheist strains of thought: Peter von Matt, *Liebesverrat: Die Treulosen in der Literatur* (Munich: Deutscher Taschenbuch Verlag, 1991), pp. 212–13.
113 Dormann distinguishes 'Briefe zweier Freunde' from the rhetorical and logical structure of the Socratic model: Dormann, p. 198.

Manen', takes the lead. As with the 'Zueignung', the unnamed speaker approaches Eusebio[114] as a child would a high priest, where the language of friendship assumes a religious dimension by analogy.[115] Whilst Günderrode may have taken some inspiration from Schiller's early *Philosophische Briefe* [Philosophical Letters] (1786) — in both cases, a crisis is caused by the destructive potential of scepticism, and the metaphysical narratives are inflected with Platonic vocabulary of perfection —[116] such a parallel may overlook the significance of the status of poetry for the text itself. In the first letter, the unnamed speaker diagnoses the ills of the present age. This amounts to a continuation of Günderrode's earlier critiques of a 'pygmäisches Zeitalter' [pygmy age]. But the focus in this opening lies specifically on the status of the poet and their vocation:

> Ist es da auch noch ein Wunder, wenn die Ökonomie in jedem Sinn und in allen Dingen zu einer so beträchtlichen Tugend herangewachsen ist. Diese Erbärmlichkeit des Lebens, laß es uns gestehen, ist mit dem Protestantismus aufgekommen. Sie werden alle zum Kelch hinzugelassen, die Layen wie die Geweihten, darum kann Niemand genugsam trinken um des Gottes voll zu werden, der Tropfen aber ist Keinem genug; da wissen sie denn nicht was ihnen fehlt, und gerathen in ein Disputiren und Protestiren darüber. [...] Genug also von dem aufgeblasenen Jahrhundert, an dessen Thorheiten noch ferne Zeiten erkranken werden. [...] Denn, abgeschlossen sind wir durch enge Verhältnisse von der Natur, durch engere Begriffe vom wahren Lebensgenuß, durch unsere Staatsformen von aller Thätigkeit im Großen. So fest umschlossen ringsum, bleibt uns nur übrig den Blick hinauf zu richten zum Himmel, oder brütend in uns selbst zu wenden. Sind nicht beinahe alle Arten der neuern Poesie durch diese unsere Stellung bestimmt? Liniengestalten entweder, die körperlos hinaufstreben im unendlichen Raum zu zerfließen, oder bleiche, lichtscheue Erdgeister, die wir grübelnd aus der Tiefe unsers Wesens herauf beschwören; aber nirgends kräftige, markige Gestalten. Der Höhe dürfen wir uns rühmen und der Tiefe, aber behagliche Ausdehnung fehlt uns durchaus. Wie Shakspeare's Julius Cäsar möcht' ich rufen: 'Bringt fette Leute zu mir, und die ruhig schlafen, ich fürchte diesen hagern Cassius.' — Da ich nun selbst nicht über die Schranken meiner Zeit hinaus reiche, dünkt es dir nicht besser für mich, den Weg eigner poetischer Produktion zu verlassen, und ein ernsthaftes Studium der Poeten der Vorzeit, und besonders des Mittelalters zu beginnen?
>
> [So is it an even a surprise that the idea of economic utility has become such a considerable virtue in all senses and in all things. This pitiful notion of life, let us be open about this, came about through Protestantism. All were allowed to approach the Communion cup, the lay and the ordained, and therefore no one can drink enough to become consumed by God, a single drop is not enough for anyone; and since they do not know what they are lacking, they end up disputing and protesting with one another [...] So enough, I say, of this

---

114 Whilst this is the name used in the correspondence between Günderrode and Creuzer to refer to Creuzer, this does not reduce the text to a biographical reading.
115 The sanctification of personal relationships is common across early Romanticism, particularly in the context of love relationships. See Julia Augart, *Eine romantische Liebe in Briefen: Zur Liebeskonzeption im Briefwechsel von Sophie Mereau und Clemens Brentano* (Würzburg: Königshausen & Neumann, 2006), p. 83.
116 Hilliard, *Freethinkers*, pp. 59–61.

bloated century, whose folly will cause disease for ages yet to come [...] For we are separated from nature through these narrower confines, through a narrow conception of the true pleasure of life, and through the composition of our states, we are held back from all agency as a whole. As tightly constricted as we are all around us, all that remains is for us to cast our gaze up toward heaven, or to turn it inward, brooding. Are almost all forms of recent poetry not determined by this, by our position? They are either delicate line-compositions, lacking corporeal form and striving upward, dissipating into infinite space, or they are pale earth-spirits that shun the light, which we have conjured up from the depths of our being through rumination. Nowhere can we find powerful, forceful figures. We may pride ourselves on the dizzying heights and depths we can reach, but we completely lack suitable dimension and body. Just as Shakespeare's Julius Caesar does, I would like to cry out: Let me have men around me that are fat, and such as sleepe a-nights: 'I fear this lean Cassius.'[117] — Since I cannot extend beyond the limits of my own time, do you not think it better for me, to leave the path of poetic creativity, and to start studying in earnest the poets of an earlier age, particularly those of the Middle Ages?] (*SW* I, 351–52)

This is a dense social and cultural critique. The democratising force of Protestantism is dismissed on the basis that it occludes the true essence of religion. The image of theophagic communion ('darum kann Niemand genugsam trinken um des Gottes voll zu werden') establishes the imagery of involuntary emaciation that continues throughout this section. The principles of economic utility ('Ökonomie') have become something of a virtue. This is the only instance of Günderrode using the term, and so it deserves some elaboration: the term derives from the Greek *oikonomia*, but can also refer to processes of efficiency and rationalisation, by analogy with the Latin *oeconomia*.[118] Decrying such principles is part and parcel of the speaker's self-stylisation as an aspirational artist and poet.[119] It also points to the desire for art to enjoy an autonomous existence, freed from the shackles of thinking that is orientated around means and ends.

But this act of critique also points to the irreconcilable tension in which the speaker finds him- or herself. The phrase from the letter 'denn auch sie [diese Zeit] ist arm an begeisternden Anschauungen für den Künstler jeder Art' [For it [this age] is also poor in moments of inspiration for artists of all kinds] (*SW* I, 351) echoes Hölderlin's famous line of 'wozu Dichter in dürftiger Zeit' [who wants poets at all in lean years?][120] from the elegy 'Brod und Wein' [Bread and Wine] (c. 1800). The urgency of the poet's calling collides painfully with the paucity of inspiring

---

117 Adapted from Shakespeare, *Julius Caesar*, p. 2947. Günderrode is condensing part of August Wilhelm Schlegel's translation: see William Shakespeare, *Shakspeare's dramatische Werke*, trans. by August Wilhelm Schlegel, 9 vols (Berlin: Johann Friedrich Unger, 1797–1810), II: *Julius Cäsar, Was ihr wollt* (1797), pp. 20–21.

118 Gisela Harras, '"Ökonomie" in deutschen Wörterbüchern', in *Ökonomie: Sprachliche und literarische Aspekte eines 2000 Jahre alten Begriffs*, ed. by Theo Stemmier (Tübingen: Narr, 1985), pp. 37–50 (p. 37).

119 This is a trope: see Reinhard Saller, *Schöne Ökonomie: Die poetische Reflexion der Ökonomie in frühromantischer Literatur* (Würzburg: Königshausen & Neumann, 2007), p. 8.

120 Friedrich Hölderlin, *Selected Poems and Fragments*, ed. by Jeremy Adler, trans. by Michael Hamburger (London: Penguin, 1998), p. 157.

material. To follow the linguistic patterning of the letter, the present age is not suffering from a narrowing of human experience. Rather, the present age is sick, decentred, parched, desiccated, whether it be in terms of religion, social structures, or more abstract principles of *eudaemonia* — and therefore, by extension, so the artist or poet too must be infected with the sickness of the age. Hence the appeal of abandoning the poetic vocation altogether in favour of studying ancient and medieval poetry. This would, however, amount to little more than an admission of defeat and resignation to the sickness of the present.

It is more than the poetic vocation that cannot be salvaged. In the speaker's professed moroseness — 'oft bin ich mißmuthig' [often I am morose] (*SW* I, 351) — lies the potential for nihilistic despair that is far more than a vocational impasse, but rather reflects a latent *spiritual* crisis. Here 'Briefe zweier Freunde' follows the narrative logic of 'Geschichte eines Braminen': a disregard of worldly matters in favour of metaphysical and spiritual consolation. Returning to first principles — of how the individual is metaphysically grounded in the world — offers a means to quell the speaker's initial lament. Thus Eusebio's fragmentary response to this letter offers a degree of relativising comfort and serenity, because the variety of complaints are nothing more than a paroxysm, symptomatic of the speaker's own psychological state.

Eusebio offers the solution of an inner *katabasis*, a variant of the familiar motif of the descent into the self to uncover the pantheist monism that underpins all existence — here, Hinduism is equated with *hen kai pan*.[121] Recognising the monist unity of all things has, for Eusebio, the effect of a consolation narrative:

> Es gibt eine Ergebung, in der allein Seligkeit und Vollkommenheit und Friede ist, eine Art der Betrachtung, welche ich Auflößung [*sic*] im Göttlichen nennen möchte; dahin zu kommen laß uns trachten und nicht klagen um die Schicksale des Universums. Damit du aber deutlicher siehst, was ich damit meine, so sende ich dir hiermit einige Bücher über die Religion der Hindu. Die Wunder uralter Weisheit, in geheimnisvollen Symbolen niedergelegt, werden dein Gemüth berühren, es wird Augenblicke geben, in welchen du dich entkleidet fühlst von dieser persönlichen Einzelheit und Armuth und wieder hingegeben dem großen Ganzen; wo du es mehr als nur denkst, daß Alles, was jezt Sonne und Mond ist, und Blume und Edelstein, und Äther und Meer, ein Einziges ist, ein Heiliges, das in seinen Tiefen ruht ohne Aufhören, selig in sich selbst, sich selbst ewig umfangend, ohne Wunsch nach dem Thun und Leiden der Zweiheit, die seine Oberfläche bewegt. In solchen Augenblicken, wo wir uns nicht mehr besinnen können, weil das, was das einzle [*sic*] und irrdische Bewußtseyn weckt, dem äußern Sinn verschwunden ist unter der Herrschaft der Betrachtung des Innern; in solchen Augenblicken versteh' ich den Tod, der Religion Geheimniß, das Opfer des Sohnes und der Liebe unendliches Sehnen.
>
> [There is a form of surrender, in which there is alone bliss, perfection and peace, a form of contemplation, which I would term dissolution into the divine:

---

121 Hindu texts, such as the *Bhavagad Gita*, would go on to be associated with and interpreted as a form of pantheism by Friedrich Schlegel and Wilhelm von Humboldt, among others: Vishwa Adluri and Joydeep Bagchee, *The Nay-Science: A History of German Indology* (New York: Oxford University Press, 2014), pp. 171–75.

let us strive to reach it and not lament about the fate of the universe. So that you can more clearly see what I mean, I am sending you along with this some books about the religion of the Hindus. The miracles of ancient wisdom, recorded in mysterious symbols, will touch your soul, and there will be moments in which you feel liberated from your own individuality and your sense of want and instead are returned to the great whole; where you can go beyond thinking that everything which now we know as sun and moon, flower or precious stone, aether and the sea, is One, sacred, which ceaselessly rests in its depths, blessed in itself, eternally embracing itself, without any desire for the actions and sufferings of the divided beings which stir its surface. In moments such as these, where we cannot remember ourselves, because, through the power of inner contemplation, that which awakens individual and earthly consciousness has receded from the external senses. In moments such as these I understand death, the mystery of religion, the sacrifice of the Son and the endless longing of love.] (*SW* I, 354–55)

Eusebio's perspective has a touch of fatalism: the peace found in surrendering to the whole derives from a Manichaean understanding of individuation as a sinful act of emanation from the divine ('Ich erblicke die rechte Verdammniß in dem selbstsüchtigen Stolz, der nicht ruhen konnte in dem Schooß des Ewigen' [I see true damnation in the selfish pride which could not rest in the eternal womb] (*SW* I, 355)). A return to the point from which the individual has emanated, that is, death, can only be welcomed.[122] What Eusebio exhorts is a retreat into the self as a means to paradoxically escape the bounds of individuality.

The phrase 'in solchen Augenblicken versteh' ich den Tod, der Religion Geheimniß, das Opfer des Sohnes und der Liebe unendliches Sehnen' is jarring because it is a stray Christian element in what is otherwise an expression of pantheism.[123] Yet this also suggests the kind of narrative weight that this pantheism carries: an alternative to the core salvation narrative. Instead of Christ's Passion, the idea of emanation is used in this context as a salve to the idea of death: to be redeemed means to exist no longer as an individual.

What Eusebio suggests is, therefore, for the unnamed poet to repeat this creative and anagogical process of *katabasis*, since Eusebio dismisses the possibility of a return to a supposed prelapsarian state of ancient or medieval poetry. In one sense,

---

122 Whether there are elements of Neoplatonism behind this are open to debate: Creuzer provided Günderrode and Susanne von Heyden with drafts of his translation of Plotinus's *Enneads*: see Preisendanz, p. 76. Creuzer himself pointed out the similarities between 'Briefe zweier Freunde' and Plotinus: Preisendanz, pp. 171–72. The idea of emanation and return is a trope in Günderrode, most clearly in 'Ein apokaliptisches Fragment'. Werner Michler reads 'Briefe zweier Freunde' as having a debt to Plotinus: see Werner Michler, *Kulturen der Gattung: Poetik im Kontext, 1750–1950* (Göttingen: Wallstein, 2015), p. 422. On a more general level, Plotinus is significant for German Idealism, specifically for Schelling from 1804 onwards, aided by Creuzer's translation of the *Enneads*: see Thomas Leinkauf, 'Schelling and Plotinus', trans. by Stephen Gersh, in *Plotinus's Legacy: The Transformation of Platonism from the Renaissance to the Modern Era*, ed. by Stephen Gersh (Cambridge: Cambridge University Press, 2019), pp. 183–216 (p. 184).
123 There are clear points of contact between ideas of Neoplatonic emanationism, Hinduism and Christianised pantheism, of the kind that Creuzer would uphold in the *Symbolik*: see Margot Kathleen Louis, *Persephone Rises, 1860–1927: Mythography, Gender, and the Creation of a New Spirituality* (Aldershot: Ashgate, 2009), p. 7.

the entirety of 'Briefe zweier Freunde' reflects the typical stages of *katabasis* going back to classical pretexts, from Orpheus and Odysseus to Aeneas,[124] except in metaphorical or poetic form. The first letter marks the initial stage of despair and hopelessness, whereas the third stages the poet's confrontation with death and the overcoming of the fear of death.

This confrontation with death gives rise to the revelation ('da war mir plözlich in einer Offenbarung Alles deutlich, und wird es mir ewig bleiben' [then, suddenly, everything became clear to me in a revelation, and will remain eternally so] (*SW* I, 359)) that forms the poetic inspiration for eschatological theory that follows. On one level, this is a salvation history framed in terms inspired by Schelling, but it is one that, more importantly, makes recourse to the notion of perfectibility.

This eschatological cosmology assuages the original anguish of the poet because it is the means to find a cure — and that cure is found in the act of poetic creativity itself, in creating and giving expression to a new master-narrative, a new non-Christian salvation history that acts as a self-cure. The speaker rediscovers enthusiasm through the experience of a profound revelation, and so resolves the creative blockage that was so concerning in the first letter. In what follows, the poetic, philosophical and the sacred are entwined.

What the same unnamed speaker formulates in its second and final letter is an eschatological theory tinged with vocabulary from the philosophy of nature, except that, as in 'Die Malabarischen Witwen', Günderrode focuses on the affinities and sympathies within elements of matter:

> Zwar weiß ich, das Leben ist nur das Produkt der innigsten Berührung und Anziehung der Elemente; weiß, daß alle seine Blüten und Blätter, die wir Gedanken und Empfindungen nennen, verwelken müssen, wenn jene Berührung aufgelöst wird, und daß das einzelne Leben dem Gesetz der Sterblichkeit dahin gegeben ist; aber so gewiß mir Dieses ist, ebenso über allem Zweifel ist mir auch das Andre, die Unsterblichkeit des Lebens im Ganzen; denn dieses Ganze ist eben das Leben, und es wogt auf und nieder in seinen Gliedern den Elementen, und was es auch sey, das durch Auflösung (die wir zuweilen Tod nennen) zu denselben zurück gegangen ist, das vermischt sich mit ihnen nach Gesetzen der Verwandtschaft, d. h. das Ähnliche zu dem Ähnlichen. Aber anders sind diese Elemente geworden, nachdem sie einmal im Organismus zum Leben hinauf getrieben gewesen, sie sind lebendiger geworden, wie Zwei, die sich in langem Kampf übten, stärker sind wenn er geendet hat als ehe sie kämpften; so die Elemente, denn sie sind lebendig, und jede lebendige Kraft stärkt sich durch Übung. Wenn sie also zurükkehren zur Erde, vermehren sie das Erdleben. Die Erde aber gebiert den ihr zurückgegebenen Lebensstoff in andern Erscheinungen wieder, bis, durch immer neue Verwandlungen, alles Lebensfähige in ihr ist lebendig geworden.

> [To be sure, I know that life is just the product of the most intimate contact and attraction between elements, I know that its blossoms and leaves — which we call thoughts and sensations — have to wilt when this contact ceases, and that the individual life is given over to the dictate of mortality. But as certain as I am of this, I have no doubt about another point: the immortality of life as a whole.

---

124 *Ägyptische Mysterien*, pp. 7–8.

For this whole is life, and it surges upward and downward in its limbs, the elements, and whatever it may be that dissolves (the process that we otherwise call death) and so returns to the original elements, it mixes with these according to the laws of affinity, that is, like attracts like. But these elements have become different after having once been compelled into life in the organism; they have become more alive, just as two who have practised a long fight are stronger at its end than at the beginning — so too are the elements. For they are alive, and each living force strengthens itself through practice. When they return to the Earth in this way, they augment the life of the Earth. The Earth then gives birth to the stuff of life that had been returned it to once more, in other manifestations, until everything that has the capacity for life within the Earth becomes alive through ever new transfigurations.] (*SW* I, 359–60)

Each individual life contributes to the teleological development of the universe, in which all matter eventually becomes alive and organic. For Günderrode, there appears to be a slippage in meaning between what is alive and what is organic: both are positively connoted, meaning that which is alive and dynamic. Death is not an endpoint. Rather, it is understood, with a nod to chemistry, as being about the composition of matter, and is therefore a transition, a threshold to the future, more perfect form of being: 'die Einzelheit lebt unsterblich fort in der Allheit, deren Leben sie lebend entwickelte, und nach dem Tode selbst erhöht und mehrt, und so durch Leben und Sterben die Idee der Erde realisiren hilft' [the individual lives eternally on in the All, whose life it developed through its individual life, and after its death, even heightens and augments it, and so through life and death helps to realise the idea of the Earth] (*SW* I, 360). The individual gains the emotional consolation that its life and death contribute to the self-realisation of the world, which itself is an indirect form of immortality.

With this invocation of self-realisation, Günderrode returns to the familiar construct of perfectibility.[125] The self-realisation of the world is couched in terms of harmony and perfection, but also extends the thought derived from Schelling's *Bruno* about the status of materialism. The endpoint of this process of perfectibility is the creation of a transfigured divine body,[126] an embodiment of perfection where mind and body interpenetrate to the extent that they are identical. This divine body is distinguished from conventional understandings of flawed matter: 'ein wahrhaft verklärter Leib, ohne Fehl und Krankheit und unsterblich' [a truly transfigured body, without flaw or disease and eternal] (*SW* I, 360).

Günderrode combines two narratives in these metaphysical speculations: an

---

125 For Schelling, the endpoint of nature's productivity is self-consciousness. Although Schelling dealt with the problem of the Fall in the essay *Philosophie und Religion* (1804), his later writings are concerned with how the development of nature contributes to divine life: see Klaus Vondung, 'Apokalyptisch-esoterische Grundierungen des Strebens nach einer Universalwissenschaft — Bengel, Oetinger, Schelling', in *Aufklärung und Esoterik: Wege in die Moderne*, ed. by Monika Neugebauer-Wölk and others, Hallesche Beiträge zur Europäischen Aufklärung, 50 (Berlin: De Gruyter, 2013), 311–21 (p. 320).

126 This idea of 'Gottesleiblichkeit' may, as Dormann argues, derive from the Swabian theologian Friedrich Christoph Oetinger's notion of *apokatastasis* in his *Biblisches und Emblematisches Wörterbuch* (1776): see Dormann, p. 194.

amalgamation of a linear teleology of eschatological perfectibility and the cyclical account of birth as fall and return — a variant of Neoplatonist emanation. Vitally, however, this vision of perfection is repeatedly cast in doubt, if not eternally deferred. This is more than a gesture of humility on the part of the speaker. It has implications for the salvation narrative that the text upholds.

There is an esoteric aspect to Günderrode's interpretation of living nature as pantheistic. The soteriological narrative hinges on the idea that nature — and therefore God — suffers for and from the lack of its perfection that has become manifest in the universe.[127] If the divine is within every individual, then salvation history has been radically reformulated in an egalitarian mode. In this monist conception of the universe, Christ is not needed to descend to mankind as a saviour, but rather, the individual participates in the divine and is responsible for *nature*'s salvation by realising its perfection — that is, eternal life, a state that would eliminate death entirely.[128] Implicit here is moral universalism and also an inner sense that would give promptings to the individual. The impulses of love, virtue, and justice are simply means to the perfective end of dissolving into oneness, to bring to an end the sin of individuation. This presents a modified argument from Günderrode's earlier metaphysical texts, such as 'Ein apokaliptisches Fragment' and 'Geschichte eines Braminen'. Both of these hold onto the idea of individuality alongside a return to the generative source of life; in 'Briefe zweier Freunde', it is no more than a precursor to a higher state of being in an enlivened cosmos. 'Briefe zweier Freunde' pushes the problem of individuation further than all previous texts: gone is any emphasis on individual agency, self-development, or freedom. Instead, what is desired is, in a Neoplatonist sense, a state of *henosis*, of perfect oneness with the divine.

Yet this state of perfection remains necessarily utopian and unobtainable, which is emphasised at the end: 'der Gott der Erde [...] klagt, daß sein seliges, göttliches Leben noch fern sei' [the god of the Earth [...] laments, that his blessed, divine life is still distant] (*SW* I, 362). The idea of *apokatastasis*, of restitution or salvation of all things in the form of the perfect divine body, is nonetheless held onto, even if it may never be realised. Whilst this state may be eternally deferred, the appeal of this soteriological narrative lies in its dynamism and fecundity. This fascination with vital animation owes a debt to late eighteenth-century scientific and biological theories of the generation of life.[129] Any endpoint to this dynamism would amount to its dissolution. What this means is that there is a tension between the two narratives Günderrode upholds here — between the progressive, perfective cycle of

---

127 Antoine Faivre derives this notion of an esoteric philosophy of nature from an interpretation of the teachings of St Paul: see Antoine Faivre, *Access to Western Esotericism* (Albany: SUNY Press, 1994), p. 11.
128 The idea of the universe participating in God's perfection is an element of panentheism: see Keith Ward, 'The World as the Body of God: A Panentheistic Metaphor', in *In Whom We Live and Move and Have Our Being: Panentheistic Reflections on God's Presence in a Scientific World*, ed. by Philip Clayton and Arthur Peacocke (Grand Rapids: Eerdmans, 2004), pp. 62–72 (p. 69).
129 See, for example, Timothy Lenoir, *The Strategy of Life: Teleology and Mechanics in Nineteenth-Century German Biology* (Chicago: University of Chicago Press, 1989).

productivity and the *henosis* that would amount to stasis, to the dissolution not just of the individual, but of the entirety of imperfect phenomenal reality.

The appeal of this narrative lies in its expression of hope, and it is one that crafts a reciprocal and dialectical relationship between the individual and divinised nature: it writes the individual back into nature, and nature into the individual. On one level, this is a performative action of the text, as the speaker overcomes a creative blockage through the revelation of how he or she necessarily participates in and perfects the cosmos. The individual's worth is purely relational, in how it contributes to the teleological development of the cosmos. It also provides an adequate response to a need for a spiritual or metaphysical ground away from the dogmatic trappings of institutionalised religion.[130]

Unlike other narratives that are concerned with human perfection, such as Herder's *Ideen zu einer Philosophie der Geschichte der Menschheit*, or Lessing's *Die Erziehung des Menschengeschlechts*, Günderrode pursues the thought of the primacy of nature to the point of removing the human element altogether — and with that its distinctiveness, ethical or otherwise. There is a logical consistency to this thought: if one proceeds from the premise of *hen kai pan*, then this brings with it the concession of the essential unity of all things. This is a feature that is particular to *Melete* as a whole, where the poems give voice to the forces of nature that tacitly suggest a metaphysical reorientation for the reader; Günderrode's syncretic use of cultural rituals and customs, reflecting an underlying metaphysical reality, serves to bolster its supposed universality. What unites the discursive 'Briefe zweier Freunde' with other poems in the collection is the textual move of stripping back to a metaphysical core, to the continuing revelation of a naturalist principle of dynamic, generative life. *Melete*, like Günderrode's metaphysical texts as a whole, depends on a naturalist fallacy, that is, on deriving norms from nature. At the same time, this allows for the conceptual move of nullifying the sting of materialism by absorbing it into panentheism and pantheism as an alternative to Christian models of salvation.

---

130 Michael Murphy argues that it is the simplicity of panentheism that makes it appealing as an alternative to established forms of religion: Michael Murphy, 'The Emergence of Evolutionary Panentheism', in *Panentheism across the World's Traditions*, ed. by Loriliai Biernacki and Philip Clayton (Oxford: Oxford University Press, 2013), pp. 177–98 (pp. 186–87).

CHAPTER 7

Perspectives on Pantheism: Mereau, Hölderlin, Novalis

The preceding chapters have explored Günderrode's metaphysical commitments and shown that the persistent recourse to modes of Spinozist pantheism and panentheism is essential to an understanding of her literary and philosophical *oeuvre*. An important question remains: how to assess Günderrode's significance overall. To do this, it is worth situating Günderrode's pantheism in the period to account for its distinctiveness. As is well known, the Romantic generation, alongside Herder, Goethe, and Lessing, were drawn to the metaphysical commitments that were associated with Spinoza and Spinozism — ones that could exist independently of engaging with Spinoza's writings.[1] This revival of interest in Spinoza went hand in hand with a dynamic understanding of life. This notion of life is a dominant concept across Romanticism, both in the German-speaking context and beyond.[2] Pantheism, then, is an important metaphysical category in literature and philosophy at the turn of the nineteenth century and in Romanticism in particular.

Associated with pantheism is an interest in notions of force, vitality, productivity, animation, and generation, and these metaphysical and philosophical aspects of pantheism run in parallel with developments in the nascent life sciences at the turn of the nineteenth century, which proposed indwelling or even occult forces that caused matter to form bodies and organisms.[3] The language of vitality became a creative repository, available to be adapted for both the literature and philosophy of the time. An appreciation of the interconnectedness of all life had been previously present in seventeenth-century ripostes to materialism and mechanism and early eighteenth-century physico-theology.[4] What makes Romantic theories of nature

---

1   Benjamin D. Crowe, 'On "The Religion of the Visible Universe": Novalis and the Pantheism Controversy', *British Journal of the History of Philosophy*, 16.1 (2008), 125–46 (p. 127).
2   See Gigante, *Life: Organic Form and Romanticism*; Abrams, *Natural Supernaturalism*.
3   For accounts of Enlightenment and late eighteenth-century interest in concepts of vitality and vitalism, see Reill, *Vitalizing Nature in the Enlightenment*; Joan Steigerwald, *Experimenting at the Boundaries of Life: Organic Vitality in Germany around 1800* (Pittsburgh, PA: University of Pittsburgh Press, 2019); Zammito, *The Gestation of German Biology*.
4   Kondylis, *Die Aufklärung im Rahmen des neuzeitlichen Rationalismus*, p. 245; Steffen Martus, *Aufklärung: Das deutsche Jahrhundert. Ein Epochenbild* (Hamburg: Rowohlt, 2018), p. 369. Heinrich Detering has traced the proto-ecological strands of thought in earlier and later eighteenth-century poetry (Brockes, Haller, Goethe), which manifest in the appreciation of the connections between

distinctive is not only their vitalism and naturalization of human beings and natural objects, and their understanding of the self and nature by analogy with one another, but also the move into a vitalised pantheism.[5] The Spinozist slogan of *hen kai pan* was the motto shared between Hegel, Hölderlin, and Schelling at the Tübingen seminary,[6] and its monist metaphysics complemented the political radicalism and egalitarian hopes initially buoyed by the French Revolution.[7] Spinozism, too, proved philosophically useful in Romantic philosophy's responses to Kantian and post-Kantian idealism.[8]

Read in this context, Günderrode's metaphysical commitments, on the whole, align in particular with those of Novalis and Hölderlin. It may be accidental that they had similarly unhappy lives; that their philosophical commitments were similar was not.[9] But such broad similarities themselves obscure differences. Günderrode did read Hölderlin's *Hyperion*. Her sonnet addressed to Novalis celebrates his notion of a golden age. But this evidence of reading practices does not take us very far. We need to look deeply into the specific direction of Günderrode's thought to see where the similarities and differences are. I have shown above how far works like *Melete* and 'Briefe zweier Freunde' advance Günderrode towards a thoroughgoing Spinozist naturalism. In what follows I will compare Günderrode's position with that of her contemporaries, in order to draw out fully what makes her approach, and her work, distinctive.

Pantheism as Nihilism: Sophie Mereau, *Das Blütenalter der Empfindung* (1794)

Before turning to Hölderlin and Novalis, who are both engaged in the recuperation of Spinoza and Spinozist metaphysics, there is an instructive negative example of Spinozism to be found at the close of Sophie Mereau's first novel, *Das Blütenalter der Empfindung* [The Spring of Sensibility]. Mereau's own lyric poetry shares with Günderrode some Platonist tendencies — such as the aestheticised eroticism of 'Die Gottheit' [The Deity] (1803). Alongside these thematic commonalities, both Mereau and Günderrode did know one another, although Mereau herself claimed to not have been entirely convinced of Günderrode's poetic talents or originality.[10] Her deployment of pantheism absorbs Herder's 'vitalised' interpretation of Spinoza in its language, whilst making recourse to the popular belief that Spinoza was a fatalist and an atheist — which Mereau pushes further into nihilism.

---

all life: see Heinrich Detering, *Menschen im Weltgarten: Die Entdeckung der Ökologie in der Literatur von Haller bis Humboldt* (Göttingen: Wallstein, 2020), p. 10.
5   Nina Amstutz, *Caspar David Friedrich: Nature and the Self* (New Haven: Yale University Press, 2020), pp. 8–13.
6   William S. Davis, *Romanticism, Hellenism, and the Philosophy of Nature* (Basingstoke: Palgrave Macmillan, 2018), pp. 20–22.
7   Beiser, *Enlightenment, Revolution, and Romanticism*, p. 243.
8   Frank, *Unendliche Annäherung*; Beiser, *The Romantic Imperative*.
9   For the commonalities with Hölderlin, see Waltraud Howeg, *Karoline von Günderrode und Hölderlin* (Halle, 1953); for those with Novalis, see Dormann, p. 160; Weigert, p. 250.
10 Günderrode, *Briefe*, p. 169.

Mereau's short novel is not primarily concerned with metaphysical matters. As the title suggests, it is primarily an exploration of feeling, with a large debt to Rousseau and *Die Leiden des jungen Werthers* [The Sorrows of Young Werther] (1774).[11] The short novel also bears comparison with Hölderlin's later epistolary novel *Hyperion* — itself written in the shadow of *Werther*. As Adrian Daub has argued, both novels feature protagonists who oscillate between introspection bordering on solipsism and bursts of action.[12] Matters of the heart are filtered through the prism of the French Revolution, so that the novel is as much about the struggle for ideals of freedom and equal rights as it is about personal development. In *Das Blütenalter der Empfindung*, America functions as an idealised cipher for individual freedoms, and indeed functions as a refuge from the oppressions experienced in Europe for the two protagonists, Albert and Nanette, at the novel's conclusion.[13]

Pantheism comes into the equation when the plot turns to Lorenzo, Nanette's brother, in a twist which relies on borrowings from contemporary popular literature, known as *Trivialliteratur*.[14] Lorenzo had been forced into a monastery, the victim of an older brother's scheme to have him disinherited. He escapes but is unable to earn a living as an artist. Albert then finds him in a state of melancholy. His spiritual desolation stems from an overwhelming sense of transcendental loneliness. Lorenzo had fallen in love with Luise, the daughter of a local merchant, whose father, a staunch Catholic, refuses to allow their union to go ahead, since Lorenzo naively gives an account of his monastic past. He is even forbidden from associating with Luise further. Lorenzo's response to this emotional shock — in a nod to *Werther* — is to commit suicide by shooting himself in the head.

The first stage in Lorenzo's descent into nihilistic pantheism is brought about by the loss of faith in a personal, loving God:

> Für ihn [Lorenzo] gab es keinen Beschützer in den Wolken, er hielt es für einen kindlichen Stolz der Menschen, einen Gott zu glauben, der jeden ihrer Tage bewachte und mit eignen Händen die kleinsten Begegnisse ihres Lebens bildete und lenkte. Er sah nur den einsamen unabänderlichen Gang eines unbezwinglichen Schicksals, das über Menschenleben und Menschenglück [...] dahinschreitet, und die Natur mit allen ihren Erscheinungen und den Menschen mit allem seinen Willen, darin aufnimmt und berechnet. Aufopferung einzelner Teile zu höhern Zwecken fürs Ganze, glaubte er, sei ein allenthalben befolgtes Gesetz.
>
> [For him there was no protector in the heavens; he thought it to be infantile pride of humanity to believe in a God who was watching over them every day and with his own hands would shape and guide the smallest events of their lives. He saw only the desolate, unalterable course of an indomitable fate that proceeds through human life and happiness, and absorbs nature in all its

---

11 Kontje, *Women, the Novel, and the German Nation*, p. 77.
12 Adrian Daub, *Uncivil Unions: The Metaphysics of Marriage in German Idealism and Romanticism* (Chicago: University of Chicago Press, 2012), p. 215.
13 Katharina von Hammerstein, '"Au bonheur de tous": Sophie Mereau on Human Rights and (Gender) Politics in the French Revolution and American Republic', *Colloquia Germanica*, 42.2 (2009), 97–117.
14 Dennis F. Mahoney, *Der Roman der Goethezeit (1774–1829)* (Stuttgart: Metzler, 1988), pp. 94–95.

manifestations and humankind with all its will into itself and its calculations. He thought that the sacrifice of individual parts for higher purposes for the sake of the whole was a law universally followed.][15]

Lorenzo's rejection of what he considers a naïve fantasy and trust in a personal God is part and parcel of a fragile intellectual superiority, whose disdain for others masks its unarticulated self-directed character. Humankind and nature are part of one and the same system of mechanistic naturalism and determinism — here framed as fate. Fate itself assumes a personal character, in possessing will, but it is distinguished from providence because it does not attend to human happiness. This notion of fate has the same dire consequences for the notion of individual development as Günderrode's dream-narrative exposing the problem of determinism (see pp. 25–28 above). Here, for Lorenzo, it empties the individual of meaning and makes him or her subject to the vicissitudes of deterministic laws of fate.

For Lorenzo, suicidal despair then becomes mapped onto pantheism: a form of pantheism that has been transfigured into nihilism.[16] Far from offering consolation, pantheism instead absorbs the language of determinism and necessity that, for Lorenzo, becomes tantamount to spiritual despondency. Mereau even makes explicit recourse to Herder's ontology of force, adopting his terminology of 'Urkraft'. The specific problem with pantheism, for Lorenzo, is how it jettisons the consolations provided by religious orthodoxy — specifically the hope of eternal life.

The danger of this atheist nihilism ought to serve as a warning. But instead it proves infectious. In an act of empathetic identification, Albert absorbs Lorenzo's despair. In so doing, he mediates it to the reader:

> Ich verzweifelte an allem Vortrefflichen, an allem Glück in der Welt. Was war der Zweck des Daseins? — Eine trostlose Notwendigkeit schien allenthalben den freien Blick der Untersuchung zu hemmen. Was sollte mir eine Welt, wo Rechtschaffenheit foltert und inniges Gefühl zum Mörder macht, wo zwischen Pflicht und Neigung ein quälender Widerspruch waltet? — Und wenn mir nur dies ein Recht gegeben hätte, auf eine bessre Welt zu hoffen! [...] Alle Kraft entwikkelt sich und wirkt, *wo* und *wie* sie kann. Aus der unendlichen Masse des Urseins fließt alles; zu ihr kehret alles wieder zurück. Alles Gute findet seinen Lohn; es findet ihn in sich, darf ihn nicht außer sich suchen. Wo ist das Rätsel, das zur Auflösung einer andern Welt bedürfte?

> [I despaired of all that is virtuous, of all happiness in the world. What was the purpose of existence? — Bleak necessity seemed to restrict my ability to pursue the matter further at every turn. What is the purpose to me of a world that torments virtue, and where inner feeling becomes murderous, where there is an agonising contradiction between duty and inclination? — And if only this had given me a right to hope for a better world! [...] All force develops and acts, *where* and *how* it can. Out of the endless mass of primordial being everything flows; and everything returns to it as well. All that is good finds its reward, it finds it in itself, and must not seek it outside itself. Where is the mystery that would require another world as its solution?][17]

---

15 Sophie Mereau, *Das Blütenalter der Empfindung: Amanda und Eduard* (Munich: Deutscher Taschenbuch Verlag, 1996), p. 52.
16 Kontje, *Women, the Novel, and the German Nation*, p. 92.
17 Mereau, *Das Blütenalter der Empfindung*, pp. 52–53.

In the thrall of empathetic melancholy, Albert comes close to the sin of despair. When the world is viewed through the prism of necessity, there appears to be little moral order or sense of virtue or righteousness being rewarded, and nothing that could suggest that the afterlife could offer any improvement. Indeed, Mereau's turn to the language of pantheistic vitalism is used here to justify an explicit denial of the existence of an afterlife. If all emerges from a primordial ground of being and returns to it, then heavenly reward is instead to be found in the individual. Whilst this locates moral goodness in the self, this possibility is compromised by the immoral or amoral conditions prevailing between the individual and society. Albert pushes pantheist nihilism to its logical endpoint, to the destruction of the transient individual, so emptying the individual of any meaning:

> Das einmal gewesene Sein mischt sich, wenn es nun schwindet, wieder mit der unerschöpflichen, schaffenden Urkraft, ohne Spur, daß es war; es ist nun immer und ewig nicht mehr, und mein eignes Dasein ist bloß an Erinnerung geknüpft. Wenn diese schwindet, so bin ich selbst nicht mehr, so ist ein andres Wesen an meine Stelle getreten. Der Staub vermischt sich mit dem Staube; der Lebensfunke mit der ewigen Urkraft. Er verlischt nicht; in andern Körpern wird er flammen; aber mein Ich ist dann auf ewig untergegangen.

> [What has already existed mixes, at the point of dissolution, once more with the inexhaustible, creative primordial force, without leaving a trace of its own existence. Thereafter it is then always and forever no more, and my own existence is merely sustained by remembrance. When this disappears, I myself am no more, and another being has taken my place. Dust mixes with dust; the spark of life fuses with the primordial force. That spark cannot be extinguished: it will ignite in other bodies, but my self has then perished for eternity.][18]

Where for Günderrode, Spinozist pantheism serves a heterodox consolation narrative, for Albert and Mereau, pantheism becomes an object of fear. In this it resembles the negative Spinozism of Günderrode's 'Magie und Schicksal'. It amounts to little more than justification for existential despair — indeed, for a metaphysics of despair. The de-souled form of palingenesis that Albert outlines supports the idea of an eternal, self-sustaining life force, but one that intrinsically bound up with a bleak nihilism.

Whilst Albert himself does not succumb to this vision, the psychological strain exerted on him by the import of Lorenzo's nihilism nonetheless leads him to seek another consolation narrative, one that will perform the same function as that of Christian orthodoxy, which is to assuage doubt and fear:

> Ich fühlte — was ich noch nie in so unbezwinglicher Stärke gefühlt hatte — das Bedürfnis, ein System zu haben, das in seiner göttlichen Erhabenheit alle Zweifel aufnehmen und entscheiden, das den sinkenden Geist aufrecht halten und ihn vor Verzweiflung bewahren könnte.

> [I felt — which I had hitherto never felt in such uncontrollable intensity — the need to have a system that, in its divine majesty, could absorb and give certainty to all doubt, one that could be a prop to a faltering spirit and could protect it from despair.][19]

---

18   Ibid.
19   Ibid., p. 53.

Albert does not himself find a fully-fledged system to ease his existential anxieties, breezily claiming that there is enough inspiration already present in society and the world to reignite optimism.

Mereau provides an account of pantheism that cleaves close to the fears roused by Jacobi: that pantheism is intrinsically linked with atheism, fatalism, and nihilism, and that this negative Spinozism eliminates both human freedom and morality. In the context of the novel, these are more than abstract philosophical fears, but rather prove infectious in the pressure exerted on Albert.

Hölderlin: from *Hyperion* to *Der Tod des Empedokles*

Hölderlin may be more commonly discussed in the context of Romantic pantheism than Mereau, but there are useful parallels: the oscillations of mood in the latter anticipate the extremes experienced by Hyperion in his eccentric path.[20] Hölderlin's view of pantheism is altogether more positively inflected than in Mereau, and he shares with Günderrode a fusion of Platonist and Spinozist sympathies — indeed, of the three authors examined in this chapter, Hölderlin is the closest to Günderrode in his metaphysical commitments in both *Hyperion* and the *Der Tod des Empedokles* [The Death of Empedocles] (1797–1800).

Hölderlin is closest to Günderrode in a literal sense as well, although there is no evidence of any meeting between the two. As a tutor to the children of the Gontard family, Hölderlin resided in their house on the Großer Hirschgraben in Frankfurt between 1796 and 1798. From 1797, Günderrode lived only stone's throw away, at the intersection of the Roßmarkt and Kaiserstraße, in the Damenstift operated by a charitable foundation, the Cronstett- and Hynspergische evangelische Stiftung. Beyond this topographical coincidence, Hölderlin studied Jacobi's tract on Spinoza; his summary notes survive. He drew on his friend Wilhelm Heinse's erotic pantheism from the novel *Ardinghello oder die glückseligen Inseln* [Ardinghello or the Blissful Islands] (1787) for his early hymns, as well as for *Hyperion*.[21]

Where Hölderlin does display similarities with Günderrode is in the deployment of the term 'Leben' [life]. 'Leben' or 'das Lebendige' are both freighted with metaphysical meaning. Whilst they are not central terms for him as they are for Günderrode, these terms assume prominence in *Der Tod des Empedokles*,[22] and take on a significant role in Hölderlin's thought and poetics around 1798.[23] Compared to Günderrode, the extent to which Hölderlin engaged with scientific discourses of

---

20 Lawrence Ryan, *Hölderlins 'Hyperion': Exzentrische Bahn und Dichterberuf* (Stuttgart: Metzler, 1965).
21 Leonhard Herrmann, *Klassiker jenseits der Klassik: Wilhelm Heinses 'Ardinghello' — Individualitätskonzeption und Rezeptionsgeschichte*, Communicatio, 41 (Berlin: De Gruyter, 2010), pp. 157–65; Max L. Baeumer, *Heinse-Studien* (Stuttgart: Metzler, 1966), pp. 57–62.
22 Charlie Louth, *Hölderlin and the Dynamics of Translation*, Studies in Comparative Literature, 2 (Oxford: Legenda, 1998), p. 81.
23 Jennifer Anna Gosetti-Ferencei, *Heidegger, Hölderlin, and the Subject of Poetic Language: Towards a New Poetics of Dasein*, Perspectives in Continental Philosophy, 38 (New York: Fordham University Press, 2004), p. 157.

the time remains an open question.[24] At the very least, his attraction to pantheism is on the whole devoid of the scientific vocabulary inherited from vitalism and theories of chemistry that becomes absorbed into Günderrode's pantheism.

Der Tod des Empedokles can be productively read alongside Günderrode's 'Mahomed, der Prophet von Mekka' in particular, as a play that is equally concerned with the possibility of religious and political renewal. Both Empedokles and Mahomed are mediators between the earthly and the divine. The primary distinction is one of genre: whereas *Empedokles* is Hölderlin's attempt to write tragedy, Günderrode instead writes a classicising play without adhering to strict genre definitions of comedy and tragedy. This accounts for the differences in mood: whereas Mahomed overcomes a series of trials and the play is sustained by eschatological hope, *Empedokles* is more reflective, at times elegiac, oscillating between moments of rhetorical fervour and Empedokles' despair at having lost the favour of the gods. Where 'Mahomed' has concentrated moments of dramatic action, *Empedokles*'s action is condensed into language and is more focused on the consequences of these utterances.[25] This is not because the play was left uncompleted. Its intrinsic dramatic structure is more elliptical than that of 'Mahomed', which is more linear, reaching closure. The uncertainty of how Mahomed's mission will be realised is resolved in its proleptic end. Günderrode's play points to a different philosophical conception of history compared to Hölderlin. The play 'Mahomed' points to greater confidence in the process of history, a belief that it can be shaped to further human ends. Hölderlin's *Empedokles* project is instead far more ambivalent about what might be achieved by revolutionary action.

One of the tensions central to the conception of *Empedokles* is that between the conditioned and unconditioned, and how to strive towards the unconditioned — an element that is also central to the motif of the epistemological quest in Günderrode. It is a tension present in the famous opening to the Frankfurt plan of *Der Tod des Empedokles* from September 1797, which characterises Empedokles through his totalising but constantly thwarted desire for the apprehension of all that lives:

> zu Kulturhaß gestimmt, zu Verachtung alles sehr bestimmten Geschäffts, alles nach verschiedenen Gegenständen gerichteten Interesses, ein Todtfeind aller einseitigen Existenz, und deswegen auch in wirklich schönen Verhältnissen unbefriedigt, unstät, leidend, blos weil sie besondere Verhältnisse sind und, nur im großen Akkord mit allem Lebendigen empfunden ganz ihn erfüllen, blos weil er nicht mit allgegenwärtigem Herzen innig, wie ein Gott, und frei und ausgebreitet, wie ein Gott, in ihnen leben und lieben kan, blos weil er, so bald sein Herz und sein Gedanke das Vorhandene umfaßt, ans Gesez der Succession gebunden ist.

---

24 Leif Weatherby has, for example, argued for the importance of the physician and anatomist Samuel Thomas Soemmerring's *Über das Organ der Seele* (1796) for Hölderlin's thought: see Leif Weatherby, *Transplanting the Metaphysical Organ: German Romanticism between Leibniz and Marx* (New York: Fordham University Press, 2016), pp. 131–70.

25 Angela Esterhammer, *The Romantic Performative: Language and Action in British and German Romanticism* (Stanford: Stanford University Press, 2000), pp. 203–17.

[Predisposed to despise his culture, to scorn all neatly circumscribed affairs, every interest directed to sundry objects; a mortal enemy of all one-sided existence, and therefore unsatisfied even in truly harmonious circumstances, restive, suffering, simply because they are particular ones, ones that fulfil him utterly only when they form part of the great harmony of all living things; simply because he cannot live in them and love them intimately, with omnipresent heart, like a god, and freely and expansively, like a god; simply because as soon as his heart and his thought embrace anything at hand he finds himself bound to the law of succession.][26]

The proposed all-unity of all that lives is necessarily metaphysical in nature. As laid out in this plan, Empedokles is a titanic, transgressive figure whose extraordinary suffering results from the wholesale rejection of human particularity, which is, at its core, an ontological problem of individuation.[27]

In sketching out the oscillations between the extremes of Empedokles' character — deep hatred of 'alle[] einseitige Existenz', alongside the Promethean self-elevation and self-deification, Hölderlin anticipates the tensions between *physis* and *techne* which form the starting point of the essay 'Grund zum Empedokles' [Basis for Empedocles], which was composed between the second and third versions of the play. While the plan stages an absolute distinction between the unconditioned and conditioned, an element central to all three drafts of the play is lacking: the question of Empedokles' role as mediator between the finite and the infinite, and between the supersensible and sensible. By recalibrating Empedokles as more of a fusion of prophet, poet (as *poeta vates*), and political revolutionary in the extant versions of the play, mediation therefore takes on prominence, particularly in the first two versions.[28]

What is distinct about the metaphorical and figurative construction of nature — both mythopoetic and religious — in the first two versions of *Der Tod des Empedokles* is the consistent recourse to poetically vitalist language that stresses the dynamism of the generative, divine forces both in and of nature. This is where Hölderlin and Günderrode can be brought into dialogue with one another: not only is Empedokles a medial figure and divinely inspired prophet — however much this may be sullied by egotism — the language used to describe Empedokles as a mediator is inextricably bound to the metaphysical understanding of 'Leben' and generative forces.

---

26 Friedrich Hölderlin, *Sämtliche Werke*. ed. by Friedrich Beissner and Adolf Beck, 8 vols (Stuttgart: Kohlhammer, 1943–85), IV.1: *Der Tod des Empedokles. Aufsätze. Erste Hälfte. Texte und Erläuterungen*, ed. by Friedrich Beissner (1961), p. 145; Friedrich Hölderlin, *The Death of Empedocles: A Mourning Play*, trans. by David Farrell Krell (Albany, NY: State of University of New York Press, 2008), p. 29 (translation adapted).
27 David Constantine, *Hölderlin* (Oxford: Clarendon Press, 1988), p. 133.
28 The figure of Empedocles was sufficiently capacious in the eighteenth century to allow for these layers of meaning and interpretation: see Theresia Birkenhauer, *Legende und Dichtung: Der Tod des Philosophen und Hölderlins Empedokles* (Berlin: Vorwerk, 1996). For Hölderlin's sources, see Uvo Hölscher, *Empedokles und Hölderlin* (Frankfurt a.M.: Insel, 1965); see also, Charles Lewis, *The Law of Poetry: Studies in Hölderlin's Poetics*, Germanic Literatures, 18 (Cambridge: Legenda, 2019), pp. 37–38.

In reading Hölderlin's *Der Tod des Empedokles* through the play's vital or vitalist language, I am drawing on suggestions in recent Hölderlin scholarship that emphasise, in Kristina Mendecino's pithy formulation, how 'logic of life (*biology*) amounts to a logic of force (*bialogy*)'.[29] The concept of force can be productively combined with Jennifer Anna Gosetti-Ferencei's suggestive formulation of Hölderlin's 'elegiac biopoetics'.[30] This term — if only tentatively — seeks to account for the emphasis on division in Hölderlin's poetry and other works. This manifests itself, for example, in the divide between the individual and nature in both *Hyperion* and *Der Tod des Empedokles*, where unity and plenitude can be intimated or reconstituted through the intensity of lyrical language. In the tensions between separation and the desire for (re-)unification, it is the flow of forces, simultaneously physical and metaphysical, that mediate between the individual and nature — and Empedokles functions as their conduit. More specifically: Empedokles occupies the position of a *daimon*,[31] an intermediary between the divine world of nature and that of material reality — although in the first two versions of the play, Empedokles' role as an intermediary is necessarily compromised by his loss of a state of grace.[32]

Aesthetic Platonism in *Hyperion*

Before turning to *Empedokles* itself, it is worth briefly considering *Hyperion*. It is in this novel and its paratexts that Hölderin's attraction to pantheism and its genealogical link to the pantheism controversy becomes most explicit. This attraction to pantheism or panentheism is well known in scholarship, and its character has been variously traced to sources such as Platonism, Neoplatonism, Herder, Leibniz, and Schiller's early *Philosophische Briefe*.[33] It is in *Hyperion* where Hölderlin proclaims pantheist sympathies, most strikingly in the use of the motto *hen kai pan*. The novel is, on the whole, more Platonist than Spinozist. In it, aesthetic Platonism is fused with Hyperion's egalitarian and republican hopes in the famous formulation of 'die

---

29 Kristina Mendecino, 'Vivisections: Scripting Life in Hölderlin's "Das Belebende"', *The German Quarterly*, 91.3 (2018), 270–85 (p. 272).
30 Jennifer Anna Gosetti-Ferencei, 'Nature and Poetic Consciousness from Hölderlin to Rilke', in *Hölderlin's Philosophy of Nature*, ed. by Rochelle Tobias (Edinburgh: Edinburgh University Press, 2020), pp. 23–43 (p. 31).
31 As suggested, but not elaborated on, by Klaus Düsing: Klaus Düsing, 'Christus und die antiken Götter in der Mythologie der späten Hölderlin', in *Vernunft und Glauben: Ein philosophischer Dialog der Moderne mit dem Christentum. Père Xavier Tillette zum 85. Geburtstag*, ed. by Steffen Dietzsch and Gian Franco Figo (Berlin: Akademie, 2006), pp. 177–89 (p. 180).
32 The historical Empedocles proposed the conception of the *daimon* as a being cast into exile because of a polluting sin: see Nicholls, pp. 37–38.
33 An early commentator on Hölderlin's pantheism or panentheism was Wilhelm Dilthey: see Anthony Curtis Adler, *Politics and Truth in Hölderlin:* Hyperion *and the Choreographic Project of Modernity* (Rochester, NY: Camden House, 2021), p. 7; see also Franz Gabriel Nauen, *Revolution, Idealism and Human Freedom: Schelling, Hölderlin and Hegel and the Crisis of Early German Idealism*, International Archives of the History of Ideas/Archives Internationales d'histoire des idées, 45 (The Hague: Nijhoff, 1971), p. 58; for sources of Hölderlin's 'vitalism', see Frederick C. Beiser, *German Idealism: The Struggle Against Subjectivism* (Cambridge, MA: Harvard University Press, 2002), pp. 381–82.

Theokratie des Schönen' [Theocracy of Beauty].[34] References to Plato can be found prominently in the preface to the penultimate preface to the novel, as well as the opening letter of its final version.[35] Whilst *Hyperion*, by contrast with *Der Tod des Empedokles*, does not make use of the language of forces or energies consistently, the novel nonetheless anticipates the vitalism found in Hölderlin's later attempt at writing tragedy.

Hyperion has been productively read as a novel in which Hyperion constitutes himself by retrospectively recounting his experiences to Bellarmin. As Jochen Schmidt has convincingly argued, the novel enacts a form of Stoic self-therapy, in which pantheistic effusions make it possible for Hyperion to absorb the psychic shocks caused by the dashing of revolutionary hopes and the death of Hyperion's beloved and mentor, Diotima.[36] The function of pantheistic metaphysics, in this sense, is not dissimilar to Günderrode's consolation narratives, in particular 'Briefe zweier Freunde'. The ecstatic hymn to nature that brings *Hyperion* to a close is propelled by its lyrical intensity that invokes monist plenitude, tinged with Neoplatonist emanationism, and is framed in biological terms:

> Es fallen die Menschen, wie faule Früchte von dir, o laß sie untergehn, so kehren sie zu deiner Wurzel wieder, und ich, o Baum des Lebens, daß ich wieder grüne mit dir und deine Gipfel umathme mit all deinen knospenden Zweigen! friedlich und innig, denn alle wuchsen wir aus dem goldnen Saamkorn herauf! [...] Wie der Zwist der Liebenden, sind die Dissonanzen der Welt. Versöhnung ist mitten im Streit und alles Getrennte findet sich wieder.
>
> Es scheiden und kehren im Herzen die Adern und einiges, ewiges, glühendes Leben ist Alles.
>
> [Men fall from you like rotting fruit, oh, let them perish, for then they return to your root, and I, O tree of life, may I green again with you and breathe around your crown with all your budding branches! peacefully and deeply, for we've all of us grown high from that seed of golden grain! [...] The dissonances of the world are like lovers' tiffs. There's reconciliation in the middle of strife, and all that's apart comes together again.
>
> The arteries part and return in the heart and one eternal glowing life is All.][37]

Günderrode tends to shy away from the paradox of reconciliation in strife that is a central tension in Hyperion's metaphysical proclamation. Nonetheless, there are productive points of contact between the two authors. Hölderlin crafts a narrative of palingenesis through the biblical reference to the tree of life that overcomes and nullifies death, to the point of imagining Hyperion's own resurrection at the source of life, that is, at the source of pure being.[38] The final, physiological

---

34 Hölderlin, *Sämtliche Werke*, III: *Hyperion*, ed. by Friedrich Beissner (1957), p. 96.
35 Michael Franz has argued for the foundational influence of Plato on Hölderlin, Hegel, and Schelling: see Michael Franz, *Tübinger Platonismus: Die gemeinsamen philosophischen Anfangsgründe von Hölderlin, Schelling und Hegel* (Tübingen: Narr Francke, 2012).
36 Schmidt, 'Stoischer Pantheismus als Medium des Säkularisierungsprozesses'.
37 Hölderlin, *Sämtliche Werke*, III, 159–60; Friedrich Hölderlin, *Hyperion, or the Hermit in Greece*, trans. by Howard Gaskill (Cambridge: OpenBook, 2019), pp. 136–37.
38 For the tree of life, see Genesis 2. 9. For a brief discussion of Hölderlin's interest in notions of

image leads to the proclamation of a dynamic, pulsating life principle, a force suggestive of the phenomenal world as a single, interconnected organism.[39] Whilst echoing the Spinozist motto of *hen kai pan*, the metaphorical equation of life with the diastolic and systolic flows of blood itself echoes the circularity of emanationism.

Like that of Günderrode, Hölderlin's pantheism owes a debt to Spinozism. Hölderlin's understanding of the relationship between the individual and nature has been variously analysed as being pantheist, if not Spinozist, in *Hyperion*.[40] Traces of Spinozism have also been detected in the apotheosis of death as a transfiguration into new life or renewal in *Der Tod des Empedokles*, with a particular emphasis on how the essay 'Grund zum Empedokles' leads to the reconceptualization of Empedokles in the third version of the tragedy.[41] Hölderlin may have absorbed Herder's famously creative misreading of Spinozism, achieved via the insertion a Leibnizian element of force into Spinoza's system, in the composition of these essays and the third version of the play.[42] But a vitalist ontology of forces is in fact more prevalent throughout the first and second versions. In the third version, the political and religious conflict in Agrigentum is stripped away, thereby moving the focus away from Empedokles' role as religious mediator and instigator of political renewal. The idea of force, then, is bound up with the potential for revolutionary agency.

In the first version, words associated with force specifically occur in contexts associated with Empedokles' status as a seer or prophet, as one accorded with privileged access to the divine in nature. This linguistic patterning remains consistent across the characters. Thus Empedokles' disciple Panthea exclaims: 'So innig liebt' | Und sah kein anderer die ewge Welt | Und ihre Genien und Kräfte nie' [No one ever loved and saw | the eternal world and all its tutelary spirits and forces | as intensely as you did].[43] Similarly, Pausanias claims that others sense Empedokles' exalted status: 'Er lebe mit den Genien der Welt | Im Bunde' [he | Was one who dwelled with all the tutelary spirits of | The world, confederate with them].[44] Empedokles himself, in elegiac despair, says: 'das Wandeln und Wirken deiner Geniuskräfte | Der Herrlichen, deren Genoß ich war, o Natur!' [the changes and the charges of | Your splendid tutelary forces, whose comrade I then was, | O nature!].[45] Hölderlin embeds this patterning of forces in the notion of genius,

---

continued existence, see Lieselotte E. Kurth-Voigt, *Continued Existence, Reincarnation, and the Power of Sympathy in Classical Weimar* (Rochester, NY: Camden House, 1999), pp. 225–26.

39 The phrase 'glühendes Leben' is lifted from Goethe's *Die Leiden des jungen Werthers*, whose monoperspectival epistolary novel was influential for Hölderlin: see Howard Gaskill, *Hölderlin's Hyperion* (Durham: University of Durham, 1984), p. 30.

40 Most prominently: Margarethe Wegenast, *Hölderlins Spinoza-Rezeption und ihre Bedeutung für die Konzeption des* Hyperion, Studien zur deutschen Literatur, 112 (Tübingen: Niemeyer, 1990).

41 See Ulrich Gaier, *Hölderlin: Eine Einführung* (Tübingen: Francke, 1993), pp. 132–34; Peter-André Alt, 'Subjektivierung, Ritual, implizite Theatralität: Hölderlins "Empedokles"-Projekt und die Diskussion des antiken Opferbegriffes im 18. Jahrhundert', *Hölderlin-Jahrbuch*, 37 (2010–11), 30–67.

42 Bell, *Spinoza in Germany*, p. 144.

43 Hölderlin, *Sämtliche Werke*, IV.1, 21.

44 Ibid., p. 43; Hölderlin, *The Death of Empedocles*, p. 72.

45 Hölderlin, *Sämtliche Werke*, IV.1, 18; Hölderlin, *The Death of Empedocles*, p. 51.

referring to a primordial creative force. Divine nature is, therefore, *natura naturans*, suffused with daimonic energies and forces to which Empedokles has a particular sensitivity. This sensitivity is even given material, sensory form in the continuation of his Etna speech, which is replete with synaesthetic detail of how he heard the voice of the gods in his first breath and sight of the world:

> Kennt ihr der Götter Stimme nicht? Noch eh'
> Als ich der Eltern Sprache lauschend lernt',
> Im ersten Othemzug, im ersten Blik
> Vernahm ich jene schon und immer hab'
> Ich höher sie, denn Menschenwort geachtet.
> Hinauf! sie riefen mich und jedes Lüftchen
> Regt mächtiger die bange Sehnsucht auf
>
> [Do you not hear the voice of the gods? whereas I, before
> I learned, through listening, the language of my parents,
> With my initial breath, in my primordial vision,
> Already I was hearkening to that voice, and always
> I thought it higher than the human word.
> Upward! They called out to me and every breeze
> Incited more mightily the agonizing longing in me][46]

Empedokles positions himself as having privileged access to the gods, and indeed is (or at least claims to be) an inherently medial figure — whereas in Günderrode Mahomed's 'doppeltes Leben' or 'zweifaches Leben' only develops later. Where Mahomed experiences difficulties in coming to understand the nature of divine insights and requires the intervention of the angel Gabriel to resolve his doubt, such cognitive problems do not afflict Empedokles. What is at stake in *Empedokles* is how self-dissolution reinstates a primordial unity — similar to how self-immolation heralds a return to primordial unity in Günderrode's 'Die Malabarischen Witwen' — but also how self-dissolution functions as a politically symbolic act.

Empedokles' receptivity to the daimonic energies and forces of divine nature is important for the conception of his character, which aligns with the ancient notion of the poet as second creator or *alter deus*.[47] The vitalist metaphysics assumes political significance, too, in the context of the fallout of the French Revolution. The philosophy and metaphysics of nature maps onto a philosophy of history.[48] Indeed, all versions of the play as well as the associated essays, particularly 'Das untergehende Vaterland' [The Declining Fatherland], are interested in moments of epochal, revolutionary transition, propelled by the anticipation of a *kairos* moment, a right or opportune moment of transfiguration, which in the play is marked by Empedokles' death in the fires of Etna. In all versions of the play, the imagery of flows figuratively connects to a triadic model of history, where the desolation of

---

46 Hölderlin, *Sämtliche Werke*, IV.1, 69–70; Hölderlin, *The Death of Empedocles*, p. 94 (translation adapted).

47 Jochen Schmidt, *Die Geschichte des Genie-Gedankens in der deutschen Literatur, Philosophie und Politik 1750–1945*, 2 vols (Heidelberg: Winter, 2004), I: *Von der Aufklärung bis zum Idealismus*, pp. 404–13.

48 Ernst Mogel, *Natur als Revolution: Hölderlins Empedokles-Tragödie* (Stuttgart: Metzler, 1994), pp. 172–74.

the present age becomes transfigured through the onset of a new golden age, one that recalls a golden age from the past.[49]

Where Hölderlin differs from Novalis or Günderrode is in withholding the restitution or realisation of a golden age (such as in *Heinrich von Ofterdingen* or 'Immortalita'). On a pragmatic level this can be attributed in part to the non-completion of the drama. Narratives of perfectibility betray their own inherent fragility across Günderrode's *oeuvre* as well. What is discursively and indeed consistently articulated in Günderrode is what the endpoint of the historical and metaphysical teleology might be — and how the agency of the individual necessarily aligns with the development of the whole. The problem in *Empedokles* is one of potentiality, of how Empedokles can pass on, indeed generalise, his revelation so that all can be receptive to divine nature:

> Es sprechen, wenn ich ferne bin, statt meiner
> Des Himmels Blumen, blühendes Gestirn
> Und die der Erde tausendfach entkeimen,
> Die göttlichgegenwärtige Natur
> Bedarf der Rede nicht; und nimmer läßt
> Sie einsam euch, wo Einmal sie genaht,
> Denn unauslöschlich ist der Augenblick
> Von ihr
>
> [Let others speak on my behalf when I am far away,
> The flowers of the sky, the blossoms of the stars
> And all those myriad flowers that spring forth from the earth;
> Divinely present nature
> Needs no speech; no, never will she leave you to
> Your own devices, if but once she has drawn near.
> For inextinguishable is the moment that is hers][50]

The tension here is one of articulation: once Empedokles has successfully acted as a mediator between divine nature and the people of Agrigentum, then with him perishes the need for any linguistic enunciation of the divine — the advent of which, in the play, is indefinitely deferred.

Empedokles: Between Inspiration and Melancholy

This poetic and democratic vision of free mediation between human and the divine moves Hölderlin away from the questions that concern Günderrode — where pantheism is linked to the intersection of individual agency and determinism. Both *Hyperion* and *Empedokles* share one further commonality with Günderrode's 'Mahomed': both protagonists are given over to moments of enthusiasm and

---

49 See Claudia Nitschke, 'Zwischen Fluß und Übersprung: Geschichte und Individuum in Hölderlins "Tod des Empedokles"', in *Romantische Metaphorik des Fließens: Körper, Seele, Poesie*, ed. by Walter Pape, Schriften der Internationalen Arnim-Gesellschaft, 6 (Tübingen: Niemeyer, 2012), pp. 37–53.
50 Hölderlin, *Sämtliche Werke*, IV.I, 68–69; Hölderlin, *The Death of Empedocles*, p. 93 (translation adapted).

afflatus. They are, in short, both enthusiasts or *Schwärmer*.⁵¹ The potential for renewal, regeneration, and rejuvenation encapsulated by the language of forces, of ceaseless activity, becomes complicated in the first version by Empedokles' oscillations between enthusiasm and despondency. Indeed, in accordance with the medical psychology of the eighteenth century, where melancholy and enthusiasm were understood to be intrinsically linked, Empedokles' psychological progression is marked by the recuperation from despair into renewed enthusiasm, from spiritual desolation into a fragile appreciation of divine plenitude.⁵²

Empedokles is not a *Schwärmer* in the negative sense of the word that had gained currency in the eighteenth century. Empedokles instead is a *Schwärmer* in the more neutral sense referring to an enthusiast, just as Günderrode rehabilitates the term in 'Mahomed'.⁵³ Since Empedokles is afforded prophetic insight, one of the dramatic problems of the play, alongside the question of how to motivate Empedokles' fabled death in the fires of Etna, is one of communication: how can the free-thinking Empedokles legitimise his idiosyncratic political and metaphysical insights to the community in Agrigentum? Empedokles' religion of nature challenges the legitimacy of religious and political authority, embodied by Hermokrates.⁵⁴ Yet it is Empedokles' own authority that is immediately problematised in the first version of the play. Panthea herself very much fits the mould of the *Schwärmer* with her unbridled enthusiasm for Empedokles. She provides one of the first images of Empedokles as a visionary poet-prophet:

> Er weiß es nicht. Der Unbedürftge wandelt
> In seiner eignen Welt; in leiser Götterruhe geht
> Er unter seinen Blumen, und es scheun
> Die Lüfte sich, den Glüklichen zu stören,
>   Aus sich selber wächst
> In steigendem Vergnügen die Begeisterung
> Ihm auf, bis aus der Nacht des schöpfrischen
> Entzükens, wie ein Funke, der Gedanke springt,
> Und heiter sich die Geister künftger Thaten
> In seiner Seele drängen, und die Welt,
> Der Menschen gährend Leben und die größre
> Natur um ihn erscheint — hier fühlt er, wie ein Gott
> In seinen Elementen sich, und seine Lust
> Ist himmlischer Gesang, dann tritt er auch
> Heraus ins Volk

---

51   Alabanda mocks Hyperion by calling him a *Schwärmer*: Hölderlin, *Sämtliche Werke*, III, 32.

52   Schings, *Melancholie und Aufklärung*, p. 67. *Hyperion*, too, stages these shifts between enthusiasm and melancholy, to the extent that it has even been suggested to be a 'Melancholie-Roman' [novel of or about melancholy]: see Ulrich Port, *'Die Schönheit der Natur erbeuten': Problemgeschichtliche Untersuchungen zum ästhetischen Modell von Hölderlins* Hyperion, Epistemata: Reihe Literaturwissenschaft, 194 (Würzburg: Königshausen & Neumann, 1996), p. 304.

53   On Empedokles as a *Schwärmer*, see Martín Rodríguez Baigorria, 'Hölderlin und die Sattelzeit: Enthusiastische Rhetorik und geschichtliche Beschleunigung', *Archiv für Begriffsgeschichte*, 57 (2015), 145–74.

54   Karin Schutjer, *Narrating Community after Kant: Schiller, Goethe, and Hölderlin* (Detroit: Wayne State University Press, 2001), pp. 163–207.

> [He doesn't know. He needs nothing, traverses
> His own world; reposing gently like a god
> He walks among his flowers; the very breeze
> Forbears disturbing this most fortunate one,
> and from out of himself there waxes
> In ever-enhancing enjoyment an enthusiasm
> Within, until from the night of his creative rapture
> The thought, like a spark, leaps,
> And cheerfully the spirit of deeds that are
> To come crowd his soul, and the world,
> The leavening life of humankind, and the larger
> Natural world about him radiate — here he feels like
> A god within his element; his joy intones
> A canticle of heaven; he then steps forth
> To face his people][55]

This characterisation contains *in nuce* the dramatic problem that animates the first version of the play — Empedokles' false self-elevation. Panthea suggests Empedokles' visions are contained within the self. The enjambement of the lines generates a rising cadence that anticipates the fulfilment of the revelatory moment ('Aus sich selber wächst | In steigendem Vergnügen die Begeisterung | Ihm auf'). Panthea perceives Empedokles not to be a conduit of the divine but instead deifies him. This opens up the problem of authority inherent in a figure mediating between the earthly and the divine, but it is different in quality from the displacement of Mahomed's agency and self-interest in 'Mahomed, der Prophet von Mekka'. Instead, Empedokles suffers from an excess of self-interest. In particular, the suggestion of transgression in 'hier fühlt er, wie ein Gott' [here he feels like a god] echoes the Frankfurt plan and intimates Empedokles' possession or at least command over all things, paratactically linking the world, nature, and the sphere of human political activity.[56] Set against the image of Empedokles's godlike authority, Panthea equally emphasises the respect and reciprocity between Empedokles and nature. This takes place specifically the botanical world, and stages how nature discloses itself to him:

> ihn zieht in seine Schatten
> Die stille Pflanzenwelt, wo er sich schöner findet,
> Und ihr geheimnißvolles Leben, das vor ihm
> In seinen Kräften allen gegenwärtig ist.
>
> [into its shade the silent plant world
> Will draw him, where he finds himself more readily,
> And its enigmatic life is present to him
> In all its multifarious force.][57]

The serenity of such metaphysical vitality is contrasted with Empedokles' spiritual

---

55 Hölderlin, *Sämtliche Werke*, IV.I, 5–6; Hölderlin, *The Death of Empedocles*, p. 40.
56 Metaphors of fermentation, that is, 'gährend' and its cognates, are Hölderlin's terms for referring to the intense political instability in France and German-speaking lands in the mid- to late-1790s: see Günter Mieth, *Friedrich Hölderlin: Dichter der bürgerlich-demokratischen Revolution* (Würzburg: Königshausen & Neumann, 2001), pp. 44–50.
57 Hölderlin, *Sämtliche Werke*, IV.I, 6; Hölderlin, *The Death of Empedocles*, p. 40.

crisis, his self-incurred sin of Promethean overreaching and hubris when he declares himself a god.[58] Whilst Hölderlin makes dramatic use of the slippage from enthusiasm into melancholy, Empedokles' spiritual despair represents the blockage of precisely those vital forces to which he had previously had access. In the spirit of the textual logic of the first version, Hermokrates notes the problem of Empedokles' false self-aggrandisement:

> Weil er des Unterschieds zu sehr vergaß
> Im übergroßen Glük, und sich allein
> Nur fühlte; so ergieng es ihm, er ist
> Mit gränzenloser Oede nun gestraft
>
> [Because he proved forgetful of the difference
> In his extravagant delight, feeling for
> Himself alone; so it went with him, he is
> Now punished, in arid wastes abandoned][59]

The language — or indeed the metaphorical landscape of despondency — is adopted by Empedokles himself, referring to his 'stumme todesöde Brust' [mute breast, desolate as death].[60] Wastelands and deserts had been standard topoi in melancholic landscapes from at least the seventeenth century onward.[61] In a moment of urgent apostrophe, Empedokles refers to the binary of vital flows of water to quell his spiritual desiccation:

> in mir
> In mir, ihr Quellen des Lebens, strömet ihr einst
> Aus Tiefen der Welt zusammen und es kamen
> Die Dürstenden zu mir — vertroknet bin
> Ich nun, und nimmer freun die Sterblichen
> Sich meiner —
>
> [in me
> In me, you founts of life, you once flowed all
> Together from the world's depths;
> The parched ones then came to me — desiccated now
> Am I, no more do mortals take their joy
> In me][62]

In accordance with the medical psychology of the period, it is only fitting that,

---

58 Such parallels to Prometheus are worked out in the opening of the second version of the play, when Hermokrates speaks of Empedokles: 'Sie dankens ihm, | Daß er vom Himmel raubt | Die Lebensflamm' und sie | Verräth den Sterblichen' [They thank him | For having robbed the sky of | The flame of life, | Betraying it to mortals], Hölderlin, *Sämtliche Werke*, IV.1, p. 92; Hölderlin, *The Death of Empedocles*, p. 115.
59 Hölderlin, *Sämtliche Werke*, IV.1, 11; Hölderlin, *The Death of Empedocles*, p. 45.
60 Hölderlin, *Sämtliche Werke*, IV.1, 18; Hölderlin, *The Death of Empedocles*, p. 51 (translation adapted).
61 Helen Watanabe O'Kelly, *Melancholie und die melancholische Landschaft: Ein Beitrag zur Geistesgeschichte des 17. Jahrhunderts*, Basler Studien zur deutschen Sprache und Literatur, 54 (Bern: Francke, 1978), pp. 80–84.
62 Hölderlin, *Sämtliche Werke*, IV.1, 14; Hölderlin, *The Death of Empedocles*, pp. 47–48 (translation adapted).

therefore, the solution to Empedokles' melancholy is a water cure, where his intense suffering and enervation are alleviated through the ritualized act of imbibing water. This naturalised form of communion ('Nim | Dein Trinkgefäß, die hohle Kürbis, daß der Trank | Die Seele mir erfrische' [Take | Your drinking vessel, the hollow gourd, and fetch a draft | To freshen my parched soul])[63] elevates Empedokles' spirit, but to an almost terrible sublimity.

Beyond these shifts between the language of desiccation and vitality, Empedokles' sin itself implicitly points to the tensions in a vitalised understanding of divinised nature, since he assumes that his absorption of divine forces is tantamount to possessing them. It is a problem of titanic egotism, one that has been associated with the spectre or caricature of a Fichtean ego.[64] The play is not analytical and does not directly reconstruct the psychological motivation for his fall from a state of grace into self-imposed isolation. Empedokles' hubris itself is a product of a crude misunderstanding. He believes the plenitude of the self to be superior to divine, generative forces in nature. By differentiating himself from them, he objectifies nature through an artificial act of self-elevation. Far from the solace provided by the fleeting appreciation of pantheistic plenitude in *Hyperion*, Empedokles's pantheistic understanding of how the individual is grounded in nature tips instead into solipsistic nihilism and atheism.[65] Empedokles' forgetting of his status as a mediator or *daimon* leads to his sin. Instead of engaging in the self-emptying of the true enthusiast (as implied in the etymology of the word), he presumes to mastery of nature. The relationship between humankind and nature should instead be based on mutual reciprocity and respect. Empedokles' visionary gift is based on the love granted to him by divine forces:[66]

> Verachtet hab' ich dich und mich allein
> Zum Herrn gesetzt, ein übermüthiger
> Barbar! an eurer Einfalt hielt ich euch,
> Ihr reinen immerjugendlichen Mächte!
> Die mich mit Freud erzogen, mich mit Wonne genährt
> Und weil ihr immergleich mir wiederkehrtet,
> Ihr Guten, ehrt' ich eure Seele nicht!
> Ich kannt' es ja, ich hatt' es ausgelernt,
> Das Leben der Natur, wie sollt' es mir
> Noch heilig seyn, wie einst! Die Götter waren
> Mir dienstbar nun geworden, ich allein
> War Gott, und sprachs im frechen Stolz heraus.
>
> [I spurned you, declared myself alone

---

63 Hölderlin, *Sämtliche Werke*, IV.I, 51; Hölderlin, *The Death of Empedocles*, p. 78 (translation adapted).
64 Constantine, *Hölderlin*, p. 145; see also Michael Allen Gillespie, *Nihilism before Nietzsche* (Chicago: University of Chicago, 1995), p. 80.
65 Prior to the re-evaluation and valorisation of Spinoza's system from the 1780s onward, pantheism had long had polemical associations with nihilism and atheism: see Zammito, 'Herder, Kant, Spinoza', p. 113.
66 Mark Ogden, *The Problem of Christ in the Work of Friedrich Hölderlin*, Bithell Series of Dissertations, 16 (London: Modern Humanities Research Association, 1991), pp. 96–97.

> Your lord and master, arrogant
> Barbarian that I am! I held you fast to your simplicity,
> You pure powers, ever youthful!
> And you who raised me joyously, and with delight
> Did nourish me, you who always came back
> To me, you good ones, I did not respect your soul!
> Oh, yes, I knew it all, had fully learned
> The life of nature; how should it have
> Remained as sacred as it once was; the gods had
> Become mere menials to me, I alone
> Was god, and spoke it out in haughty insolence][67]

The justification for Empedokles' blasphemy stems in part from the problem of privileged knowledge, that intimacy with the operations of nature leads to the loss of its revered status ('Ich kannt' es ja, ich hatt' es ausgelernt, | Das Leben der Natur, wie sollt' es mir | Noch heilig seyn, wie einst!'). Whilst Empedokles recovers from his atheism and nihilism over the course of the first version — where self-abasement is the necessary consequence of the proclamation of Empedokles' unbridled agency as a god — these very tensions point to the problem of his character. Empedokles functions as an exemplar of how an individual should relate to nature, which is founded on an ethic of reciprocity and respect rather than domination and control.

'Vater Aether': The Metaphysics of Breath from *pneuma* to *logos*

Whereas Empedokles' self-incurred spiritual crisis results in a blockage of precisely those forces which accord him with special insight, there is another element of mediation in the play that is worth attending to. Central to Empedokles' role as a mediator and *daimon* is the question of articulating the divine. The gods themselves are silent and dependent on a human mediator to provide divine revelation that is unsullied by human interest.[68] The highest of the divine forces is 'Vater Aether' [Father Ether].[69] Ether permeates and operates on the boundary between the physiological and the metaphysical.[70] The recourse throughout *Der Tod des*

---

67 Hölderlin, *Sämtliche Werke*, IV.1, 20–21; Hölderlin, *The Death of Empedocles*, p. 53.
68 As Empedokles details: 'Es offenbart die göttliche Natur | Sich göttlich oft durch Menschen, so erkennt | Das vielversuchende Geschlecht sie wieder. | Doch hat der Sterbliche, dem sie das Herz | Mit ihrer Wonne füllte, sie verkündet, | O laßt sie dann zerbrechen das Gefäß, | Damit es nicht zu andrem Brauche dien', | Und Göttliches zum Menschenwerke werde' [Divine as nature is, she oft reveals herself | Divinely through humanity, and only thus does | Our ever-probing race come to know of her again. | This mortal, he whose heart she's filled with sheer | Delight, has faithfully announced her; | Oh, let her now destroy the vessel so | That it may never serve some other use | And turn divinity into mere human work], in Hölderlin, *Sämtliche Werke*, IV.1, 73; Hölderlin, *The Death of Empedocles*, pp. 96–97.
69 Hölderlin, *Sämtliche Werke*, IV.1, 18; 44; 107.
70 See Hölderlin's hymn 'An den Aether', as well Jochen Schmidt's notes on the importance of *pneuma* for Hölderlin, tracing the sources to Cicero, to the notion of *pneuma* as a world-soul, and to Stoicism: Friedrich Hölderlin, *Sämtliche Werke und Briefe*, ed. by Jochen Schmidt, 3 vols (Frankfurt a.M.: Deutscher Klassiker Verlag, 1992–94), I: *Sämtliche Gedichte*, pp. 598–600.

Empedokles to ether as the primal, vital force,[71] as the ensouling breath of *pneuma*, brings into focus the problem of how to think of the divine or God in Hölderlin. The term 'Aether' functioned as a solution for Hölderlin until 1801.[72]

The metaphysics of breath has a long genealogy, going back to the Presocratic philosophers. In the eighteenth century it had rich associations, where the equation of *pneuma* and Latin *spiritus* allowed for *pneuma* to be linked to poetic inspiration, to *logos*.[73] It is precisely this linkage which can be traced throughout *Der Tod des Empedokles*. It runs in parallel with Günderrode's own transfiguration of *pneuma* into *logos* in the poem 'Die Töne' [The Sounds] (1802–03), which concerns the creative flow of sonic energies. Individual sounds long to be released from their material bonds (and silence) — longing to become *pneuma* or 'Lebensodem' [breath of life] (*SW* I, 380, l. 2). Upon their liberation, they resonate through 'der Nachtigallen Brust' [the nightingales' breast] (ibid., l. 14) — a proxy for poetic activity — until settled within individuals, 'unterm Herzen' [beneath the heart] (ibid., l. 19).

For Hölderlin, however, the move from *pneuma* into *logos* is altogether more metaphysical than in Günderrode. One of the first invocations of 'Aether' by Empedokles is in a moment of lyrical plenitude. Ether is the source of the ceaseless generative activity of other forces in nature:

> Ihr wuchst indessen fort und täglich tränkte
> Des Himmels Quelle die Bescheidenen
> Mit Licht und Lebensfunken säte
> Befruchtend auf die Blühenden der Aether.
> O innige Natur!
>
> [You grew so steadily and daily drank
> From heaven's source, you humble ones
> With light and sparks of life well sated,
> The ether pollinating all your blossoms.
> O intimate nature!][74]

For humans, too, Empedokles frames air as the ensouling, enlivening, and nurturing force, one that is ever rejuvenating, through the individual's residual memory of primal immersion:

> o Luft,
> Luft, die den Neugeborenen umfängt,
> Wenn droben er die neuen Pfade wandelt,
> Dich ahnd' ich, wie der Schiffer, wenn er nah
> Dem Blüthenwald der Mutterinsel kömt,

---

[71] Jürgen Link, *Hölderlins Fluchtlinie Griechenland* (Göttingen: Vandenhoeck & Ruprecht, 2020), p. 152.

[72] After which semi-divine medial figures (Dionysus, Christ) become important in the poetry. See Wolfgang Binder, *Friedrich Hölderlin: Studien* (Frankfurt a.M.: Suhrkamp, 1987), pp. 115–16.

[73] K. F. Hilliard, 'Atemübungen: Geist und Körper in der Lyrik des 18. Jahrhunderts', in *Body Dialectics in the Age of Goethe*, ed. Marianne Henn and Holger A. Pausch, Amsterdamer Beiträge zur neueren Germanistik, 55 (Amsterdam: Rodopi, 2003), pp. 293–313 (pp. 296–97).

[74] Hölderlin, *Sämtliche Werke* IV.I, 14; see also pp. 101–02 for the equivalent in the second version; Hölderlin, *The Death of Empedocles*, p. 47.

> Schon athmet liebender die Brust ihm auf
> Und sein gealtert Angesicht verklärt
> Erinnerung der ersten Wonne wieder!
>
> [O air!
> You, air, embrace this newborn
> When upward he traverses unseen paths;
> I catch your scent as does the mariner who nears
> The forest blossoms of the mother isle,
> A memory transfigures now his weathered face,
> Remembering his first delights once more!][75]

It is in the Etna speech, where he adopts a similar patterning of lyrical intensity, that Empedokles' ecstatic invocation of 'Aether' shifts from *pneuma* to *logos*. Indeed, Empedokles makes the causal link between *pneuma* and *logos* explicit after his reconciliation with the people of Agrigentum:

> In heiteren Nächten oft, wenn über mir
> Die schöne Welt sich öffnet, und die heilge Luft
> Mit ihren Sternen allen als ein Geist
> Voll freudiger Gedanken mich umfieng,
> Da wurd es oft lebendiger in mir;
> Mit Tagesanbruch dacht' ich euch das Wort,
> Das ernste langverhaltene, zu sagen.
>
> [In brilliant nights, when overhead the universe
> Disclosed itself, and when the holy air
> Of night, with all its stars, as one spirit
> Surrounded me with joyous thoughts, then
> I often felt in me a burgeoning vitality;
> At break of day I found the words
> To tell you, earnest words, long held back.][76]

Empedokles' inspiration translates into the intoxicating rhetoric of his farewell speech to the people of Agrigentum. A renewed appreciation of divine nature should lead, Empedokles suggests, to a democratization of the daimonic and to political and social renewal:

> Wenn dann der Geist sich an des Himmels Licht
> Entzündet, süßer Lebensothem euch
> Den Busen, wie zum erstenmale tränkt,
> Und goldner Früchte voll die Wälder rauschen
> Und Quellen aus dem Fels, wenn euch das Leben
> Der Welt ergreift, ihr Friedensgeist, und euchs
> Wie heilger Wiegensang die Seele stillet,
> Dann aus der Wonne schöner Dämmerung
> Der Erde Grün von neuem euch erglänzt
> Und Berg und Meer und Wolken und Gestirn,
> Die edeln Kräfte, Heldenbrüdern gleich,

---

75 Hölderlin, *Sämtliche Werke*, IV.I, 74; Hölderlin, *The Death of Empedocles*, pp. 97–98 (translation adapted).
76 Hölderlin, *Sämtliche Werke*, IV.I, 64; Hölderlin, *The Death of Empedocles*, p. 89.

> Vor euer Auge kommen, daß die Brust
> Wie Waffenträgern euch nach Thaten klopft
>
> [And then your spirit will take flame from
> The light of heaven, sweet breath of life
> Will then suffuse your breast anew,
> And forests full of golden fruits will sway beneath
> The wind, and springs will jet from rocks, when
> The world's life, her spirit of peace, embraces you;
> She'll nurse your soul and calm you with a blessed lullaby;
> And from the beautiful twilight of delight
> The green of earth will glisten once again
> And mountains, seas, clouds and stars,
> The noble forces, all heroic brothers bound to you,
> Will then appear before your eyes, that like a warrior
> Your breast will clamour mightily for deeds][77]

Here, the all-encompassing experience of nature assumes a normative function, and will, Empedokles intimates, lead to political and social renewal.[78] What is encapsulated by this instance of naming *pneuma* as 'Lebensothem' is how pantheism can be reconfigured as the metaphysics that can give rise to revolution. It is not therefore not merely the metaphysics that happens to complement the ideals that were associated with the French Revolution. In the context of *Der Tod des Empedokles*, this suggestion of renewal remains necessarily proleptic. Empedokles as the visionary orator enacts the force of *poiesis*, bringing into being revolutionary potential. Its realisation is left tantalisingly open. Here Hölderlin comes close to the connection between poetic or metaphysical vitalism and revolutionary agency that is embedded in Günderrode's 'Mahomed', but shorn of Günderrode's teleology and determinism.

Novalis: Making Sense of Nature

At first glance, Günderrode would appear to be most closely aligned with Novalis: she was sufficiently drawn to his work that she wrote a sonnet dedicated to him in the *Nachlass* (*SW* I, 391). In later generations they were both turned into icons of otherworldliness.[79] The lines of connection between Novalis and the legacy of the pantheism controversy are surprisingly more diffuse when compared with Hölderlin. This is in part a product of traditions in philosophical scholarship. Novalis is positioned in the development of Idealist and Romantic philosophy and specifically in his responses to Kant, most famously to Fichte, and to the second edition of Jacobi's *Über die Lehre des Spinoza* [On the Teachings of Spinoza]

---

77 Hölderlin, *Sämtliche Werke*, IV.1, 65–66; Hölderlin, *The Death of Empedocles*, pp. 90–91 (translation adapted).
78 Joachim von der Thüsen, '"Vater Ätna": Vulkan und Geschichte in Hölderlins Empedokles', in *Poesie als Auftrag: Festschrift für Alexander von Bormann*, ed. by Dagmar Ottmann and Markus Symmank (Würzburg: Königshausen & Neumann, 2001) pp. 93–102 (p. 97).
79 William Arctander O'Brien, *Novalis: Signs of a Revolution* (Durham, NC: Duke University Press, 1995), pp. 11–26; Rauchenbacher, pp. 55–67.

(1785; second edition: 1789).[80] Whilst there is a tendency to write Novalis into a narrative of Romantic enthusiasm for Spinoza, this is in the limited sense of how Spinoza's realism or naturalism was perceived to be useful for critically exceeding Fichte's idealism, indeed as an anti-Fichte.[81] Precisely how Novalis responded to Spinoza's naturalism remains an open question.[82] Equally, Novalis's use of the term 'pantheism' in both the *Vermischte Bemerkungen* [Assorted Comments] and its published version, 'Blüthenstaub', is consciously idiosyncratic and rooted in a discussion of what constitutes an adequate religious mediator.[83]

Alongside the elastic use of terminology and the fragmentary and non-systematising nature of Novalis's *oeuvre*, there is a particular difficulty that emerges when unpicking Novalis's metaphysical commitments. To speak anachronistically: the issue lies in his interdisciplinarity, where he modulates between philosophical, poetic, scientific, and mathematical vocabularies and formulae. This manifests itself in particular in the unfinished notebooks *Das allgemeine Brouillon* [The General Brouillon] (1798–99), which synthesises knowledge from a variety of fields, as well as in the *Fragmente und Studien* [Fragments and Studies] (1799–1800). For example, the term 'Leben' does not carry metaphysical weight in these notebooks, as it does for Hölderlin and Günderrode, but instead draws on debates about the origins of natural beings, the laws of nature, and organic forces at the turn of the nineteenth century.[84] Whilst it is in part understood philosophically, Novalis deploys it as a vitalist term and it is grounded in his critical studies of science, in particular physiology and the medical theories of John Brown (especially the notion of excitability).[85] Life is 'Kraftäußerung — mithin Produkt entgegengesetzter Factoren' [an expression of force — therefore the product of opposing factors].[86] The idea that processes of life are an expression of an indeterminate force is part and parcel of scientific vitalism of the late eighteenth century.[87] In a closing section

---

80 Ludwig Stockinger, '"Die Poesie heilt die Wunden, die der Verstand schlägt": Novalis' Poesiebegriff im begriffs- und literaturgeschichtlichen Kontext', in *Novalis: Poesie und Politik*, ed. by Herbert Uerlings (Tübingen: Niemeyer, 2004), pp. 63–79 (p. 66).

81 See, for example, Michael Mack, 'Spinoza and Romanticism', in *The Palgrave Handbook of German Romantic Philosophy*, ed. by Elizabeth Millán Brusslan (Cham: Palgrave Macmillan, 2020), pp. 65–94 (pp. 86–88); Beiser, *German Idealism*, p. 419.

82 See Jane Kneller, 'Novalis' nüchterne Rezeption der spinozistischen "Gott-Trunkenheit"', in *Affektenlehre und amor dei intellectualis: Die Rezeption Spinozas im deutschen Idealismus*, ed. by Violetta Waibel (Hamburg: Meiner, 2012), pp. 62–76. On Novalis and Spinozan materialism, see Siarhei Biareishyk, 'Rethinking Romanticism with Spinoza: Encounter and Individuation in Novalis, Ritter, and Baader', *The Germanic Review*, 94.4 (2019), 271–98.

83 Novalis, *Schriften*, II, 440–42.

84 For Novalis's use of the language of vitalism as part of these philosophical and scientific debates, see Gabriele Rommel, 'Friedrich von Hardenberg (Novalis) — Gedanken über "die inner *chiffrirende* Kraft. Spuren derselben in der *Natur*"', in *Physik um 1800 — Kunst, Wissenschaft oder Philosophie?*, ed. by Olaf Breidbach and Roswitha Burwick, Laboratorium Aufklärung, 5 (Munich: Fink, 2012), pp. 67–102.

85 For a detailed account of Novalis's reception of Brunonian medicine and its relation to his responses to Fichte, see John Neubauer, 'Dr. John Brown (1735–88) and Early German Romanticism', *Journal of the History of Ideas*, 28.3 (1967), 367–82.

86 Novalis, *Schriften*, III: *Das philosophische Werk II*, ed. by Richard Samuel (1983), p. 660.

87 See Jessica Riskin, *The Restless Clock: A History of the Centuries-Long Argument of What Makes*

of *Das Allgemeine Brouillon*, Novalis refers to the functions of life interchangeably as irritability, as 'Erregbarkeit' or 'Reitzbarkeit', or as sensibility ('Sensibilitaet'), terminology which is indebted to the influential physiology of Albrecht von Haller.[88] Novalis pushes this vitalism further in a note that elevates oxygen — first discovered by Joseph Priestley in 1771 — to the organising principle of natural processes: 'Alle Naturkräfte sind nur Eine Kraft. Das Leben der ganzen Natur ist ein Oxyd[ations] Process' [All forces of nature are only one force. The life of the whole of nature is an oxidation process].[89] Novalis, then, was engaged in the lively scientific debates of the time about how to explain processes of organisation, generation, and their origins.

Despite these differences between Novalis and Günderrode, there are productive overlaps in their metaphysical commitments. Indeed, there are commonalities between Hölderlin, Novalis, and Günderrode in their shared monism. What fundamentally links Günderrode and Novalis is a question of epistemology: how — and by what sensory or other means — can knowledge and metaphysical knowledge be generated, if at all? Traces of Spinozism and pantheism, too, are found in Novalis in the context of questions of religious mediation, cognition, and the articulation of divine revelation.[90] Novalis famously declared Spinoza to be a 'gotttrunkener Mensch' [God-intoxicated man].[91] There is also a genealogical connection between the language of Idealism and Romantic reworkings of the Spinozist slogan *hen kai pan*.[92] Novalis's *Fichte-Studien* are also concerned with the question of how consciousness can be connected to the pre-conscious, or to the ground of being.[93] This is a question that Hölderlin addresses in the short essay 'Urtheil und Seyn' [Judgment and Being] (1795). In these texts, Hölderlin and Novalis were critically thinking through the legacy of Fichtean idealism.[94] This lineage of these epistemological questions is, as I have shown (pp. 126–30), more Kantian in Günderrode, although she too makes recourse to an idea of a ground of being. Whilst Novalis and Hölderlin are concerned with the status of the self and self-consciousness, what differentiates Günderrode from them is how self-consciousness is not a concern in her work.[95] Rather, her interests are altogether more epistemological. They concern the act of writing the individual back into a primordial sense of being, which is coterminous with divinised nature.

There have been allusions in the preceding chapters to other points of connection

Living Things Tick (Chicago: University of Chicago Press, 2016); Reill, *Vitalizing Nature in the Enlightenment*, p. 9.
88   Novalis, *Schriften*, III, 324–25: Novalis adapts Haller for his own interpretation of physiology: see Lothar Pikulik, *Frühromantik: Epoche — Werke — Wirkung*, 2nd edn (Munich: Beck, 2000), pp. 256–57.
89   Novalis, *Schriften*, III, 659; see also Maria Tatar, *Spellbound: Studies on Mesmerism and Literature* (Princeton: Princeton University Press, 1971), pp. 70–71.
90   Auerochs, *Die Entstehung der Kunstreligion*, pp. 465–66.
91   Novalis, *Schriften*, III, 651.
92   Timm, *Die heilige Revolution*, p. 78.
93   Frank, *Unendliche Annäherung*, p. 802.
94   Bowie, *Aesthetics and Subjectivity*, pp. 82–101.
95   As Anna Ezekiel has rightly noted: Günderrode, *Poetic Fragments*, pp. 146–49.

between Günderrode and Novalis, such as reminiscences of the structure of *Erinnerung* [remembrance] und *Ahnung* [anticipation]. Both studied — although in Novalis's case, more extensively — the Platonist philosophy of Frans Hemsterhuis.[96] To be sure, Novalis shares with Günderrode an attraction to both Platonist and Neoplatonist thought. He wrote approvingly on Plotinus when compared to Fichte.[97] There are also productive parallels between 'Briefe zweier Freunde' and Novalis's *Die Christenheit oder Europa*. Both diagnose the sickness of the present age and both deplore the rise of Protestantism, which resulted, they claim, in the suppression of a unified revelation and religious community.[98] Novalis's turn towards an aestheticised Catholicism allows for transcendent moments of perception in phenomenal reality.[99]

Equally, both privilege the poet as being accorded with special access to higher truths, and stage death as ecstatic revelation (in *Hymnen an die Nacht* [Hymns to the Night] and 'Ein apokaliptisches Fragment' respectively). The elevation of the poet finds expression most concisely in Novalis's fragmentary poem 'Wenn nicht mehr Zahlen und Figuren', as well as the salvatory function of the allegorical figure of poetry, Fabel, in the 'Klingsohrs Märchen' from *Heinrich von Ofterdingen*. This complements Günderrode's prophetic and rhetorically gifted interpretation of Muhammad and the invocation of *Kunstreligion*, even a religion of poetry, in 'Der Dom zu Cölln'.

Before turning to a discussion of Novalis's use of Spinozism and pantheism, it is worth considering how his first, fragmentary attempt at writing a novel, *Die Lehrlinge zu Sais*, stands alongside Günderrode's works. Here there are thematic similarities between Novalis and Günderrode. Günderrode also makes use of the Saïs motif, and indeed 'Der Franke in Egypten' stands alongside the inset *Märchen* in *Die Lehrlinge zu Sais*. Both promote the notion that self-knowledge and self-development can only occur through seeing oneself through the love of another. Novalis, too, was working through his study of Schelling's early writings on the philosophy of nature, specifically the *Ideen zu einer Philosophie der Natur* [Ideas for a Philosophy of Nature] (1797) — although the spectre of Fichte is present as well in the text.[100]

In *Die Lehrlinge zu Sais*, Novalis is fundamentally interested in exploring the identity of nature and the self and their interrelation — one of Günderrode's most common themes — but how this is approached is more formally experimental than in Günderrode.[101] Exploring the problem of modern subjectivity results, in Novalis,

---

96 Novalis, *Schriften*, II, 360–78.
97 Hampton, *Romanticism and the Re-invention of Modern Religion*, pp. 199–201.
98 See Alison Stone, 'Being, Knowledge, and Nature in Novalis', *Journal of the History of Philosophy*, 16.1 (2008), 141–64; also: Novalis, *Schriften*, III, 511.
99 Stefan Matuschek, *Der gedichtete Himmel: Eine Geschichte der Romantik* (Munich: Beck, 2021), pp. 148–99. The notion of transcendent perception in phenomenal reality is not dissimilar to Schleiermacher's *Reden über die Religion*, as discussed at the close of Chapter 5.
100 John Neubauer, *Bifocal Vision: Novalis' Philosophy of Nature and Disease* (Chapel Hill: University of North Carolina Press, 1971), pp. 116–17. Novalis, *Schriften*, I: *Das dichterische Werk*, ed. by Paul Kluckhohn and Richard Samuel (1977), p. 90.
101 Jürgen Daiber, *Experimentalphysik des Geistes: Novalis und das romantische Experiment* (Göttingen: Vandenhoeck & Ruprecht, 2001), p. 170.

in a polyphonic narrative structure, which is akin to the *Symphilosophie* [collaborative philosophy] and *Sympoesie* [collaborative creation of poetry or poesy] proclaimed in the pages of the *Athenaeum*.[102] This polyphony of voices is complemented by a kaleidoscopic perspective on overlapping philosophies of nature. Both express an awareness of how diffuse the concept of nature is.[103] Where in Günderrode there is a tendency towards relatively linear narrative structures, the irresolutions and shifts of narrative voice — from singular to plural, from first-person to third-person — in *Die Lehrlinge zu Sais* mean that the text depends on the active engagement of the reader to make sense of it.[104] In precisely this spirit, the aim here is to draw out points of connection between Novalis and Günderrode, rather than offering an overarching reading of the dense texture of *Die Lehrlinge zu Sais*.

Where Günderrode and Hölderlin are concerned with the problem of how to articulate a metaphysical or divine revelation, in 'Mahomed' and *Empedokles* respectively, Novalis instead asks how it is possible to discern the language of nature. In the opening paragraph, he invokes the trope of the book of nature, only for the legibility of its 'Hieroglyphenschrift' [hieroglyphic script] to escape cognition, and to escape becoming fixed in language:

> In ihnen [verschiedene Naturerscheinungen] ahndet man den Schlüssel dieser Wunderschrift, die Sprachlehre derselben; allein die Ahndung will sich selbst in keine feste Formen fügen, und scheint kein höherer Schlüssel werden zu wollen. Ein Alcahest scheint über die Sinne der Menschen ausgegossen zu seyn. Nur augenblicklich scheinen ihre Wünsche, ihre Gedanken sich zu verdichten. So entstehen ihre Ahndungen, aber nach kurzen Zeiten schwimmt alles wieder, wie vorher, vor ihren Blicken.
>
> [In them [figures of nature] we suspect a key to the magic writing, even a grammar, but our surmise takes on no definite forms and seems unwilling to become a higher key. It is as though an alkahest had been poured over the senses of man. Only at moments do their desires and thoughts seem to solidify. Thus arise their presentiments, but after a short time everything swims again before their eyes.][105]

The reader is here at a double semiotic remove from whatever the language of nature might be. Instead, the reader encounters a generalised statement about the metaphorical process of reading nature, one replete with tentative hypotheticals as well as alchemical language that focuses on the limitations of sensory mediation —

---

102 Philipp Weber, 'Romantisches Üben: *Die Lehrlinge zu Sais* von Novalis', in *Verkörperungen des Kollektiven: Wechselwirkungen von Literatur und Bildungsdiskursen seit dem 18. Jahrhundert*, ed. by Anna Dabrowska and others (Bielefeld: transcript, 2019), pp. 63–85 (p. 71); Theodore Ziolkowski, *German Romanticism and its Institutions* (Princeton: Princeton University Press, 1990), p. 259.
103 Andreas Kubik, *Die Symboltheorie bei Novalis: Eine ideengeschichtliche Studie in ästhetischer und theologischer Absicht* (Tübingen: Mohr Siebeck, 2006), pp. 207–08.
104 Herbert Uerlings, *Novalis* (Stuttgart: Reclam, 1998), pp. 164–66. This participatory role of the reader is also a feature of early Romanticism in general: see May Mergenthaler, *Zwischen Eros und Mitteilung: Die Frühromantik im Symposium der* Athenaeums-*Fragmente* (Paderborn: Schöningh, 2012), p. 16.
105 Novalis, *Schriften*, I, 79; Novalis, *The Novices of Sais*, trans. by Ralph Manheim (New York: Curt Valentin, 1949), pp. 3–5.

namely that sense-perception dissipates metaphorically through the universal solvent ('Ein Alcahest scheint über die Sinne der Menschen ausgegossen zu seyn').[106] The invocation of Saïs suggests the possibility of unveiling the hidden code — however terrible the consequences may be, such as in Schiller's 'Das verschleierte Bild zu Sais' or Günderrode's 'Der Adept'. Novalis instead suspends the possibility of a resolution: the focus is instead on how to synthesise the thoughts given by the array of speakers, particularly in the second part.[107]

In the first part, the teacher at Saïs is presented as an ideal model for how to investigate natural phenomena. This is in part grounded in the syncretic refinement of his senses:

> Oft hat er uns erzählt, wie ihm als Kind der Trieb die Sinne zu üben, zu beschäftigen und zu erfüllen, keine Ruhe ließ [...] In große bunte Bilder drängten sich die Wahrnehmungen seiner Sinne: er hörte, sah, tastete und dachte zugleich. Er freute sich, Fremdlinge zusammen zu bringen. Bald waren ihm die Sterne Menschen, bald die Menschen Sterne, die Steine Thiere, die Wolken Pflanzen, er spielte mit den Kräften und Erscheinungen, er wußte wo und wie er dies und jenes finden, und erscheinen lassen konnte

> [Often he has told us how when he was a child, the desire to practise, to busy, to fulfil his senses left him no peace. [...] The perceptions of his senses crowded into great colourful images; he heard, saw, touched and thought at once. He delighted in bringing strangers together. Sometimes the stars were men for him and sometimes men were stars, sometimes the stones were beasts, the clouds plants; he played with forces and phenomena, he knew where and how he could find this and that, or make this and that manifest itself][108]

The correspondences he finds are distinct from the petrifying Baconian mode of *dissecare naturam* or Linnaean taxonomies that are anathema to Günderrode (see 'Vorzeit, und Neue Zeit'). His method draws instead on the Hermetic tradition.[109] In the teacher's pluralistic deployment of his senses, analytical reflection also operates alongside the imagination ('In große bunte Bilder drängten sich die Wahrnehmungen seiner Sinne'). Another speaker equally highlights the importance of embodied cognition, and how it is the body that ties the individual to nature:

> Den Inbegriff dessen, was uns rührt, nennt man die Natur, und also steht die Natur in einer unmittelbaren Beziehung auf die Gliedmaßen unsers Körpers, die wir Sinne nennen. Unbekannte und geheimnißvolle Beziehungen unsers Körpers lassen unbekannte und geheimnißvolle Verhältnisse der Natur vermuthen, und so ist die Natur jene wunderbare Gemeinschaft, in die unser Körper uns einführt, und die wir nach dem Maaße seiner Einrichtungen und Fähigkeiten kennen lernen.

---

106 Jörg Paulus, *Der Enthusiast und sein Schatten: Literarische Schwärmer- und Philisterkritik im Roman um 1800*, Quellen und Forschungen zur Literatur- und Kulturgeschichte, 13 (Berlin: De Gruyter, 1998), pp. 277–78. Novalis's debt to Paracelsus and Jan Baptist van Helmont for the composition of *Die Lehrlinge zu Sais* is well known: Novalis, *Schriften*, I, 76–78.

107 Dennis F. Mahoney, 'Human History as Natural History in *The Novices of Sais* and *Heinrich von Ofterdingen*', *Historical Reflections / Réflexions Historiques*, 18.3 (1992), 111–24 (p. 114).

108 Novalis, *Schriften*, I, 79–80; Novalis, *The Novices of Sais*, pp. 7–9 (translation adapted).

109 Jeanne Riou, *Imagination in German Romanticism: Re-thinking the Self and its Environment* (Oxford: Peter Lang, 2004), pp. 100–01.

[The epitome of what stirs our feeling is called nature, hence nature stands in an immediate relation to the functions of our body that we call senses. Unknown and mysterious relations within our body cause us to surmise unknown and mysterious states in nature; nature is a community of the marvellous, into which we are initiated by our body, and which we learn to know in the measure of our body's faculties and abilities.][110]

Locating the site of knowledge in the body is a riposte to Kantian epistemology, but the analogous and porous relations between the body and nature point too to the interactions between the Paracelsan microcosm and the macrocosm.[111] This porosity between nature and the body does not mean that Novalis restricts perception to the sensible realm alone. Indeed, in 'Blüthenstaub', he advocates a delicate, extrasensory faculty that has to be held in balance with the intellect, one that would allow the individual to proceed beyond phenomenal, conditioned reality, and outside the self:

> Das willkührlichste Vorurtheil ist, daß dem Menschen das Vermögen außer sich zu seyn, mit Bewußtseyn jenseits der Sinne zu seyn, versagt sey. Der Mensch vermag in jedem Augenblick ein übersinnliches Wesen zu seyn. Ohne dies wäre er nicht Weltbürger, er wäre ein Thier. [...] Je mehr wir uns aber dieses Zustandes bewußt zu seyn vermögen, desto lebendiger, mächtiger, genügender ist die Überzeugung, die daraus entsteht; der Glaube an ächte Offenbarungen des Geistes. Es ist kein Schauen, Hören, Fühlen; es ist aus allen dreyen zusammengesetzt, mehr als alles Dreyes: eine Empfindung unmittelbarer Gewißheit, eine Ansicht meines wahrhaftesten, eigensten Lebens.
>
> [It is the most arbitrary prejudice to deny the individual the capacity to be outside oneself, and to be outside the senses in consciousness. An individual has the ability to become a supersensible being at any time. Without this, he or she would not be a world citizen, he or she would be an animal. [...] The more we are able to become aware of this state, the more lively, powerful, and forceful is the conviction that is generated by it; the belief in true revelations of the spirit. It is not a seeing, hearing, or feeling; is it composed of all three, more than all three; a sensation of immediate certainty, a vision of my truest and most singular life.][112]

Novalis is here working through a concept of extrasensory perception. Novalis suggests a metaphysics of spirit, in which the intuitions generated by this supersensible state lead back to a higher apprehension of the self, rather than beyond it.[113] What is side-stepped by the possibility of supersensible cognition is the problem of mediation through the senses, which Novalis consistently probes in the *Logologische Fragmente* [Logological Fragments] (1798). In one fragment, Novalis discusses the interpenetrating and reciprocal sensory systems of the soul and the body.[114] A longer fragment, entitled 'Von der *unsinnlichen*, oder *unmittelbaren* Erkenntnis'

---

110 Novalis, *Schriften*, I, 97; Novalis, *The Novices of Sais*, p. 77.
111 As Hartmut Böhme notes: Böhme, pp. 205–07. See also Novalis, *Schriften*, II, 594: 'Die Idee des Microcosmos. / Cosmometer sind wir ebenfalls' [The idea of the microcosm. / We are equally cosmometers].
112 Novalis, *Schriften*, II, 421.
113 Helmut Schanze, *Erfindung der Romantik* (Stuttgart: Metzler, 2018), pp. 133–34.
114 Novalis, *Schriften*, II, 546.

[On *non-sensory* or *unmediated* perception], Novalis systematically works through epistemological questions, stating that perception is always mediated as well as outlining a dialectical relationship between the self and the world.[115] The nub of the problem that *Die Lehrlinge zu Sais* and *Logologische Fragmente* address is derived from Novalis's response to Kantian and Fichtean philosophy: how to account for interactions between the body and the world, the self and the world, the subject and object, and how knowledge is gained through a dual movement of appropriation and alienation between the subject and object.[116]

What is conspicuous by its absence in Novalis is the 'innerer Sinn' or inner sense that Günderrode repeatedly turns to as a source of specifically metaphysical knowledge, and one that allows the individual to be grounded in the whole.[117] Whilst Novalis makes space for intuition in 'Blüthenstaub', he places limits on what sensory knowledge can yield. In the *Allgemeines Brouillon*, Novalis quotes Hemsterhuis's notion of a moral sense only to proceed to a metacritical analysis of 'Sinn' itself:

> Nur durch den Moralischen Sinn wird uns Gott vernehmlich [...] der Sinn fürs Ding an sich — der ächte *Divinationssinn*./ diviniren, etwas ohne Veranlassung, Berührung, vernehmen./Das Wort Sinn, das auf mittelbares Erkenntniß, *Berührung, Mischung*, hindeutet, ist hier freylich nicht recht schicklich [...] Es ist *Nichtsinn*, oder Sinn, gegen den jenes Nichtsinn ist.
>
> [It is only through the moral sense that God will become perceptible to us — [...] the sense for the thing in itself — the true sense of *divination*./ Divining, to perceive something without cause or contact./ The word 'sense' [*Sinn*] which suggests indirect knowledge, *contact*, and *combination*, is certainly not particularly apt here [...] It is a *non-sense*, or a sense, for which the latter is a non-sense.][118]

Novalis playfully invokes the notion of a sense *ex negativo*, where sense functions as a placeholder for a capacity that operates outside the conditioned or phenomenal world and allows for metaphysical knowledge. This note pulls in two directions, by setting limits on what sense perception can do, whilst also opening up the possibility of divining metaphysical knowledge and the connection to a higher, unconditioned reality.[119]

---

115 Ibid., pp. 550–52.

116 Frederick C. Beiser makes this argument in the context of *Das Allgemeine Brouillon*, but the interaction between appropriation and alienation between the subject and object is worked through in the *Logologische Fragmente* as well. This is an expansion of the Kantian-Fichtean model of knowledge that derives from appropriation alone: Beiser, *German Idealism*, pp. 431–32.

117 The term 'innerer Sinn' was used to refer to a higher form of perception, such as by the physicist Johann Wilhelm Ritter: 'Wir haben einen innern Sinn zur Welterkenntnis, der noch ganz zurück ist. Er sieht nicht, hört nicht usw. aber er *weiß* [...] Jener innere Sinn sollte wohl mehr hervorgerufen werden' [We have an inner sense for perceiving the world that is still completely undeveloped. It does not see, does not hear, etc., but it *knows* [...] This inner sense should perhaps be induced], in Johann Wilhelm Ritter, *Fragmente aus dem Nachlasse eines jungen Physikers: Ein Taschenbuch für Freunde der Natur* (Leipzig and Weimar: Gustav Kiepenheuer, 1984), p. 258.

118 Novalis, *Schriften*, III, 250; Novalis, *Notes for a Romantic Encyclopaedia: Das Allgemeine Brouillon*, trans. and ed. by David W. Wood (Albany: SUNY Press, 2007), pp. 9–10.

119 Barbara Senckel, *Individualität und Totalität: Aspekte zu einer Anthropologie bei Novalis*, Studien zur deutschen Literatur, 74 (Tübingen: Niemeyer, 1983), pp. 107–09.

This critical approach to how sense perception operates is equally present in *Die Lehrlinge zu Sais*. In the opening paragraph of the second part of the text, 'Die Natur', Novalis sketches out the problem of modern subjectivity: how the conscious naming of objects of sense perception leads to the self-imposed alienation of the individual from nature:

> Es mag lange gedauert haben, ehe die Menschen darauf dachten, die mannichfachen Gegenstände ihrer Sinne mit einem gemeinschaftlichen Namen zu bezeichnen und sich entgegen zu setzen. Durch Uebung werden Entwickelungen befördert, und in allen Entwickelungen gehn Theilungen, Zergliederungen vor, die man bequem mit den Brechungen des Lichtstrahls vergleichen kann. So hat sich auch nur allmählich unser Innres in so mannichfaltige Kräfte zerspaltet, und mit fortdauernder Uebung wird auch diese Zerspaltung zunehmen. Vielleicht ist es nur krankhafte Anlage der späteren Menschen, wenn sie das Vermögen verlieren, diese zerstreuten Farben ihres Geistes wieder zu mischen und nach Belieben den alten einfachen Naturstand herzustellen, oder neue, mannichfaltige Verbindungen unter ihnen zu bewirken.
>
> [It must have been a long time before men thought of giving a common name to the manifold objects of their senses, and of placing themselves in opposition to them. Through practice developments were furthered, and in all developments occur separations and divisions that may well be compared with the splitting of a ray of light. It was only gradually that our inwardness split into such various forces, and with continued practice this splitting will increase. Perhaps it is only the sickly predisposition of later men that makes them lose the power to mix again the scattered colours of their spirit and at will restore the old, simple, natural state, or bring about new and varied relations between the colours.][120]

A double split is outlined: between the individual and nature, but also the inner fragmentation that results from the deployment of the senses. This is quite contrary to the harmonic fusion of sense perception practised by the teacher in the first part. By dissecting the world, sense perception also dissects the self.[121] But the operation of the prismatic faculty of mind, which begins by refracting sense impressions as one would beams of light, can be reversed — although the Rousseauian ideal of a state of nature ['Naturstand'] may be irrevocably lost.[122] In suggesting the possibility of a recuperation of a more holistic state of mind, the text creates its own combinatorial poetics, shifting from the metaphors of light to language drawn from chemistry that enact the mixture of disparate elements ['diese zerstreuten Farben ihres Geistes wieder zu mischen [...] oder neue, mannichfaltige Verbindungen unter ihnen zu bewirken'].[123]

---

120 Novalis, *Schriften*, I, 82–83; Novalis, *The Novices of Sais*, pp. 19–21 (translation adapted).
121 Utz, pp. 224–25.
122 Frederick Burwick, *The Damnation of Newton: Goethe's Color Theory and Romantic Perception* (Berlin: De Gruyter, 1986), pp. 104–05.
123 Michel Chaouli has read Friedrich Schlegel's use of chemical metaphors as functioning analogously to his combinatorial and experimental poetics: see Michel Chaouli, *The Laboratory of Poetry: Chemistry and Poetics in the Work of Friedrich Schlegel* (Baltimore, MD: Johns Hopkins University Press, 2002), pp. 108–36.

Such attention to the creative possibilities of language is significant because of the position the poet occupies in the text. Novalis shares with Günderrode a tendency towards the religious elevation of the poet.[124] In Günderrode's case, this is grounded in the lyrical poet's enhanced inner sense perception (as with Mahomed). Her insight into this distinctive power is most concisely expressed in a *Nachlass* fragment: 'Herrlicher Sänger es schloß ein Gott dir die sterblichen Augen | Aber mit den Augen des Sinns siehst du die Fülle der Welt' [Wondrous singer, a god closed your mortal eyes, | But with the eyes of a higher sense you see the plenitude of the world] (*SW* I, 398).

In *Die Lehrlinge zu Sais*, Novalis emphasises the limitations of the purely analytical intellect compared to the poet's imagination:

> Naturforscher und Dichter haben durch Eine Sprache sich immer wie Ein Volk gezeigt. Was jene im Ganzen sammelten und in großen, geordneten Massen aufstellten, haben diese für menschliche Herzen zur täglichen Nahrung und Nothdurft verarbeitet, und jene unermeßliche Natur zu mannichfaltigen, kleinen, gefälligen Naturen zersplittert und gebildet. Wenn diese mehr das Flüssige und Flüchtige mit leichtem Sinn verfolgten, suchten jene mit scharfen Messerschnitten den innern Bau und die Verhältnisse der Glieder zu erforschen. Unter ihren Händen starb die freundliche Natur, und ließ nur todte, zuckende Reste zurück, dagegen sie vom Dichter, wie durch geistvollen Wein, noch mehr beseelt, die göttlichsten und muntersten Einfälle hören ließ, und über ihr Alltagsleben erhoben, zum Himmel stieg, tanzte und weißagte, jeden Gast willkommen hieß, und ihre Schätze frohen Muths verschwendete.

> [Scientists and poets have, by speaking *one* language, always shown themselves to be *one* people. What the scientists have gathered and arranged in huge, well-ordered stores, has been made by the poets into the daily food and consolation of human hearts; the poets have broken up the one, great, immeasurable nature and moulded it into various small, amenable natures. Poets have lightheartedly pursued the liquid and fugitive, while scientists have cut into the inner structure and sought after the relations between its members. Under their hands friendly nature died, leaving behind only dead, quivering remnants, while the poet inspired her like a heady wine till she uttered the blithest, most god-like fancies, till, lifted out of her everyday life, she soared to heaven, danced and prophesised, bade everyone welcome, and squandered her treasures with a happy heart.][125]

The poetic sensibility, by contrast to the that of scientist, does not dissect and thus kill the natural world, but enlivens it. By responding to nature and casting it in poetic language, nature becomes not only ennobled, ensouled, but also intoxicated — and this intoxication plays out in the ecstatic hyperbole of personified nature ['zum Himmel stieg, tanzte und weißsagte, jeden Gast willkommen hieß, und ihre Schätze frohen Muths verschwendete'].

---

124 Novalis, *Schriften*, III, 685–86. The elevation of the poet to prophet is a tendency across Romanticism: see Kate Rigby, *Reclaiming Romanticism: Towards an Ecopoetics of Decolonization* (Bloomsbury: London, 2020), pp. 113–47.
125 Novalis, *Schriften*, I, 84; Novalis, *The Novices of Sais*, pp. 25–27.

Read in response to the opening of *Die Lehrlinge zu Sais*, which questions how the language of nature can be divined, here Novalis is making a weighty claim on behalf of literature: that it is part of how nature discloses itself.[126] Indeed, it is a claim that is borne out in the text, where the aesthetic reception of the inset *Märchen* proves a stimulus for the concluding discussion. The text resists a final resolution or indeed a systematic narrative. Instead of fixity, what remains is the creative reciprocity between the individual and nature, and between the polyphony of voices and the reader.[127]

Novalis and Spinozist Metaphysics

Novalis does come close to Günderrode's metaphysical positions in a series of notes in the *Allgemeine Brouillon*, where Spinoza's philosophy is understood through the prism of Fichtean idealism:

> Es ist *einerley*, ob ich das Weltall in mich, oder mich ins Weltall setze. Spinotza sezte alles heraus — Fichte alles hinein. So mit der Freyheit. Ist Freyheit im Ganzen, so ist Freyheit auch in mir. Nenn ich die Freyheit Nothw[endigkeit], und Nothw[endigkeit] ins Ganze, so ist Noth[wendigkeit] in mir und umgek[ehrt].
>
> [It is *immaterial* whether I posit the universe within myself, or myself in the universe. Spinoza posited everything outside — Fichte everything within. So too with freedom. If freedom is within the whole, then freedom is also in me. If I call freedom necessity, and necessity is in the whole, then necessity is in me, and vice versa.][128]
>
> Fichtes Ich ist die Vernunft — Sein Gott und *Spinotzas* Gott haben große Aehnlichkeit. Gott ist die übersinnliche Welt rein — wir sind ein unreiner Theil derselben. Wir denken uns Gott persönlich, wie wir uns selbst persönlich denken.
>
> [Fichte's ego is reason — His God and *Spinoza*'s God are strikingly similar. God is the pure supersensible world — we are an impure part of it. We conceive of God personally, just as we conceive ourselves personally.][129]

The first statement draws on the conceptual fluidity of necessity and freedom in terms familiar from the pantheism controversy: that internal necessity is the freedom to act in accordance with the impulses of one's own nature. Novalis reaches this conclusion not via Herder, as Günderrode does, but by proceeding from a synthesis of Spinoza's absolute substance and the Fichtean absolute subject. This associative logic carries over to the second note, which emphasises Spinoza's rationalism but also the possibility of a perfective metaphysics ['Gott ist die übersinnliche Welt rein

---

126 Maximilian Bergengruen, 'Signatur, Hieroglyphe, Wechselrepräsentation: Zur Metaphysik der Schrift in Novalis' *Lehrlingen*', *Athenäum*, 14 (2004), 43–67 (pp. 61–62).
127 Terry Pinkard, *German Philosophy 1760–1860: The Legacy of Idealism* (Cambridge: Cambridge University Press, 2002), pp. 147–48.
128 Novalis, *Schriften*, III, 382; Novalis, *Notes for a Romantic Encyclopedia*, p. 114.
129 Novalis, *Schriften*, III, 469; Novalis, *Notes for a Romantic Encyclopedia*, p. 193.

— wir sind ein unreiner Theil derselben']. Whilst these notes demonstrate Novalis thinking through the philosophical possibilities of how to conceptualise God, he consistently holds God and nature apart.[130] In further notes on cosmology in the *Allgemeine Brouillon*, Novalis is keen to separate God from the world — indeed, in one pithy formulation, God is the perfective goal of nature, which is bound up in a narrative of its gradual spiritualisation.[131] Elsewhere, in the *Fichte-Studien*, Novalis upholds this distinction whilst also outlining a dual-aspect monism. Both nature and the individual are transcendent and immanent, albeit in a qualitatively distinct matter.[132]

These disparate notes show that Novalis touches on the issues that overlap with Günderrode's Spinozist metaphysics. His thoughts share many of the same concerns with Günderrode, but they do not coalesce into a consistent pantheism or panentheism. In a draft of the 'Astralis-Lied' [Song of Astralis] in the second part of *Heinrich von Ofterdingen*, Novalis makes use of the Spinozist slogan of *hen kai pan*. Astralis, an ethereal spirit brought forth by Heinrich and Mathilde's love, invokes the utopian transfiguration of the world into a new golden age:

> Es bricht die neue Welt herein
> Und verdunkelt den hellsten Sonnenschein[,]
> Man sieht nun aus bemooßten Trümmern
> Eine wunderseltsame Zukunft schimmern
> Und was vordem alltäglich war
> Scheint jetzo fremd und wunderbar.
> ⟨Eins in allem und alles im Einen
> Gottes Bild auf Kräutern und Steinen
> Gottes Geist in Menschen und Thieren,
> Dies muß man sich zu Gemüthe führen.
> Keine Ordnung mehr nach Raum und Zeit
> Hier Zukunft in der Vergangenheit[.]⟩
> Der Liebe Reich ist aufgethan
> Die Fabel fängt zu spinnen an.[133]

> [The new world is breaking forth
> And eclipses the brightest sunlight[.]
> Now you can see gleaming from
> The moss-grown ruins a wondrous and strange future
> And what before was commonplace
> Seems now to be strange and wonderful.
> One in all and all in one
> God's image on herbs and stones,
> God's spirit in humans and animals,
> To this we must take heed.

---

130 Novalis's concept of God is flexible, as Frederick C. Beiser details: Beiser, *German Idealism*, p. 410.
131 Novalis, *Schriften*, III, 250. Heinrich Schipperges, 'Der Mensch — Ein Kosmometer: Präludium einer Anthropologie bei Novalis', in *Esotérisme, gnoses et imaginaire symbolique: mélanges offerts à Antoine Faivre*, ed. by Richard Caron and others, Gnostica, 3 (Leuven: Peeters, 2001), pp. 325–35 (p. 332).
132 Novalis, *Schriften*, II, 157.
133 The angled brackets indicate a crossing out in the manuscript.

No more order according to space and time,
Here future in the past[.]
The kingdom of love has been revealed;
Fable begins to spin at her wheel.]¹³⁴

This synthesising vision invokes a trans-spatial and transtemporal unity and moves close to Jacob Böhme's theosophy.¹³⁵ It also has linguistic parallels with, and thus responds to, the dream of the blue flower that opens the novel.¹³⁶ Astralis' proclamation of the perfect reciprocity of spiritualised nature ['Eins in allem und alles im Einen'] is only extant as a section that had been struck out in the manuscript. It is nonetheless revealing about the metaphysical implications of the new world, since it highlights different levels of divine revelation. In an indirect response to the opening conundrum of *Die Lehrlinge zu Sais*, God's image in nature becomes legible to those to whom God's spirit is imparted.¹³⁷ This distinction between orders of being in nature dissolves in a series of intriguing notes on the continuation of the novel, where Novalis develops the idea that, since God can become flesh, then it holds that God can manifest in all the elements of creation:

> Wenn Gott Mensch werden konnte, kann er auch Stein, Pflanze[,] Thier und Element werden, und vielleicht giebt auf diese Art eine fortwährende Erlösung in der Natur.
> Die Individualitaet in der Natur ist ganz unendlich. Wie sehr belebt diese Ansicht unsre Hoffnungen von der Personalitaet des Universums.
> Bemerkungen über das, was die Alten Sympathie nannten?
>
> [If God can become human, He can also become a stone, plant[,] animal and element, and perhaps in this manner there is perpetual salvation in nature.
> Individuality in nature is completely endless. How greatly this insight stimulates our hopes about the personal character of the universe!
> Notes on what the ancients call sympathy?]¹³⁸

These intriguing notes even include the suggestion of Heinrich's own continual metamorphoses ('Heinrich von Afterd[ingen] wird Blume — Thier — Stein — Stern' [Heinrich von After[dingen] becomes a flower — animal — stone — star]).¹³⁹ What lies at the heart of these notes is the Neoplatonist notion of the sympathetic correspondences between all elements of the universe.¹⁴⁰ More importantly, Novalis's rewriting of a salvation history combines with a notion of eschatological

---

134 Novalis, *Schriften*, I, 318.
135 Christoph Jamme, *Mythos und Aufklärung: Dichten und Denken um 1800* (Munich: Fink, 2013), p. 59.
136 James R. Hodkinson, *Women and Writing in the Works of Novalis: Transformation beyond Measure?* (Rochester, NY: Camden House, 2007), p. 228; Friedrich Strack, *Im Schatten der Neugier: Christliche Tradition und kritische Philosophie im Werk Friedrichs von Hardenberg* (Tübingen: Niemeyer, 1982), p. 37.
137 Sophie Vietor, *Astralis von Novalis: Handschrift — Text — Werk* (Würzburg: Königshausen & Neumann, 2001), pp. 119–20.
138 Novalis, *Schriften*, III, 664–65.
139 Novalis, *Schriften*, I, 341. See also Kurth-Voigt, *Continued Existence*, pp. 225–26 for the importance of Lessing in Novalis's thinking on metempsychosis and human perfectibility.
140 Irene Bark, *'Steine in Potenzen': Konstruktive Rezeption der Mineralogie bei Novalis* (Tübingen: Niemeyer, 1999), pp. 308–09.

perfectibility in the narrative of the gradual spiritualisation of all nature. The narrative structure of *Heinrich von Ofterdingen* corresponds, then, to the cyclical and linear structure of perfectibility in Günderrode's *oeuvre*. In spite of these similarities in Novalis's salvation narrative, what is fundamentally lacking is the framework of Spinozism and the spiritualisation of matter that informs Günderrode's metaphysics. Where Novalis generally holds on to the concept of God as distinct from nature, in *Melete*, Günderrode's position is altogether more naturalist by collapsing the divine into nature entirely — hence 'der Gott der Erde' [the god of the Earth] (*SW* 1, 362) in the soteriological narrative of 'Briefe zweier Freunde'.

Neither Novalis nor Hölderlin is as consistently Spinozist as Günderrode in their metaphysics, much as the material that they draw on and develop in their writings overlaps with Günderrode's vocabulary of Platonism, Neoplatonism, and Schellingian philosophy of nature. By contrast, Sophie Mereau differs from the Romantic poets, by showing how the fatalist clichés around Spinozism persisted even beyond Herder's rehabilitation of Spinoza's philosophy. Novalis's poetic and philosophical project, where Spinoza has little more than a guest appearance, functions in part analogously with Günderrode's interests in the valorisation of art and in questions of epistemology. Whereas the structure of the eschatological narratives may present productive parallels, they have fundamentally different emphases. Novalis stresses the poetic transfiguration of the world, whereas Günderrode falls back on problems inherited from the pantheism controversy in her metaphysical texts. Novalis, too, draws more on scientific vitalism than Günderrode or Hölderlin, who both use the language of vitalism in metaphysical contexts.

Whereas Hölderlin may stray further towards Spinozism than Novalis, both *Hyperion* and *Empedokles* oscillate between elegiac and ecstatic moods, which differ from the more optimistic tenor of Günderrode's metaphysics. The sources for Günderrode's metaphysics are also unique in Romanticism and indeed in the period as a whole. Whereas Novalis and Hölderlin, for example, mine the Christian and Hellenic traditions as sources for pursuing their hopes for religious renewal, in her religious and philosophical syncretism, Günderrode instead turns to non-Christian and non-European traditions as sources of revelation. In essence, it is the absolute consistency with which Günderrode addresses metaphysical and philosophical questions through the lens of Spinozist pantheism and panentheism that makes her stand out in her time.

CONCLUSION

It is common in scholarly discussions of Romanticism and Spinozism to turn to Heinrich Heine's declaration in *Zur Geschichte der Religion und Philosophie in Deutschland* [On the History of Religion and Philosophy in Germany] (1835) that 'Der Pantheismus ist die verborgene Religion Deutschlands' [Pantheism is the hidden religion of Germany].[1] This is because Heine offers a pithy characterisation of the revival of Spinozism around 1800.[2] Pantheism carries a specific political weight for Heine that chimes with revolutionary ideals: Schelling's philosophy of nature, among other forms of German Idealism, necessarily entailed a political, social, and sensual revolution by giving value to the material world.[3] Heine's linkage between pantheism and its political import, although specific to his nineteenth-century context, can also be made productive for Günderrode and panentheism: the moral principle of equality of all things merges with the metaphysical tenet of *hen kai pan*; hopes for political progress are, however, more difficult to map onto narratives of perfectibility that forgo closure.

Where Heine diverges from Günderrode is that whilst the ideals of Republicanism can be contained within panentheism, her metaphysical texts, on the whole, are marked by a detachment from contingent reality.[4] Her poetic metaphysics rely on a retreat from the messiness of everyday life and generate a form of solace that is found in the uncovering of the truth of Spinozist panentheism and pantheism, such as in 'Geschichte eines Braminen' and 'Briefe zweier Freunde'. The entwined roles of poetry and philosophy correspond to Günderrode's aphorism that the search for metaphysical truths must involve hermit-like estrangement from society: 'Es giebt nur zwei Arten recht zu leben irrdisch, oder himlisch; man kann der Welt dienen, u nüzen [...] Oder man lebt himlisch in der Betrachtung des Ewigen' (*SW* I, 437) [There are only two ways to live properly: earthly, or heavenly. One can serve the world and use it [...] Or one lives in a heavenly fashion in the contemplation of

---

1   Heinrich Heine, *Historisch-kritische Gesamtausgabe der Werke*, ed. by Manfred Windfuhr, 16 vols (Hamburg: Hoffmann & Campe, 1973–97), VIII.1: *Zur Geschichte der Religion und Philosophie in Deutschland, Die romantische Schule* (1979), p. 62.
2   Most prominently, Frederick C. Beiser, see for example, in *The Fate of Reason*, p. 52; also Williamson, p. 256; also B. A. Gerrish, *Continuing the Reformation: Essays on Modern Religious Thought* (Chicago: University of Chicago Press, 1993), pp. 109–10.
3   Ritchie Robertson, *Mock-Epic Poetry from Pope to Heine* (Oxford: Oxford University Press, 2009), pp. 396–97.
4   The notable exception would be 'Mahomed, der Prophet von Mekka', but the narrative thrust of the play supports the wider point since it brings together metaphysical truths with lived practices of religion and politics.

the Eternal]. This, in turn, recalls the role ascribed to the philosopher by Plato's Socrates in the dialogue *Theaetetus*, whose freedom lies in the unencumbered pursuit of truth (173e–174a).[5] Even the most audacious attempt to bring together the worldly and the metaphysical, such as in the play 'Mahomed', hinges on non-closure. Poetry and literature also act as receptacles for ideals that may be reactivated and realised at some unspecified point in time: such is the reflexive function of the poems dedicated to Brutus. The problem of narrative closure lies in the inability of such ecstatic narratives to sustain themselves: a utopian moment of perfection is not understood as an empirical possibility but rather remains a regulative idea.[6] Nonetheless, the simplicity of panentheism offers a non-orthodox alternative to Christian narratives of salvation: panentheism, or pantheism more broadly, became something of a religion to the heterodox Lutheran, away from the authority of the Bible.[7]

These tensions between the political and the metaphysical, between internal and exterior worlds, between the individual and nature, and how philosophical matters are given poetic voice, are central to Günderrode's work as a whole, and have been previously discussed in critical literature.[8] Grounding discussions of Günderrode's work in the context of the pantheism controversy instead allows for a more nuanced assessment of Günderrode's significance in the literary and intellectual environment of the late eighteenth century. To conclude, I will therefore give a summary of what makes Günderrode's poetic metaphysics distinctive, and also provide a sketch comparing Günderrode's position or positions to those of other prominent writers of the period beyond those active in the 1790s, such as Sophie Mereau, Novalis, and Hölderlin.

Metaphysical commitments are a main narrative thread in Günderrode, from her *Studienbuch* all the way through to *Melete* and its associated texts. So central are they that even the non-metaphysical texts, such as 'Nikator' and 'Hildgund', contain hints that individual agency has to be grounded in a metaphysical understanding of the world. Focusing on Günderrode through the lens of panentheism reveals her development as a poet and philosopher during the relatively short period during which she was active. Where the importance of the interaction between religious concerns and poetic concerns has been noted in general for Romanticism,[9] Günderrode has hitherto been absent from such narratives, and indeed, from any narratives concerned with the intellectual fallout of the pantheism controversy. This is a curious omission, since Günderrode was a remarkably consistent poet and thinker of panentheism in the period.

For the Jena Romantics, Spinozism was a central ingredient in their *Sympoesie* and *Symphilosophie*, which manifests in the interrelations between Novalis's 'Blüthenstaub'

---

5   See Plato, *Theaetetus*, trans. by John McDowell (Oxford: Oxford University Press, 2019), p. 52.
6   Hans-Joachim Mähl, *Die Idee des goldenen Zeitalters im Werk des Novalis: Studien zur Wesensbestimmung der frühromantischen Utopie und zu ihren ideengeschichtlichen Voraussetzungen* (Heidelberg: Winter, 1965), p. 249.
7   As Beiser notes: *The Fate of Reason*, p. 52.
8   Such as in Christmann, Dormann, Licher, and Westphal.
9   See, for example, Ziolkowski, p. 329.

— where a fragment explicitly discusses pantheism and monotheism[10] — Schlegel's 'Ideen' and Schleiermacher's *Reden über die Religion*. Schlegel's 'Gespräch über die Poesie' [Dialogue on Poesy] (1800) is suffused with the vocabulary of Spinozism; the final section of Fichte's *Die Bestimmung des Menschen*, for example, contains phrasing with pantheistic overtones. For the Jena circle, though, the appeal of Spinozism was also to do with the figure of Spinoza himself, who, in his singularity, mirrored their ideal of the artistic genius.[11]

If Günderrode draws on eclectic currents, from the Jena Romantics to Platonism, Neoplatonism, to Herder and Schelling's philosophy of nature, then what precisely remains distinctive about her work? The main questions that Günderrode pursues in these metaphysical texts reflect, at first glance, what Dalia Nassar has classified as the central questions and concerns of philosophical Romanticism: how mind and nature, how the one and many, how the infinite and finite relate to each one another.[12] Yet in Günderrode one finds a poet and philosopher who consistently returns to Spinozist panentheism, drawing on Herder's vitalist and Leibnizian rendering of Spinoza. Indeed, so consistent are Günderrode's metaphysical concerns that she is *the* most consistent adherent of panentheism and pantheism in Romanticism and in the period more generally.

Whilst the plot of history for Günderrode is consistent with that found in Schelling's philosophy and prefigures that of Hegel's *Phänomenologie des Geistes* [Phenomenology of Spirit] (1807), one of the tensions in these metaphysical narratives and poems derives not just from their commonalities, but from repetition. In the case of 'Adonis Todtenfeyer', the act of repetition is subtextual as part of how ritual practices generate meaning. In the metaphysical narratives where closure remains elusive, the structural repetitions create the transient illusion of permanence.

These narrative repetitions, together with tension of non-closure, are part of a broader project of naturalisation: poetic attempts to anchor the individual in the whole that has the effect of inoculating against the dangers of materialism, fatalism, and atheism by transfiguring panentheism and pantheism into a form of spiritualised materialism. This means that certain cherished concepts, such as teleology, individual agency and self-development, can be maintained. This process of naturalisation is particularly evident in *Melete*, where Günderrode, partly drawing on Schelling, takes panentheism to this logical pantheistic endpoint, where everything becomes part of the subjectivity of nature: humans and nature are no longer distinct orders of being.

---

10   Novalis defines pantheism and monotheism idiosyncratically in the context of a *Mittlerreligion* [a mediated religion]. The original version of the fragment in the *Vermischte Bemerkungen* substitutes monotheism for the neologism 'Entheismus'. For a discussion of this fragment and Novalis's reception of Spinoza and Fichte, see Monika Tokarzewska, 'Der "Pantheismus" und "Entheismus" im 73. Fragment der "Vermischten Bemerkungen" und in den "Fichte-Studien" von Novalis', in *Literatur und Theologie: Schreibprozesse zwischen biblischer Überlieferung und geschichtlicher Erfahrung*, ed. by Karol Sauerland and Ulrich Wergin (Würzburg: Königshausen & Neumann, 2005), pp. 73–86.
11   Julia A. Lamm, 'Romanticism and Pantheism', in *The Blackwell Companion to Nineteenth-Century Theology*, ed. by David Ferguson (Chichester: Wiley-Blackwell, 2010), pp. 165–86 (pp. 166–67).
12   Dalia Nassar, *The Romantic Absolute: Being and Knowing in Early German Romantic Philosophy, 1795–1804* (Chicago: University of Chicago Press, 2014), p. 2.

Günderrode's naturalisation of the individual is distinctive for her time. In other eighteenth-century perspectives, other approaches come to the fore. In his unpublished lecture 'Ein Blick in das Ganze der Natur: Einleitung zu Anfangsgründen der Thiergeschichte' [A View on the Whole of Nature: Introduction to the Foundations of the Animal Kingdom] (1781–83), Georg Forster runs closer to scientific models of objectifying nature. This text, which betrays Forster's debt to the French naturalist Buffon,[13] adopts an aesthetic of *Nützlichkeit* [utility], where the notion of utility and an appreciation of nature cohere.[14] Forster makes use of a Christian notion of stewardship as the relation between man and nature. What remains untouched by human hand remains forbidding:

> Zur Anbetung des Schöpfers gemacht, gebietet er über alle Geschöpfe; als Vasall des Himmels, und König der Erde, veredelt, bevölkert, und bereichert er sie: er zwingt die lebenden Geschöpfe zur Ordnung, Unterwürfigkeit und Eintracht; er selbst verschönert die Natur; er bauet, erweitert und verfeinert sie. Er rottet Disteln und Dornen aus, pflanzt Weinstöcke und Rosen an ihre Stätte. Dort liegt ein wüster Erdstrich, eine traurige, von Menschen nie bewohnte Gegend, deren Höhen mit dichten schwarzen Wäldern überzogen sind.
>
> [Made for the worship of the Creator, he holds command over all creatures: as the vassal of heaven, and king of the Earth, he ennobles, populates and enriches the Earth: he enforces order, subservience and harmony among living creatures. He himself beautifies nature; he constructs, expands, and refines it. He roots out thistles and thorns, plants vines and roses in their place. Out there is a desolate strip of land, a sombre region, never inhabited by man, whose hills are covered with dense, black woods.][15]

This perspective on nature, where human society crafts the landscape into order and beauty, rests on the hierarchical assumption of human superiority to and responsibility towards the natural world.

A contrasting view can be found in the nature poetry of the latter half of the eighteenth century that in some ways acts as a precursor to Günderrode. In the poetry of Friedrich Stolberg, such as 'An die Natur' [To Nature] (1775) and 'Hymne an die Erde' [Hymn on the Earth] (1778),[16] the experience of nature assumes a quasi-religious function. The individual is cast in the role of a dependent infant, reliant on the Earth or nature as its nurturing mother. As Matthias Löwe argues,

---

13 The essay includes direct translations from Buffon: see Clarence J. Glacken, *Traces on the Rhodian Shore: Nature and Culture in Western Thought from Ancient Times to the End of the Eighteenth Century* (Berkeley: University of California Press, 1967), p. 703.
14 This melding of utility and an appreciation of nature was common in the late eighteenth century. See Denise Phillips, *Acolytes of Nature: Defining Natural Science in Germany, 1770–1850* (Chicago: University of Chicago Press, 2012), p. 33. For an overview of the development of 'nützliche Naturwissenschaften' in the eighteenth century, see Ursula Klein, *Nützliches Wissen: Die Erfindung der Technikwissenschaften* (Göttingen: Wallstein, 2016).
15 Georg Forster, 'Ein Blick in das Ganze der Natur: Einleitung zu Anfangsgründen der Thiergeschichte', in Georg Forster, *Werke: Sämtliche Schriften, Tagebücher, Briefe*, ed. by Deutsche Akademie der Wissenschaften zu Berlin, 18 vols (Berlin: Akademie, 1958–), VIII: *Kleine Schriften zu Philosophie und Zeitgeschichte*, ed. by Siegfried Scheibe (1991), p. 94.
16 A copy of Stolberg's 'Hymne an die Erde' is in Günderrode's *Nachlass*.

for Stolberg, transcendence becomes immanent in nature, and the poems exemplify a form of monism in the late Enlightenment that valorises sensory experience — without tipping into pantheism.[17]

In philosophical terms, Günderrode moves, by way of Schelling, roughly from a Leibnizian to a Spinozist position. The tensions and strains of Günderrode's texts derive from the question of how to constitute the relationship between the individual and the whole. The Leibnizian position can be best outlined by a fragment similar in sentiment to Stolberg's poetry: 'Die Natur' [Nature] (c. 1781) by the Swiss theologian and writer Georg Christoph Tobler.[18] Once erroneously ascribed to Goethe, Tobler's hymnic fragment describes how the individual is caught up in the bosom of all-encompassing, productive, and personified maternal nature, understood in pantheistic terms. The Leibnizian aspect of Tobler's fragment derives from the endless production of individuals, of monads, who cannot penetrate further into the depths of nature, and whose existence appears to be nothing more than the result of the capricious play of creation.[19]

The essential point of this Leibnizian position is that the individual monad is invulnerable, and yet reflects the entirety of the cosmos. For Günderrode, this reaches its apotheosis in 'Ein apokaliptisches Fragment', where the individual communes with the whole. The conclusion of the fragment can be neatly summarised by the ecstatic conclusion to Zeus's seduction of Ganymed in Goethe's poem 'Ganymed' (1774): 'Umfangend umfangen!' [Embracing and embraced!].[20] The poetic movement of ascent and descent becomes strained precisely because individuation is framed as a problem to be overcome. Yet the Leibnizian concept of the monad that Günderrode explicitly refers to in 'Des Wandrers Niederfahrt' makes the undoing of individuation impossible, since it presupposes that the individual is invulnerable. The solution, provided in 'Ein apokaliptisches Fragment', is to push the individual to the point that it does reflect the entirety of the cosmos, but this solution is one that comes at a heavy cost — death is the price to be paid for an expansion of consciousness. 'Ein apokaliptisches Fragment' is, in this sense, an ecstatic defeat in the pursuit of knowledge.

The pressure exerted on the individual by this question is so severe that Günderrode's invocation of a Manichaean conception of individuation as sinful in 'Briefe zweier Freunde' comes as no surprise, nor does the recasting of nature as subject rather than object in *Melete* as a whole. Indeed, there is an echo of Goethe's 'Ganymed' — whether intentional or not — in 'Briefe zweier Freunde' that marks the dissolution of the individual. For Eusebio, perfect oneness is 'sich selbst ewig

---

17   Matthias Löwe, 'Epochenbegriff und Problemgeschichte: Aufklärung und Romantik als konkurriende Antworten auf dieselben Fragen', in *Aufklärung und Romantik: Epochenschnittstellen*, ed. by Daniel Fulda and others, Laboratorium Aufklärung, 28 (Paderborn: Fink, 2015), pp. 45–68 (p. 61).
18   For Daniel Steuer, Tobler's fragment anticipates the complex understanding of nature in Idealism and Romanticism: see Daniel Steuer, 'Nature', in *Encyclopedia of the Romantic Era, 1760–1850*, ed. by Christopher John Murray, 2 vols (New York: Fitzroy Dearborn, 2004), II, 792–94 (p. 792).
19   Nicholas Boyle, *Goethe: The Poet and the Age*, 2 vols (Oxford: Oxford University Press, 1992–2003), I: *The Poetry of Desire* (1992), p. 339.
20   Goethe, *Sämtliche Werke, Briefe, Tagebücher und Gespräche*, I.I: *Gedichte 1759–1799*, ed. by Karl Eibl (1987), p. 205.

umfangend' [eternally embracing itself] (*SW* I, 354). This marks an explicit textual move into Spinozism, where the loss of singularity is to be welcomed. Whilst Günderrode repeatedly stresses the importance of self-development across her *oeuvre*, this deployment of Spinozist panentheism and pantheism not only bolsters the overarching and more familiar narrative of how Spinozism was rehabilitated at the end of the eighteenth century, but also demonstrates how it could be cast as a meaningful consolation narrative that appealed to heterodox Lutherans.

BIBLIOGRAPHY

Manuscript Sources

BRENTANO, CLEMENS, letter to Karoline von Günderrode, 1806, Freies Deutsches Hochstift (FDH) Frankfurt a.M., MS 8298

SAVIGNY, FRIEDRICH KARL VON, letter to Karoline von Günderrode, 8 January 1804, Freies Deutsches Hochstift (FDH), Frankfurt a.M., MS 8305

GÜNDERRODE, KAROLINE VON, letter to Claudine Piautaz, 1801–03, Freies Deutsches Hochstift (FDH), Frankfurt a.M., MS 20369

NEES VON ESENBECK, LISETTE, letter to Karoline von Günderrode, 28 February 1805, Freies Deutsches Hochstift (FDH), Frankfurt a.M., MS 8345

NACHLASS KAROLINE VON GÜNDERRODE, Frankfurt a.M., Universitätsbibliothek J. C. Senckenberg (SUF), MS Ff. K. v. Günderrode Abt. 1; Abt. 2 A1–A5; Abt. 3

Printed Sources

Primary Sources (Günderrode)

GEIGER, LUDWIG, *Karoline von Günderode und ihre Freunde: Mit dem Porträt der Dichterin* (Stuttgart, Leipzig, Berlin, Vienna: Deutsche Verlags-Anstalt, 1895)

GÜNDERRODE, KAROLINE VON, *Der Schatten eines Traumes. Gedichte. Prosa. Briefe*, ed. by Christa Wolf (Berlin: Buchverlag der Morgen, 1979)

—— *Ich sende dir ein zärtliches Pfand: Die Briefe der Karoline von Günderrode*, ed. by Birgit Weißenborn (Frankfurt a.M.: Insel, 1992)

—— *Gedichte, Prosa, Briefe* (Stuttgart: Reclam, 1998)

—— *Sämtliche Werke und ausgewählte Studien*, ed. by Walter Morgenthaler, 3 vols (Frankfurt a.M.; Basel: Stroemfeld/Roter Stern, 2006)

—— *Poetic Fragments*, trans. by Anna Ezekiel (Albany: SUNY Press, 2016)

PREISENDANZ, KARL, *Die Liebe der Günderode: Friedrich Creuzers Briefe an Caroline von Günderode* (Berlin: Lang, 1975)

PREITZ, MAX, 'Karoline von Günderrode in ihrer Umwelt, I: Briefe von Lisette und Christian Gottfried Nees von Esenbeck, Karoline von Günderrode, Friedrich Creuzer, Clemens Brentano und Susanne von Heyden', *Jahrbuch des freien deutschen Hochstifts* (1962), 208–302

—— 'Karoline von Günderrode in ihrer Umwelt. II. Karoline von Günderrodes Briefwechsel mit Friedrich Karl und Gunda von Savigny', *Jahrbuch des freien deutschen Hochstifts* (1964), 158–235

PREITZ, MAX, and HOPP, DORIS, 'Karoline von Günderrode in ihrer Umwelt, III. Karoline von Günderrodes Studienbuch', *Jahrbuch des freien deutschen Hochstifts* (1975), 223–323

ROHDE, ERWIN, *Friedrich Creuzer und Karoline von Günderode: Briefe und Dichtungen* (Heidelberg: Winter, 1896)

Primary Sources (Other Authors)

ARNIM, ACHIM VON, *Werke in sechs Bänden*, ed. by Roswitha Burwick and others, 6 vols (Frankfurt a.M.: Deutscher Klassiker Verlag, 1989–92)

ARNIM, BETTINE VON, *Goethe's Briefwechsel mit einem Kinde* (Frankfurt a.M.: Deutscher Klassiker Verlag, 1992)

——*Clemens Brentano's Frühlingskranz: Die Günderode* (Frankfurt a.M.: Deutscher Klassiker Verlag, 2006)

Classical Literary Criticism, ed. by T. S. Dorsch and Penelope Murray (London: Penguin, 2004)

CREUZER, FRIEDRICH, 'Philologie und Mythologie, in ihrem Stufengang und gegenseitigem Verhalten', *Heidelberger Jahrbücher der Literatur für Philologie, Historie, Literatur und Kunst*, 1.1 (1808), 3–24

——*Friedrich Creuzers Symbolik und Mythologie* (Leipzig: Heyer und Leske, 1819)

FESSLER, IGNAZ AURELIUS, *Attila: König der Hunnen* (Breslau: Korn, 1794)

FORSTER, GEORG, *Werke: Sämtliche Schriften, Tagebücher, Briefe*, ed. by Deutsche Akademie der Wissenschaften zu Berlin, 18 vols (Berlin: Akademie, 1958–)

'Frankfurt a. M., b. Wilmanns: Poetische Fragmente von Tian', *Jenaische Allgemeine Literatur-Zeitung*, 138, 13 June 1807, pp. 489–91

GATTERER, JOHANN CHRISTIAN, *Einleitung in die synchronistische Universalhistorie* (Göttingen: Vandenhoek, 1771)

GOETHE, JOHANN WOLFGANG, *Werke, herausgegeben im Auftrage der Großherzogin Sophie von Sachsen*, 143 vols (Weimar: Hermann Böhlau, 1887–1919)

——*Sämtliche Werke, Briefe, Tagebücher und Gespräche*, ed. by Dieter Borchmeyer and others, 40 vols (Frankfurt a.M.: Deutscher Klassiker Verlag, 1985–2013)

GÜNDERRODE, HECTOR WILHELM VON, *Geschichte des römischen Königs Adolphs nach denen Urkunden und gleichzeitigen Geschichtsschreibern* (Frankfurt a.M.: Johann Philipp Reifferstein, 1779)

HEDERICH, BENJAMIN, *Gründliches mythologisches Lexicon*, ed. by Johann Joachim Schwabe (Leipzig: Gleditsch, 1770)

HEGEL, GEORG WILHELM FRIEDRICH, *Werke in zwanzigen Bänden*, ed. by Eva Moldenhauer und Karl Markus Michel, 20 vols (Frankfurt a.M.: Suhrkamp, 1969–71)

HEINE, HEINRICH, *Historisch-kritische Gesamtausgabe der Werke*, ed. by Manfred Windfuhr, 16 vols (Hamburg: Hoffmann & Campe, 1973–97)

HENNINGS, AUGUST, *Der Musaget: Ein Begleiter des Genius der Zeit. Sechstes Stück* (Altona: Hammerich, 1799)

HERDER, JOHANN GOTTFRIED, *Werke in zehn Bänden*, ed. Jürgen Brammack und Martin Bollacher, 10 vols (Frankfurt a.M.: Deutscher Klassikerverlag, 1985–2000)

—— *God, Some Conversations*, trans. by Frederick H. Burkhardt (Bobbs-Merrill: Indianapolis, 1940)

HÖLDERLIN, FRIEDRICH, *Sämtliche Werke*, ed. by Friedrich Beissner and Adolf Beck, 8 vols (Stuttgart: Kohlhammer, 1943–85)

——*Sämtliche Werke und Briefe*, ed. by Jochen Schmidt, 3 vols (Frankfurt a.M.: Deutscher Klassiker Verlag, 1992–94)

——*Selected Poems and Fragments*, ed. by Jeremy Adler, trans. by Michael Hamburger (London: Penguin, 1998)

——*The Death of Empedocles: A Mourning Play*, trans. by David Farrell Krell (Albany, NY: State of University of New York Press, 2008)

——*Hyperion, or the Hermit in Greece*, trans. by Howard Gaskill (Cambridge: OpenBook, 2019)

HUME, DAVID, *An Enquiry Concerning Human Understanding*, ed. by Peter Millican (Oxford: Oxford University Press, 2007)

IVES, EDWARD, *Reisen nach Indien und Persien*, trans. by Christian Willhelm Dohm, 2 vols (Leipzig: Weidmanns Erben und Reich, 1774)
JACOBI, FRIEDRICH HEINRICH, *Werke: Gesamtausgabe*, ed. by Klaus Hammacher and Walter Jaeschke, 7 vols (Hamburg: Meiner, 1998–)
KANT, IMMANUEL, *Kant's Gesammelte Schriften: Akademieausgabe*, ed. by Königlich-Preussische Akademie der Wissenschaften zu Berlin and others, 29 vols (Berlin: Reimer; De Gruyter 1900–)
——*The Critique of Pure Reason*, trans. and ed. by Paul Guyer and Allen W. Wood (Cambridge: Cambridge University Press, 1998)
KIESEWETTER, J. G. C. C., *Grundriß einer allgemeinen Logik nach Kantischen Grundsätzen zum Gebrauch für Vorlesungen begleitet mit einer weitern Auseinandersetzung für diejenigen die keine Vorlesung darüber hören können. Zweiter Theil welcher die angewandte allgemeine Logik enthält* (Berlin: Lagarde, 1796)
KLEUKER, JOHANN FRIEDRICH, *Anhang zum Zend-Avesta*, II.1 (Leipzig: Hartknoch, 1783)
Der Koran, oder das Gesetz für die Muselmänner . . . Nebst einigen feyerlichen koranischen Gebeten . . . mit Anm. und einem Register vers., und auf Verlangen hrsg. von Friedrich Eberhard Boysen, trans. by Friedrich Eberhard Boysen (Halle: Gebauer, 1773)
KOSEGARTEN, LUDWIG GOTTHARD, *Poesieen: Erster Band* (Leipzig: Gräff, 1798)
LESSING, GOTTHOLD EPHRAIM, *Werke und Briefe in zwölf Bänden*, ed. by Wilfried Barner and others, 12 vols (Frankfurt a.M.: Deutscher Klassiker Verlag, 1985–2003)
LUDEN, HEINRICH, 'Frankfurt u. Heidelberg, b. Mohr: *Studien*. Herausgegeben von Carl Daub u. Friedrich Creuzer, etc. (Beschluss der im vorigen Stücke abgebrochenen Recension.)', *Jenaer Allgemeine Literaturzeitung*, 260, 31 October 1805, pp. 209–16
MAJER, FRIEDRICH, 'Ueber die mythologischen Dichtungen der Indier: an Alwina', in *Poetisches Journal*, ed. by Ludwig Tieck (Jena: Frommann, 1800), 165–216
MEREAU, SOPHIE, *Das Blütenalter der Empfindung: Amanda und Eduard* (Munich: Deutscher Taschenbuch Verlag, 1996)
MENDELSSOHN, MOSES, *Gesammelte Schriften: Jubiläumsausgabe*, ed. by Fritz Bamberger and others, 32 vols (Stuttgart-Bad Canstatt: frommann-holzboog, 1971–)
'Nachrichten für die Kunst; in einem Briefe aus Weimar. An den Herausgeber', *Zeitung für die elegante Welt*, 36, 24 March 1803, pp. 279–80
'Nachrichten für die Kunst. (Beschluß).', *Zeitung für die elegante Welt*, 37, 26 March 1803, pp. 287–88.
NOVALIS, *The Novices of Sais*, trans. by Ralph Manheim (New York; Curt Valentin, 1949)
——*Schriften*, ed. by Paul Kluckhohn and others, 3rd edn, 5 vols (Stuttgart: Kohlhammer, 1960–88)
——*Notes for a Romantic Encyclopaedia: Das Allgemeine Brouillon*, trans. and ed. by David W. Wood (Albany: SUNY Press, 2007)
PAUL, JEAN, *Sämtliche Werke*, ed. by Norbert Miller, 10 vols (Munich: Hanser, 1959–; repr. Darmstadt: Wissenschaftliche Buchgesellschaft, 2000)
PLATO, *Phaedrus*, trans. by Robin Waterfield (Oxford: Oxford University Press, 2002)
——*Symposium*, trans. by Robin Waterfield (Oxford: Oxford University Press, 2008)
——*Theaetetus*, trans. by John McDowell (Oxford: Oxford University Press, 2019)
PLUTARCH, *Plutarch's De Iside et Osiride*, ed. and trans. by J. Gwyn Griffiths (Cambridge: University of Wales Press, 1970)
QUINTILIAN, *The Orator's Education*, ed., trans. by Donald A. Russell, 5 vols (Cambridge, MA: Harvard University Press, 2001)
REMER, JULIUS AUGUST, *Handbuch der ältern Geschichte von der Schöpfung der Welt bis auf die große Völkerwanderung* (Braunschweig, 1794)
RITTER, JOHANN WILHELM, *Fragmente aus dem Nachlasse eines jungen Physikers: Ein Taschenbuch für Freunde der Natur* (Leipzig and Weimar: Gustav Kiepenheuer, 1984)

ROLAND DE LA PLATIÈRE, MARIE-JEANNE, *Œuvres de J. M. Ph. Roland, Femme de l'ex-ministre de l'intérieur*, ed. by L. A. Champagneux, 3 vols (Paris: Bidault, 1799)

SCHELLING, FRIEDRICH WILHELM JOSEPH VON, *Ausgewählte Schriften*, ed. by Manfred Frank, 6 vols (Frankfurt: Suhrkamp, 1985)

SCHILLER, FRIEDRICH, *Schillers Werke: Nationalausgabe*, ed. by Julius Petersen and others, 43 vols (Weimar: Böhlaus Nachfolger, 1943–2010)

SCHLEGEL, FRIEDRICH, *Kritische Friedrich-Schlegel-Ausgabe*, ed. by Ernst Behler and others, 31 vols (Munich: Schöningh, 1958–)

SCHLEIERMACHER, FRIEDRICH DANIEL ERNST, *Kritische Gesamtausgabe*, ed. by Hans-Joachim Birkner and others, 58 vols (Berlin: De Gruyter, 1980–)

SHAKESPEARE, WILLIAM, *Shakspeare's dramatische Werke*, trans. by August Wilhelm Schlegel, 9 vols (Berlin: Johann Friedrich Unger, 1797–1810)

——, *The New Oxford Shakespeare: Critical Reference Edition*, ed. by Gary Taylor and others, 2 vols (Oxford: Oxford University Press, 2017–)

SPALDING, JOHANN JOACHIM, *Kritische Ausgabe*, ed. by Albrecht Beutel, 12 vols (Tübingen: Mohr Siebeck, 2001–13)

SPINOZA, BENEDICTUS DE, *The Collected Works of Spinoza*, ed. and trans. by Edwin Curley, 2 vols (Princeton: Princeton University Press, 1985–2016)

WIELAND, CHRISTOPH MARTIN, *C. M. Wieland's Sämmtliche Werke*, 36 vols (Leipzig: Göschen, 1853–58)

WÜNSCH, CHRISTIAN ERNST, *Unterhaltungen über den Menschen: Erster Theil: über die Kultur und äußerliche Bildung desselben*, 2nd edn (Leipzig: Breitkopf, 1796)

WYTTENBACH, JOHANN HUGO, *Aussprüche der philosophirenden Vernunft und des reinen Herzens über die der Menschheit wichtigsten Gegenstände, mit besonderer Rücksicht auf die kritische Philosophie zusammen getragen aus den Schriften älterer und neuerer Denker*, 2 vols (Leipzig, Vienna: Rötzel, 1796–98)

Secondary Sources

Relating to Günderrode

BARRY, KELLY, '1804, May 18: The Subject and Object of Mythology', in *A New History of German Literature*, ed. by David Wellbery and others (Cambridge, MA: Belknap Press, 2004), pp. 494–500

BATTERSBY, CHRISTINE, *The Sublime, Terror and Human Difference* (London: Routledge, 2007)

BECKER-CANTARINO, BARBARA, *Schriftstellerinnen der Romantik: Epoche — Werke — Wirkung* (Munich: Beck, 2000)

—— 'Mythos und Symbolik bei Karoline von Günderrode und Friedrich Creuzer', in *200 Jahre Heidelberger Romantik*, ed. by Friedrich Strack and Barbara Becker-Cantarino (Berlin: Springer, 2008), pp. 281–98

—— 'The "New Mythology": Myth and Death in Karoline von Günderrode's Literary Work', in *Women and Death 3: Women's Representations of Death in German Culture since 1500*, ed. by Claire Bielby and Anna Richards (Rochester, NY: Camden House, 2010), pp. 51–70

—— 'Liebestod: Goethe "Der Gott und die Bajadere" und Günderrode "Die Malabarischen Witwen"', in *Emotionen in der Romantik: Repräsentation, Ästhetik, Inszenierung*, ed. by Antje Arnold and Walter Pape (Berlin: De Gruyter, 2012), pp. 21–32

BERMAN, NINA, *German Literature on the Middle East: Discourses and Practices, 1000–1989* (Ann Arbor: University of Michigan Press, 2011)

BERWALD, OLAF, *Visuelle Gewalt und Selbstverlust bei Günderrode, Hölderlin und Fichte* (Ann Arbor: UMI, 2006)
BLACKWELL, JEANNINE and ZANTOP, SUSANNE, eds, *Bitter Healing: German Women Writers 1700–1800. An Anthology* (Lincoln: University of Nebraska Press, 1990)
BLANKENSHIP, ROBERT, *Suicide in East German Literature: Fiction, Rhetoric, and the Self-Destruction of Literary Heritage* (Rochester, NY: Camden House, 2017)
BOHRER, KARL HEINZ, *Der romantische Brief: Die Entstehung ästhetischer Subjektivität* (Munich: Hanser, 1987)
BUNZEL, WOLFGANG, 'Bis(s) zum Morgengrauen. Clemens Brentanos erster Brief an Karoline von Günderrode: Kontext, Funktion, Materialität', in *Romantik kontrovers: Ein Debattenparcours zum zwanzigjährigen Jubiläum der Stiftung für Romantikforschung*, ed. by Gerhart von Graevenitz, Stiftung für Romantikforschung, 58 (Würzburg: Königshausen & Neumann, 2015), pp. 229–44
BURDORF, DIETER, '"Diese Sehnsucht ist ein Gedanke, der ins Unendliche starrt": Über Karoline von Günderrode — aus Anlaß neuer Ausgaben ihrer Werke und Briefe', *Wirkendes Wort*, 43 (1993), 49–67
BURWICK, ROSWITHA, 'Liebe und Tod in Leben und Werk der Günderode', *German Studies Review*, 3.2 (1980), 207–23
CHRISTMANN, RUTH, *Zwischen Identitätsgewinn und Bewußtseinsverlust: Das philosophisch-literarische Werk der Karoline von Günderrode (1780–1806)*, Trierer Studien zur Literatur, 44 (Frankfurt a.M.: Peter Lang, 2005)
DAUBERT, KARIN R., 'Karoline von Günderrode's "Der Gefangene und der Sänger": New Voices in Romanticism's Desire for Cultural Transcendence', *New German Review*, 8 (1992), 1–17
DORMANN, HELGA, *Die Kunst des inneren Sinns: Mythisierung der inneren und äußeren Natur im Werk Karoline von Günderrodes* (Würzburg: Königshausen & Neumann, 2004)
EICKENRODT, SABINE, '"Die Vergangenheit war mir dahin!" Karoline von Günderrodes apokalyptische Vision', in *Geschriebenes Leben: Autobiographik von Frauen*, ed. by Michaela Holdenried (Berlin: Schmidt, 1995), pp. 185–97
——*Augen-Spiel: Jean Pauls optische Metaphorik der Unsterblichkeit* (Göttingen: Wallstein, 2006)
EZEKIEL, ANNA, 'Metamorphosis, Personhood, and Power in Karoline von Günderrode', *European Romantic Review*, 25.6 (2014), 773–91
GALASSO, STEPHANIE, 'Form and Contention: *Sati* as Custom in Günderrode's "Die Malabarischen Witwen"', *Goethe Yearbook*, 24 (2017), 197–220
GERSDORFF, DAGMAR VON, *Die Erde ist mir Heimat nicht geworden: Das Leben der Karoline von Günderrode* (Frankfurt a.M.: Insel, 2011)
GÖLZ, SABINE I., 'Günderrode Mines Novalis', in *'The Spirit of Poesy': Essays on Jewish and German Literature and Thought in Honor of Géza von Molnár*, ed. by Richard Block and Peter Fenves (Evanston, IL: Northwestern University Press, 2000), pp. 89–130
HERMANN, IRIS, 'Theater ist schöner als Krieg: Kleists Hermannsschlacht auf der Bühne', in *Hermanns Schlachten: Zur Literaturgeschichte eines nationalen Mythos*, ed. by Martina Wagner-Egelhaaf, Veröffentlichungen der Literaturkommission für Westfalen, 32 (Bielefeld: Aisthesis, 2008), pp. 239–60
HILGER, STEPHANIE M., *Women Write Back: Strategies of Response and the Dynamics of European Literary Culture, 1790–1805*, Internationale Forschungen zur Allgemeinen und Vergleichenden Literaturwissenschaft, 124 (Amsterdam, New York: Rodopi, 2009)
HILLE, MARKUS, *Karoline von Günderrode* (Reinbek: Rowohlt, 1999)
HILLIARD, K. F., 'Orient und Mythos: Karoline von Günderrode', *Frauen: MitSprechen — MitSchreiben: Beiträge zur literatur- und sprachwissenschaftlichen Frauenforschung*, ed. by Marianne Henn and Britta Hufeisen, Stuttgarter Arbeiten zur Germanistik, 349 (Stuttgart: Heinz, 1997), pp. 244–55

HILMES, CAROLA, 'Unbotmäßig: Karoline von Günderrodes literarische Inszenierungen der "Jungfrau in Waffen"', *Jahrbuch des freien deutschen Hochstifts* (2017), 147–68

HOCK, LISABETH M., *Replicas of a Female Prometheus: The Textual Personae of Bettin von Arnim*, Northern American Studies in Nineteenth-Century German Literature, 27 (Peter Lang: New York, 2001)

HOFF, DAGMAR VON, *Dramen des Weiblichen: Deutsche Dramatikerinnen um 1800* (Opladen: Westdeutscher Verlag, 1989)

——'Aspects of Censorship in the Work of Karoline von Günderrode', *Women in German Yearbook*, 11 (1995), 99–112

HOWEG, WALTRAUD, *Karoline von Günderrode und Hölderlin* (Halle, 1953)

HUMMEL, ADRIAN, 'Lebenszwänge, Schreibräume, unirdisch: Eine kulturanthropologische orientierte Deutung des "Mythos Günderrode"', *Athenäum*, 13 (2003), 61–91

KASTINGER-RILEY, HELENE C., 'Zwischen den Welten: Ambivalenz und Existentialproblematik im Werk Caroline von Günderrodes', in *Die weibliche Muse: Sechs Essays über künstlerisch schaffende Frauen der Goethezeit* (Columbia, SC: Camden House, 1986), pp. 91–119

KEMPF, EDITH, 'Karoline von Günderrode', in *Deutsche Literatur: Aus fünf Jahrhunderten*, ed. by Hermann Korte (Stuttgart: Metzler, 2015), pp. 228–29

KORD, SUSANNE, *Ein Blick hinter die Kulissen: Deutschsprachige Dramatikerinnen im 18. und 19. Jahrhundert*, Ergebnisse der Frauenforschung, 27 (Stuttgart: Metzler, 1992)

——*Sich einen Namen machen: Anonymität und weibliche Autorschaft, 1700–1900* (Stuttgart: Metzler, 1996)

KRIMMER, ELISABETH, *In the Company of Men: Cross-Dressed Women around 1800* (Detroit: Wayne State University Press, 2004)

KRÜGER-FÜRHOFF, IRMELA MAREI, *Der versehrte Körper: Revisionen des klassizistischen Schönheitsideals* (Göttingen: Wallstein, 2001)

KÜHNEL, FLORIAN, *Kranke Ehre? Adlige Selbsttötung im Übergang zur Moderne* (Munich: Oldenbourg, 2013)

LAVERS, JORDAN ROSS, '*Schwesterstimme*: Gender, Emotion and Kinship in the Correspondence of the von Günderrode Sisters' (unpublished doctoral thesis, University of Western Australia, 2020)

LAZAROWICZ, MARGARETE, *Karoline von Günderrode: Portrait einer Fremden* (Frankfurt a.M.: Peter Lang, 1986)

LICHER, LUCIA, '"Der Völker Schicksal ruht in meinem Busen": Karoline von Günderrode als Dichterin der Revolution', in *Der Menschheit Hälfte blieb noch ohne Recht': Frauen und die französische Revolution*, ed. by Helga Brandes (Wiesbaden: Deutscher Universitätsverlag, 1991), pp. 113–32

——*Mein Leben in einer bleibenden Form aussprechen: Umrisse einer Ästhetik im Werk Karoline von Günderrodes (1780–1806)* (Heidelberg: Winter, 1996)

——'A Sceptical Mohammedan: Aesthetics as a Theory of Life's Practice in the Writings of Caroline von Günderrode', in *Transactions of the Ninth International Congress on the Enlightenment, Münster, 23–29 July 1995*, Studies on Voltaire and the Eighteenth Century, 346–48, 3 vols (Oxford: Voltaire Foundation, 1996), III, 1450–52

MICHLER, WERNER, *Kulturen der Gattung: Poetik im Kontext, 1750–1950* (Göttingen: Wallstein, 2015)

NAUMANN, ANNELORE, *Caroline von Günderrode* (Berlin: Freie Universität, 1957)

NIELSEN, WENDY C., *Women Warriors in Romantic Drama* (Newark: University of Delaware Press, 2013)

ÖLKE, MARTINA, 'Verhinderter Ausbruch? Zur Konzeption des (weiblichen) Genies in Karoline von Günderrodes Gedichten *Aegypten* und *Der Nil*', in *Bei Gefahr des Untergangs:*

Phantasien des Aufbrechens. Festschrift für Irmgard Roebling, ed. by Ina Brueckel and others (Würzburg: Königshausen & Neumann, 2000), pp. 117–31

PURVER, JUDITH, 'Revolution, Romanticism, Restoration (1789–1830)', in *A History of Women's Writing in Germany, Austria and Switzerland*, ed. by Jo Catling (Cambridge: Cambridge University Press, 2000), pp. 68–87

RAUCHENBACHER, MARINA, **Karoline von Günderrode*: Eine Rezeptionsstudie* (Würzburg: Königshausen & Neumann, 2014)

REEVES, MINOU, 'Pantheism, Heroism, Sensualism, Mysticism: Muhammed and Islam in German Literature from Goethe to Rilke', in *Traces of Transcendency/Spuren des Transzendenten: Religious Motifs in German Literature and Thought*, ed. by Rüdiger Görner, Publications of the Institute of Germanic Studies, 77 (Munich: Iudicium, 2001), pp. 89–103

REGEN, ERICH, *Die Dramen Karolinens von Günderode* (Berlin: Ebering, 1910)

REHM, WALTER, *Der Todesgedanke in der deutschen Dichtung vom Mittelalter bis zur Romantik*, 2nd edn (Darmstadt: Wissenschaftliche Buchgesellschaft, 1967)

RUNTE, ANNETTE, *Über die Grenze: Zur Kulturpoetik der Geschlechter in Literatur und Kunst* (Bielefeld: transcript, 2006)

SCHULZ, GERHARD, 'Träume eines Stiftfräuleins: Zum 200. Geburtstag der Karoline von Günderrode', *Frankfurter Allgemeine Zeitung*, 9 February 1980, p. 23

SCHWARTZ, KARL, 'GÜNDERRODE (Karoline Friederike Louise Maximiliane von)', in *Allgemeine Encyklopädie der Wissenschaften und Künste*, ed. by Johann Samuel Ersch and Johann Gottfried Gruber, 167 vols (Leipzig: Brockhaus, 1818–89), XCVII: *Gulaþingslög — Gussonea* (1878), pp. 167–231

SIMONIS, ANNETTE, '"Das verschleierte Bild": Mythopoetik und Geschlechterrollen bei Karoline von Günderrode', *Deutsche Vierteljahrsschrift für Literaturwissenschaft*, 74.2 (2000), 254–78

SIMPSON, PATRICIA ANNE, *The Erotics of War in German Romanticism* (Lewisburg, PA: Bucknell University Press, 2006)

SOLBRIG, INGEBORG, 'The Contemplative Muse: Karoline von Günderode's Religious Works', *Germanic Notes*, 18 (1987), 18–20

—— 'Die Orientalische Muse Meletes: Zu den Mohammed-Dichtungen Karoline von Günderrodes', *Jahrbuch der deutschen Schillergesellschaft*, 33 (1989), 299–322

WAGENBÄUR, BIRGIT, '"habe getaumelt in den Räumen des Aethers": Karoline von Günderrodes ästhetische Identität', in *Frauen: MitSprechen — MitSchreiben: Beiträge zur literatur- und sprachwissenschaftlichen Frauenforschung*, ed. by Marianne Henn and Britta Hufeisen, Stuttgarter Arbeiten zur Germanistik, 349 (Stuttgart: Heinz, 1997), pp. 201–21

WEIGERT, ASTRID, 'Gender and Genre in the Works of German Romantic Women Writers', in *The Oxford Handbook of European Romanticism*, ed. by Paul Hamilton (Oxford: Oxford University Press, 2016), pp. 240–55

WESTPHAL, WOLFGANG, *Karoline von Günderrode und 'Naturdenken um 1800'* (Essen: Blaue Eule, 1993)

WILLSON, A. LESLIE, *A Mythical Image: The Ideal of India in German Romanticism* (Durham, NC: Duke University Press, 1964)

ZAGARI, LUCIANO, '"Die Leiche der Venus": Griechische Mythologie und Kunst der Deformation in romantischen Gedichten und Erzählungen. 1. Novalis, Karoline von Günderrode', in *Deutsche und italienische Romantik: Referate des Bad Homburger Colloquiums in der Werner-Reimers-Stiftung*, ed. by Enrico de Angelis and Ralph-Rainer Wuthenow (= *Jacques e i suoi quaderni*, 13 (1989)), 249–62

General Secondary Literature

ABRAMS, M. H., *Natural Supernaturalism: Tradition and Revolution in Romantic Literature* (New York: Norton, 1971)

ADLER, JEREMY, '*Eine fast magische Anziehungskraft*': *Goethes 'Wahlverwandtschaften' und die Chemie seiner Zeit* (Munich: Beck, 1987)

ADLER, ANTHONY CURTIS, *Politics and Truth in Hölderlin:* Hyperion *and the Choreographic Project of Modernity* (Rochester, NY: Camden House, 2021)

ADLURI, VISHWA and BAGCHEE, JOYDEEP, *The Nay-Science: A History of German Indology* (New York: Oxford University Press, 2014)

Ägyptische Mysterien: Reisen in die Unterwelt in Aufklärung und Romantik, ed. by Jan Assmann and Florian Ebeling (Munich: Beck, 2011)

ALI, KECIA, *The Lives of Muhammad* (Cambridge, MA: Harvard University Press, 2014)

ALLISON, HENRY E., *Lessing and the Enlightenment: His Philosophy of Religion and its Relation to Eighteenth-Century Thought* (Ann Arbor: University of Michigan Press, 1966)

ALT, PETER-ANDRÉ, 'Subjektivierung, Ritual, implizite Theatralität: Hölderlins "Empedokles"-Projekt und die Diskussion des antiken Opferbegriffes im 18. Jahrhundert', *Hölderlin-Jahrbuch*, 37 (2010–11), 30–67

AMSTUTZ, NINA, *Caspar David Friedrich: Nature and the Self* (New Haven and London: Yale University Press, 2020)

ASMUTH, CHRISTOPH, *Interpretation — Transformation: Das Platonbild bei Fichte, Schelling, Hegel, Schleiermacher und Schopenhauer und das Legitimationsproblem der Philosophiegeschichte* (Göttingen: Vandenhoeck & Ruprecht, 2006)

ASSMANN, JAN, *Moses the Egyptian: The Memory of Egypt in Western Monotheism* (Cambridge, MA: Harvard University Press, 1997)

ASSMANN, JAN, *Religio Duplex: How the Enlightenment Reinvented Egyptian Religion*, trans. by Robert Savage (Cambridge: Polity, 2014)

AUEROCHS, BERND, 'Platon um 1800: Zu seinem Bild bei Stolberg, Wieland, Schlegel und Schleiermacher', *Wieland-Studien*, 3 (1996), 161–93

—— *Die Entstehung der Kunstreligion* (Göttingen: Vandenhoeck & Ruprecht, 2006)

AUGART, JULIA, *Eine romantische Liebe in Briefen: Zur Liebeskonzeption im Briefwechsel von Sophie Mereau und Clemens Brentano* (Würzburg: Königshausen & Neumann, 2006)

BARK, IRENE, '*Steine in Potenzen*': *Konstruktive Rezeption der Mineralogie bei Novalis* (Tübingen: Niemeyer, 1999)

BARON, KONSTANZE, and SOBOTH, CHRISTIAN, 'Einleitung', in *Perfektionismus und Perfektibilität: Theorien und Praktiken der Vervollkommnung in Pietismus und Aufklärung*, ed. by Konstanze Baron and Christian Soboth, Studien zum achtzehnten Jahrhundert, 35 (Hamburg: Meiner, 2018) pp. 9–28

BAEUMER, MAX L., *Heinse-Studien* (Stuttgart: Metzler, 1966)

BECKER-CANTARINO, BARBARA, 'Zur Rezeption "Bettinas" in England und in Neuengland', in *Bettina von Arnim Handbuch*, ed. by Barbara Becker-Cantarino (Berlin: De Gruyter, 2019), pp. 609–21

BEGEMANN, CHRISTIAN, 'Erhabene Natur: Zur Übertragung des Begriffs des Erhabenen auf Gegenstände der äußeren Natur in den deutschen Kunsttheorien des 18. Jahrhunderts', *Deutsche Vierteljahrsschrift für Literaturwissenschaft und Geistesgeschichte*, 58 (1984), 74–110

BEHLER, ERNST, 'Friedrich Schlegel's "Rede über die Mythologie" im Hinblick auf Nietzsche', *Nietzsche-Studien*, 8.1 (1979), 182–209

—— *Unendliche Perfektibilität: Europäische Romantik und Französische Revolution* (Paderborn: Schöningh, 1989)

—— *German Romantic Literary Theory* (Cambridge: Cambridge University Press, 1993)

BEIERWALTES, WERNER, *Platonismus und Idealismus* (Frankfurt a.M.: Klostermann, 1972)
—— *Denken des Einen: Studien zur neuplatonischen Philosophie und ihrer Wirkungsgeschichte* (Frankfurt a.M.: Klostermann, 1985)
BEISER, FREDERICK C., *The Fate of Reason: German Philosophy from Kant to Fichte* (Cambridge, MA: Harvard University Press, 1987)
—— *Enlightenment, Revolution, and Romanticism: The Genesis of Modern German Political Thought, 1790–1800* (Cambridge, MA: Harvard University Press, 1992)
—— 'Introduction: Hegel and the Problem of Metaphysics', in *The Cambridge Companion to Hegel*, ed. by Frederick C. Beiser (Cambridge: Cambridge University Press, 1993), pp. 1–24
—— (ed. and trans.), *The Early Political Writings of the German Romantics* (Cambridge: Cambridge University Press, 1996)
—— *German Idealism: The Struggle Against Subjectivism* (Cambridge, MA: Harvard University Press, 2002)
—— *The Romantic Imperative: The Concept of Early German Romanticism* (Cambridge, MA: Harvard University Press, 2003)
—— *The German Historicist Tradition* (Oxford: Oxford University Press, 2011)
BELL, DAVID, *Spinoza in Germany from 1670 to the Age of Goethe*, Bithell Series of Dissertations, 7 (London, 1984)
BELL, MATTHEW, *Goethe's Naturalistic Anthropology: Man and Other Plants* (Oxford: Oxford University Press, 1994)
—— *The German Tradition of Psychology in Literature and Thought, 1700–1840* (Cambridge: Cambridge University Press, 2005)
BERGENGRUEN, MAXIMILIAN, 'Signatur, Hieroglyphe, Wechselrepräsentation: Zur Metaphysik der Schrift in Novalis' *Lehrlingen*', *Athenäum*, 14 (2004), 43–67
BESSLICH, BARBARA, *Der deutsche Napoleon-Mythos: Literatur und Erinnerung 1800 bis 1945* (Darmstadt: Wissenschaftliche Buchgesellschaft, 2007)
BEUTEL, ALBRECHT, 'Spalding und Goeze und *Die Bestimmung des Menschen*: Frühe Kabalen um ein Erfolgsbuch der Aufklärungstheologie', in *Literatur und Theologie im 18. Jahrhundert: Konfrontationen — Kontroversen — Konkurrenzen*, ed. by Hans-Edwin Friedrich and others, Hallesche Beiträge zur europäischen Aufklärung, 41 (Berlin: De Gruyter, 2011), pp. 108–21
BEWELL, ALAN J., 'The Political Implication of Keats's Classicist Aesthetics', *Studies in Romanticism*, 25 (1986), 220–29
BIAREISHYK, SIARHEI, 'Rethinking Romanticism with Spinoza: Encounter and Individuation in Novalis, Ritter, and Baader', *The Germanic Review*, 94.4 (2019), 271–98
BINDER, WOLFGANG, *Friedrich Hölderlin: Studien* (Frankfurt a.M.: Suhrkamp, 1987)
BINOCHE, BERTRAND, *L'homme perfectible* (Seyssel: Éditions Champs Villon, 2004)
BIRD, STEPHANIE, *Recasting Historical Women: Female Identity in German Biographical Fiction* (Oxford: Berg, 1998)
BIRKENHAUER, THERESIA, *Legende und Dichtung: Der Tod des Philosophen und Hölderlins Empedokles* (Berlin: Vorwerk, 1996)
BODE, CHRISTOPH, 'Absolut Jena: A Second Look at Lacoue-Labarthe's and Nancy's Representation of the Literary Theory of *Frühromantik*', in *Romanticism and Philosophy: Thinking with Literature*, ed. by Thomas Constantisco and Sophie Laniel-Musitelli (New York: Routledge, 2015), pp. 19–39
BÖDEKER, HANS ERICH, 'Die Religiosität der Gebildeten', in *Religionskritik und Religiosität in der deutschen Aufklärung*, ed. by Karlfried Gründer and Karl Heinrich Rengstorf, Wolfenbütteler Studien zur Aufklärung, 11 (Heidelberg: Schneider, 1989), pp. 145–95
BÖHME, HARTMUT, *Natur und Subjekt* (Frankfurt a.M.: Suhrkamp, 1988)

BOLLACHER, MARTIN, *Der junge Goethe und Spinoza: Studien zur Geschichte des Spinozismus in der Epoche des Sturms und Drangs*, Studien zur deutschen Literatur, 18 (Niemeyer: Tübingen, 1969)

BOVENSCHEN, SILVIA, *Die imaginierte Weiblichkeit: Exemplarische Untersuchungen zu kulturgeschichtlichen und literarischen Präsentationsformen des Weiblichen*, 3rd edn (Frankfurt a.M.: Suhrkamp, 2016)

BOWIE, ANDREW, 'The Philology of Philosophy: The Early Romantic Critical Heritage and Contemporary Literary Theory', *Publications of the English Goethe Society*, 65 (1996), 116–35

—— *Aesthetics and Subjectivity*, 2nd edn (Manchester: Manchester University Press, 2003)

BOYLE, NICHOLAS, *Goethe: The Poet and the Age*, 2 vols (Oxford: Oxford University Press, 1992–2003)

BRANDES, HELGA, 'Die Entstehung eines weiblichen Lesepublikums im 18. Jahrhundert: Von den Frauenzimmerbibliotheken zu den literarischen Damengesellschaften', in *Lesen und Schreiben im 17. und 18. Jahrhundert: Studien zu ihrer Bewertung in Deutschland, England, Frankreich*, ed. by Paul Goetsch, ScripOralia, 65 (Tübingen: Narr, 1994), pp. 125–33

BRANDES, UTE, 'Quotation as Authentication: *No Place on Earth*', in *Responses to Christa Wolf*, ed. by Marilyn Sibley Fries (Detroit: Wayne State University Press, 1989), pp. 326–48

BRAUNBECK, HELGA G., 'Das weibliche Schreibmuster der Doppelbiographie: Bettine von Arnims und Christa Wolfs Günderrode-Biographik', in *Frauen — Literatur — Revolution*, ed. by Helga Grubitzsch and others, THETIS — Literatur im Spiegel der Geschlechter, 3 (Pfaffenweiler: Centaurus-Verlagsgesellschaft, 1992), pp. 231–44

BUBNER, RÜDIGER, *The Innovations of Idealism*, trans. by Nicholas Walker (Cambridge: Cambridge University Press, 2003)

BURWICK, FREDERICK, *The Damnation of Newton: Goethe's Color Theory and Romantic Perception* (Berlin: De Gruyter, 1986)

CALAME, CLAUDE, *The Poetics of Eros in Ancient Greece*, trans. by Janet Lloyd (Princeton: Princeton University Press, 1999)

CAPPER, CHARLES, *Margaret Fuller: An American Romantic Life*, 2 vols (Oxford: Oxford University Press, 1992–2007)

CHAOULI, MICHEL, *The Laboratory of Poetry: Chemistry and Poetics in the Work of Friedrich Schlegel* (Baltimore, MD: Johns Hopkins University Press, 2002)

CIEŚLA-KORYTOWSKA, MARIA, 'On Romantic Cognition', in *Romantic Poetry*, ed. by. Angela Esterhammer (Amsterdam: John Benjamins, 2002), pp. 39–53

CLAYTON, PHILIP, *The Problem of God in Modern Thought* (Grand Rapids: Eerdmans, 2000)

COLEMAN, CHARLY, 'Resacralizing the World: The Fate of Secularization in Enlightenment Historiography', *The Journal of Modern History*, 82.2 (2010), 368–95

COLISH, MARCIA L., *The Stoic Tradition from Antiquity to the Early Middle Ages*, 2 vols (Leiden, Brill, 1990)

CONSTANTINE, DAVID, *Hölderlin* (Oxford: Clarendon Press, 1988)

COOPER, IAN, *The Near and Distant God: Poetry, Idealism and Religious Thought from Hölderlin to Eliot* (London: Legenda, 2008)

COOPER, LAURENCE D., *Rousseau, Nature, and the Problem of the Good Life* (University Park: Pennsylvania State University Press, 1999)

COPE, CHRISTOPHER, *Phoenix Frustrated: The Lost Kingdom of Burgundy* (London: Constable, 1986)

COWAN, ROBERT, *The Indo-German Identification: Reconciling South Asian Origins and European Destinies 1765–1885* (Rochester, NY: Camden House, 2010)

CRAMER, KEVIN, *The Thirty Years' War and German Memory in the Nineteenth Century* (Lincoln, NB: University of Nebraska Press, 2007)

CROUTER, RICHARD, *Friedrich Schleiermacher: Between Enlightenment and Romanticism* (Cambridge: Cambridge University Press, 2005)

CROWE, BENJAMIN D., 'On "The Religion of the Visible Universe": Novalis and the Pantheism Controversy', *British Journal of the History of Philosophy*, 16.1 (2008), 125–46

CULLER, JONATHAN, *The Pursuit of Signs: Semiotics, Literature, Deconstruction* (London: Routledge, 2005)

CYRANKA, DANIEL, *Mahomet: Repräsentationen des Propheten in deutschsprachigen Texten des 18. Jahrhunderts*, Beiträge zur Europäischen Religionsgeschichte, 6 (Göttingen: Vandenhoeck & Ruprecht, 2018)

DAIBER, JÜRGEN, *Experimentalphysik des Geistes: Novalis und das romantische Experiment* (Göttingen: Vandenhoeck & Ruprecht, 2001)

DAUB, ADRIAN, *Uncivil Unions: The Metaphysics of Marriage in German Idealism and Romanticism* (Chicago: University of Chicago Press, 2012)

DAUBERT, KARIN R., 'Reflexive Authorship in Bettina Brentano-von Arnim's *Die Günderode*: Narrative Disunity, Hölderlin, and Günderrode', in *Gender, Collaboration, and Authorship in German Culture: Literary Joint Ventures, 1750–1850*, ed. by Laura Deiulio and John B. Lyon, New Directions in German Studies, 27 (New York: Bloomsbury Academic, 2019), pp. 253–72

DAVIES, STEFFAN, *The Wallenstein Figure in German Literature and Historiography 1790–1920*, Bithell Series of Dissertations, 36 (Leeds: Maney Publishing, 2010)

DAVIS, WILLIAM S., *Romanticism, Hellenism, and the Philosophy of Nature* (Basingstoke: Palgrave Macmillan, 2018)

DEBUS, ALLEN G., *Man and Nature in the Renaissance* (Cambridge: Cambridge University Press, 1978)

DÉCULTOT, ELISABETH, 'Einleitung: Die Kunst des Exzerpierens. Geschichte, Probleme, Perspektiven', in *Lesen, Kopieren, Schreiben: Lese- und Exzerpierkunst in der europäischen Literatur des 18. Jahrhunderts*, ed. by Elisabeth Décultot (Berlin: Ripperger & Kremers, 2014), pp. 7–47

DEHRMANN, MARK-GEORG, *Das 'Orakel der Deisten': Shaftesbury und die deutsche Aufklärung* (Göttingen: Wallstein, 2008)

DETERING, HEINRICH, 'Was ist Kunstreligion? Systematische und historische Bemerkungen', in *Kunstreligion: Ein ästhetisches Konzept der Moderne in seiner historischen Entfaltung*, ed. by Albert Meier and others, 3 vols (Berlin: De Gruyter, 2011–14), I: *Der Ursprung des Konzepts um 1800* (2011), pp. 11–27

—— *Menschen im Weltgarten: Die Entdeckung der Ökologie in der Literatur von Haller bis Humboldt* (Göttingen: Wallstein, 2020)

DETIENNE, MARCEL, *The Gardens of Adonis: Spices in Greek Mythology*, trans. by Janet Lloyd (Hassocks: Harvester Press, 1977)

DISSELKAMP, MARTIN, *Barockheroismus: Konzeptionen 'politischer' Größe in Literatur und Traktatistik des 17. Jahrhunderts*, Frühe Neuzeit, 65 (Tübingen: Niemeyer, 2002)

DOLE, ANDREW C., *Schleiermacher on Religion and the Natural Order* (Oxford: Oxford University Press, 2009)

DÜSING, KLAUS, 'Christus und die antiken Götter in der Mythologie der späten Hölderlin', in *Vernunft und Glauben: Ein philosophischer Dialog der Moderne mit dem Christentum. Père Xavier Tillette zum 85. Geburtstag*, ed. by Steffen Dietzsch and Gian Franco Figo (Berlin: Akademie, 2006), pp. 177–89

EDWARDS, CATHARINE, 'Introduction: Shadow and Fragments', in *Roman Presences: Receptions of Rome in European Culture, 1789–1945*, ed. by Catharine Edwards (Cambridge: Cambridge University Press, 1999), pp. 1–18

ERLER, MICHAEL, *Die Philosophie der Antike: Platon* (Basel: Schwabe, 2007)

ESTERHAMMER, ANGELA, *The Romantic Performative: Language and Action in British and German Romanticism* (Stanford: Stanford University Press, 2000)

FAIVRE, ANTOINE, *Access to Western Esotericism* (Albany: SUNY Press, 1994)

—— 'Renaissance Hermeticism and the Concept of Western Esotericism', in *Gnosis and Hermeticism from Antiquity to Modern Times*, ed. by Roelof van den Broek and Wouter J. Hanegraff (Albany: SUNY Press, 1998), pp. 109–23

FIGUEIRA, DOROTHY M., 'Die Flambierte Frau: Sati in European Culture', in *Sati: The Blessing and the Curse: The Burning of Wives in India*, ed. by John Stratton Hawley (New York: Oxford University Press, 1994), pp. 55–78

FORSTER, FELIX, *Dante Gabriel Rossetti und der Romantische Desillusionismus* (Göttingen: V&R unipress, 2014)

FORSTER, LEONARD, 'Faust and the Sin of Sloth', in *The Discontinuous Tradition: Studies in German Literature in Honour of Ernst Ludwig Stahl*, ed. by Peter F. Ganz (Oxford: Clarendon Press, 1971), pp. 54–66.

FORSTER, MICHAEL N., 'Herder and Spinoza', in *Spinoza and German Idealism*, ed. by Eckart Förster and Yitzhak Y. Melamed (Cambridge: Cambridge University Press, 2012), pp. 59–84

FORSTMAN, JACK, *A Romantic Triangle: Schleiermacher and the Early German Romantics* (Missoula, MT: Scholars Press, 1977)

FRANK, MANFRED, *Der kommende Gott: Vorlesungen über die Neue Mythologie: 1. Teil* (Frankfurt a.M.: Suhrkamp, 1982)

—— *'Unendliche Annäherung': Die Anfänge der philosophischen Frühromantik* (Frankfurt a.M.: Suhrkamp, 1997)

FRANK, MANFRED, and MILLÁN-ZAIBERT, ELIZABETH, *The Philosophical Foundations of Early German Romanticism* (Albany: SUNY Press, 2004)

FRANZ, MICHAEL, *Schellings Tübinger Platon-Studien* (Göttingen: Vandenhoeck & Ruprecht, 1996)

—— *Tübinger Platonismus: Die gemeinsamen philosophischen Anfangsgründe von Hölderlin, Schelling und Hegel* (Tübingen: Narr Francke, 2012)

FRIED, JOCHEN, *Die Symbolik des Realen: Über alte und neue Mythologie in der Frühromantik* (Munich: Fink, 1985)

GAIER, ULRICH, *Hölderlin: Eine Einführung* (Tübingen: Francke, 1993)

GARRETT, AARON, 'Human Nature', in *The Cambridge History of Eighteenth-Century Philosophy*, ed. by Knud Haakonssen, 2 vols (New York: Cambridge University Press, 2006), I, pp. 160–233

GASKILL, HOWARD, *Hölderlin's Hyperion* (Durham: University of Durham, 1984)

GAUKROGER, STEPHEN, *The Collapse of Mechanism and the Rise of Sensibility: Science and the Shaping of Modernity, 1680–1760* (Oxford: Clarendon Press, 2010)

GERMANA, NICHOLAS A., 'Herder's India: The "Morgenland" in Mythology and Anthropology', in *The Anthropology of the Enlightenment*, ed. by Marco Cipollini and Larry Wolff (Stanford: Stanford University Press, 2007), pp. 118–40

GERRISH, B. A., *Continuing the Reformation: Essays on Modern Religious Thought* (Chicago: University of Chicago Press, 1993)

GIER, ALBERT, '"O Richard, o mon roi": Richard Löwenherz im Musiktheater', in *Richard Löwenherz, ein europäischer Herrscher im Zeitalter der Konfrontation von Christentum und Islam*, ed. by Ingrid Bennewitz and Klaus von Eickels, Bamberger interdiziplinäre Mittelalterstudien, Vorträge und Vorlesungen, 8 (Bamberg: University of Bamberg Press, 2019), pp. 171–96

GIGANTE, DENISE, *Life: Organic Form and Romanticism* (New Haven: Yale University Press, 2009)

GILLESPIE, MICHAEL ALLEN, *Nihilism before Nietzsche* (Chicago: University of Chicago, 1995)

GIOVANNI, GEORGE DI, 'Kant's Metaphysics of Nature and Schelling's Ideas for a Philosophy of Nature', *Journal of the History of Philosophy*, 17.2 (1979), 197–215

—— *Freedom and Religion in Kant and his Immediate Successors: The Vocation of Humankind, 1774–1800* (Cambridge: Cambridge University Press, 2005)
GLACKEN, CLARENCE J., *Traces on the Rhodian Shore: Nature and Culture in Western Thought from Ancient Times to the End of the Eighteenth Century* (Berkeley: University of California Press, 1967)
GÖRNER, RÜDIGER, *Romantik: Ein europäisches Ereignis* (Stuttgart: Reclam, 2021)
GOSETTI-FERENCEI, JENNIFER ANNA, *Heidegger, Hölderlin, and the Subject of Poetic Language: Towards a New Poetics of Dasein*, Perspectives in Continental Philosophy, 38 (New York: Fordham University Press, 2004)
—— 'Nature and Poetic Consciousness from Hölderlin to Rilke', in *Hölderlin's Philosophy of Nature*, ed. by Rochelle Tobias (Edinburgh: Edinburgh University Press, 2020), pp. 23–43
GRAEVENITZ, GERHART VON, *Mythos: Zur Geschichte einer Denkgewohnheit* (Stuttgart: Metzler, 1987)
GRAFTON, ANTHONY, *Defenders of the Text: The Traditions of Scholarship in an Age of Science, 1450–1800* (Cambridge, MA: Harvard University Press, 1991)
GRANT, IAIN HAMILTON, *Philosophies of Nature after Schelling* (London: Continuum, 2008)
GRATZKE, MICHAEL, *Feuer und Blut: Heldentum bei Lessing, Fontane, Jünger und Heiner Müller* (Würzburg: Königshausen & Neumann, 2011)
GREINEDER, DANIEL, *From the Past to the Future: The Role of Mythology from Winckelmann to Schelling* (Oxford: Peter Lang, 2007)
GRIMM, CATHERINE, ' "Wie ist Natur so hold und gut, die mich am Busen hält": Nature Philosophy and Feminine Subjectivity in the Epistolary Memoirs of Bettine von Arnim', in *Schwellenüberschreitungen: Politik in der Literatur von deutschsprachigen Frauen 1780–1918*, ed. by Caroline Bland and Elisa Müller-Adams (Berlin: Aisthesis, 2007), pp. 151–68
GROETSCH, ULRICH, 'The Miraculous Crossing of the Red Sea: What Lessing and his Opponents during the *Fragmentenstreit* Did Not See', in *Lessings Religionphilosophie im Kontext: Hamburger Fragmente und Wolfenbütteler Axiomata*, ed. by Christoph Bultmann and Friedrich Vollhardt, Frühe Neuzeit, 159 (Berlin: De Gruyter, 2011), pp. 181–99
GROOT, H. B. DE, 'The Ouroboros and the Romantic Poets', *English Studies*, 50 (1969), 553–64
GUASTELLA, GIANNI, *Word of Mouth: Fama and its Personifications in Art and Literature from Ancient Rome to the Middle Ages* (Oxford: Oxford University Press, 2017)
GUNDELFINGER, FRIEDRICH, *Caesar in der deutschen Literatur* (Berlin: Mayer & Müller, 1904)
HADOT, PIERRE, *Philosophy as a Way of Life: Spiritual Exercises from Socrates to Foucault*, trans. by Michael Chase (Oxford: Blackwell, 1995)
HALMI, NICHOLAS, *The Genealogy of the Romantic Symbol* (Oxford: Oxford University Press, 2007)
HAMMERSTEIN, KATHARINA VON, ' "Au bonheur de tous": Sophie Mereau on Human Rights and (Gender) Politics in the French Revolution and American Republic', *Colloquia Germanica*, 42.2 (2009), 97–117
HAMPTON, ALEXANDER J. B., *Romanticism and the Re-invention of Modern Religion: The Reconciliation of German Idealism and Platonic Realism* (Cambridge: Cambridge University Press, 2019)
HANSERT, ANDREAS, *Geburtsaristokratie in Frankfurt am Main* (Vienna: Böhlau, 2014)
HARRAS, GISELA, ' "Ökonomie" in deutschen Wörterbüchern', in *Ökonomie: Sprachliche und literarische Aspekte eines 2000 Jahre alten Begriffs*, ed. by Theo Stemmier (Tübingen: Narr, 1985), pp. 37–50
HEDLEY, DOUGLAS, 'God and Giants: Cudworth's Platonic Metaphysics and his Ancient Theology', *British Journal of the History of Philosophy*, 25.5 (2017), 932–53
HENTSCHEL, THIERRY, *Imagining the Middle East* (Montreal: Black Rose, 1992)

HERLING, BRADLEY L., *The German Gita: Hermeneutics and Discipline in the Early German Reception of Indian Thought, 1778–1831* (New York: Routledge, 2006)

HERRMANN, BRITTA, 'Von der Macht der Worte und der Gewalttätigkeit des Dichters: Zur Erzeugung virtueller Realität im 18. Jahrhundert', *Annali di Ca' Foscari: Serie occidentale*, 52 (2018), 89–105

HERRMANN, LEONHARD, *Klassiker jenseits der Klassik: Wilhelm Heinses 'Ardinghello' — Individualitätskonzeption und Rezeptionsgeschichte*, Communicatio, 41 (Berlin: De Gruyter, 2010)

HEUSER-KESSLER, MARIE-LUISE, *Die Produktivität der Natur: Schellings Naturphilosophie und das neue Paradigma der Selbstorganisation in den Naturwissenschaften* (Berlin: Duncker & Humblot, 1986)

HIGH, JEFFREY L., 'Clever Priests and the Missions of Moses and Schiller: From Monotheism to the Aesthetic Civilization of the Individual', in *Religion, Reason, and Culture in the Age of Goethe*, ed. by Elisabeth Krimmer and Patricia Anne Simpson (Rochester, NY: Camden House, 2014), pp. 79–98

HILLIARD, K. F., 'Goethe and the Cure for Melancholy: "Mahomets Gesang", Orientalism and the Medical Psychology of the 18th Century', *Oxford German Studies*, 23 (1994), 71–103

—— 'Atemübungen: Geist und Körper in der Lyrik des 18. Jahrhunderts', in *Body Dialectics in the Age of Goethe*, ed. Marianne Henn and Holger A. Pausch, Amsterdamer Beiträge zur neueren Germanistik, 55 (Amsterdam and New York: Rodopi, 2003), pp. 293–313

—— *Freethinkers, Libertines and Schwärmer: Heterodoxy in German Literature, 1750–1800*, igrs books, 1 (London: Institute of Germanic and Romance Studies, 2011)

HINSKE, NORBERT, 'Das stillschweigende Gespräch: Prinzipien der Anthropologie und Geschichtsphilosophie bei Mendelssohn und Kant', in *Moses Mendelssohn und die Kreise seiner Wirksamkeit*, ed. by Michael Albrecht and others, Wolfenbütteler Studien zur Aufklärung, 19 (Tübingen: Niemeyer, 1994), pp. 135–56

HODKINSON, JAMES R., *Women and Writing in the Works of Novalis: Transformation beyond Measure?* (Rochester, NY: Camden House, 2007)

—— 'Der Islam im Dichten und Denken der deutschen Romantik: zwischen Kosmopolitismus und Orientalismus', in *Islam in der deutschen und türkischen Literatur*, ed. by Michael Hofmann and Klaus von Stosch, Beiträge zur komparativen Theologie, 4 (Paderborn: Schöningh, 2012), pp. 60–79

HÖLSCHER, UVO, *Empedokles und Hölderlin* (Frankfurt a.M.: Insel, 1965)

HOOLSEMA, DANIEL J., 'The End of an Impossible Future in "The Literary Absolute"', *Modern Language Notes*, 110.4 (2004), 845–68

HORNIG, GOTTFRIED, 'Perfektibilität', *Archiv für Begriffsgeschichte*, 24 (1979), 221–57

HORSCH, SILVIA, '"Was findest Du darinne, das nicht mit der allerstrengsten Vernunft übereinkomme?": Islam as Natural Theology in Lessing's Writings and in the Enlightenment', in *Cultural Exchange in German Literature*, ed. by Eleoma Joshua and Robert Vilain (Rochester, NY: Camden House, 2007), pp. 45–62

HUMPHREYS, S. C., *The Strangeness of Gods: Historical Perspectives on the Interpretation of Athenian Religion* (Oxford: Oxford University Press, 2004)

ISER, WOLFGANG, 'The Reading Process: A Phenomenological Approach', *New Literary History*, 3.2 (1972), 279–99

ISRAEL, JONATHAN, *Radical Enlightenment: Philosophy and the Making of Modernity 1650–1750* (Oxford: Oxford University Press, 2001)

IZENBERG, GERALD N. N., *Impossible Individuality: Romanticism, Revolution, and the Origins of Modern Selfhood* (Princeton: Princeton University Press, 1992)

JACOB, MARGARET C., *The Radical Enlightenment: Pantheists, Freemasons and Republicans* (London: Allen & Unwin, 1981)

JAMME, CHRISTOPH, '"Göttersymbole": Friedrich Creuzer als Mythologe und seine philosophische Wirkung', in *200 Jahre Heidelberger Romantik*, ed. by Friedrich Strack and Barbara Becker-Cantarino (Berlin: Springer, 2008), pp. 486–98

—— *Mythos und Aufklärung: Dichten und Denken um 1800* (Munich: Fink, 2013)

JANKE, WOLFGANG, 'Amor Dei intellectualis (Spinoza — Jacobi — Fichte — F. Schlegel — Schelling): Vom Aufstieg des Geistes zur Gottesliebe', in *Geist, Eros und Agape: Untersuchungen zu Liebesdarstellungen in Philosophie, Religion und Kunst*, ed. by Edith Düsing and Hans-Dieter Klein (Würzburg: Königshausen & Neumann, 2009), pp. 291–310

JONG, ALBERT F. DE, *Traditions of the Magi: Zoroastrianism in Greek and Latin Literature* (Leiden: Brill, 1997)

JUNG, THEO, *Zeichen des Verfalls: Semantische Studien zur Entstehung der Kulturkritik im 18. und frühen 19. Jahrhunderts*, Historische Semantik, 18 (Göttingen: Vandenhoeck & Ruprecht, 2012)

KANTERIAN, EDWARD, *Kant, God and Metaphysics: The Secret Thorn* (London: Routledge, 2018)

KASCHUBA, WOLFGANG, 'Revolution als Spiegel: Reflexe der Französischen Revolution in deutscher Öffentlichkeit und Alltagskultur um 1800', in *Französische Revolution und deutsche Öffentlichkeit: Wandlungen in Presse*, ed. by Helger Böning (Munich: Saur, 1991), pp. 381–98

KAUFMANN, FRANZ-XAVER, *Religion und Modernität: Sozialwissenschaftliche Perspektiven* (Tübingen: Mohr, 1989)

KEMPER, HANS-GEORG, '"Eins im All! Und all in Eins!": "Christliche Hermetik" als trojanisches Pferd der Aufklärung', in *Aufklärung und Esoterik: Rezeption — Integration — Konfrontation*, ed. by Monika Neugebauer-Wölk (Tübingen: Niemeyer, 2008), pp. 29–52

KENNEDY, CLARE, *Paradox, Aphorism and Desire in Novalis and Derrida*, Texts and Dissertations, 71 (London: Maney, 2008)

KHAN, RUQAYYA YASMINE, *Self and Secrecy in Early Islam* (Columbia, SC: University of South Carolina Press, 2008)

KIRKLAND, SEAN D., *The Ontology of Socratic Questioning in Plato's Early Dialogues* (Albany: SUNY Press, 2012)

KLATT, NORBERT, '". . . des Wissens heißer Durst": ein literarischer Beitrag zu Schillers Gedicht "Das verschleierte Bild zu Sais"', *Jahrbuch der deutschen Schillergesellschaft*, 29 (1985), 98–112

KLEIN, URSULA, *Nützliches Wissen: Die Erfindung der Technikwissenschaften* (Göttingen: Wallstein, 2016)

KLEINGELD, PAULINE, *Kant and Cosmopolitanism: The Philosophical Ideal of World Citizenship* (Cambridge: Cambridge University Press, 2011)

KLOSS, ALFRED, *Die Heidelbergischen Jahrbücher der Literatur in den Jahren 1808–1816* (Leipzig: Voigtländer, 1916)

KNELLER, JANE E., 'Romantic Conceptions of the Self in Novalis and Hölderlin', in *Figuring the Self: Subject, Absolute, and Others in Classical German Philosophy*, ed. by David E. Klemm and Günter Zöller (Albany: SUNY Press, 1997), pp. 134–48

—— 'Novalis' nüchterne Rezeption der spinozistischen "Gott-Trunkenheit"', in *Affektenlehre und amor dei intellectualis: Die Rezeption Spinozas im deutschen Idealismus*, ed. by Violetta Waibel (Hamburg: Meiner, 2012), pp. 62–76

KONDYLIS, PANAJOTIS, *Die Aufklärung im Rahmen des neuzeitlichen Rationalismus* (Stuttgart: Klett-Cotta, 1981)

KONTJE, TODD, *Women, the Novel, and the German Nation 1771–1871: Domestic Fiction in the Fatherland* (Cambridge: Cambridge University Press, 1998)

—— *German Orientalisms* (Ann Arbor: University of Michigan Press, 2004)

KOOPMANN, HELMUT, *Freiheitssonne und Revolutionsgewitter: Reflexe der Französischen*

Revolution im literarischen Deutschland zwischen 1789 und 1840, Untersuchungen zur deutschen Literaturgeschichte, 50 (Tübingen: Niemeyer, 1989)

KORD, SUSANNE, 'All's Well That Ends Well? Marriage, Madness, and Other Happy Endings in Eighteenth-Century Women's Comedies', *Lessing Yearbook*, 28 (1996), 181–97

KNUDSEN, JONATHAN B., *Justus Möser and the German Enlightenment* (Cambridge: Cambridge University Press, 1986)

KRUEGER, JAMES, and LIPSCOMB, BENJAMIN, 'Towards a Synoptic Vision: Reading Kant Metaphysically, Reading him Whole', in *Kant's Moral Metaphysics: God, Freedom, and Immortality*, ed. by James Krueger and Benjamin J. Bruxvoort Lipscomb (Berlin: De Gruyter, 2010), pp. 1–19

KUBIK, ANDREAS, *Die Symboltheorie bei Novalis: Eine ideengeschichtliche Studie in ästhetischer und theologischer Absicht* (Tübingen: Mohr Siebeck, 2006)

KUEHN, MANFRED, *Kant: A Biography* (Cambridge: Cambridge University Press, 2001)

KUHN, ANNA K., 'The "Failure" of Biography and the Triumph of Women's Writing: Bettina von Arnim's *Die Günderode* and Christa Wolf's *The Quest for Christa T.*', in *Revealing Lives: Autobiography, Biography, and Gender*, ed. by Susan Groag Bell and Marilyn Yalom (Albany: SUNY Press, 1990), pp. 19–28

KURTH-VOIGT, LIESELOTTE E., 'Existence after Death: Changing Views in Wieland's Writings', *Lessing Yearbook*, 17 (1985), 153–76

—— 'Existence after Death in Eighteenth-Century Literature: Prolegomena to a Study of Poetic Visions of the Beyond and Imaginative Speculations about Continued Life in a Future State', *South Atlantic Review*, 52.2 (1987), 3–14

—— *Continued Existence, Reincarnation, and the Power of Sympathy in Classical Weimar* (Rochester, NY: Camden House, 1999)

KUZNIAR, ALICE, *Delayed Endings: Nonclosure in Novalis and Hölderlin* (Athens: University of Georgia Press, 1987)

LACOUE-LABARTHE, PHILIPPE, and NANCY, JEAN-LUC, *The Literary Absolute: The Theory of Literature in German Romanticism*, trans. by Philip Barnard and Cheryl Lester (Albany: SUNY Press, 1988)

LAMM, JULIA A., 'Romanticism and Pantheism', in *The Blackwell Companion to Nineteenth-Century Theology*, ed. by David Ferguson (Chichester; Malden, MA: Wiley-Blackwell, 2010), pp. 165–86

LAMPENSCHERF, STEPHAN, '"Heiliger Plato, vergieb. . .": Hölderlins "Hyperion" und Die neue Platonische Mythologie', *Hölderlin-Jahrbuch*, 28 (1992–1993), 128–51

LARGE, WILLIAM, 'From German Romanticism to Critical Theory, by Andrew Bowie', *Journal of the British Society for Phenomenology*, 31.1 (2000), 108–09

LAZIER, BENJAMIN, *God Interrupted: Heresy and the European Imagination between the World Wars* (Princeton: Princeton University Press, 2008)

LEINKAUF, THOMAS, 'Schelling and Plotinus', trans. by Stephen Gersh, in *Plotinus's Legacy: The Transformation of Platonism from the Renaissance to the Modern Era*, ed. by Stephen Gersh (Cambridge: Cambridge University Press, 2019), pp. 183–216

LENOIR, TIMOTHY, *The Strategy of Life: Teleology and Mechanics in Nineteenth-Century German Biology* (Chicago: University of Chicago Press, 1989)

LE RIDER, JACQUES, 'War die Klassik farbenfeindlich und die Romantik farbengläubig? Von Lessings *Laokoon* zu Goethes *Farbenlehre* und deren Nachwirkung', in *Goethe und das Zeitalter der Romantik*, ed. by Walter Hinderer (Würzburg: Königshausen & Neumann, 2007), pp. 31–50

LEVENTHAL, ROBERT S., '"Eins und Alles": Herders Spinoza-Aneignung in *Gott, einige Gespräche*', *Publications of the English Goethe Society*, 86.2 (2017), 67–89

LEWIS, CHARLES, *The Law of Poetry: Studies in Hölderlin's Poetics*, Germanic Literatures, 18 (Cambridge: Legenda, 2019)

LINDNER, HERBERT, *Das Problem des Spinozismus im Schaffen Goethes und Herders* (Weimar: Arion, 1960)
LINK, JÜRGEN, *Hölderlins Fluchtlinie Griechenland* (Göttingen: Vandenhoeck & Ruprecht, 2020)
LÖCHTE, ANNE, *Johann Gottfried Herder: Kulturtheorie und Humanitätsidee der Ideen, Humanitätsbriefe und Adrastea*, Epistemata: Würzburger Wissenschaftliche Schriften, 540 (Würzburg: Königshausen & Neumann, 2005)
LOKKE, KARI, *Tracing Women's Romanticism: Gender, History, and Transcendence* (London: Routledge, 2004)
LORENZ, STEPHAN, 'Leibniz als Denker der Vollkommenheit und der Vervollkommnung: Mit Hinweisen zur Rezeption', in *Perfektionismus und Perfektibilität: Theorien und Praktiken der Vervollkommnung in Pietismus und Aufklärung*, ed. by Konstanze Baron and Christian Soboth, Studien zum achtzehnten Jahrhundert, 35 (Hamburg: Meiner, 2018), pp. 75–96
LOUIS, MARGOT KATHLEEN, *Persephone Rises, 1860–1927: Mythography, Gender, and the Creation of a New Spirituality* (Aldershot: Ashgate, 2009)
LOUTH, CHARLIE, *Hölderlin and the Dynamics of Translation*, Studies in Comparative Literature, 2 (Oxford: Legenda, 1998)
LOVEJOY, ARTHUR O., *The Great Chain of Being: A Study in the History of an Idea* (Cambridge, MA: Harvard University Press, 1936)
LÖWE, MATTHIAS, 'Epochenbegriff und Problemgeschichte: Aufklärung und Romantik als konkurriende Antworten auf dieselben Fragen', in *Aufklärung und Romantik: Epochenschnittstellen*, ed. by Daniel Fulda and others, Laboratorium Aufklärung, 28 (Paderborn: Fink, 2015), pp. 45–68
LÜTZELER, PAUL MICHAEL, '"Die grosse Linie zu einem Brutuskopfe": Republikanismus und Cäsarismus in Schillers *Fiesco*', *Monatshefte*, 70.1 (1978), 15–28
MALCOLM, NOEL, *Useful Enemies: Islam and the Ottoman Empire in Western Political Thought, 1450–1750* (Oxford: Oxford University Press, 2019)
MILLÁN-ZAIBERT, ELIZABETH, *Friedrich Schlegel and the Emergence of Romantic Philosophy* (Albany: SUNY Press, 2007)
MACK, MICHAEL, 'Spinoza and Romanticism', in *The Palgrave Handbook of German Romantic Philosophy*, ed. by Elizabeth Millán Brusslan (Cham: Palgrave Macmillan, 2020), pp. 65–94
MACLEOD, CATRIONA, *Embodying Ambiguity: Androgyny and Aesthetics from Winckelmann to Keller* (Detroit: Wayne State University Press, 1998)
MACOR, LAURA ANNA, *Die Bestimmung des Menschen (1748–1800): Eine Begriffsgeschichte*, Monographien zur Philosophie der deutschen Aufklärung, 25 (Stuttgart-Bad Canstatt: frommann-holzboog, 2013)
MÄHL, HANS-JOACHIM, *Die Idee des goldenen Zeitalters im Werk des Novalis: Studien zur Wesensbestimmung der frühromantischen Utopie und zu ihren ideengeschichtlichen Voraussetzungen* (Heidelberg: Winter, 1965)
MAENCHEN-HELFEN, J. OTTO, *The World of the Huns: Studies in their History and Culture*, ed. by Max Knight (Berkeley: University of California Press, 1973)
MAHONEY, DENNIS F., *Der Roman der Goethezeit (1774–1829)* (Stuttgart: Metzler, 1988)
—— 'Human History as Natural History in *The Novices of Sais* and *Heinrich von Ofterdingen*', *Historical Reflections / Réflexions Historiques*, 18.3 (1992), 111–24
MAILLARD, CHRISTINE, '"Indomanie" um 1800: ästhetische, religiöse und ideologische Aspekte', in *Der Deutschen Morgenland: Bilder des Orients in der deutschen Literatur und Kultur von 1770 bis 1850*, ed. by Charis Goer and Michael Hofmann (Munich: Wilhelm Fink, 2008), pp. 67–84
MARTUS, STEFFEN, *Aufklärung: Das deutsche Jahrhundert. Ein Epochenbild* (Hamburg: Rowohlt, 2018)

MATT, PETER VON, *Liebesverrat: Die Treulosen in der Literatur* (Munich: Deutscher Taschenbuch Verlag, 1991)
MATTHEWS, BRUCE, *Schelling's Organic Form of Philosophy: Life as the Schema of Freedom* (Albany: SUNY Press, 2011)
MATUSCHEK, STEFAN, 'Die Macht des Gastmahls: Schlegels *Gespräch über die Poesie* und Platons *Symposion*', in *Wo das philosophische Gespräch ganz in Dichtung übergeht: Platons Symposion und seine Wirkung in der Renaissance, Romantik und Moderne*, ed. by Stefan Matuschek (Heidelberg: Winter, 2002), pp. 81–96
—— *Der gedichtete Himmel: Eine Geschichte der Romantik* (Munich: Beck, 2021)
MAYER, PAOLA, *Jena Romanticism and its Appropriation of Jakob Böhme: Theosophy, Hagiography, Literature* (Montreal and Kingston: McGill-Queen's University Press, 1999)
MEE, JON, 'Millenarian Visions and Utopian Speculations', in *The Enlightenment World*, ed. by Martin Fitzpatrick, Peter Jones, Christa Knellwolf and Iain McCalman (Abingdon: Routledge, 2004), pp. 536–50
MENDECINO, KRISTINA, 'Vivisections: Scripting Life in Hölderlin's "Das Belebende"', *The German Quarterly*, 91.3 (2018), 270–85
MERGENTHALER, MAY, *Zwischen Eros und Mitteilung: Die Frühromantik im Symposium der Athenaeums-Fragmente* (Paderborn: Schöningh, 2012)
MERRILL, THOMAS, *Christian Criticism: A Study of Literary God-talk* (Amsterdam: Rodopi, 1976)
MEYER-LANDRUT, EHRENGARD, *Fortuna: Die Göttin des Glücks im Wandel der Zeiten* (Munich: Deutscher Kunstverlag, 1997)
MIETH, GÜNTER, *Friedrich Hölderlin: Dichter der bürgerlich-demokratischen Revolution* (Würzburg: Königshausen & Neumann, 2001)
MILES, GEOFFREY, *Shakespeare and the Constant Romans* (Oxford: Clarendon Press, 1996)
MISCHER, SIBILLE, *Der verschlungene Zug der Seele: Natur, Organismus und Entwicklung bei Schelling, Steffens und Oken* (Würzburg: Königshausen & Neumann, 1997)
MOGEL, ERNST, *Natur als Revolution: Hölderlins Empedokles-Tragödie* (Stuttgart: Metzler, 1994)
MOMMSEN, KATHARINA, *Goethe und die arabische Welt* (Frankfurt a.M.: Insel, 1988)
MONTEFUSCO, LUCIA CALBOLI, 'Exercitatio', in *Der Neue Pauly*, ed. by Hubert Cancik and others. <http://dx.doi.org/10.1163/1574-9347_dnp_e407880> [accessed 3 July 2019].
MOORE, BRYAN L., *Literature and Ecology: Ecocentric Personification from Antiquity to the Twenty-first Century* (New York: Palgrave Macmillan, 2008)
MORTIMER, SARAH, and ROBERTSON, JOHN, 'Nature, Revelation, History: The Intellectual Consequences of Religious Heterodoxy 1600–1750', in *Intellectual Consequences of Religious Heterodoxy, 1600–1750*, ed. by Sarah Mortimer and John Robertson, Brill's Studies in Intellectual History, 211 (Leiden: Brill, 2012), pp. 1–46
MURPHY, MICHAEL, 'The Emergence of Evolutionary Panentheism', in *Panentheism across the World's Traditions*, ed. by Loriliai Biernacki, Philip Clayton (Oxford: Oxford University Press, 2013), pp. 177–98
NASSAR, DALIA, *The Romantic Absolute: Being and Knowing in Early German Romantic Philosophy, 1795–1804* (Chicago: University of Chicago Press, 2014)
—— 'The Human Vocation and the Question of the Earth: Karoline von Günderrode's Philosophy of Nature', *Archiv für Geschichte der Philosophie*, 104.1 (2022), 108–30
The Nature of Melancholy: From Aristotle to Kristeva, ed. by Jennifer Radden (Oxford: Oxford University Press, 2002)
NAUEN, FRANZ GABRIEL, *Revolution, Idealism and Human Freedom: Schelling, Hölderlin and Hegel and the Crisis of Early German Idealism*, International Archives of the History of Ideas/Archives Internationales d'histoire des idées, 45 (The Hague: Nijhoff, 1971)
NEILLY, JOANNA, *E.T.A. Hoffmann's Orient. Romantic Aesthetics and the German Imagination* (Cambridge: Legenda, 2016)

NEUBAUER, JOHN, 'Dr. John Brown (1735–88) and Early German Romanticism', *Journal of the History of Ideas*, 28.3 (1967), 367–82
—— *Bifocal Vision: Novalis' Philosophy of Nature and Disease* (Chapel Hill: University of North Carolina Press, 1971)
NEUMANN, MICHAEL, '"Das Fatum als Gegensatz der freien Selbstbestimmung" in der Schauerliteratur', in *Inevitabilis Vis Fatorum: Der Triumph des Schicksalsdramas auf der europäischen Bühne um 1800*, ed. by Roger Bauer and others (= *Jahrbuch für internationale Germanistik*, Reihe A, Kongressberichte, 27 (1990)), pp. 210–20
NICHOLLS, ANGUS, *Goethe's Concept of the Daemonic: After the Ancients* (Rochester, NY: Camden House, 2006)
NIGOSIAN, S. A., *Islam: Its History, Teaching, and Practices* (Bloomington: Indiana University Press, 2004)
NITSCHKE, CLAUDIA, 'Zwischen Fluß und Übersprung: Geschichte und Individuum in Hölderlins "Tod des Empedokles"', in *Romantische Metaphorik des Fließens: Körper, Seele, Poesie*, ed. by Walter Pape, Schriften der Internationalen Arnim-Gesellschaft, 6 (Tübingen: Niemeyer, 2012), pp. 37–53
O'BRIEN, WILLIAM ARCTANDER, *Novalis: Signs of a Revolution* (Durham, NC: Duke University Press, 1995)
OGDEN, MARK, *The Problem of Christ in the Work of Friedrich Hölderlin*, Bithell Series of Dissertations, 16 (London: Modern Humanities Research Association, 1991)
OZ-SALZBERGER, FANIA, 'Scots, Germans, Republic and Commerce', in *Republicanism: A Shared European Heritage*, ed. by Martin van Gelderen and Quentin Skinner, 2 vols (Cambridge: Cambridge University Press, 2002), II: *The Values of Republicanism in Early Modern Europe*, pp. 197–226
PAGDEN, ANTHONY, 'The Immobility of China: Orientalism and Occidentalism in the Enlightenment', in *The Anthropology of the Enlightenment*, ed. by Marco Cipollini and Larry Wolff (Stanford: Stanford University Press, 2007), pp. 50–64
PARKER, ROBERT, *Polytheism and Society at Athens* (Oxford: Oxford University Press, 2007)
PAULIN, ROGER, *The Life of August Wilhelm Schlegel: Cosmopolitan of Art and Poetry* (Cambridge: OpenBook, 2016)
PAULUS, JÖRG, *Der Enthusiast und sein Schatten: Literarische Schwärmer- und Philisterkritik im Roman um 1800*, Quellen und Forschungen zur Literatur- und Kulturgeschichte, 13 (Berlin: De Gruyter, 1998)
PEROVICH JR., ANTONY N., 'Fichte, Hegel, and the Senses of "Revelation"', in *Fichte, German Idealism and Early Romanticism*, ed. by Daniel Breazeale and Tom Rockmore (Amsterdam: Rodopi, 2010), pp. 259–74
PETERSDORFF, DIRK VON, *Mysterienrede: Zum Selbstverständnis romantischer Intellektueller*, Studien zur deutschen Literatur, 139 (Tübingen: Niemeyer, 1996)
PEUCKER, BRIGITTE, *Lyric Descent in the German Romantic Tradition* (New Haven: Yale University Press, 1987)
PFANNKUCHEN, ANTJE, and WEATHERBY, LEIF, 'Writing Polarities: Romanticism and the Dynamic Unity of Poetry and Science', *The Germanic Review*, 92 (2017), 335–39
PHILLIPS, DENISE, *Acolytes of Nature: Defining Natural Science in Germany, 1770–1850* (Chicago: University of Chicago Press, 2012)
PIKULIK, LOTHAR, *Frühromantik: Epoche — Werke — Wirkung*, 2nd edn (Munich: Beck, 2000)
PINKARD, TERRY, *German Philosophy 1760–1860: The Legacy of Idealism* (Cambridge: Cambridge University Press, 2002)
PIPER, HERBERT W., *The Active Universe: Pantheism and the Concept of Imagination in the English Romantic Poets* (London: Athlone Press, 1962)
PIZER, JOHN D., *Imagining the Age of Goethe in German Literature, 1970–2010* (Rochester, NY: Camden House, 2011)

PORT, ULRICH, *'Die Schönheit der Natur erbeuten': Problemgeschichtliche Untersuchungen zum ästhetischen Modell von Hölderlins Hyperion*, Epistemata: Reihe Literaturwissenschaft, 194 (Würzburg: Königshausen & Neumann, 1996)

POTT, MARTIN, *Aufklärung und Aberglaube: Die deutsche Frühaufklärung im Spiegel ihrer Aberglaubenskritik*, Studien zur deutschen Literatur, 119 (Tübingen: Niemeyer, 1992)

PUGH, DAVID, *Dialectic of Love: Platonism in Schiller's Aesthetics* (Montreal; Buffalo; London: McGill-Queen's University Press, 1997)

QUINN, FREDERICK, *The Sum of All Heresies: The Image of Islam in Western Thought* (Oxford: Oxford University Press, 2008)

RAISBECK, JOANNA, '"Diese Unwissenheit ist mir der unerträglichste Mangel, der gröste Widerspruch": The Pursuit of Pre-rational Knowledge in Günderrode', in *Anti\Idealism: Re-interpreting a German Discourse*, ed. by Juliana de Albuquerque and Gert Hofmann (Berlin: De Gruyter, 2019), pp. 131–45

——'Daimonic Energies in Hölderlin's *Tod des Empedokles*', in *Forces of Nature: Dynamism and Agency in German Romanticism*, ed. by Adrian Renner and Frederike Middelhoff (Berlin: De Gruyter, 2022), pp. 127–46

REED, T. J., *Light in Germany: Scenes from an Unknown Enlightenment* (Chicago: University of Chicago Press, 2015)

REHLINGHAUS, FRANZISKA, *Die Semantik des Schicksals: Zur Relevanz des Unverfügbaren zwischen Aufklärung und Erstem Weltkrieg*, Historische Semantik, 22 (Göttingen: Vandenhoeck & Ruprecht, 2015)

REICHERT, KLAUS, 'Zur Geschichte der christlichen Kabbala', in *Kabbala und die Literatur der Romantik: Zwischen Magie und Trope*, ed. by Eveline Goodman-Thau and others, Conditio Judaica, 27 (Tübingen: Niemeyer, 1999), pp. 1–16

REILL, PETER HANNS, 'Between Mechanism and Hermeticism: Nature and Science in the Late Enlightenment', in *Frühe Neuzeit — Frühe Moderne? Forschungen zur Vielschichtigkeit von Übergangsprozessen*, ed. by Rudolf Vierhaus (Göttingen: Vandenhoeck & Ruprecht, 1992), pp. 393–421

——*Vitalizing Nature in the Enlightenment* (Berkeley: University of California Press, 2005)

——'Between Theosophy and Orthodox Christianity: Johann Salomo Semler's Hermetic Religion', in *Polemical Encounters: Esoteric Discourse and its Others*, ed. by Olav Hammer and Kocku von Stuckrad, Aries Book Series, 7 (Boston: Brill, 2007), pp. 157–79

REITZAMMER, LAURIALAN, *The Athenian Adonia in Context: The Adonis Festival as Cultural Practice* (Madison: University of Wisconsin Press, 2016)

RIASANOVSKY, NICHOLAS V., *The Emergence of Romanticism* (New York, Oxford: Oxford University Press, 1992)

RICHARDS, ROBERT J., *The Romantic Conception of Life* (Chicago: University of Chicago Press, 2002)

RIFFATERRE, MICHAEL, 'Prosopopoeia', *Yale French Studies*, 69 (1983), 107–23

RIGBY, KATE, *Reclaiming Romanticism: Towards an Ecopoetics of Decolonization* (Bloomsbury: London, 2020)

RIOU, JEANNE, *Imagination in German Romanticism: Re-thinking the Self and its Environment* (Oxford: Peter Lang, 2004)

RISKIN, JESSICA, *Science in the Age of Sensibility: The Sentimental Empiricists of the French Enlightenment* (Chicago: University of Chicago Press, 2002)

——*The Restless Clock: A History of the Centuries-Long Argument of What Makes Living Things Tick* (Chicago: University of Chicago Press, 2016)

ROBERTSON, RITCHIE, *Mock-Epic Poetry from Pope to Heine* (Oxford: Oxford University Press, 2009)

ROBICHAUD, DENIS J. J., 'Competing Claims on the Legacies of Renaissance Humanism in Histories of Philology', *Erudition and the Republic of Letters*, 3 (2018), 177–222

DELLA ROCCA, MICHAEL, *Spinoza* (Abingdon: Routledge, 2008)
RODRÍGUEZ BAIGORRIA, MARTÍN, 'Hölderlin und die Sattelzeit: Enthusiastische Rhetorik und geschichtliche Beschleunigung', *Archiv für Begriffsgeschichte*, 57 (2015), 145–74
ROHLS, JAN, 'Herders "Gott"', in *Johann Gottfried Herder: Aspekte seines Lebenswerks*, ed. by Martin Kessler and Volker Leppin (Berlin: De Gruyter, 2005), pp. 271–91
ROMMEL, GABRIELE, 'Friedrich von Hardenberg (Novalis) — Gedanken über "die inner *chiffrirende* Kraft. Spuren derselben in der *Natur*"', in *Physik um 1800 — Kunst, Wissenschaft oder Philosophie?*, ed. by Olaf Breidbach and Roswitha Burwick, Laboratorium Aufklärung, 5 (Munich: Fink, 2012), pp. 67–102
ROSENKRANZ, KARL, *Geschichte der Kant'schen Philosophie*, ed. by Steffen Dietzsch (Berlin: Akademie, 1987)
ROSNER, ROBERT, and SOUKUP, RUDOLF WERNER, 'Die chemischen Institute der Universität Wien', in *Reflexive Innensichten aus der Universität: Disziplinengeschichten zwischen Wissenschaft, Gesellschaft und Politik*, ed. by Karl Anton Fröschl and others (Göttingen: V&R unipress, 2015), pp. 211–24
RYAN, LAWRENCE, *Hölderlins 'Hyperion': Exzentrische Bahn und Dichterberuf* (Stuttgart: Metzler, 1965)
SAINE, THOMAS P., *The Problem of Being Modern or the German Pursuit of Enlightenment from Leibniz to the French Revolution* (Detroit: Wayne State University Press, 1997)
SALLER, REINHARD, *Schöne Ökonomie: Die poetische Reflexion der Ökonomie in frühromantischer Literatur* (Würzburg: Königshausen & Neumann, 2007)
SAUL, NICHOLAS, 'The Pursuit of the Subject: Literature as Critic and Perfecter of Philosophy 1790–1832', in *Philosophy and German Literature, 1700–1900*, ed. by Nicholas Saul (Cambridge: Cambridge University Press, 2002), pp. 57–101
SCHANZE, HELMUT, *Erfindung der Romantik* (Stuttgart: Metzler, 2018)
SCHINGS, HANS-JÜRGEN, *Melancholie und Aufklärung: Melancholiker und ihre Kritiker in Erfahrungsseelenkunde und Literatur des 18. Jahrhunderts* (Stuttgart: Metzler, 1977)
SCHIPPERGES, HEINRICH, 'Der Mensch — Ein Kosmometer: Präludium einer Anthropologie bei Novalis', in *Esotérisme, gnoses et imaginaire symbolique: mélanges offerts à Antoine Faivre*, ed. by Richard Caron and others, Gnostica, 3 (Leuven: Peeters, 2001) pp. 325–35
SCHMIDT, JOCHEN, 'Stoischer Pantheismus als Medium des Säkularisierungsprozesses und als Psychotherapeutikum um 1800: Hölderlins *Hyperion*', *Jahrbuch der deutschen Schillergesellschaft*, 51 (2007), 183–204
—— *Die Geschichte des Genie-Gedankens in der deutschen Literatur, Philosophie und Politik 1750–1945*, 2 vols (Heidelberg: Winter, 2004)
—— 'Grundlagen, Kontinuität und geschichtlicher Wandel des Stoizismus', in *Stoizismus in der europäischen Philosophie, Literatur, Kunst und Politik: Eine Kulturgeschichte von der Antike bis zur Moderne*, ed. by Barbara Neymeyr and others, 2 vols (Berlin: De Gruyter, 2008), I, pp. 3–133
SCHMIDT, WOLF GERHARD, *'Homer des Nordens' und 'Mutter der Romantik': James Macphersons 'Ossian' und seine Rezeption in der deutschsprachigen Literatur*, 4 vols (Berlin: De Gruyter, 2003–04)
SCHMIDT-BIGGEMANN, WILHELM, *Baruch de Spinoza, 1677–1977: Werk und Wirkung* (Wolfenbüttel: Herzog August Bibliothek, 1977)
SCHOTTELIUS, SASKIA, *Fatum, Fluch und Ironie: Zur Idee des Schicksals in der Literatur von der Aufklärung bis zur Romantik*, Europäische Hochschulschriften, 1: Deutsche Sprache und Literatur, 1505 (Frankfurt a.M.: Peter Lang, 1995)
SCHUCHARD, MARSHA KEITH, *Restoring the Temple of Vision: Cabalistic Freemasonry and Stuart Culture* (Leiden: Brill, 2002)
SCHULLER, MARIANNE, '". . . da wars mir immer als wär hinter mir der mirs einflüstre . . .": Schreibszenen in Bettine von Arnims Günderode-Buch', in *'Mir ekelt vor diesem*

tintenklecksenden Säkulum': Schreibszenen im Zeitalter der Manuskripte, ed. by Martin Stingelin (Fink: Munich, 2004), pp. 238–44

SCHULZ, GERHARD, *Geschichte der deutschen Literatur: Die deutsche Literatur zwischen Französischer Revolution und Restauration*, 2 vols, Geschichte der deutschen Literatur, 7 (Munich: Beck, 1983)

SCHUTJER, KARIN, *Narrating Community after Kant: Schiller, Goethe, and Hölderlin* (Detroit: Wayne State University Press, 2001)

SCHWAIGER, CLEMENS, 'Zur Frage nach den Quellen von Spaldings Bestimmung des Menschen: Ein ungelöstes Rätsel der Aufklärungsforschung', in *Die Bestimmung des Menschen*, ed. by Norbert Hinske (= *Aufklärung*, 11.1 (1999)), pp. 7–19

SENCKEL, BARBARA, *Individualität und Totalität: Aspekte zu einer Anthropologie bei Novalis*, Studien zur deutschen Literatur, 74 (Tübingen: Niemeyer, 1983)

SHARP, HASANA, *Spinoza and the Politics of Naturalization* (Chicago: University of Chicago Press, 2011)

SHEA, LOUISA, *The Cynic Enlightenment: Diogenes in the Salon* (Baltimore, MD: Johns Hopkins University Press, 2010)

SHEEHAN, JONATHAN, *The Enlightenment Bible: Translation, Scholarship, Culture* (Princeton: Princeton University Press, 2005)

SMITH, JOHN H., 'Living Religion as Vanishing Mediator: Schleiermacher, Early Romanticism, and Idealism', *The German Quarterly*, 84.2 (2011), 137–58

—— 'Leibniz Reception around 1800: Monadic Vitalism and Aesthetic Harmony', in *Religion, Reason, and Culture in the Age of Goethe*, ed. by Elisabeth Krimmer and Patricia Anne Simpson (Rochester, NY: Camden House, 2013), pp. 209–43

SNOW, DALE E., *Schelling and the End of Idealism* (Albany: SUNY Press, 1996)

SOMMER, ANDREAS URS, 'Sinnstiftung durch Individualgeschichte: Johann Joachim Spaldings *Bestimmung des Menschen*', *Zeitschrift für Neuere Theologiegeschichte*, 8 (2001), 163–200

SORKIN, DAVID, 'Reclaiming Theology for the Enlightenment: The Case of Siegmund Jacob Baumgarten (1706–1757)', *Central European History*, 36.4 (2003), 503–30

STEIGERWALD, JOAN, *Experimenting at the Boundaries of Life: Organic Vitality in Germany around 1800* (Pittsburgh, PA: University of Pittsburgh Press, 2019)

STEPHAN, INGE, 'Gewalt, Eros und Tod: Metamorphosen der Charlotte Corday-Figur vom 18. Jahrhundert bis in die Gegenwart', in *Die Marseillaise der Weiber: Frauen, die Französische Revolution und ihre Rezeption*, ed. by Inge Stephan and Sigrid Weigel, Literatur im historischen Prozeß, 26 (Hamburg: Argument, 1989), pp. 128–53

STEUER, DANIEL, 'Nature', in *Encyclopedia of the Romantic Era, 1760–1850*, ed. by Christopher John Murray, 2 vols (New York: Fitzroy Dearborn, 2004), II, 792–94

STOCKER, MARGARITA, *Judith: Sexual Warrior: Women and Power in Western Culture* (New Haven: Yale University Press, 1998)

STOCKINGER, LUDWIG, '"Die Poesie heilt die Wunden, die der Verstand schlägt": Novalis' Poesiebegriff im begriffs- und literaturgeschichtlichen Kontext', in *Novalis: Poesie und Politik*, ed. by Herbert Uerlings (Tübingen: Niemeyer, 2004), pp. 63–79

STONE, ALISON, 'Being, Knowledge, and Nature in Novalis', *Journal of the History of Philosophy*, 16.1 (2008), 141–64

STONE, LAUREN SHIZUKO, 'Beilage zum Brief: On "Epistolarity" and Materiality in Bettine von Arnim's *Die Günderode*', *Colloquia Germanica*, 47.3 (2014), 287–305

STRACK, FRIEDRICH, *Im Schatten der Neugier: Christliche Tradition und kritische Philosophie im Werk Friedrichs von Hardenberg* (Tübingen: Niemeyer, 1982)

STROUP, JOHN, *The Struggle for Identity in the Clerical Estate: Northwest German Opposition to Absolutist Policy in the Eighteenth Century* (Leiden: Brill, 1984)

TATAR, MARIA, *Spellbound: Studies on Mesmerism and Literature* (Princeton: Princeton University Press, 1971)

TAUTZ, BIRGIT, 'Revolution, Abolition, Aesthetic Sublimation: German Responses to News from France in the 1790s', in *(Re-)Writing the Radical: Enlightenment, Revolution and Cultural Transfer in 1790s Germany, Britain and France*, ed. by Maike Oergel, Spectrum Literaturwissenschaft, 32 (Berlin and Boston: De Gruyter, 2012), pp. 72–87

TAYLOR, CHARLES, *Sources of the Self: The Making of the Modern Identity* (Cambridge: Cambridge University Press, 1989)

TAYLOR, JOAN E., *Christians and the Holy Places: The Myth of Jewish-Christian Origins* (Oxford: Clarendon Press, 1993)

THOMALLA, ERIKA, *Anwälte des Autors: Zur Geschichte der Herausgeberschaft im 18. und 19. Jahrhundert* (Göttingen: Wallstein, 2020)

THUMS, BARBARA, 'Religion — Kunst — Lebenskunst: Romantische Tendenzen aufs Unendliche', in *Romantische Religiosität*, ed. by Alexander von Bormann (Würzburg: Königshausen & Neumann, 2005), pp. 19–44

THÜSEN, JOACHIM VON DER, '"Vater Ätna": Vulkan und Geschichte in Hölderlins Empedokles', in *Poesie als Auftrag: Festschrift für Alexander von Bormann*, ed. by Dagmar Ottmann and Markus Symmank (Würzburg: Königshausen & Neumann, 2001) pp. 93–102

TIMM, HERMANN, *Gott und die Freiheit*, Studien zur Religionsphilosophie der Goethezeit, 1 (Frankfurt a.M.: Klostermann, 1974)

—— *Die heilige Revolution: Das religiöse Totalitätskonzept der Frühromantik. Schleiermacher — Novalis — Friedrich Schlegel* (Frankfurt a.M.: Syndikat, 1978)

TOKARZEWSKA, MONIKA, 'Der "Pantheismus" und "Entheismus" im 73. Fragment der "Vermischten Bemerkungen" und in den "Fichte-Studien" von Novalis', in *Literatur und Theologie: Schreibprozesse zwischen biblischer Überlieferung und geschichtlicher Erfahrung*, ed. by Karol Sauerland and Ulrich Wergin (Würzburg: Königshausen & Neumann, 2005), pp. 73–86

TOLAN, JOHN V., 'European Accounts of Muhammad's Life', in *The Cambridge Companion to Muhammad*, ed. by Jonathan E. Brockopp (Cambridge: Cambridge University Press, 2010), pp. 226–50

—— *Faces of Muhammad: Western Perceptions of the Prophet of Islam from the Middle Ages to Today* (Princeton: Princeton University Press, 2019)

TROP, GABRIEL, *Poetry as a Way of Life: Aesthetics and Askesis in the German Eighteenth Century* (Evanston, IL: Northwestern University Press, 2015)

UERLINGS, HERBERT, *Novalis* (Stuttgart: Reclam, 1998)

UTZ, PETER, *Das Auge und das Ohr im Text: Literarische Sinneswahrnehmung in der Goethezeit* (Munich: Fink, 1990)

VASSÁNYI, MIKLÓS, *Anima Mundi: The Rise of the World Soul Theory in Modern German Philosophy* (Dordrecht: Springer, 2011)

VECCHIATO, DANIELE, 'Eine "lächerliche Fratze"? Zur Bedeutung und Funktion des astrologischen Motivs in literarischen Wallenstein-Darstellungen des späten achtzehnten Jahrhunderts', *Jahrbuch der deutschen Schillergesellschaft*, 59 (2015), 87–107

VICKERS, BRIAN, *In Defence of Rhetoric* (Oxford: Clarendon Press, 1988)

VIERHAUS, RUDOLF, *Deutschland im 18. Jahrhundert: Politische Verfassung, soziales Gefüge, geistige Bewegungen* (Göttingen: Vandenhoeck & Ruprecht, 1987)

VIETOR, SOPHIE, *Astralis von Novalis: Handschrift — Text — Werk* (Würzburg: Königshausen & Neumann, 2001)

VONDUNG, KLAUS, 'Apokalyptisch-esoterische Grundierungen des Strebens nach einer Universalwissenschaft — Bengel, Oetinger, Schelling', in *Aufklärung und Esoterik: Wege in die Moderne*, ed. by Monika Neugebauer-Wölk and others, Hallesche Beiträge zur Europäischen Aufklärung, 50 (Berlin: De Gruyter, 2013), 311–21

La Vopa, Anthony J., 'The Philosopher and the "Schwärmer": On the Career of a German Epithet from Luther to Kant', *Huntingdon Library Quarterly*, 60 (1997), 85–115

Waldstein, Edith, *Bettine von Arnim and the Politics of Romantic Conversation*, Studies in German Literature, Linguistics, and Culture, 33 (Rochester, NY: Camden House, 1988)

Walker, D. P., *The Ancient Theology: Studies in Christian Platonism from the Fifteenth to the Eighteenth Century* (London: Duckworth, 1972)

Ward, Keith, 'The World as the Body of God: A Panentheistic Metaphor', in *In Whom We Live and Move and Have Our Being: Panentheistic Reflections on God's Presence in a Scientific World*, ed. by Philip Clayton and Arthur Peacocke (Grand Rapids: Eerdmans, 2004), pp. 62–72

Watanabe O'Kelly, Helen, *Melancholie und die melancholische Landschaft: Ein Beitrag zur Geistesgeschichte des 17. Jahrhunderts*, Basler Studien zur deutschen Sprache und Literatur, 54 (Bern: Francke, 1978)

Watkins, Eric, 'Kant on the Hiddenness of God', *Kantian Review*, 14.1 (2009), 81–122

Weatherby, Leif, *Transplanting the Metaphysical Organ: German Romanticism between Leibniz and Marx* (New York: Fordham University Press, 2016)

Weber, Philipp, 'Romantisches Üben: Die Lehrlinge zu Sais von Novalis', in *Verkörperungen des Kollektiven: Wechselwirkungen von Literatur und Bildungsdiskursen seit dem 18. Jahrhundert*, ed. by Anna Dabrowska and others (Bielefeld: transcript, 2019), pp. 63–85

Wegenast, Margarethe, *Hölderlins Spinoza-Rezeption und ihre Bedeutung für die Konzeption des* Hyperion, Studien zur deutschen Literatur, 112 (Tübingen: Niemeyer, 1990)

Whaley, Joachim, *Germany and the Holy Roman Empire*, 2 vols (Oxford: Oxford University Press, 2012)

Whistler, Daniel, *Schelling's Theory of Symbolic Language: Forming the System of Identity* (Oxford: Oxford University Press, 2013)

Williamson, George S., *The Longing for Myth in Germany: Religion and Aesthetic Culture from Romanticism to Nietzsche* (Chicago: University of Chicago Press, 2004)

Wirth, Jason M., *Conspiracy of Life: Meditations on Schelling and his Time* (Albany: SUNY Press, 2003)

Woodard, Ben, *Schelling's Naturalism: Motion, Space and the Volition of Thought* (Edinburgh: Edinburgh University Press, 2019)

Wundt, Max, 'Die Wiederentdeckung Platons im 18. Jahrhundert', *Blätter für deutsche Philosophie*, 15 (1941), 149–58

Wünsch, Marianne, 'Schicksal am Ende der Romantik: Das Beispiel von Grabbes "Herzog Theodor von Gothland"', in *Inevitabilis Vis Fatorum: Der Triumph des Schicksalsdramas auf der europäischen Bühne um 1800*, ed. by Roger Bauer and others (= *Jahrbuch für internationale Germanistik*, Reihe A, Kongressberichte, 27 (1990)), pp. 130–50

Würtenberger, Thomas, *Symbole der Freiheit: Zu den Wurzeln westlicher politischer Kultur* (Cologne: Böhlau, 2017)

Zammito, John H., 'Herder, Kant, Spinoza und die Ursprünge des deutschen Idealismus', in *Herder und die Philosophie des deutschen Idealismus*, ed. by Marion Heinz (Amsterdam: Rodopi, 1997), pp. 106–44

—— *The Gestation of German Biology: Philosophy and Physiology from Stahl to Schelling* (Chicago: University of Chicago Press, 2018)

Zeller, Rosmarie, 'Das Schicksalsdrama: Zacharias Werners "Der vierundzwanzigste Februar", seine Imitationen und Variationen', in *Dynamik und Dialektik von Hoch- und Trivialliteratur im deutschsprachigen Raum im 18. und 19. Jahrhundert*, ed. by Anne Feler and others, 2 vols (Würzburg: Königshausen & Neumann, 2015), I, pp. 125–42

Zimmermann, Rolf Christian, *Das Weltbild des jungen Goethe: Studien zur hermetischen Tradition des deutschen 18. Jahrhunderts*, 2 vols (Munich: Fink, 1969–79)

ZIMMERMANN, KARIN, *Die polyfunktionale Bedeutung dialogischer Sprechformen um 1800. Exemplarische Analysen: Rahel Varnhagen, Bettine von Arnim, Karoline von Günderrode*, Europäische Hochschulschriften Reihe I: Deutsche Sprache und Literatur, 1302 (Frankfurt a.M.: Peter Lang, 1992)

ZIOLKOWSKI, THEODORE, *German Romanticism and its Institutions* (Princeton: Princeton University Press, 1990)

ZÖLLER, GÜNTER, '"An Other and Better World": Fichte's *The Vocation of Man* as a Theologico-Political Treatise', in *Fichte's Vocation of Man: New Interpretive and Critical Essays*, ed. by Daniel Breazeale and Tom Rockmore (Albany: SUNY Press, 2013), pp. 19–32

INDEX

Abrams, M. H. 142, 191 n. 2
Gustavus Adolphus, king of Sweden, 62–63
amor dei intellectualis 32 n. 44, 119
anamnesis 95, 138–39, 141, 146, 153
Arnim, Achim von 13, 14 n. 26
Arnim, Bettine von 1, 5, 10, 11, 13
  Die Günderode 14–18
autonomy 3, 25, 44–46, 49, 53–54, 58, 63, 66–67, 69, 74, 77–79, 106, 109, 114, 116, 120

Battersby, Christine 123
Behler, Ernst 52–54, 171
Beiser, Frederick C. 3, 21, 28 n. 22, 29–30, 32 n. 44, 36, 53 n. 39, 89 n. 28, 101 n. 97, 155 n. 82, 180 n. 103, 192 n. 7, 199 n. 33, 212 n. 81, 218 n. 116, 222 n. 130, 225 n. 2, 226 n. 7
Berwald, Olaf 152–53
Bode, Christoph 3
Brentano, Clemens 13, 19, 152
Brutus, Marcus Junius (Caesar's assassin) 5, 37–38, 49, 53–63, 65, 75, 80, 226

Caesar, Julius 5, 37–38, 54–55, 57–60, 184
Cartesian philosophy 22, 29, 34, 91, 169, 182
Chastellet, Achille François du 56
Corday, Charlotte 65
Corpus Hermeticum, see Hermeticism
Creuzer, Friedrich 9–10, 13–15, 19. 39, 118, 157–59, 164–65, 170–72, 173 n. 70, 176, 178–79, 183 n. 114, 186 n. 122
Cronstetten-Hynspergische Damenstift 12–13, 196
Cynicism 116

Das älteste Systemprogramm des deutschen Idealismus 171
Daub, Adrian 193
Daub, Carl 15, 39, 178
determinism 25, 27–30, 32, 38–39, 79, 109, 119–20, 171, 194, 203, 211
deus sive natura 29–30, 105
Diderot, Denis 122
Diefenbach, Johann Georg 30, 51, 127–30, 148
dissecare naturam 125, 216
Dormann, Helga 1 n. 3, 62 n. 65, 99 n. 89, 132 n. 31, 148 n. 67, 145, 159, 160 n. 22, 164, 182 n. 113, 188 n. 126

Eickenrodt, Sabine 136 n. 39, 152

Enlightenment 21–22, 36, 38, 50, 77, 87, 90, 97, 126–27, 171, 229
  and humanism 88
  legacy of the Enlightenment 19–20
  and myth 170
  and progress 52, 108
  and religious scepticism 92–93, 95
  and sense perception 132
eros 51, 138–42, 144, 146, 154

fatalism 5, 28–32, 37–39, 47–49, 79, 186, 196, 227
  see also Spinozism
Fichte, Johann Gottlieb 3, 16, 75, 207, 211–14, 218, 221
  Die Bestimmung des Menschen 33, 113, 227
  Einige Vorlesungen über die Bestimmung des Gelehrten 114
Forster, Georg 228
Forster, Michael N. 31
Fragmentenstreit 89
Frank, Manfred 3, 4 n. 13, 34, 171 n. 57
Franz, Michael 138–39, 200 n. 35
French Revolution 5, 19–20, 35, 37 n. 7, 38, 50, 52–54, 78, 192–93, 202, 211
  and the Terror 5, 50

Geiger, Ludwig 9–10
Giovanni, George di 38–39, 180 n. 107
Goethe, Johann Wolfgang von 9, 12, 16, 22–23, 29, 45, 66 n. 83, 85, 138, 158, 172, 174, 191, 229
  'Ganymed', 229
  Mahomet 109–10
Gosetti-Ferencei, Jennifer Anna 199
Günderrode, Karoline von:
  life:
    circumstances of death 9–10
    family 11–14
  studies:
    Fichte 33, 75 n. 101, 113, 114 n. 156
    Hemsterhuis 76–77
    Kantian epistemology 129–31
    Schelling 169, 182
    Schleiermacher 155–56
    Studienbuch 30, 33, 51, 74–75, 78, 115 nn. 159 & 160
  works:
    'Adonis Todtenfeyer' 164–68
    'Aegypten' 174–75
    'Briefe zweier Freunde' 182–90
    'Buonaparte in Egypten' 81–82

'Brutus' 57–58
'Der Adept' 147–48
'Der Caucasus' 176–77
'Der Dom zu Cölln' 132–35
'Der Franke in Egypten' 82–83
'Der Gefangene und der Sänger' 162
Der Kanonenschlag oder das Gastmahl des Tantalus 82
'Der Luftschiffer' 135–37
'Der Nil' 175–76
'Des Wandrers Niederfahrt' 148–51
'Die Manen' 61–62, 131–32
'Die Sonne taugte sich' 58–61
'Die Töne' 209
dream-narratives (untitled) 25–28
'Ein apokaliptisches Fragment' 151–56
'Eine persische Erzählung' 172–74
'Einstens lebt' ich süßes Leben' 137–38
'Geschichte eines Braminen' 78–79, 112–20
'Hildgund' 63–69, 77–79
'Immortalita' 142–46
'Liebe' 139
'Liebe und Schönheit' 140–41
'Magie und Schicksal' 39–49
'Mahomed, der Prophet von Mekka' 82–83, 86–111
'Mahomets Traum in der Wüste' 85–86
Melete 157–60
'Nikator' 63, 69–75, 77–79
'Novalis deinen heilgen Seherblikken' 142
'Tendenz des Künstlers' 4
'Vorzeit, und Neue Zeit' 124–25
'Zueignung' 160–63

Hadot, Pierre 163
Heine, Heinrich 225
Hemsterhuis, Frans 16, 76–77, 132, 139, 214, 218
hen kai pan 155, 164, 172, 177, 185, 190, 192, 199, 201, 213, 222, 225
Herder, Johann Gottfried 22, 23, 29, 35, 38, 45, 54, 75 n. 100, 78, 82, 85, 88, 105–06, 112, 119, 149, 191–92, 194, 199, 221, 224, 227
  Briefe zur Beförderung der Humanität 51
  Gott. Einige Gespräche 23, 31–34, 106 n. 122, 181
  Ideen zu einer Philosophie der Geschichte der Menschheit 33–34, 173 n. 69, 181 n. 110, 190
Hermeticism 43, 88, 97–98, 216
Heyden, Susanne von 13, 158, 186 n. 122
Hilger, Stephanie M. 91
Hilliard, Kevin 53 n. 41, 174, 183 n. 116, 209 n. 73
Hinduism 117–19, 159, 181, 185–86
Hölderlin, Friedrich 8, 16, 20, 34, 171, 184, 192, 212–13, 215, 224, 226
  Der Tod des Empedokles 196–211
  Hyperion, oder der Eremit in Griechenland 29, 88, 139, 192–93, 196, 199–201, 203, 207, 224
Hume, David:
  An Essay Concerning Human Understanding 92

Hutcheson, Francis 72, 132

'der innere Sinn' 99, 131–32, 134
Iser, Wolfgang 162
Islam 50, 84–94, 96, 100, 102, 105, 111, 159
Izenberg, Gerald N. N. 78

Jacobi, Friedrich Heinrich 5, 31–32, 38, 49, 96–97, 101, 139, 196
  Über die Lehre des Spinoza 28–29, 211–12

Kant, Immanuel 3, 16, 21, 30–31, 38, 53, 75–76, 96–98, 115, 117, 125–32, 148, 172, 180, 192, 211, 217–18
  Die Religion innerhalb der Grenzen der bloßen Vernunft 95
  Kritik der reinen Vernunft 30–31, 96, 126
  Kritik der Urteilskraft 98
Kastinger-Riley, Helene M. 146
katabasis 168, 185–87
  and *anabasis* 123
kenosis 109, 112, 120
Kieswetter, Johann Gottfried:
  Grundriss einer reinen allgemeinen Logik nach Kantischen Grundsätzen 127, 120 n. 30
Klopstock, Friedrich Gottlieb 54, 164
Kondylis, Panajotis 21–22, 191 n. 4
Kord, Susanne 20, 45 n. 19, 63–64, 70 n. 96
Kosegarten, Ludwig Gotthard 33–34, 34 n. 52
Krause, Karl Christian Friedrich 24
Kunstreligion 4, 134, 164, 214
Kuzniar, Alice 63, 142 n. 57

Lacoue-Labarthe, Philippe, and Nancy, Jean-Luc 3–4
La Roche, Sophie von 112
Lavers, Jordan 12 n. 18, 13
Leibniz, Gottfried Wilhelm 25, 34, 50. 76, 85, 117, 129, 153, 181, 199, 201, 227, 229
  Leibnizian monad 7, 43, 151, 229
  Leibniz-Wolffian optimism 31, 105, 113, 180
Lessing, Gotthold Ephraim 22, 29, 31, 54, 85, 89, 153, 191, 223 n. 139
  'Daß mehr als fünf Sinne für den Menschen sein können' 121–23, 131
  Die Erziehung des Menschengeschlechts 101, 118–19 n. 172, 171, 190
  Eine Duplik 147–48
life:
  as a metaphysical construct 7, 24–25, 105–08, 143–45, 149–50, 154–55, 165–68, 172, 175, 187–91, 195–96, 199–201, 205, 209, 211–13
  see also vitalism; pantheism
Löwe, Matthias 228–29

Mainz Republic 37
materialism 19–21, 23, 25, 27, 29, 106–07, 114, 169, 182, 188, 190–91, 227

Matthews, Bruce 178
mechanistic naturalism 21–23, 27, 194
Mendecino, Kristina 199
Mendelssohn, Moses:
  Morgenstunden oder Vorlesungen über das Dasein Gottes 31
  Phädon oder über die Unsterblichkeit der Seele 139
Mereau, Sophie 8, 11, 37, 224, 226
  Das Blütenalter der Empfindung 192–96
  'Die Gottheit' 192
Miles, Geoffrey 54
Morgenthaler, Walter 1, 15 n. 35, 55 n. 48, 56 n. 56,
  81 n. 2, 112 n. 147, 132 n. 34, 158 n. 8, 164 n. 34,
  166 n. 45, 172 n. 64, 173, 176 n. 79
myth 169–72

Nancy, Jean-Luc, *see* Lacoue-Labarthe, Philippe
Napoleon 6, 37, 49, 50, 65, 80–86, 94 n. 62, 120
Nassar, Dalia 33 n. 46, 227
natura naturans 202–03
  and *natura naturata* 106, 146, 149, 177
Naturphilosophie, *see* philosophy of nature
Nees von Esenbeck, Christian 10, 13–14, 138, 140, 151,
  158, 179
Nees von Esenbeck, Lisette 13, 138
Neoplatonism 7, 55, 88, 186 n. 122, 150, 154, 159, 199,
  214, 223–24, 227
  and emanation 24 n. 11, 186, 189, 200
  and Plotinus 181 n. 111, 186 n. 122, 214
new mythology, *see* myth
nihilism 29, 74, 192, 194–96, 207–08
Novalis 8–9, 29, 32 n. 44, 53, 132, 135 n. 37, 192, 203,
  211–24
  'Blüthenstaub' 97, 150–51, 212, 217–18, 226–27
  Das allgemeine Brouillon 212–23, 218 n. 116, 221–22
  Die Christenheit oder Europa 88, 214
  Die Lehrlinge zu Sais 70, 83, 98, 214–21, 223
  Fichte-Studien 3, 213, 222
  Heinrich von Ofterdingen 142, 203, 214, 222–24
  Logologische Fragmente 217–18, 218 n. 116
  Vermischte Bemerkungen 212, 227 n. 10
  'Wenn nicht mehr Zahlen und Figuren' 124, 214

Ossian 62, 64, 169

panentheism, *see* pantheism
pantheism 2, 5–8, 16–17, 21–25, 29–31, 36, 38, 49,
  78–80, 105, 112, 114, 117–18, 120–21, 146, 163,
  168–69, 182, 185 n. 121, 186, 189 n. 128, 190–97,
  199, 201, 203, 207 n. 65, 211–14, 222, 224–27,
  229, 230
pantheism controversy 2, 5, 21, 28, 31, 38, 155, 199,
  211, 221, 224, 226
Pantheismusstreit, *see* pantheism controversy
perennial philosophy 6, 88, 170
perfectibility 5, 7, 35, 50–53, 63, 86, 114, 119, 123,
  187–89, 203, 224–25

perfection 7, 25, 31–32, 34, 36, 50–51, 55, 75, 79, 114,
  118–19, 123, 140, 154, 168, 183, 185, 188–90, 224,
  226
Peucker, Brigitte 123
philosophy of nature 7, 24, 33, 106, 169, 178–80, 187,
  214, 224–25, 227
Plato 118, 138–39, 144, 200
  Ion 134 n. 35
  Phaedrus 141
  Symposium 139
  Theaetetus 226
Platonism 4–5, 7, 50 n. 31, 51, 76–77, 98, 132, 137–42,
  145–46, 153–54, 159, 177, 182–83, 192, 196, 199,
  214, 224, 227
Plutarch 35, 54–55, 98
  De Iside et Osiride 35 n. 53
poeta vates 164, 198
Preitz, Max 11
prisca theologia 88, 121
prosopopoeia 176–78
Pugh, David 4

Reinhold, Karl Leonhard 21, 95, 98 n. 84, 127
religion 6, 24, 62, 80, 83, 87–88, 91, 93–96, 105–07,
  109, 111–13, 117–20, 126–27, 129, 131–32, 155–56,
  170, 173, 184–86, 190, 204, 226
  and heterodoxy 6, 88–89
  and knowledge of God 96–105
  and legitimacy 87, 89–90, 92, 94–95, 98, 102–04,
    125–26, 204
  and the origin or foundation of religion 82, 90, 111,
    117, 176
  and Romantic religion 30, 97, 171
  and syncretism 88, 92, 94, 118, 159, 164–65, 170,
    172–73, 190, 224
  and universal religion 6, 86, 88, 94, 96, 111
  see also Islam; *Kunstreligion*; pantheism; Spinozism
Republicanism 5, 37–38, 50, 53–61, 81, 120, 199, 225
Riasanovsky, Nicholas V. 21
Richter, Jean Paul 17, 75 n. 100, 136
  'Rede des toten Christus vom Weltgebäude herab'
    (from *Siebenkäs*) 26–27
Ritter, Johann Wilhelm 172, 181, 218 n. 117
Rousseau, Jean Jacques 5, 52, 75–76, 78, 84 n. 14, 139,
  219

Savigny, Friedrich Karl von 13–14, 19, 37 n. 7, 152
Schelling, Friedrich 7, 16, 24, 170–72, 178–82, 187,
  188 n. 125, 192, 227, 229
  Identitätsphilosophie 178
  influence on Günderrode 24, 178–82
  works:
    *Bruno oder über das göttliche und natürlich Prinzip der
      Dinge* 25, 188
    Ideen zu einer Philosophie der Natur 214
    see also philosophy of nature

Schiller, Friedrich:
    influence on Günderrode 4, 39–40, 54–55,
        75 n. 100, 132, 138 n. 44, 145–46
    works:
        'Das Reich der Schatten' 132, 145–46
        'Das verschleierte Bild zu Sais' 98, 147, 216
        Die Braut von Messina 39–40
        'Die Götter Griechenlands' 143
        Die Räuber 47–48 n. 20, 54–55
        Die Sendung Moses 94–96
        Geschichte des dreißigjährigen Krieges 61
        Philosophische Briefe 183, 199
        Über die ästhetische Erziehung des Menschen 53, 143
        Wallenstein 39
Schlaffer, Hannelore 9
Schlegel, August Wilhelm 159
    translation of Shakespeare 184 n. 117
Schlegel, Friedrich 3, 9, 29–30, 53, 83, 138, 159, 170
    'Gespräch über die Poesie' 227
    'Ideen' 30 n. 33, 97, 171, 227
    'Rede über die Mythologie' 170–71
    'Über Lessing' 83 n. 8
Schlegel-Schelling, Caroline 11, 37
Schleiermacher, Friedrich 29, 101, 109 n. 132, 135, 138–39
    Reden über die Religion 29 n. 30, 97, 112–13, 126, 155, 171, 214 n. 99, 227
Schottelius, Saskia 39
Schulz, Gerhard 9, 169 n. 49
Schwärmer 85, 88, 121, 132, 204
Shaftesbury, Earl of (Anthony Ashley Cooper) 76, 113, 139
Shakespeare, William 54–55, 57 n. 59, 184
Simonis, Annette 1 n. 5, 23 n. 8, 35 n. 53, 98 n. 83, 169 n. 47, 170
Soboth, Christian 52
Spalding, Johann Joachim:
    Betrachtung über die Bestimmung des Menschen 6, 107, 112–13

Spinoza, Benedictus de 2, 5, 21, 23, 28–34, 38, 105 n. 117, 106, 109, 119, 149, 179, 191–92, 196, 201, 212–13, 221, 224, 227
    Tractatus theologio-politicus 89, 92
Spinozastreit, *see* pantheism controversy
Spinozism 5–7, 23, 29–35, 96, 191–92, 201, 213–14, 224–27, 230
    negative or fatalist Spinozism 5, 32, 38–39, 48–49, 78, 195–96, 224
    see also pantheism
Stoicism 54–55, 56–58, 60, 200, 208 n. 70
    and cosmic sympathies 62
Stolberg-Stolberg, Friedrich Leopold zu 54, 138, 228–29

teleology 31, 36, 50–52, 75, 88, 108, 189, 203, 211, 227
The Terror, *see* French Revolution
Tieck, Ludwig 9, 11, 118 n. 169
Timm, Hermann 23 n. 7, 32–33, 149 n. 69, 213 n. 92
Tobler, Georg Christoph:
    'Die Natur' 229

'Urkraft' 33, 119, 149, 194–95

Vanini, Giulio Cesare 33–34
vitalism 22–23, 192, 195, 197, 200, 211–13, 224
Voltaire 85

Wagenbäur, Birgit 10
Whistler, Daniel 179
Wieland, Christoph Martin:
    Briefe von Verstorbenen an hinterlassene Freunde 122–23
Williamson, George S. 170, 225 n. 2
Winckelmann, Johann Joachim 75 n. 100, 82, 132, 169 n. 48, 170
Wolf, Christa 1, 5, 10–11, 18–20
    'Der Schatten eines Traumes: Karoline von Günderrode — ein Entwurf' 18–20